MAN-OF-WAR

MAN-OF-WAR

A HISTORY OF THE COMBAT VESSEL

DONALD MACINTYRE · BASIL W. BATHE

PREFACE BY EDWARD L. BEACH

CASTLE BOOKS   NEW YORK

Opposite title-page: The Austrian super-dreadnought
Viribus Unitis with its two superfiring triple turrets.
The picture was painted by Harry Heusser in 1913
and is now in Heeresgeschichtliches Museum, Vienna.

ACKNOWLEDGEMENTS

THE MAN-OF-WAR *is the result of comprehensive international teamwork.*

The book has been designed by Tre Tryckare on the basis of an idea by EWERT CAGNER.

Author: DONALD MACINTYRE

After thirty years in the Royal Navy of Great Britain, Captain Macintyre retired in 1952 to take up a career as a writer, in which he has since established an international reputation as a naval historian. After an autobiographical book on his wartime experiences, 'U-Boat Killer', he has published a number of books including 'Jutland', 'Fighting Admiral' (a biography of Admiral Sir James Somerville), 'Narvik', 'Admiral Rodney' and the trilogy 'Battle of the Atlantic', Battle for the Mediterranean' and 'Battle for the Pacific'.

In THE MAN-OF-WAR *Captain Macintyre writes about the development of the warship from the beginning of the steam age up to the present day.*

Co-writer: BASIL W. BATHE

Mr. Bathe writes about the development of the warship from 4000 B.C. until about 1840 (the first ten chapters).

Mr. B. W. Bathe joined the Department of Aeronautics and Sailing Ships at the Science Museum, London, in 1949 and since 1962 he has been in charge of the Sailing Ships and Small Craft Collections. In 1967 he was appointed Assistant Keeper First Class and is now also in charge of the Steamship Collection. He was elected to the Council of the Society for Nautical Research in 1966 and has since 1965 been Hon. Treasurer of the Committee for Nautical Archaeology.

The manuscript has been reviewed by the following maritime experts, who have also given valuable help with pictures, and/or contributed forewords, etc.

ALFREDO AQUILERA GARCIA, former Colonel of the Army Law Service, Doctor in Law, Professor at the Escuela Social de Valencia, contributor to many maritime publications, annuals, etc., author of articles on naval subjects.

EDWARD L. BEACH, Captain U.S.N. (ret.), occupies the Chair of Naval Science at the U.S. Naval War College, Newport, Rhode Island. He has contributed a foreword to the American edition and has reviewed the text. Submarine officer and commander during the Second World War, Naval Aide to President Eisenhower, commander of *Triton* during submerged world circumnavigation (1960), he is the author of four books about the U.S. Navy.

HOWARD I. CHAPELLE, Curator of Transportation of the Museum of History and Technology, U.S. National Museum, Smithsonian Institution, Washington, D.C., naval architect and author of seven books on the history of American naval architecture in the days of sail and of four books on small craft, design and construction.

ARNE EMIL CHRISTENSEN Jr., M.A. of Scandinavian archaeology from the University of Oslo. Research associate at the University Collection of National Antiquities, Oslo. Author of scientific and popular articles on the Viking ships and early shipbuilding in Scandinavia and of a book on Norwegian ships through the ages.

STIG H:SON ERICSON, Admiral (ret.), Commander-in-Chief of the Royal Swedish Navy (1953–61), A.D.C. to H.M. the King of Sweden since 1937, Grand Marshal of the Royal Court since 1962, G.C.V.O. Publications: several books on naval matters. Admiral Ericson has contributed a foreword to the Swedish edition.

GIORGIO GIORGERINI, editor and author of the Italian naval annual 'Almanacco Navale', author of several naval books and naval freelance writer. Former assistant Professor at the University of Genoa.

DIETER JUNG, assistant Professor in Zoology at the Free University of Western Berlin. Co-editor of 'Die deutschen Kriegsschiffe 1815–1945' (with Erich Gröner and Martin Maass). Contributor to 'Das Bertelsmann Lexikon'.

ALLAN KULL, Commander, Royal Swedish Navy, former gunnery officer afloat and in the Naval Administration, Naval Attaché in Helsingfors and Warsaw, Naval Staff, now in the Defence Staff, member of the World Ships Society, editor of the 'Marinalmanacka' (1931–37) and the 'Svensk Marinkalender' since 1937.

HENRI LE MASSON, of the Académie de Marine, Honorary Lieutenant-Commander (I.T.), French Naval Reserve. Served in 1939–40 as one of the French liaison officers at the British Admiralty. Has published ten books about the navy and the sea. Editor of 'Les Flottes de Combat' since 1943.

L. L. VON MUNCHING, maritime journalist, historian contributor to various naval publications. Librarian at the Department of Defence, Royal Netherlands Navy, author of a number of books on shipping and naval subjects.

F. C. VAN OOSTEN, Lieutenant-Commander in the Royal Netherlands Navy. Historian. Serving with the Naval Historical Section of the Naval Staff at The Hague. Author of many articles in naval magazines and of a book on maritime historical subjects.

NORMAN POLMAR, leading authority on twentieth-century warships, has written extensively on naval subjects for several newspapers and magazines. His own books include 'Atomic Submarines' and 'Death of the *Thresher*'. Contributor to the British 'Brassey's Annual' and the French 'Les Flottes de Combat'. 1963–67 assistant editor of the U.S. Naval Institute 'Proceedings'. Since 1967 Public Relations Co-ordinator for Deep Submergence Systems at the Northrop Corporation.

R. STEEN STEENSEN, Captain, Royal Danish Navy (ret.), founder of the Navy's Recognition School, chairman of the Marinehistorisk Selskab, author of many books on maritime subjects.

Original drawings by Tre Tryckare artists.

List of acknowledgement of other illustrations on page 274.

CONTENTS

PREFACE

By Captain Edward L. Beach, U.S.N.(ret.)

Wooden castles floating on the sea, God's winds on white canvas held aloft by slender spars and drum-taut line, rows of black cannon in sides of oak . . . Two long, white-sailed fleets coming on the wind to seek decision, broadside guns spouting thunder, flame and billowing smoke, solid iron shot hurtling across the narrow waters, smashing the heavy walls opposing . . . The scarred, crippled Admiral signalling his country's demand that every man do his duty . . . These are some of the images of the days of fighting sail.

In the beginning there were crude trading vessels propelled by oars and rudimentary sails, plying the rivers and only occasionally venturing to cruise along coastlines exposed to open sea. All were armed in modest degree and in cases of extreme danger of attack they banded together in loosely organised fleets. As commerce developed, organisational responsibility moved likewise and the design of some ships emphasised fighting above trading qualities.

We have record of the triremes of the Greeks and their victory over the Persians at Salamis. Then came the galleys of the Romans with the many innovations they introduced, while to the north there were the longships with their dragon-carved stems and berserk tactics. Gradually the sizes of warships evolved, oars gave way to sail and the tactics and designs of ships changed accordingly.

Then came the early frigates, the smooth-bore cannon, the galleon—a combination trading and fighting ship—and finally the battleship of sail, the Ship-of-the Line. Soon, however, inventors brought boilers, bunkers of coal, tortuously turning engines. Smokestacks sprouted between the tall masts, the white sails became smudged with soot, but the paddle-wheels and screw-propellers drove the ships independent of the wind. Other men invented the rifled gun and explosive shells to shatter and tear out the heretofore solid sides of wood, and ships were clad in iron to survive.

The ironclad gave way to the steel ship with a belt of armour. Guns became more powerful, more accurate, longer-ranged, and were mounted in turrets which could turn in all directions. Engines were perfected, and then came the turbines, followed quickly by oil-fuelled boilers, to add speed and endurance. Nations rivalled each other in design and building of these mobile forts of steel, for the dreadnought battleship had come to be the measure of sea power among rivals.

Soon there were submarines beneath and aircraft above, and a new queen of battles appeared, the aircraft carrier, which extended her reach far beyond the range of guns by launching fighting planes from her flight deck.

The submarine brought other changes to the tactics and science of navies, and when nuclear power freed it from the atmosphere, there was produced the untrackable, invulnerable, mobile missile system upon which rests much of freedom's hope of survival.

This is where we are today. The new dreadnoughts of the sea hold the land in thrall. Battles like Lepanto, Trafalgar, Jutland and Midway are of the past, but the power of the sea to influence and even to command the shore has never been greater. We have not seen the end of an epoch, but only the prelude to the uses of sea power.

In this thoroughly researched book two well-known authors and professionals in naval lore, Mr. B. W. Bathe of the Science Museum in London, member of the Council of the Society for Nautical Research, and Captain Donald Macintyre, Royal Navy (Retired), a British naval officer of long standing and England's ace U-boat hunter in the Second World War, have combined their knowledge, experience of the sea and proven scholarship to tell us about the old ships of our naval heritage and how they became what they are. This is a labour of love, for which two better qualified Man-of-War's men could not be found.

THE COUNTER ARMADA, 1589

Sir Francis Drake's Commission appointing John Martin to be Captain of the Bark Thomas

To all Christian people who shall see, heare or read these presents Sir John Norrice and Sir Francis Drake Knights give to witt that wheras it hath pleased the Queenes most excellent Majestie ELIZABETH our gracious Soveraigne to committ unto us the charge and conduction of this Armie and Fleet for Portugall, and the coastes of Spaine, giving us expresse and full authoritie to make and constitute all Officers necessarie both by Land and Sea, for the better government of the Shipps and men under our commandement; as appeareth more at Large in her Majesties Commissions to us graunted in that behalfe, bearing date from Westminster the xi of October last in the yeare of our Lord 1588. And forasmuch as among the necessarie Officers Capitaines for the Sea to have speciall care for the mariners and Shipps during the whole time of this Service: Wee have therfore conceaved such firme opinion of the valor and sufficiencie of John Martin gentleman, that wee have authorized him, and by these presents do establish him to bee Capitaine of the Barke Thomas, beeing a Shipp of Sixscore tonne, to execute all such services by Sea, as shalbee thought requisite to be followed by that Office. Giving him full power and authoritie to doe all such actions, and receave all such dueties as are incident unto the reputation and dignitie of that Place. Willing therfore and expressly charging all Souldiers and Mariners whatsoever to whom it may appertaine for Sea Service, to be obedient and respective unto the sayd John Martin as they will answer the Contrarie at their perille. And it shalbee his sufficient warrant in that behalf. Geven under our hands and seales the 18th of April in the one and thirtieth yeare of the raigne of our Soveraigne Lady ELIZABETH by the grace of God Queen of England France and Ireland defender of the faith &c.

J. NORREYS   FRA DRAKE

To all xp̃ian people who shall see, heare or read these presentz Sr. John Norrice and Francis Drake Knights give to witt, that wheras it hath pleased the Queenes most excellent Majestie ELIZABETH o.r. grācious soveraigne, to comitt vnto vs the charge & conduct of this armie and Fleet for Portugall, and the coastes of Spaine, giving vs expresse and full authoritie to make and constitute all Officers necessarie both by Land & Sea, for the better goverm.t of the Shipps and men vnder o.r comandement; as appeareth more at large in her Majesties Comission to vs graunted in that behalfe, bearing date from Westmin̄ster the xj.th of October last in the yeare of o.r Lord 1588. And forasmuch as emong the necessarie Officers Capitaines for the Sea to have speciall care for the mariners & Shipps during the whole time of this Service: Wee have therfore conceaved such firme opinion of the valor and sufficiencie of John Martin gentleman, that wee have authorized him, and by these presents doe establish him to bee Capitaine of the Barke Thomas, beeing a Shipp of Sixscore tonne, to execute all such services by Sea, as shalbee thought requisite to be followed by that Office. Giving him full power and authoritie to doe all such actions, and receave all such dueties, as are incident vnto the reputation & dignitie of that Place. Willing therfore & expressly charging all Souldiers & Mariners whatsoever to whom it may apperteine, appointed for Sea Service, to be obedient & respective vnto the sayd John Martin as they will answer the Contrarie at their perill. And this shalbee his sufficient warrant in that behalf. Yeven vnder o.r handes and seales the 18.th of April in the one and thirtieth yeare of the raigne of o.r Soveraign Lady ELIZABETH by the grace of God Queen of England France and Ieeland defendor of the faith &c

An Egyptian river boat with crew and warriors.

Middle Kingdom, *c.* 2000 B.C.

THE FIRST FOUR THOUSAND YEARS—

EGYPT, PHOENICIA, GREECE AND ROME

Defining the term 'warship' in the broadest way as 'a ship used in war', it is not possible to say when or where primitive people first used a floating object as a fighting platform or for the transport of warriors. The first vessels used in warfare were not specially designed for fighting purposes but were the normal trading or even fishing vessels of the particular region.

Drawings of ships carrying tribal standards on Egyptian vases of the period before 3400 B.C. are possibly the earliest extant representations of ships of war. These crude drawings—some authorities even doubt that they represent ships—appear to show river craft, about 50 feet in length, with cabins amidships.

Other vases of about the same date from southern Egypt show for the first time a sail, and a steering oar used over the stern quarter of the vessel.

In ancient Egypt shipbuilders had always to contend with the difficulty of obtaining suitable local timber, and a form of construction was employed which suited the short and irregular timber of the acacia or 'sunt' tree. The hull was built without stem, sternpost, keel or ribs. The planking consisted of short thick pieces pinned together by wooden pegs and wedge-shaped dovetails. In the absence of ribs, the use of numerous heavy deck beams supplied to some extent the necessary structural strength. Contemporary Egyptian records, however, show that as early as 2900 B.C. cedar wood for shipbuilding was being imported from Phoenicia; so it would seem that some of the larger ships were constructed in a manner more akin to later shipbuilding practice, with at least the more important members of the vessel made from timber of a larger compass.

The first pictorial evidence for a sea-going naval expedition is an Egyptian bas-relief of about 2600 B.C., which shows vessels employed by the Pharaoh Sahure. These vessels were probably some 60 feet in length and constructed in the usual Egyptian manner, but to make them more suitable for sea voyages a special strengthening device was introduced. This consisted of a heavy rope truss secured at the bow and stern of the vessel, supported at intervals along the deck by vertical props and tightened by means of a rod pushed through the truss and then twisted. The purpose of this truss was to prevent sagging of the ends of the vessel, a fault to which, in view of their peculiar construction, these vessels must have been particularly vulnerable. These early sea-going ships were propelled primarily by rowers, but in fair weather conditions a single square sail would have been hoisted on the bipod mast which is shown in the lowered position on the bas-relief.

In a temple at Deir el-Bahari, reliefs of about 1500 B.C. show in much detail the sea-going ships used in an expedition sent by Queen Hatshepsut to the land of Punt, probably in the country now known as Somalia.

The expedition was primarily a trading voyage, but in the absence of contemporary evidence for ships designed specially for war, it may perhaps be accepted that vessels of the type shown were used for purposes of both war and peace.

The ships appear to be about 80 to 100 feet in length and their basic design is similar to that of the vessels already described, of some thousand years earlier. It is not clear from the reliefs whether a strong keel, or frames, were incorporated in the structure of the ship, but it was still considered necessary to fit a strong hogging truss to supplement longitudinal strength. The ends of sixteen deck beams can be seen projecting through the side planking. Large steering-oars are shown lashed to port and starboard quarters, with additional support from upright posts on the deck. From each steering-oar a tiller projects downwards and could be operated by a steersman standing on deck. The bipod mast of the earlier ship was replaced by a single pole mast placed amidships. A wide sail was spread between an upper and lower yard. The lower yard was supported by a number of ropes led up to blocks on the mast.

About 1190 B.C., a naval battle took place in which the fleet of Rameses III defeated the vessels of an invading force known as the 'Sea Peoples'.

The representation of this action on the wall of a temple at Medinet Habu is the earliest extant picture of a great naval engagement. It shows for the first time vessels designed and built as warships. The vessels are shown in a somewhat conventional style and without as much detail as those on the earlier Deir el-Bahari reliefs, but significant changes are apparent.

The hull of the Egyptian warship is long and narrow but a hogging truss is not shown. It would seem therefore that Egyptian ship construction had changed, possibly from contact with other seafarers of the Mediterranean whose vessels had developed from dugouts instead of the 'small pieces' construction of the Nile. Other new features shown in the Egyptian ship are high bulwarks to protect the rowers, a 'fighting top' on the mast and the projecting prow terminating in a carved lion's head. It has been suggested that this projecting prow was a ram for offensive purposes, but its position high above the water makes this most doubtful. The single mast carried a square sail, without the lower yard of the earlier Egyptian ships.

In the battle scene the sails are shown furled up to the yards and it is evident that the vessels were manœuvred by rowers when in action. The relief shows that the ships of the defeated 'Sea Peoples' were generally similar to the Egyptian vessels, but had high straight stems and sterns ornamented with animal or bird heads.

The 'Sea Peoples' probably came from the northern coasts of the eastern Mediterranean and may have included elements of Minoans, Greeks, Philistines and Etruscans. Contemporary representations of very early Mediterranean ships, the vessels of the Minoan civilisation, of Homeric Greece and of the Phoenicians, are very crude, and attempts to interpret the form of ships, the date of the introduction of the ram, and of oarsmen in two tiers, one above the other, from the distorted designs on pottery and seals or from the scanty literary references, must be regarded as very conjectural. It is at least evident, however, that—apart from the vessels of the Egyptians—sea-going ships were in use in the Mediterranean

Top: Egyptian ship, *c.* 1500 B.C., the type of vessel used for the expedition to Punt. Drawing based on relief at Deir el-Bahari.

Bottom: Egyptian sea-going ship, *c.* 2600 B.C.

before 2000 B.C., that the earliest fighting galley was an undecked vessel rowed by up to twenty-five oarsmen a side, arranged at one level; and that ships were fitted with rams before 800 B.C.

It would seem probable that the galley developed primarily as a ram, which played such a great part in the maritime history of the later Greek and Roman eras, evolved from a dugout canoe. Suitable trees from which the dugouts could be made were available in the Aegean littoral. Later, longitudinal planks were added to each side of the simple dugout to increase free-board and ribs or frames were added on the inside to help support and stiffen the side planks. As further development took place, the basic dugout was reduced to become the keel of a 'built' ship with stempost, sternpost and transverse frames.

In the Mediterranean from very early times vessels were carvel-built, with their longitudinal skin planking butted edge to edge. This is in contrast to the ships of northern Europe where clinker building with overlapping planks became the practice.

An important stage in the development of the galley is shown by the representations of Phoenician-Assyrian warships on bas-reliefs of about 700 B.C., from the palace of King Sennacherib at Nineveh. The hulls of these vessels were perhaps of dugout form with the bow elongated into a strong ram on the water-line, obviously designed for warfare and not ornamentation.

These reliefs are the first reliable evidence for a two-tiered oar arrangement. Above the heads of the rowers an upper deck extended from bow to stern, which was used as a fighting platform.

Despite the many surviving examples of Greek art, particularly sculptures and paintings on vases, which provide fine illustrations of the general form of galleys, precise constructional details are unknown; and the problems of how the oars and oarsmen were arranged are a matter of conjecture and controversy.

As already shown, the two-tiered galley—the bireme—first appeared in the eastern Mediterranean about 700 B.C., and the three-tiered vessel—trireme—was in use in the same waters before 500 B.C. These long and narrow vessels were designed as weapons, to ram and sink enemy ships. Their structure had to be strong enough to withstand the shock of ramming and light enough to enable sufficient speed to be obtained by the rowers. The practical difficulties of wooden shipbuilding limited the length to which a vessel of these proportions could be made; and thus the only way an increased number of oars could be used, to give more force to the ram, was by mounting them in tiers, or what is more often termed 'banks'.

From the contemporary evidence, including paintings, sculpture, written records and the known dimensions of slipways on which galleys were built, a conjectural reconstruction of a trireme of about 500 B.C. can be made. Thus the typical trireme was about 140 feet in length, with a width of hull of about 16 feet. The width of the vessel was further increased by some 4 feet by the projecting structure which extended along each side of the trireme and on which the oars of the upper and middle 'banks' were probably pivoted. Usually one hundred and seventy oars were used, arranged thirty-one a side on the top 'bank' and twenty-seven a side in the middle and lower 'banks'. The oars did not exceed 14 feet 6 inches in length and each oar was pulled by one man.

Although exact details are unknown, it seems that the trireme was built with frames and deck beams to give transverse strength; but with a hull so long in proportion to its beam, the keel and skin-planking above would not have provided sufficient longitudinal strength. Therefore, heavy bands of timber—in later ship-building known as 'wales'—were fitted outside the skin planking, extending the full length of the hull. The lower of these wales joined the forward projection of the keel. The ram, with the strength of the keel behind it and supported on each side by the wales, thus became the strongest unit of the vessel.

Triremes were the principal vessels used by both the opposing forces at the battle of Salamis in 480 B.C., and in the Peloponnesian War, 431–404 B.C.

At Salamis, the Athenians and their allies, with some three hundred triremes, were able to decisively defeat a Persian force of about a thousand vessels,

Egyptian ships, fifth dynasty. This bas-relief from the tomb of King Sahu-re (c. 2600 B.C.) is the earliest record giving a representation of sea-going vessels.

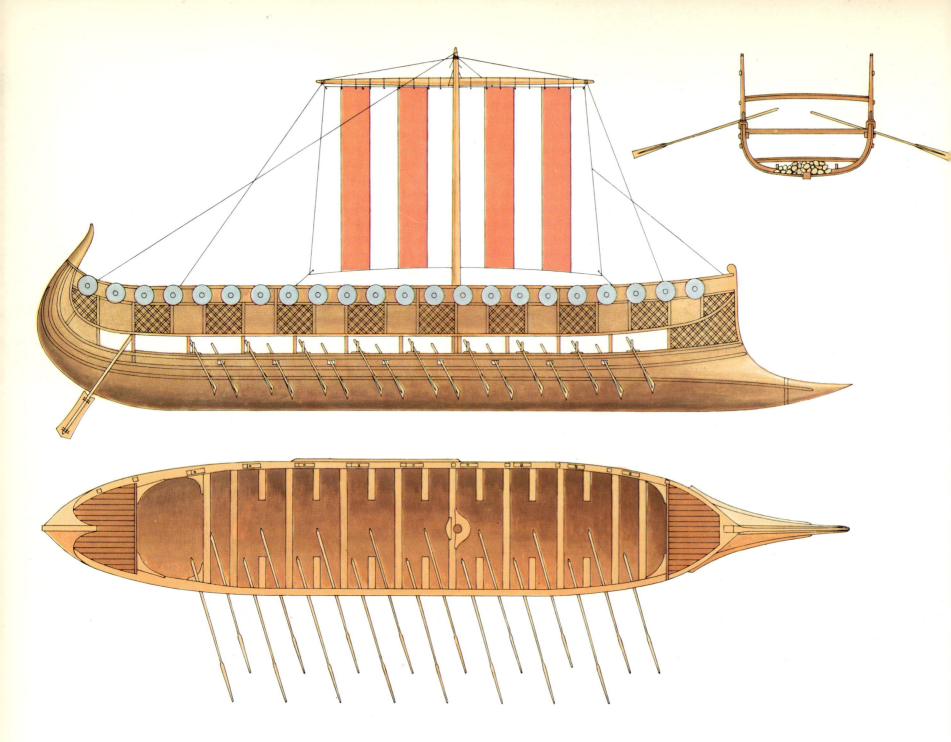

PHOENICIAN WAR GALLEY

Seventh century B.C.

14

consisting mainly of contingents from Egypt and Phoenicia. By a stratagem, the Persian fleet was enticed into a narrow channel and were thus able to fight only on a narrow front in difficult water conditions. Repeated ramming attacks by lines of Greek vessels routed the tightly packed mass of enemy vessels.

Classical writers describing the tactics of galley warfare state that the fleets were usually formed up with their vessels in lines abreast. Manœuvres are described in which the practice was to break through the enemy line of galleys and then turn and ram, or to row round the flank of the enemy line and then ram. In each case the principal point of attack was against the relatively weak stern portion of the galley.

Defensive fleet formations to counter these manœuvres could be made, and the ideal theoretical attack in which a galley rammed an adversary and then withdrew to allow the holed vessel to sink was not always possible, but other means of offensive action were employed.

The galley carried contingents of archers to harass the enemy, and of soldiers for the hand-to-hand fighting which would take place after boarding. Heavy weights and pots of burning material—the latter a forerunner of 'Greek fire'—were suspended from projecting spars so that they could be dropped on to an enemy.

After about 300 B.C., artillery, in the form of catapults, was carried in the larger galleys. These catapults could shoot spears, stones or pots containing fire, and lengthened considerably the range of attack.

According to contemporary sources, soon after 400 B.C. vessels known as quadriremes and quinqueremes were in use, and by 300 B.C. these more powerful vessels had, to a large extent, taken the place of the older type of trireme.

Various theories have been advanced as to the position of the oars and oarsmen of these vessels. Even more difficult is the problem of the oarage of galleys, which writers of the period credit with from six to forty banks of oars.

It might have been possible to construct and use quadriremes and quinqueremes with four and five rows of oars. It would not have been practical to add extra rows after this; the oars would have been too long and heavy to use, and the vessel itself unstable and unseaworthy.

Some authorities believe that the classification by 'remes' did not refer to banks of oars operating at different heights from the water but to the number of men employed on each oar or at each set of oars. Following this theory, various alternative arrangements have been thought possible; for instance, a quadrireme could have been a galley with a single horizontal row of oars and four men to each oar. If the classification is taken as referring to the number of men to each set of oars, the quadrireme could have had two rows of oars with two men at each oar, or alternatively three rows of oars with one man at each oar of the lower and middle rows and two men at the longer oar of the upper row.

It must be emphasised again that all these conclusions are conjectural and that the problem of the oarage of galleys has not yet been solved. Perhaps the activities of land and underwater archaeologists may provide further information on this subject which has so long been a matter of argument.

The same problems of design, dimensions and oarage arise in the study of Roman galleys. The Romans, a military rather than a maritime nation, copied their war vessels from the Greeks and Carthaginians to such advantage that Rome eventually became the major seapower in the Mediterranean.

Early in the third century B.C. the expanding military and commercial power of Rome led to hostility with the Carthaginians, a seafaring nation whose galleys at that time controlled the Mediterranean. When the First Punic War commenced in 264 B.C., Rome had virtually no navy to oppose the Carthaginian fleet or to prevent communications between the Carthaginian bases in Africa and their colonies in Sicily.

In 260 B.C. the Romans built a fleet, while the oarsmen were trained ashore in replicas of the galley's rowing benches.

In naval warfare, the Carthaginians employed the ramming tactics which, to be successful, demanded an ability to manœuvre the galley only to be obtained from

Detail from bas-relief depicting a galley. From the palace of King Sennacherib at Nineveh, c. 700 B.C.

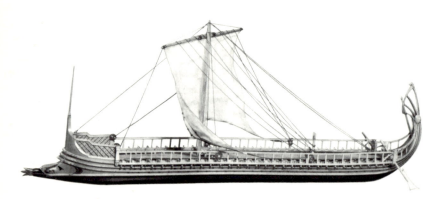

Top: Greek galley shown on a contemporary vase, eighth century B.C.

Bottom: Greek galley, fourth century B.C.

very skilled oarsmen. The Romans, lacking the skill in maritime warfare which had been acquired over the centuries by the Carthaginians, had to find a method of fighting which would enable their superb land troops to be used to advantage.

To exploit to the full the fighting qualities of the troops it was necessary to get them quickly and safely on to the enemy vessel. For this purpose a machine known as a 'corvus' was devised. The corvus was a heavy boarding plank some 30 feet in length and 4 feet wide, with a strong iron spike under its outer end. The inner end of the plank worked against an upright pole on the deck, at the bows of the galley. When going into action, the plank was raised by a tackle led to the top of the pole.

When an enemy galley closed in to ram, the plank was dropped so that the spike at its outer end became embedded in the enemy's deck. With the vessels thus fastened together the Roman troops were able to charge across the boarding plank and engage the Carthaginians in hand-to-hand fighting. The stratagem appears to have come as a surprise to the Carthaginians and to have been most successful. In 260 B.C., at the battle of Mylae, a Roman fleet defeated a Carthaginian force, capturing or sinking forty-four of their galleys.

During the earlier years of the long struggle with Carthage, Roman fleets were lost through poor seamanship, but the organising and driving power of Rome enabled the fleets to be supplied with new and improved galleys. These later galleys seem to have been heavy quinqueremes and triremes, with very substantial rams, sheathed with iron or bronze. Some protection against the rams of enemy galleys was provided in the form of belts of timber, perhaps reinforced with iron plates. Turret-like fighting platforms were fitted on deck. As trained and experienced crews became available the corvus seems to have been largely discarded. Perhaps also the Carthaginians had found a counter stratagem.

After the destruction of Carthage, in 146 B.C., these heavy galleys remained the principal fighting vessels of the Roman fleets. However, about the middle of the first century B.C., a new lighter and faster type of galley was introduced. Known as 'liburnians' these galleys were adapted from the vessels used by pirates who operated from the Illyrian coast.

There is no definite knowledge of the oarage of the liburnian, but the arrangement was most probably of 'bireme' type with two rows of oars.

Liburnians may have formed part of Julius Caesar's fleet which, in 56 B.C., defeated a force of over two hundred ships of the Veneti, a tribe from Brittany. This battle is the first recorded with northern ships, and is important in being a major action between oared vessels and vessels which relied mainly on their sails.

Caesar's description of the Veneti vessels makes it clear that they differed greatly from the galleys of the Mediterranean. Caesar relates that they were shallow-draught vessels, flat-bottomed, with high bows and sterns, and very strongly built of oak. They were rigged with leather sails and their ability, in comparison with his own vessels, to endure storms, and to be run aground without damage, is commented on by Caesar. In the action, the Romans, who found that the Veneti ships were too strong to be badly damaged by ramming, used hooks at the ends of long poles to tear away the rigging, bringing down the yards and sails, and so immobilising the enemy vessels.

At the battle of Actium in 31 B.C., galleys of the liburnian type proved successful in action against the older, heavier class of galley, and by the first century A.D. they were in extensive use in the Roman fleets.

Important developments in the design of galleys do not seem to have occurred during the next four hundred years when the Roman Empire reached its greatest size and was, for much of the time, in almost complete control of the Mediterranean and the waters surrounding her more distant provinces. During this period heavy galleys were most probably retained for use in home waters, but the naval forces employed in policing and guard duties throughout the empire used galleys of the liburnian type.

In the sixth century A.D., after the decline of the western Roman Empire and the transfer of power to Byzantium (Constantinople), a new type of galley known as a 'dromon' came into use in the Mediterranean. The name means 'runner' and

Details from a black-figured amphora showing Greek ships. *c.*
540 B.C.

the earliest dromons (warships of this name continued in use until medieval times) were light, fast craft.

Later there were different classes of dromons, the largest of which formed the most powerful units of the Byzantine navy. The dromons were fitted with fighting decks at the bows and sterns connected by gangways and were propelled by a hundred oars arranged fifty a side at two levels. The number of men pulling at each oar varied in accordance with the size of the dromon.

An important innovation of about 600 A.D. was the fitting of fore and aft sails of a triangular shape—lateen sails—to the dromon in place of the square sails which had been carried by most Greek and Roman galleys as secondary means of propulsion.

The use of fire as a weapon in sea warfare has already been mentioned, but from the seventh century A.D. a new and very effective weapon came into use in the Byzantine fleets. This was a form of flame-thrower mounted on the foredeck of the dromon and discharging 'Greek fire', a liquid combustible of which naphtha was the principal ingredient. The Byzantines became expert in the use of this destructive and terrifying weapon, and it undoubtedly accounted for their success in many naval actions.

ROMAN GALLEYS

With legionaries on board.

From a bas-relief.

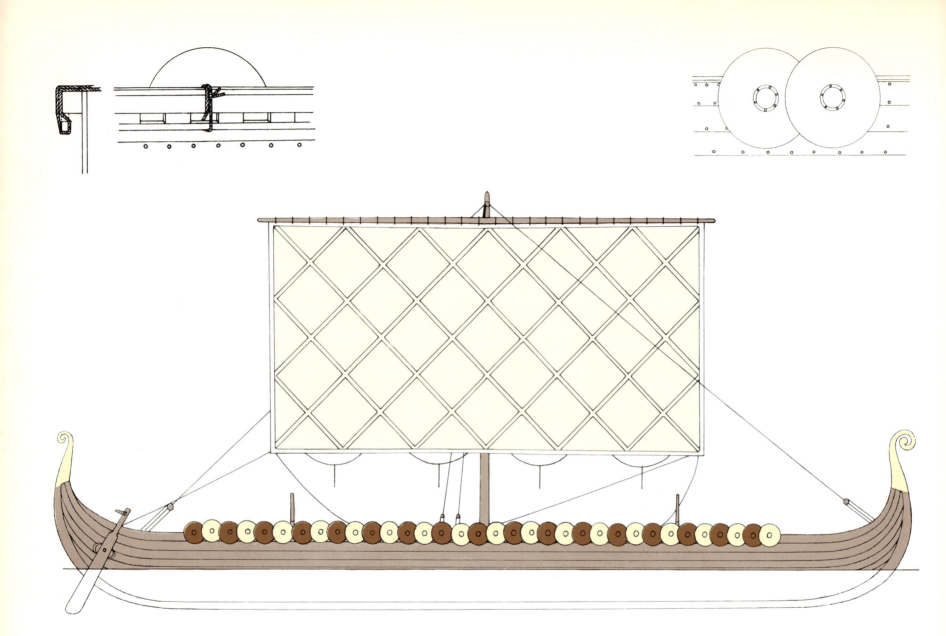

THE GOKSTAD SHIP

(A reconstruction)

Left: Midship section.

Top: The shields were fastened by ropes through the shield grips
and a batten on the inside of the rail.

In northern Europe the development of the sea-going warship started later than in Egypt and the eastern Mediterranean area.

From the Stone Age rock carvings of north Norway, which are thought to depict skin boats; from the representations of Bronze Age vessels on rocks in Norway, Sweden and Denmark, and from the dugout canoes that have been found in these areas, it has been established that the early inhabitants of Scandinavia were using boats for coastal fishing, transport and perhaps for combat purposes from about 2000 B.C. The remains of vessels which have been found in Scandinavia show how, in a period of some one thousand three hundred years, from about 300 B.C., that admirably designed and built vessel, the Viking longship, was evolved from these early primitive craft.

The first actual example of a northern warship is the remains of a sea-going boat of 300 B.C., found with a quantity of arms on the Danish island of Als.

This long vessel, 43 feet in length, was constructed from five planks sewn together with cord, and fitted with a number of thin internal ribs lashed to cleats on the planks. Ten light transverse beams—thwarts—provided seats for twenty men using paddles. The vessel was perhaps an attempt to copy in wood a boat made from animal skins, sewn together and stretched over wood framework, rather than a development from a dugout with additional planks on each side.

This vessel had a constructional feature which remained a characteristic of northern European vessels until the Middle Ages and is still used for some small craft—it was clinker built, that is, the lower edge of each longitudinal plank overlapped the upper edge of the plank immediately below it.

A further important step in the history of the longship is shown in a vessel, of the first or second century, known as the Halsnøy boat. This craft has rowlocks on the gunwale, indicating the use of oars instead of paddles, a change which had taken place on the Nile some three thousand years earlier.

A vessel of about A.D. 300, found at Nydam in Schleswig, is the earliest example in which iron rivets are used to join the overlapping edges of the planks. The Nydam boat, double-ended and undecked, is built of oak, with a length of 78 feet and a beam of 10 feet 6 inches. There is no sign that a mast was fitted, the boat being propelled by fifteen oars a side.

In the Kvalsund ship of about A.D. 700, a definite projecting keel appears for the first time instead of the keel plank of the earlier vessels.

A later stage in the progress of Viking shipbuilding is shown in a very well-preserved vessel of the second half of the ninth century, found in a burial mound at Gokstad in Norway.

This warship, nearly 80 feet in length, is a well-proportioned, double-ended vessel, built of oak, with a heavy external keel and a high stem and sternpost. Transverse strength was provided by a number of frames or ribs and by cross-beams attached to the frames and extending from side to side, with knees—right-angle timbers—at the junction of cross-beam and side plank. Movable boards were placed over the beams to form a deck. The frames were not connected directly to the keel but only indirectly by means of the garboard strakes—the planks nearest the keel.

The clinker planking of sixteen strakes a side was attached to the frames in two distinct ways. In making the planks used below the water-line, cleats or lugs were left standing on their inner surfaces. The planks were then fastened to the frames by means of lashings which passed through the cleats and through holes in the frames. Above the water-line the planks were attached to the frames by

wooden nails. The overlapping edges of the planks were fastened together with iron rivets. This unique form of construction, using thin planks, produced a strong vessel which remained light and supple and so particularly suitable for rowing.

The Gokstad ship was rowed by sixteen oars a side. These oars, which varied in length between 17 and 19 feet, were worked through small openings—oarports—cut in the side planking about 18 inches below the gunwale. When not in use the oarports could be closed on the inside by round lids which could be swung in place in front of the oar-ports. There was no evidence in the vessel of seats for the oarsmen and it is considered probable that the oarsmen used their sea-chests for seats.

Although, in common with other northern warships, the Gokstad ship was designed primarily for rowing, the vessel undoubtedly had reasonably good sailing qualities. A mast, which would have carried a single square sail, was housed amidships in a very strong and elaborate form of mast step which was designed to allow the mast to be lowered.

The vessel was steered by an oar fastened to a conical wood chock on the starboard—that is, the 'steerboard'—quarter.

A Viking warship was measured by the number of divisions which it contained. Each division, known as a 'room', consisted of the space between two successive cross-beams in which a pair of oars was worked, one to port and one to starboard. Thus the Gokstad vessel was a ship of sixteen 'rooms' and was a comparatively small warship of her period.

An augmentation in warship design took place at the end of the ninth century A.D. Anglo-Saxon records state that Alfred, King of England, had vessels built which were larger and of a different shape to the vessels used by the Danes and Frisians. Although this is the first mention of the large northern vessels of the tenth to twelfth centuries it is not certain if this class of warship, later known as 'dragons', actually originated in England or in Norway.

With his fleet, which included these larger vessels, Alfred was able for the first time to defeat the raiding Scandinavian forces at sea and so prevent landings on the coast.

No actual remains of the larger types of the longships have been found and the very few extant contemporary pictures provide only obscure representations. However, a little of their history is related in the Norse Sagas. In A.D. 900–1000 a thirty-four room, sixty-eight oared warship named the *Long Serpent* was built in Norway for Olaf Tryggvason, and at that time was described as the largest and finest longship. The length of the keel of this vessel has been recorded, and if, as seems most likely, her proportions were similar to those of the Gokstad ship, the *Long Serpent* must have been about 150 feet long overall with a beam of about 30 feet. At least sixteen of the dragon class of warships were built in the Viking era.

The largest recorded, a sixty-room longship, is stated to have been built for King Canute. The size of this vessel is probably exaggerated, as a vessel pulling sixty oars in a single horizontal row on each side would have had to be about 250 feet in length, larger than practical for wooden shipbuilding even in the nineteenth century. With the exception of a brief account of three, apparently unsuccessful, vessels built in the early years of the thirteenth century, there is no knowledge of early northern warships with more than one horizontal row or bank of oars.

The northern warships of the eleventh to fourteenth centuries have been classified into three main categories: first the 'dragon' with thirty or more rooms, then

HIC EXEVNT:CABALLI DE NAVIBVS ·-· ET HIC:MILITES: FESTINA

the longship with around twenty-five rooms, and lastly the smaller warships with from thirteen to twenty rooms.

The longships were not fitted with rams, and their design and light construction made them unsuitable for the ramming tactics used in the Mediterranean. In an engagement the northern warships provided a mobile floating platform from which archers could operate first and then, when laid alongside an enemy vessel, hand-to-hand fighting could decide the issue. An advantage of the 'dragons' was that their height above their small adversaries enabled the archers to shoot down into the enemy ships, while it was most difficult for enemy troops to board them from below. However, from the relatively small number of 'dragons' built and from the short periods of their service it would seem that they were not altogether successful. A vessel of this type and size would have been structurally weak, and the advantages of height and size of complement were outweighed by the greater manœuvring ability of the smaller longships in the same way as in the Mediterranean the liburnian class of Roman galley had proved successful against much larger and heavier multi-oared warships.

The fleet in which the army of William, Duke of Normandy, sailed in 1066, for the conquest of England, is depicted in conventional style in the famous Bayeux tapestry, which is believed to have been completed in 1077. The vessels are clearly of Viking type, clinker-built, with raised stem and sternposts and a steering-oar on the starboard quarter. Other sections of the tapestry show the vessels being constructed and also Saxon vessels, which are very similar to those of the Normans except that the uppermost strake which is pierced for oars is not continuous from bow to stern. Some Norman and Saxon ships are shown with a line of shields arranged along the gunwale, and the vessel in which Duke William sailed is distinguished by a device at the masthead which is thought to have been a lantern.

Detail from the famous Bayeux tapestry showing William the Conqueror's ships under construction.

THE THIRTEENTH AND FOURTEENTH CENTURIES

The principal, and indeed almost the only contemporary pictures of the warships used in northern European waters at the end of the twelfth century and during the thirteenth and fourteenth centuries are the representations of ships which appear on the seals of towns and offices concerned with maritime affairs. Unfortunately the shape and confined space on the seal has in many cases caused the artist to alter the proportions of the vessel and make the hull appear much too short in relation to its height.

The early seals of places as far apart as La Rochelle, Lübeck and Bergen show how double-ended, clinker-built warships of the Viking type were employed throughout the northern seas. The large warships depicted on medieval seals are shown without oars, indicating that, by that date, they were primarily sailing ships, although provision was undoubtedly made for oars to be used if necessary. After allowing for the distortion caused by the form of the seals it is evident that these sailing ships were considerably wider in proportion to their length than the Viking longships and that they had inherited something of the design of the merchant vessels of the Viking era.

A significant addition to the Viking design was the introduction—first shown in detail on thirteenth-century seals—of small castellated platforms set up on posts at each end of the vessel. These fighting castles were at first only temporary erections, but their gradual transition into permanent structures secured to the stem and sternpost is clearly shown on later seals.

At this period most of the vessels used for war were temporarily converted merchant ships. For instance in England a federation of ports known as the Cinque Ports, in return for various privileges, had to supply for the king's service a certain number of vessels for a set period annually. The only major alteration to these merchant ships seems to have been the fitting of the elevated fighting platforms at bow and stern, and even these may have been retained by the merchant ships to assist in the defence of the vessels against pirates.

A change which had an important effect on the design of ships, and produced for the first time in northern ships a stern of different shape to the bows, took place at the end of the twelfth century.

The rudder, which until then had been mounted on the side of the vessel, was transferred to a median position on the sternpost. In order to facilitate the fitting of the rudder the sternpost was made straight and more vertical, thus making it possible to run the underwater skin planking further aft. In addition to making the rudder fastening much stronger and strengthening the hull structure, this underwater planking gave an extra 'grip' in the water, thus reducing the drift to leeward when attempting to beat to windward. At the same time the length to breadth proportions of the vessel were gradually altered.

The longships, primarily rowing vessels, had a length equal to about five times their breadth. In the sailing ship then emerging, the length was reduced to about three times the breadth. This length to breadth proportion of about three to one for sailing vessels continued until the end of the eighteenth century.

The improvement in the design of the hulls of northern vessels was not accompanied by an improvement in rig, and one mast usually supporting a single sail remained the standard rig until the beginning of the fifteenth century. The retention for so long of this primitive rig, providing only a very limited ability to beat to windward, is surprising as two- and three-masted vessels and lateen fore-and-aft sails were in use in the Mediterranean area and were familiar to northern seamen.

Commercial contact between northern Europe and the Mediterranean countries was growing and in 1190 Richard I, King of England, assembled a fleet of warships and transports for the Third Crusade. This expedition to the Holy Land was the first occasion since the time of the Vikings (860, and in the eleventh century) when a large force of northern ships entered the Mediterranean and the first time a code of regulations for governing the fleet was established.

Contemporary accounts differ in describing the composition of this fleet of some two hundred vessels. The names given by medieval writers to various types of ships are confusing and on occasions the same name is apparently applied to vessels of very different appearance. Vessels known as 'esneccas' (in Swedish *snäcka*—shell) and 'busses' were the principal types of ships used in the fleet. The esnecca was, at that date, a vessel of galley type propelled by sail and oars, probably derived from the northern longship but with some features of the Mediterranean galley. Busses were designed as sailing ships and were used chiefly as transports.

The dimensions of twelfth- and thirteenth-century ships are not known, but contemporary authorities mention busses with three decks able to carry over two hundred passengers. Some Mediterranean ships were much larger. In 1191 the warships of the Crusaders' fleet fought an action off Beirut with a Saracen dromon. This vessel was the largest encountered by the fleet and is described as having three masts and a complement of one thousand five hundred. The Crusaders found it impossible to board this huge dromon, which was eventually sunk after being rammed by a number of their esneccas.

Another vessel of the early Middle Ages was the 'cog', but again we have no contemporary technical description of the vessel. The early cogs were apparently somewhat smaller than busses—an account of 1303 shows that the cargo of a particular cog was 104 tons of wine. The cog was particularly associated with the federation of German towns known as the Hanseatic League and the vessels shown on the thirteenth- and fourteenth-century seals of these towns are thought to represent cogs.

Used also as warships, the cog increased in size and numbers during the fourteenth and fifteenth centuries when it formed one of the principal vessels used in the northern sea-fighting forces.

A battle off Dover in 1217 was one of the first of the long series of great naval battles between the fleets of England and France which culminated in the Battle

Ship of the Cinque Ports, *c.* 1300. A representation of a ship of this type forms the central ornament of the Seal of Dover in use about A.D. 1300.

of Trafalgar in 1805. In the engagement off Dover the smaller English fleet, consisting for the main part of cogs from the Cinque Ports, completely defeated a French fleet. The contemporary accounts of the battle are of particular interest to the naval historian as they form one of the earliest extant descriptions of naval tactics with a fleet of sailing vessels. The English fleet deliberately sailed past the opposing force and then turned to have the advantage of the wind when bearing down on the enemy. In the tactical manipulation of a fleet in battle the ability to achieve the weather gage, which depended so much on seamanship and on the sailing qualities of the warships, was one of the decisive factors until the end of the sailing warship.

Medieval writers unfortunately tell us little more than the names of the weapons which formed the armament of dromons, galleys, busses and cogs. The exact size and range of the various stone and arrow throwing machines are unknown. In Mediterranean warships the larger machines, petrariae, mangonels and trebuchets, were frequently used, but northern vessels seem to have relied mainly on the ballista, a form of large cross-bow, as their long-range weapon.

Greek fire, now used by northern and southern ships, gradually became less important as it was found that it could be extinguished by sand, and the effectiveness of protective devices such as sheets of felt soaked in vinegar became apparent. Despite the use of these weapons and the introduction of elementary tactical manœuvres, in the final outcome the sailing warship, until the sixteenth century, was regarded as a floating fortress which could only be captured by hand-to-hand fighting.

Galleys, although used, did not form a major wing of the English fleet as they did in the fleets of France, Spain and Mediterranean powers. English galleys were different in construction and rig to the southern galleys, which in their general design and rig, that is carvel construction and lateen sails, remained practically the same from the thirteenth century until they went out of use at the end of the eighteenth century.

From the extant building accounts and inventories of galleys built at various English ports at the end of the thirteenth century and during the fourteenth century, it is known that the vessels were clinker-built and rigged with a square sail. From this contemporary evidence it has been estimated that the galleys ranged between 80 and 120 feet in length and were pulled by from fifty-four to one hundred oars. How these oars were arranged remains conjectural.

Little is known of their hull form but they were probably double ended and not fitted with rams. A line of hurdles was fitted along the bulwarks between the raised fighting platforms at bow and stern, to provide some protection for the rowers.

To revert to the Mediterranean, from the thirteenth to sixteenth centuries the oarage of most galleys was arranged in a system known as 'zenzile' rowing. In this system two and later three oars were arranged in groups with the oarsmen, one to each oar, seated at the same level.

Contemporary information is available on the war galleys of the navy of Venice in the fourteenth and fifteenth centuries, galleys which were typical of those used throughout the Mediterranean.

The ordinary Venetian galley had a hull length of about 130 feet and a breadth of 16 feet. Along each side, just above the level of the deck and projecting some 2 feet from the hull, a light structure was fitted which carried the thole-pins for about 180 oars. The thole-pins were placed about 12 inches apart in groups of three. The centre pin of each group was about 3 feet 6 inches from the centre pin of its adjacent groups. A narrow gangway extended along the centre line of the galley with the benches for the rowers on either side. The benches were not set at right angles to the gangway but were angled so that the inner end of each bench was further aft than the outer. Thus groups of three oarsmen, each with an oar of different length, worked on the port and starboard benches with the inboard rowers sitting slightly aft of the men on their outboard side.

At this date the Venetian galleys, in common with other Mediterranean galleys, were no longer fitted with rams, but at the bows a light beak extended forwards, above the water. This beak remained a distinctive feature of galleys until the

ENGLISH SHIP

of the early fifteenth century.

The sail is decorated with the arms of

John, Duke of Bedford (1389–1435).

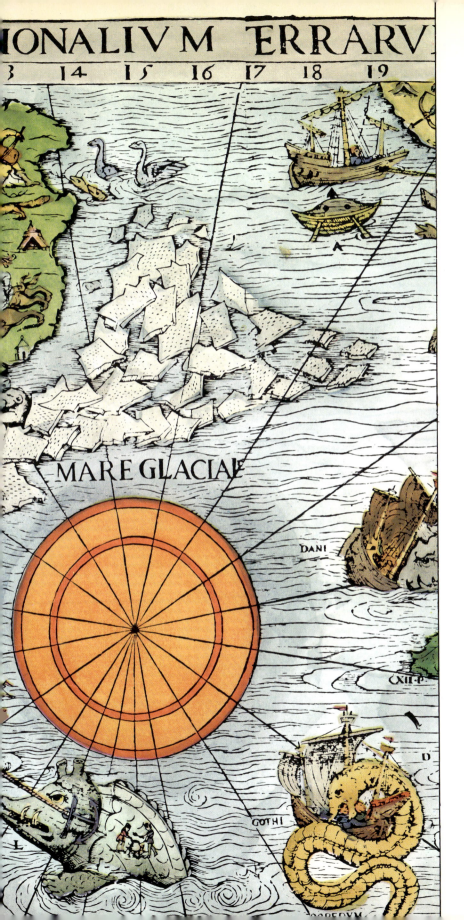

MARE GLACIAL

DANI

GOTHI

Merchant vessels, representative of the type of ship used *c.* 1500, fighting for the best market places in Iceland. Map from 'Carta Marina', published in 1539 by Olaus Magnus, Swedish scholar and historian.

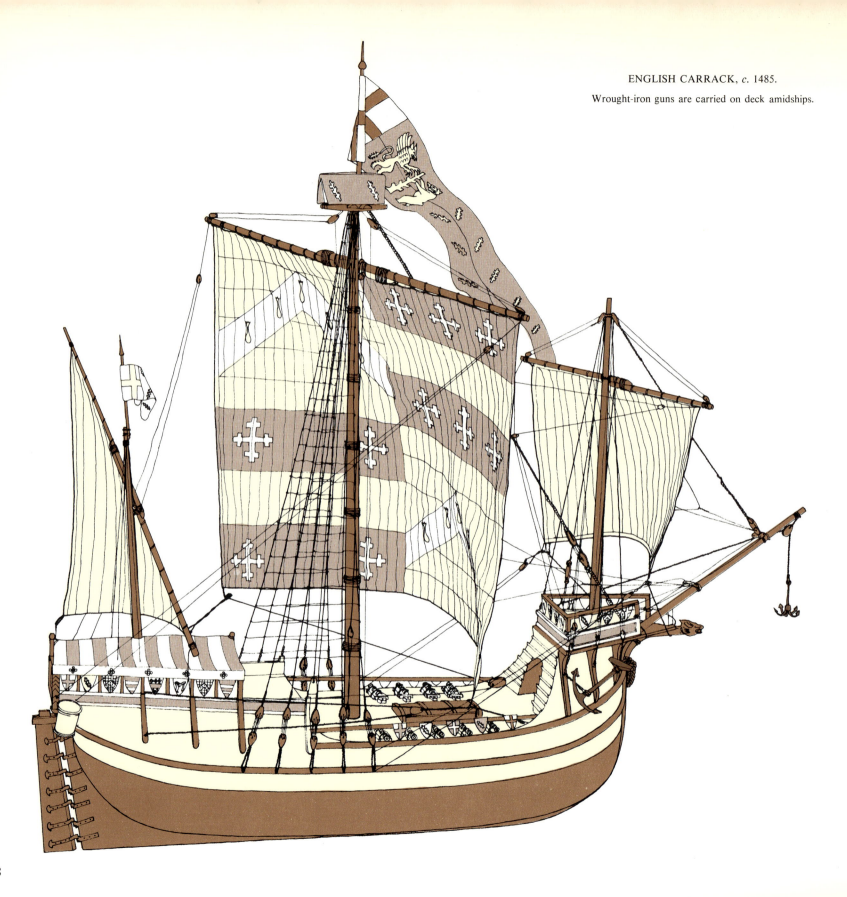

ENGLISH CARRACK, *c.* 1485.
Wrought-iron guns are carried on deck amidships.

28

eighteenth century and seems to have been developed to break the oars of the galley rammed, as the rowing-frame made the old, low ram a dangerous feature. The vessel rammed might settle on the attacker's ram and thus sink both vessels. It was better to cripple the enemy and then sink him at leisure. The galleys probably carried a stone or arrow throwing machine on a platform at the bows, forerunner of the cannon or group of cannons carried in this position by later galleys. As this machine and indeed the later cannons were fitted in such a way that they could only fire in a forward direction it was necessary to manœuvre the vessel so that the bows faced the enemy, an operation only possible with a vessel not dependent on sails alone.

In the Mediterranean the side rudder was retained much longer than in the north and two steering-oars, one on each side of the vessel, remained in common use until about 1450. In galleys the median rudder was introduced about the middle of the fourteenth century, at first in combination with steering-oars in the quarters, but in the early years of the fifteenth century the side rudders were discarded.

THE FIFTEENTH CENTURY

In the hundred years between the beginning and end of the fifteenth century very great changes and improvements took place in the design and rig of sailing ships. In this relatively short period the change from one-masted to three-masted vessels took place.

At the beginning of the century the northern ships were fitted with a single mast amidships, square sails and a rudimentary bowsprit used to extend the bowlines of the square sail. However, before 1500 the three-masted sailing ship, with a fore-and-aft sail on the mizen or after mast, and a square headsail under the bowsprit, was in general use.

It was principally the adoption of this rig that made possible the exploratory voyages of Díaz, Columbus and da Gama, and its employment for warships increased the ability of commanders to navigate their ships in action and of fleets to perform tactical movements. A two-masted, square-sail rig, with headsails, which bridged the change from one to three masts was employed for little more than fifty years. A second mast placed either before or aft of the established midships mast was unbalanced and unsuccessful in the form of vessel then used.

Contemporary representations of vessels of this period, and particularly of two-masted ships, are scarce, but fortunately some documentary and other evidence is extant. Venetian manuscripts of the early fifteenth century describe, for the first time in any detail, contemporary Mediterranean naval architecture. In England the actual remains have been discovered of the *Grâce Dieu*, an exceptionally large warship built at Southampton in 1416–18. At this date there was probably not much difference in the general appearance of the hulls of the larger sailing warships of the north and those of the Mediterranean. However, the remains of the *Grâce Dieu* show that even the largest northern vessels were still clinker-built.

In this case a most remarkable form of overlapping planking was employed. Each strake was about 7 feet in length and was built up from three layers of planking. Each 'sandwich' of planking was fastened to the one below by iron clench nails spaced about 8 inches apart and the layers of planking were fastened to the frames by treenails—wooden pins. The frames, notched to fit the planking, were about 1 foot wide by 10 inches deep and spaced 4 inches apart. Each frame was built up from short lengths of timber scarphed together. The whole structure was rendered watertight by caulking with moss, oakum and pitch.

From the constructional details it seems certain that the frames were fitted after the planking had been erected, as is general in smaller clinker-built vessels to the present day. As already stated, the *Grâce Dieu* at about 1400 tons was very large for her time. From the remains it has been calculated that she had a keel length of about 112 feet and an overall length of about 180 feet. The *Grâce Dieu* was

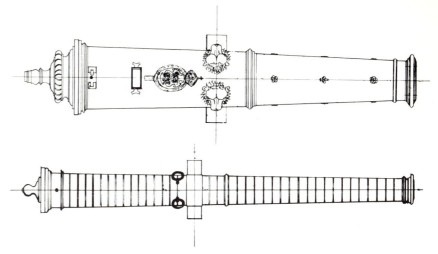

Top: Brass cannon royal from the *Mary Rose*, sunk in 1545.

Bottom: Wrought-iron serpent, *c.* 1450.

Iron hoop gun from the *Mary Rose*.

apparently a failure and remained for many years in the Hamble river until accidentally burnt in 1439, but several other large English warships—such as the *Jesus of the Tower* (1000 tons), the *Holigost of the Tower* (760 tons) and the *Trinity Royal of the Tower* (540 tons)—were in the service of King Henry V. In the names of the vessels the supplemental *of the Tower* was the old equivalent of H.M.S.

The tonnage of medieval ships is often one of the few measurements recorded, but as the exact method of calculating the tonnage is not known it is impossible to deduce the length and breadth of vessels from these recorded tonnages.

Not many large warships, such as the 'king's ships' just mentioned, had been built; the typical warship of the period was the cog of about four hundred tons. The superstructures at the bow and stern of the cog, although now permanent and much larger, were still not a continuation of the hull proper. The stern-castle in particular remained a rectangular erection superimposed on the curved lines of the hull. The stern-castle, also known as the summer-castle, was used to provide accommodation for important personages. The truncated triangular forecastle projecting above the stem was primarily a fighting platform and was therefore built much higher than the aftercastle. Wooden frames on both these superstructures supported awnings to give protection from sun and rain.

The invention of gunpowder and the use of fire-arms at sea did not at first produce any radical changes in the design of warships. Guns were employed for land warfare before 1325 and formed a small part of the armament of ships by the 1350s. The early guns used at sea were small, often weighing less than forty pounds, and were carried on the decks of the fore- and after-castles of warships, and of merchant ships used as men-of-war, and no structural alterations were necessary.

For a considerable time after the introduction of fire-arms, the principal weapons were still the bow, crossbow, darts and lances, while only a few guns were carried by each ship. Inventories of 1410–12 relating to the ships of Henry IV, King of England, record that the *Christopher of the Tower* had three iron guns, with five chambers, and one hand gun. (One of the earliest types of gun used at sea was a breech-loader which had a removable chamber at the base end of the gun.)

During the later part of the fifteenth century the fore- and after-castles gradually became larger, stronger and higher, incorporating a number of decks at ascending levels. The sides of these superstructures were pierced by gunports so that the small guns could be used at the various deck levels. These openings did not affect the strength of the main structure of the hull and presented no greater problem to the shipwright than that of the carpenter in making similar openings in a wooden building.

Towards the end of the century, when larger guns were first used in ships, they were carried on the main-deck in the waist of the vessel. At this date few large cast cannon were made, particularly in northern Europe, and the guns were usually fabricated from longitudinal wrought-iron bars over which were shrunk iron rings. These weapons were breech-loading with a separate chamber that was either screwed or wedged in position. The heavy built-up guns (some were over 9 feet in length, with a calibre of 8 inches and weighing about 8000 pounds) were mounted on wooden beds. The guns either projected through embrasures in the rail or over the top of a low rail amidships, without in any way interfering with the framing or planking of the hull.

By about 1470 a type of vessel known as a carrack was taking the place of the cog. The carrack was primarily a cargo-carrier but, like the cog, was hired by maritime powers for naval purposes and the large vessels designed as warships were carrack-built.

By the last years of the fifteenth century it is probable that most large northern vessels were also carvel-built. Perhaps the failure of such a large and important vessel as the clinker-built *Gráce Dieu* of 1418 was in part responsible for the gradual adoption by northern shipwrights of the much stronger carvel-building methods of the Mediterranean.

Contemporary illustrations and accounts show that the carrack, normally of about 600 tons, was very strongly built with closely spaced frames, and carvel

planking reinforced by four heavy longitudinal wales running from bow to stern on each side. The most typical feature of the carrack was the large forecastle projecting out over the stem and containing two or more decks. At the stern the rather lower aftercastle or summer-castle now supported a poop and poop-royal.

In England during the years 1486–88 two large carrack-type warships, the *Regent* and the *Sovereign*, were built for King Henry VII, and the accounts and inventories relating to their building and later fittings are extant.

From these accounts the statement that the *Regent* had a fore-mast, main-mast, main mizen-mast and bonaventure mizen-mast is an early record of a four-masted English ship. In addition the *Regent* carried a topmast on the fore-mast, a topgallant and topmast on the main-mast. The sailplan, consisting of foresail, mainsail, fore-topsail, main-topsail (and possibly a main topgallantsail), a lateen sail on each of the mizen-masts and a spritsail under the bowsprit, was a decided advance from that of only a few years earlier and a tremendous step forward from the single sail of the beginning of the century.

In 1495 the *Regent* was armed with two hundred and twenty-five guns, all apparently breech-loading 'serpentines'. Although most of these serpentines were small and weighed about 260 pounds, it is most likely that a few were heavier pieces. The armament of the *Regent* also included 200 bows and 400 sheaves of arrows.

The *Sovereign*, the other large warship built for King Henry VII, was three-masted and smaller than the *Regent*. The inventories state that the *Sovereign* carried 141 guns arranged as follows: Forty iron serpentines on two decks of the forecastle; one brass and sixty-five iron serpentines on three decks of the aftercastle; four iron serpentines in the stern; twenty iron 'stone-guns' in the waist, with eleven more in the aftercastle. These stone-guns fired a stone shot and were of a much larger calibre than the serpentines. They were the first attempt to provide a weapon capable of damaging, at short range, the hull of an enemy vessel, as the small serpentines firing a ball of very little weight could only be effective against the lightly built upperworks, rigging and personnel. The serpentines mounted in the stern of the aftercastle of the *Sovereign* are perhaps the first example of stern-chaser and even these light guns would have been of value as weapons for use against galleys attacking, in a calm, the stern of a sailing warship.

The inventories of the *Regent* and the *Sovereign*, and of other English vessels of the period, list numerous fittings of the type which continued in use in sailing warships until the nineteenth century.

A particularly interesting item is the reference to the main capstan of the *Regent* with another capstan in the deck above it. Thus it would seem that the double capstan with men working the capstan bars on two deck levels, so often used in later vessels, was employed before 1500.

The *Regent*, one of the largest ships afloat at that time, was copied from a French vessel, the *Colombe*, and like other vessels of Henry VII's naval forces was used as both merchant ship and warship.

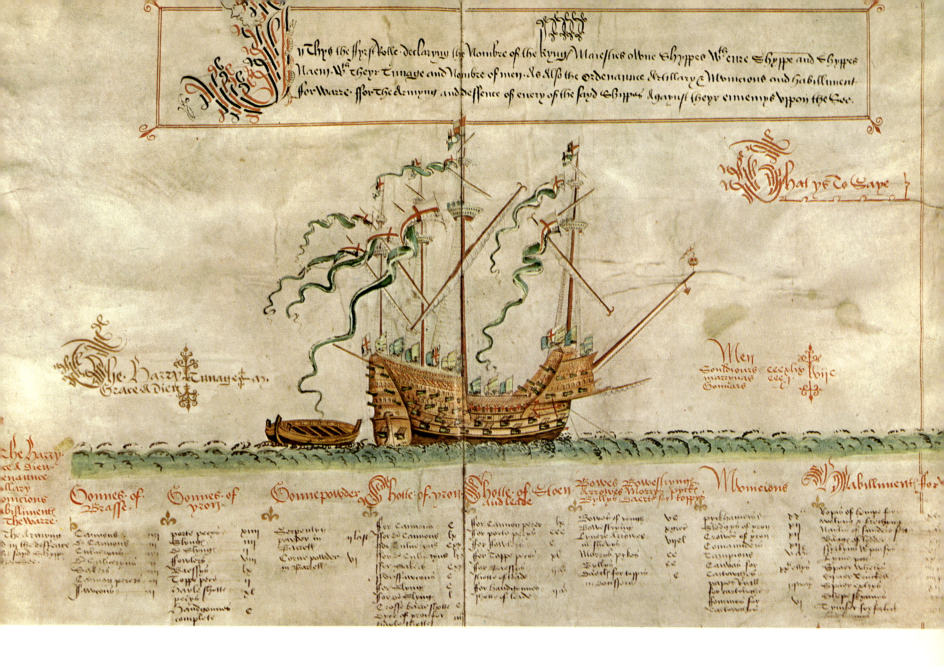

Henry Grâce à Dieu from Anthony's Roll, 1546. This drawing shows the ship as she appeared after rebuilding in 1539, when she was pierced for two almost complete tiers of guns.

Early in the sixteenth century the effect of the heavier guns then coming into use and the need, for the stability of the vessel, to mount these very heavy weapons nearer the water-line was responsible for further significant changes in the design and construction of warships.

Where or when openings for guns were first cut through the sides of the hull of a vessel is not known, although a French shipwright, Descharges of Brest, has been credited with this invention in 1501. At first these square openings—known as gunports—were few in number and placed so as not to cut the wales, which, apart from the keel and keelson, were the principal longitudinal members of the hull structure. The decks on which the guns were mounted were stepped up or down to suit the position of the gunport. This variation in the level of a deck was not a new idea, as the decks of earlier medieval ships were not flush but their height was decided by considerations of head-room in the main cabins and of cargo stowage.

Another change which took place at about the beginning of the sixteenth century was the introduction of the square transom stern. Up to this time the side planking of the hull at the stern had been rounded into the sternpost; with the new method the side planking terminated at a flat stern formed from thwartship timbers and planking. The square stern improved the design of the ship by allowing the upperworks at the after part of the vessel to merge into and become an integral part of the hull. It also made it much easier for gunports to be cut in the flat stern, in which heavy stern-chase guns could be mounted.

During the sixteenth century the trader-warship gave way to vessels designed and built for fighting.

Rivalry between the maritime powers of Europe led to the construction of a number of warships which were exceptionally large for the epoch. The vessels were probably only enlarged versions of the more conventional ships of the period, and as most of these very large warships were unsuccessful, their size was perhaps dictated by reasons of national prestige rather than by improved design giving increased sailing and fighting qualities.

The first of the sixteenth-century great ships was the *Great Michael*, built under the direction of a French shipwright at Leith, in 1505–11, for James IV of Scotland. No authentic record of the size of the *Great Michael* is available, but it has been said that the vessel had an overall length of 240 feet, with a breadth of 56 feet, and that it carried 300 sailors, 120 gunners and 1000 soldiers. The *Great Michael* was sold to France in 1514.

Most probably the dimensions given for the *Great Michael* are exaggerated, as the vessel built in England in 1514 as a rejoinder to her, the famous *Henry Grâce à Dieu* or *Great Harry*, was certainly smaller, probably of about 1500 tons, although again the exact dimensions are not known.

Other 'great ships' were the *Santa Anna* of the Knights of St. John of Malta, built about 1523, which is said to have been sheathed in lead from the bulwarks downwards; the French *La Grande Françoise*, a five-masted vessel built in 1527, and the Swedish *Store Krafweln* of 1532.

The great improvement in ordnance which took place during the first half of the sixteenth century brought about a major change in the size and distribution of the armament of warships and in the tactics of naval warfare. As the techniques of the gun-founders improved they were able to produce 'brass' guns which were cast in one piece and then bored out. These muzzle-loading guns were much more efficient and safer to use than the built-up iron breech-loading gun, with a separate chamber for the charge. As the superiority of these new weapons was realised and the destructive power of even a partial 'broadside' of heavy guns became apparent, the older iron breech-loaders were gradually replaced.

Brass muzzle-loading guns were first carried by English ships in 1509 and the change in armament is illustrated by the difference in the guns of the *Great Harry* in a period of twenty-six years. As built in 1514 the warship carried one hundred and twenty-four guns, of which forty-three can be classified as heavy pieces. Possibly five of these larger guns were cast brass muzzle-loading weapons. After being rebuilt in 1540, the hull of the *Great Harry* was pierced for two rows of guns on each side, and of her forty-nine heavy guns twenty-one were of brass.

The production by about 1550 of a whole series of cast brass guns ranging in size from the cannon-royal with a bore of $8\frac{1}{2}$ inches and weight of 8000 pounds, to the minion with a bore of $3\frac{1}{2}$ inches and a weight of 1000 pounds, allowed for the first time a degree of standardisation in the armament of a warship.

The sailing warships of the period were still of the carrack type with high poops and forecastles, but while there was a reduction in the number of lighter guns carried in these superstructures, below the upper deck with its complement of medium-weight guns, one or two almost continuous rows of heavy guns, on each side, allowed a powerful 'broadside' to be fired.

This broadside, capable of severely damaging or sinking an opponent, meant that an enemy fleet could be destroyed by gunfire. Hitherto it had been the practice to attack with the fleet in line abreast; now it was necessary to attack in line ahead and so, when sailing parallel to the enemy line, make it possible for each ship to fire its broadside. In addition to the preliminary tactical manoeuvres for the windward position, a position now even more important to a fleet on the offensive and with which it was intended to press home the attack, the ships of a fleet had to be kept in station and the fleet had to be manoeuvred as a whole during the action.

A fleet in the leeward position did have some tactical advantages. It could break off the action and turn away more easily, and in strong wind conditions its ships could use their lower deck guns while the windward opponent vessels, which would be heeled over towards the enemy line, were unable to open the gunports on the lower deck. With the guns mounted near the water-line there was always a danger of water entering the vessel if she heeled over when the gunport lids were open.

An early example of this danger was the loss of Henry VIII's warship the *Mary Rose*, which heeled over and sank in the Solent in 1545, while going out to engage a French fleet. Bad seamanship due to insubordination in the crew was undoubtedly the primary cause of the accident, although some authorities consider that the *Mary Rose*, one of the first vessels to be re-armed with heavy guns, carried her guns much nearer the water than was general practice.

Later examples of similar disasters are the loss of the Swedish warship *Wasa* at Stockholm in 1628 and the French 74-gun ship *Thésée* which at the battle of Quiberon Bay foundered because her commander, despite stormy weather conditions that were getting worse, continued to use his lower-deck guns.

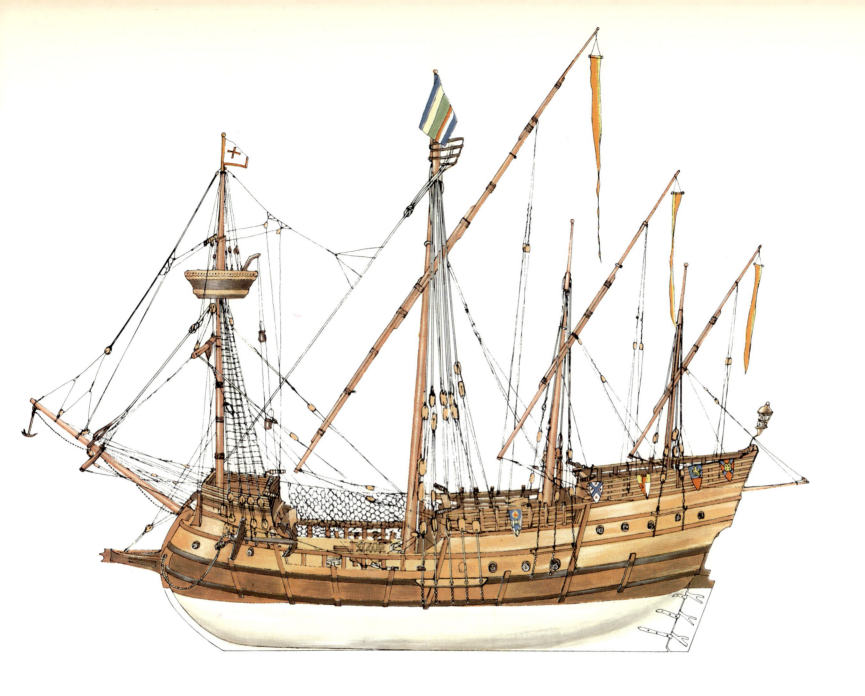

PORTUGUESE CARAVELA

One of the warships
used by the Emperor Charles V at the capture of Tunis in 1535.

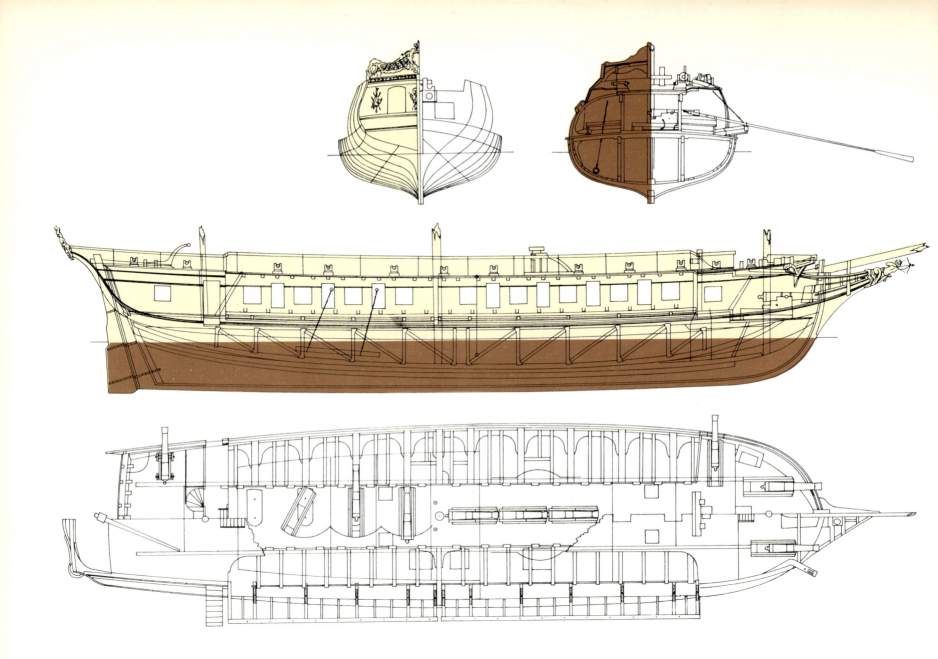

TORBORG

A frigate of 'udema' type, designed in 1770
by Fredric Henric af Chapman (1721–1808), Swedish shipbuilder and naval constructor
and author of the famous 'Architectura Navalis Mercatoria'.

OARED WARSHIPS OF THE SIXTEENTH,
SEVENTEENTH AND EIGHTEENTH CENTURIES

In the Mediterranean, oared warships were in general use throughout the sixteenth century. The galleys were of much the same design as those of the previous century, but in about 1530 a new method of arranging and operating the oars was introduced. The old method of 'zenzile' rowing, with the oars arranged in groups and one man to each oar, was replaced by a system known as 'scaloccio', in which the oars, carried as before in one horizontal row, were placed at evenly spaced intervals through the length of the vessel and each oar was pulled by a number of men.

The most usual arrangement for galleys of moderate size—about 130 feet long—was four or five men to an oar, but for the larger galley—more than 150 feet in length—six, seven or eight men pulled at the same oar. The total number of oars to a galley was reduced but the oars were longer. This new system of propulsion made it possible to increase the speed of the larger galleys.

For most of the sixteenth century the Mediterranean galleys were rigged with one mast, which supported a very large lateen sail, but towards the end of the century a second mast and lateen sail were fitted.

The galley of this period was usually armed with one large gun, possibly with a calibre of $7\frac{1}{2}$ inches, weighing about 8000 pounds and firing a fifty-pound ball. This gun was mounted on the centre-line of the platform at the bows. On each side of the heavy gun, one or two lighter guns were mounted, perhaps 'sakers' weighing about 2000 pounds and firing a six-pound ball. This group of guns on the bow platform could not be transversed and could therefore only be fired over the bows in the direction in which the galley was pointed. Only very small cannon and swivel-guns were used from the sides of the vessel.

Thus, in the Mediterranean, the fighting tactics for the galley remained almost unaltered. The principal attacking movement was still end-on, but instead of the ram, which as already stated had been replaced by a light beak, the heavy guns were used to inflict damage from a distance and, if necessary, boarding and hand-to-hand fighting followed.

During the sixteenth century a new type of warship known as a 'galleass' was introduced in the Mediterranean. The early galleass was a not very successful compromise between the galley and the sailing ship: an attempt to create a vessel in which was combined the mobility provided by oars with ability to sail long distances, to carry a heavier armament and with greater capacity for stores.

Very much more heavily built than the galley and with higher sides, the galleass carried part of her armament of heavier guns mounted to give broadside fire. The armament consisted of about twenty-five guns of the heavier type and about eighty to a hundred lighter weapons.

The galleasses originated in the very large Venetian merchant galleys. These vessels, with a length of about 160 feet and an overall breadth of 33 feet, were capable of quite long voyages, but when converted or built as fighting galleasses they were powerful but rather unsatisfactory warships. Because of the great weight of the galleass and its armament only a very slow speed was possible when propelled by oars. Their three-masted rig with lateen sails, when applied to this form of hull, was not as efficient as the mixture of square and fore-and-aft sails carried by the normal sailing warship of the period.

The lightly built galley, lying low in the water and with only enough storage capacity for operational voyages of short duration, was generally unsuitable for use in northern geographical and sea conditions. However, on occasion rowed warships were built and employed in these areas, and galleys were brought round from the French Mediterranean fleet to serve from France's northern seaboard.

In England Henry VIII's fleet also contained vessels which, although called galleasses, were of very different design to the Mediterranean galleasses and had more affinity to the sailing warship than to the lateen-rigged galley. Contemporary descriptions and drawings of the English galleasses show that they were square-rigged vessels similar to the sailing warship in general hull form but with a greater length to beam ratio. Perhaps these galleasses are best described as 'sailing ships with oars'.

The first of these large English oar and sail warships was the *Great Galley*, built in 1515. This vessel is said to have had 120 oars and four masts with square sails. Her armament included seven heavy guns on each side, mounted to give broadside fire. When first built the *Great Galley* was planked in clinker fashion, but this planking was later replaced by carvel work.

The combination of sail and oar in the northern form produced much the same difficulties as found in the Mediterranean galleasses, and the *Great Galley* was rebuilt in 1536 as a normal sailing warship. However, somewhat smaller English galleasses were built and are illustrated in a contemporary 'Roll of the Navy' of 1546. Taking the 200-ton galleass *Bull* as an example the drawing shows that the vessel was armed with at least sixteen heavy guns, carried on one flush deck. A long line of oarports is shown on a deck below that on which the guns were carried. The *Bull* was fitted with four masts, with topsails on the fore and main masts only.

The 'Roll of the Navy' illustrates one vessel, the *Galley Subtylle*, which is designed, oared, armed and rigged in the same manner as the Mediterranean galley. Henry VIII employed Italian shipwrights to help with the design and construction of oared vessels and the *Galley Subtylle*, launched in 1544, was almost certainly the result of their work.

The last great action between fleets of oared warships (except in Scandinavian waters), the Battle of Lepanto, took place in the eastern Mediterranean in 1571. A combined force of Spain, Venice, Malta, Genoa and the Papal State, consisting of some three hundred galleys and six very large galleasses, defeated a Turkish fleet of about the same number of galleys.

The opposing fleets were formed up in the ancient manner with the galleys in line-abreast formation but the allied forces placed their galleasses in advance of

At the Battle of Lepanto, 7th October 1571, the fleet of the
Holy League under Don Juan d'Austria defeated the Turkish
fleet and thus brought an end to the Turkish supremacy over
the Mediterranean. Venetian school.

the galleys. (The galleasses were towed into position, an indication of how slow they were under their own oars.) As the long line of Turkish galleys approached the allied fleet the heavy guns of the galleasses—much more powerful than any guns mounted in the galleys—opened fire and did much damage at long range, causing the Turkish line to open out to pass the galleasses. The Turks were more successful at the flanks of the three-mile-wide line of allied galleys and by skilful manœuvring were able to isolate for a time the allied right wing. However, a reserve squadron of thirty-five allied galleys was brought into the action and further successes in the centre of the line, including the capture of the Turkish commander-in-chief's galley, led to the total defeat of their fleet with some 25,000 men killed and 15,000 Christian galley slaves liberated.

It had soon become apparent that a resolutely handled sailing warship with some guns was more than a match for lightly built galleys. As early as 1499, at the Battle of Zonchio, near the island of Sapienza, although the Venetian forces were defeated, their sailing warships were able to hold off the combined attacks of a number of Turkish galleys.

The sailing warship again proved its ability to withstand galley attacks in 1538 when an indecisive battle took place near Prevesa, at the entrance of the gulf of Arta, between an allied fleet of Venetian, Papal and Spanish galleys and sailing warships, and a Turkish galley fleet. Despite calm weather conditions most suitable for galley warfare, the *Galleon of Venice*—at that time said to be the most heavily armed sailing warship in the Mediterranean—repulsed a series of determined attacks by the Turkish galleys.

Outstanding proof of the sailing warship's superiority to the galley is provided by Sir Francis Drake's famous raid on the harbour of Cadiz in 1587. In a light wind and confined waters—again ideal conditions for galleys—Drake's four sailing warships, by the use of long-range guns, sank two galleys and compelled ten more to withdraw, thus enabling Drake to destroy much of the shipping in the harbour. A further example was an action off the isle of Elba, on the 10th July 1684, when the French fifty-gun ship *Le Bon* repulsed the attacks of thirty-six Spanish galleys and finally compelled them to withdraw.

Despite, in most circumstances, the galley's obvious inferiority when opposed to a sailing warship, oared warships continued to be used in the Mediterranean throughout the seventeenth and eighteenth centuries. France's Mediterranean fleet contained galleys until the middle of the eighteenth century and the naval forces of Malta and Naples used these vessels until almost the end of that century.

The seventeenth- and eighteenth-century galleys were very similar to those of the previous century, except, in a few cases, for an increase in size and consequent ability to carry a heavier armament.

There is a great deal of information available on the later galleys and contemporary scale models and draughts exist. For instance a Swedish work of 1768 by the famous naval architect Fredric Henric af Chapman entitled 'Architectura Navalis Mercatoria' contains very detailed plans of a Maltese galley of about 1750. This galley was 179 feet long from stem to sternpost with a hull breadth of 24 feet and fitted for thirty oars on each side. The armament consisted of one 36-pounder gun, two 8-pounder guns and two 6-pounder guns, all mounted, facing forward on the bow platform. In addition eighteen swivel guns and eighteen musquetoons were carried.

In 1627 ten small warships known as the 'Lion's Whelps', armed with twelve guns and designed to row as well as sail, were built for the British Navy, but again the combination of sail and oar was not successful. Somewhat similar but larger vessels, armed with sixteen guns, were employed in the French Navy at about the same time.

The *Charles Galley* and *James Galley*, built for the British Navy in 1676, carried eleven guns on each side on the upper deck and four guns and twenty oars on each side on the lower deck. The *Charles Galley* was rebuilt in 1693 and the *James Galley* was wrecked in 1694.

Until about the end of the eighteenth century oarports were often fitted between the gunports of the smaller types of warships and oars were frequently used in a calm. Large oars—sweeps—to be used through the sternports when it was desired to turn the vessel in a calm, were supplied to even the largest warships until the middle of the nineteenth century.

For several centuries up to the beginning of the nineteenth century Barbary corsairs operated from North African ports, for much of the time using vessels of the galley type, and were an almost constant threat to merchant shipping in the Mediterranean.

Plans of an Algerine chebec, an interesting type of vessel much used by the corsairs, are also contained in the work 'Architectura Navalis Mercatoria'. This chebec, although of galley form, was only provided with nine oars on each side and was designed for sailing rather than rowing. The three-masted rig with three large lateen sails gave the chebec fast sailing qualities, which together with the relatively heavy armament produced a most formidable and efficient small warship for use in suitable conditions.

Vessels of the chebec type were also employed by the Spanish, Italian and French naval forces in the Mediterranean.

On the chebec the disposition of the guns was somewhat different to that of the galley. The heaviest guns—four 12-pounders—were still carried facing forwards on the bow platform, but as only nine oarports were required on each side it was possible to mount eight 6-pounder guns on each side between the oarports. In addition three 3-pounder guns were carried on the side of the poop, with two more mounted as stern-chasers.

At the end of the seventeenth century and during the eighteenth century oared warships were used in the Baltic, particularly in the gulf of Finland, where along much of its coastline conditions were unsuitable for inshore naval operations by ordinary sailing warships.

At the beginning of the eighteenth century galleys of a similar type, size and rig as those used in the Mediterranean were employed in the navies of Sweden and Russia, but in the latter half of the eighteenth century oared warships of a different design were introduced by af Chapman. Developed in Sweden in the 1770s these vessels, although of shallow draught, had a hull form rather like that of a small frigate of the period and many were rigged with square sails. In most cases the guns were mounted to give broadside fire. One extreme type, the 'udema', carried a number of 12-pounder guns mounted on transversing slides along the centre-line of the vessel, in such a manner that the guns could be fired to port and starboard.

Once again the combination of sails and oars was not completely successful; the vessel's shallow draught adversely affected sailing performance, and the weight of hull and armament, as in the case of the much larger galleass, made progress under oars very slow.

THE ARMAMENT OF SAILING WARSHIPS

From about 1350, when guns were first used at sea, until the end of the fifteenth century, most of these early weapons were of the wrought-iron type already briefly described.

The names given to the various sizes of guns by contemporary writers are confusing, the same name sometimes being applied to guns of very different form and size. Although a few actual pieces have survived and have been identified, the dimensions remain obscure of many of the guns—basilisks, bombards, curtalls, slings, serpentines, etc.—named in documents as forming the armament of ships.

With the transformation in naval armament which occurred in the early years of the sixteenth century, and the introduction of a family of cast brass guns, an elementary step was taken in the standardisation of naval ordnance. From this period onwards extant contemporary lists supply the theoretical weight, calibre, etc., of various naval guns. However, the actual guns did not conform closely to the stated dimensions; guns of the same class, i.e. same name and same approximate calibre, varied considerably in weight and size.

The existing examples of sixteenth-century guns rarely agree exactly with the dimensions laid down by contemporary writers. Thus the dimensions given for the guns listed below can be regarded only as a general indication of their proportions.

Name of gun	*Calibre* *ins.*	*Length* *ft. ins.*	*Weight of gun* *lbs.*	*Weight of shot* *lbs.*
Cannon Royal	8½	8 6	8000	68
Cannon	7	10 9	6000	40
Demi-cannon	6½	11 0	4500	32
Culverin	5¼	12 0	4000	18
Demi-culverin	4¼	11 6	3000	9
Saker	3½	7 9	1800	5
Minion	3¼	6 6	1200	4
Falcon	2½	6 0	680	2
Robinet	1	3 0	300	½

Although the size of the individual guns varied a great deal, many countries in Europe applied, to each general class of gun, titles derived from the same names of reptiles or birds of prey.

England
Cannon, Demi-cannon, Culverin, Saker, Falcon, Robinet

Spain
Cañon, Medio-cañon, Culebrina, Medio-culebrina, Sacre, Falcon

France
Canon, Demi-canon, Couleuvrine, Demi-couleuvrine, Sacre, Faucon, Ribandequin

The culverin, firing a shot weighing about eighteen pounds, was the long-range weapon of the period. The cannon class of guns fired a much heavier shot for a shorter distance. The question of the exact range of these guns is a matter of conjecture, but it is generally conceded that the culverin had a 'point-blank' range of about 300 yards and a 'random' range of about 2600 yards, while for the cannon the respective figures were about 250 yards and 1700 yards.

In the sixteenth and seventeenth centuries the name 'cannon' was not a generic term but was applied to a particular type of gun. The pedrero, perier or cannon-petro were short-range weapons of fairly large calibre which fired stone balls, much lighter in weight than an iron ball of the same diameter.

The 'brass' guns were cast from a mixture of copper, tin and brass, the proportions of these ingredients varying according to the dictates of individual gun-founders. It will be seen from these ingredients that these weapons, which are consistently referred to as 'brass' guns in contemporary papers, were in fact bronze.

Guns cast in iron, first made about 1500, were by the end of the century being produced in large numbers and, being much cheaper, gradually replaced the brass guns for naval use. As an indication of the pace of this process it is interesting to note that the twenty-eight 42-pounder brass guns mounted on the lower gun-deck of the *Royal George*, an English 100-gun ship launched in 1756, were not replaced by lighter iron 32-pounders until 1782. Indeed some of the small brass guns remained in use until the nineteenth century.

The early guns were lashed to heavy beds of wood known as 'stocks', which were fastened to the deck. By about 1520 two small wheels—trucks—were attached to the fore-end of the stocks and by about 1650 a gun-carriage with four small trucks had come into use.

During the seventeenth century further standardisation of naval ordnance had taken place and by the beginning of the eighteenth century the picturesque gun names were discarded, the pieces being designated by the weight of the shot which they discharged.

By the eighteenth century the guns had become, in the main, shorter. Their proportions, the thickness of the metal and the dimensions of the carriages were governed by formulas based on the calibre of the gun.

The carriage with four trucks and the method of loading and firing the guns remained almost unchanged for some two hundred years until the middle of the nineteenth century.

When a ship's gun was to be used it was drawn inboard, by a tackle fastened to the rear of the carriage, and loaded with powder and shot through the muzzle. The gun was then run outboard, by side tackles, until the muzzle protruded as far as possible from the ship's side. The gun was fired by a slow match—a length of rope soaked in a chemical solution, which included saltpetre, so that it burnt very slowly. (A flint-lock firing device was introduced about 1780.) The discharge caused the gun and its carriage to run back inboard. This recoil movement was controlled by a strong rope, known as a breeching, which was fastened to the rear end of the gun and to the bulwarks on each side of the carriage.

Mid-eighteenth-century instructions laid down the gun-drill procedure as follows:

Silence. Cast loose your guns

The muzzle lashing was taken off and the side tackles slackened so that the gun could be drawn back. The sponge, crowbar and handspike were laid out on the deck near the gun.

Level your guns

The breech end of the gun was raised by wedges.

Take out your tompions

The tompions were wooden plugs inserted into the muzzle of the gun when it was not in use.

Load with cartridge

The cartridge was a paper or cloth bag containing the correct charge of powder.

Shot your guns

Round shot and a wad were put into the gun and rammed down to the cartridge.

Run out your guns

The guns were hauled outboard by the side tackles.

Prime

The cartridge was pierced by a wire inserted down the touch hole, and the pan and touch hole filled with powder from a horn.

Point your gun

The required elevation was obtained by adjusting the wedges under the rear end of the gun, and the direction by heaving the after end of the carriage to one side or the other by crowbar and handspike.

Fire

The slow match was applied to the powder in the priming pan at the touch hole.

The number of men required to work each gun was in proportion to the size of the gun and was affected by the number and condition of the ship's crew. In a well-manned warship the figures were:

Size of gun (pdr)	No. of men	Size of gun (pdr)	No. of men
42	15	9	6
32	13	6	5
24	11	4	4
18	9	3	3
12	7		

The dimensions listed below are those laid down for English naval guns in 1753.

BRASS GUNS

Nature pdr	Length ft. ins.	Weight cwt. qr. lbs.		
42	9 6	61	2	10
32	9 5	55	2	7
24	9 5	51	1	12
18	9 0	48	1	0
12	9 0	29	0	0
9	8 5	26	0	0
6	8 0	19	0	0
3	6 5	11	0	0

IRON GUNS

Nature pdr	Length ft. ins.	Weight cwt. qr. lbs.		
42	10 0	55	1	10
32	9 6	53	3	23
24	9 5	48	0	0
18	9 0	41	1	8
12	9 0	32	3	3
9	8 5	23	2	2
6	7 0	17	1	14
4	6 0	12	2	13
3	4 6	7	1	7

Other nations also had sequences of guns identified by the weight of their shot. The French denominations were 36-, 24-, 18-, 12-, 8-, 6-, and 4-pounders. Due to difference in the standard of weights a French 36-pounder fired a shot weighing nearly thirty-nine English pounds. In the same way the Swedish 48-pounder fired

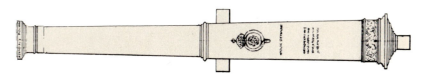

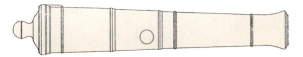

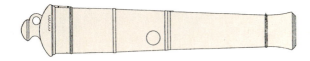

Top: Brass saker, 1529.

Centre: Iron 32-pounder, recovered from the *Royal George.* sunk in 1782.

Bottom: Iron 32-pounder, c. 1800.

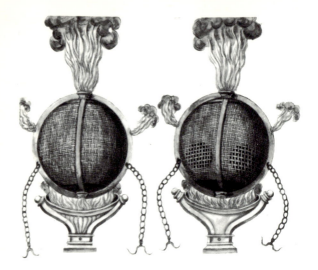

Projectiles for sea warfare as depicted in contemporary manuscript, Rudolf van Deventer: 'Bericht von Pulver und Feuerwerken', *c.* 1585.

a ball weighing nearly forty-five English pounds, and the Russian 42-pounder, one of almost thirty-eight English pounds.

At the beginning of the nineteenth century the sizes of English naval guns—all iron—were as follows:

Size pdr	Length ft. ins.	Weight cwt. qr. lbs.			Calibre ins.	Size pdr	Length ft. ins.	Weight cwt. qr. lbs.			Calibre ins.
32	9 6	55	2	0	6·4	9	7 6	26	2	0	4·2
24	9 6	50	2	0	5·8		7 0	25	1	0	
	9 0	47	3	0		6	8 6	22	1	0	3·7
18	9 0	42	2	0	5·3		8 0	21	2	0	
	8 0	37	3	0			7 6	20	1	0	
12	9 0	34	3	0	4·7		7 0	19	1	0	
	8 6	33	1	0			6 6	18	2	0	
	7 6	29	1	0			6 0	17	2	0	
	7 0	21	0	0		4	5 6	11	3	0	3·2
9	9 0	31	0	0	4·2	3	4 6	7	1	0	2·9
	8 6	29	2	0							

The first real innovation in ships' ordnance since the sixteenth-century cast brass guns occurred in 1779 when a new type of gun, the carronade, was introduced into the British Navy. First cast at the ironworks of the Carron Co., in Scotland, these guns were very short and thin-walled with a relatively large calibre. A smaller charge was used and a smaller gun crew was required.

The great difference in weight and size can be seen by comparing the dimensions of carronades, given in the following table, with those for the standard naval guns previously listed.

CARRONADES

Size pdr	Length ft. ins.	Weight cwt. qr. lbs.			Calibre ins.
68	5 2	36	0	0	8·05
	4 0	29	0	0	
42	4 3½	22	1	0	6·84
32	4 0½	17	0	14	6·35
24	3 7½	13	0	0	5·68
	3 0	11	2	25	
18	3 3	9	0	0	5·16
	2 4	8	1	25	
12	2 2	5	3	10	4·52

The carronades were normally used with a special type of carriage, consisting of a slide—which allowed the recoil movement—mounted on a platform, the front end of which was pivoted to the deck and the rear end provided with rollers. This arrangement permitted some traversing movement.

Like the pedreros of the sixteenth century, carronades were short-range 'smashers' and were most effective at 'point-blank' range, a distance of about 400 yards in the case of the 68-pounder and about 200 yards for the 12-pounder carronade.

After some preliminary tests a few British warships were armed, as an experiment, wholly with carronades. The initial surprise of receiving very large shot from a vessel of a size normally armed with much smaller calibre guns led to some spectacular successes. However, it was realised that the short range of the carronades made a vessel armed only with them very vulnerable, under most sailing

Swedish ship under gunfire. Illustration from Rudolf van Deventer: 'Bericht von Pulver und Feuerwerken'.

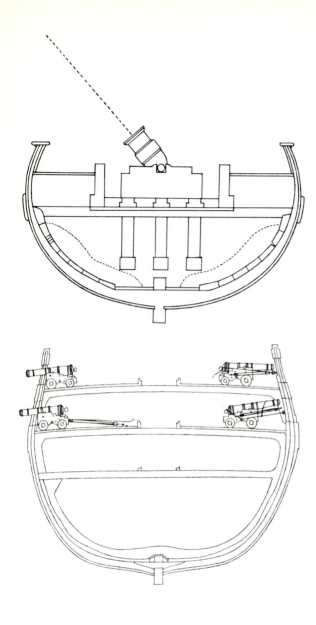

Top: Midship section with mortar, *c.* 1780.

Bottom: Midship section with guns, *c.* 1780.

conditions, to warships armed with longer-range guns. Therefore the largest carronades were used to supplement the armament of ships-of-the-line while the 12-, 18- and 24-pounder carronades were used very extensively on the forecastles and quarter-decks of smaller naval vessels.

After about 1785, carronades were employed on board the warships of other nations although to a more limited extent than in the British Navy.

The United States of America, in particular, made use of this type of weapon for their warships and also experimented with vessels armed almost entirely with carronades. One of their vessels—a frigate—so armed, after losing her main topmast in a squall, was immobilised and captured by two British warships using long-range guns. This defeat led to the relegation of the carronade, in the U.S. Navy, to a secondary role, where the gun was also used mainly from the quarter-deck and forecastle.

The mortar, a very short piece of ordnance, used for firing projectiles so that they would fall nearly vertically, was also employed at sea from the fifteenth century onwards. The mortar was usually fired at a fixed angle of elevation, the charge of powder being varied according to the range required. In the eighteenth century large mortars with a calibre of 10 or 13 inches were fitted to specially designed vessels known as bomb ketches. These mortars, which could usually be elevated or depressed, fired an explosive projectile and were used principally for bombarding shore fortifications. Smaller mortars were used from the decks and tops of ordinary warships.

The projectiles used for the smooth-bore, muzzle-loading gun remained almost the same from the seventeenth century until the middle of the nineteenth century. These projectiles were of four main types:

(1) Solid balls made from cast iron (stone balls were rarely used after the end of the sixteenth century) to fit the calibres of the various guns. A solid ball from the larger-calibre guns, fired at 'point-blank' range, could pierce four or five feet of solid timber. Varieties of these projectiles were chain-shot—two solid balls linked by a chain—and bar-shot—two half-balls joined by an iron bar—which were used to damage the masts and rigging of an enemy vessel.

(2) Scatter-shot, of two kinds, first grape-shot consisting of several tiers of iron balls contained in a thick canvas bag strongly corded together so as to form a sort of cylinder of suitable diameter to fit the calibre of the gun; and secondly, case-shot formed by putting a large number of musket balls in a cylindrical metal box designed to suit the gun from which it was to be fired.

(3) Explosive-shot or 'bombs': these were hollow cast-iron balls filled with gunpowder and provided with a fuse. The fuses of the earlier bombs were lighted before the shot was put into the gun, but this very dangerous practice was discontinued when it was found that the explosion of the propellent powder in the gun automatically lit the fuse. The explosive shot was usually fired from mortars.

(4) Incendiary projectiles, such as hot-shot and carcasses. The hot-shot was an ordinary iron round shot which was heated until it was red hot before it was inserted into the gun. To prevent the premature firing of the propellent charge an extra wad of wet straw or clay was put into the gun barrel before the hot-shot. The carcass was an iron framework, something like the ribs of a human carcass, filled with combustible materials and of a shape and size suitable for firing from a mortar, gun or carronade.

Small swivel- or pivot-guns with a calibre of about $1\frac{1}{2}$ inches, used as anti-personnel weapons, were mounted in forks on the bulwarks and timber-heads of warships. In the sixteenth century swivel-guns were breech-loading with a separate chamber for the charge. Muzzle-loading swivel-guns were used in the seventeenth century and throughout the eighteenth century.

From this chapter it will be seen that naval gunnery made no outstanding advances for the whole period under review, and a gunner of the sixteenth century would have been quite capable of successfully loading, aiming and firing the guns used on ships at the end of the eighteenth century.

LA COURONNE

French 72-gun two-decker, launched in 1638

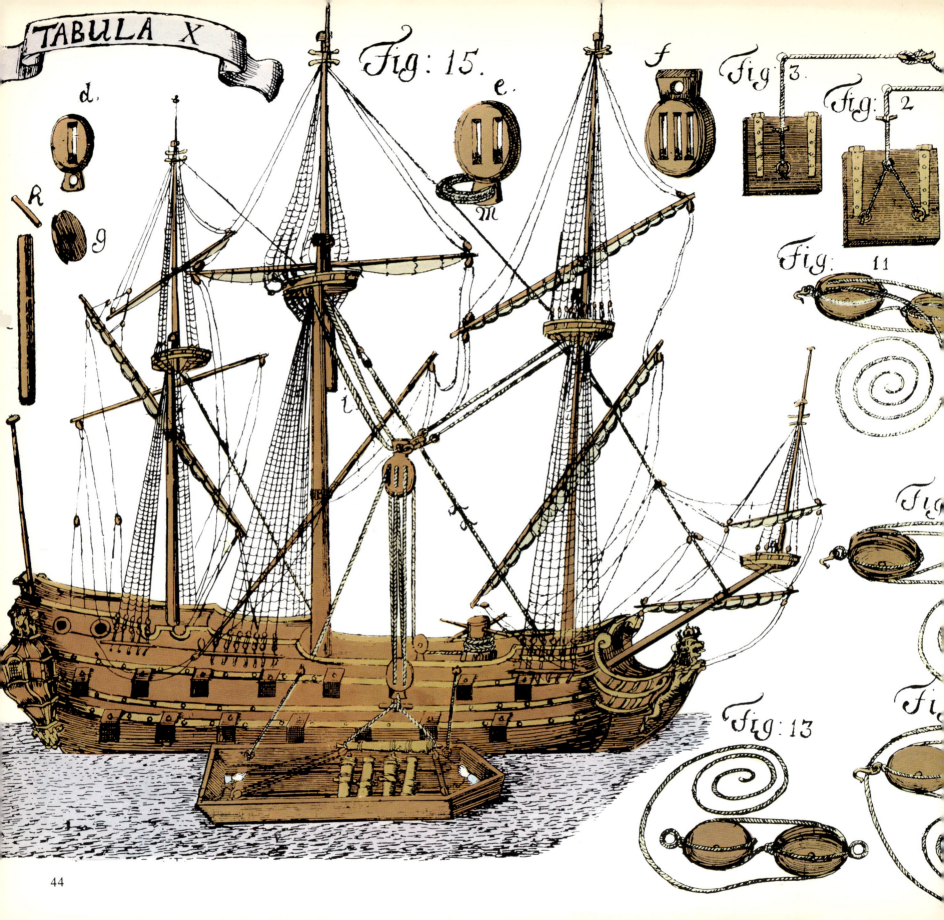

TABULA X

Fig: 15.

Fig: 3

Fig: 2

Fig: 11

Fig: 13

d.

e.

f.

k

g

m

i

44

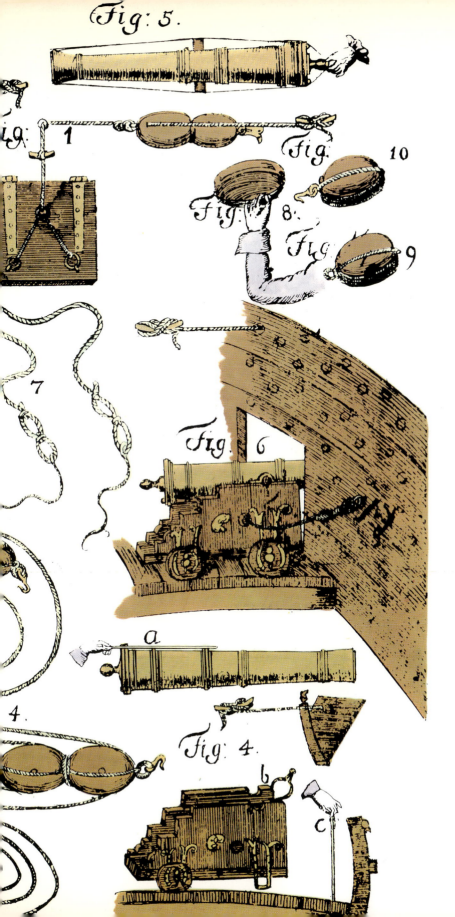

Guns being taken aboard a warship.

Illustrations from a Swedish book on artillery, 1705. (Daniel Grundell: 'Nödig Underrättelse om Artilleriet till Lands och Siös'—'Necessary Information about the Artillery by Land and Sea'.)

Figs. 1–3   Gunports
Figs. 4, 6   Gun-carriages
Fig. 5   Gun
Fig. 7   Crowfoot
Figs. 8–10   Blocks
Figs. 11–14   Blocks and tackle
Fig. 15   Guns being taken aboard a warship

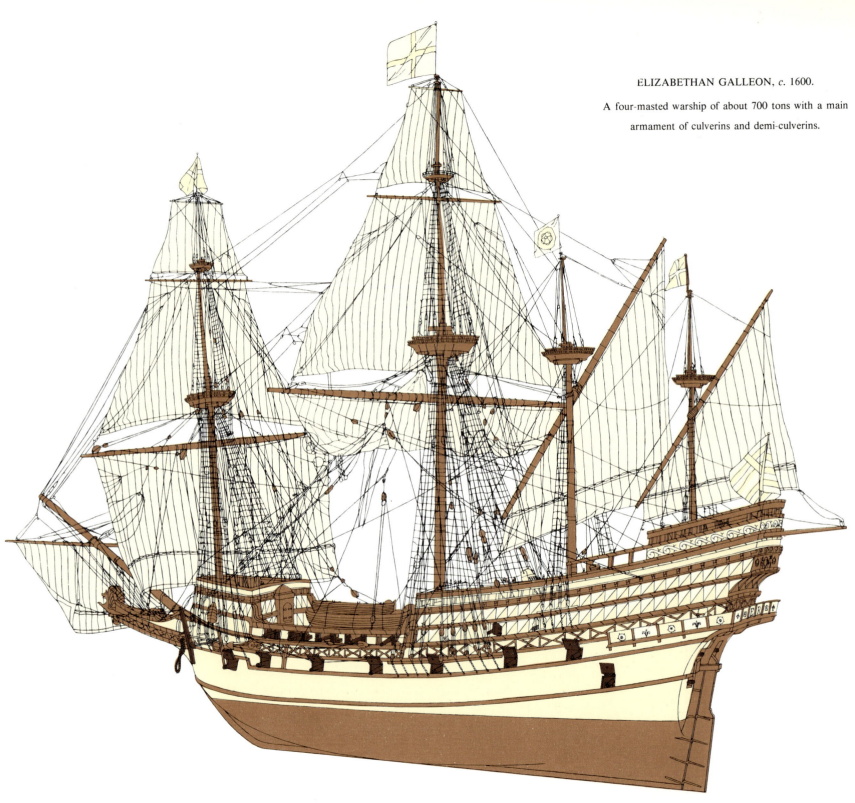

ELIZABETHAN GALLEON, *c.* 1600.

A four-masted warship of about 700 tons with a main armament of culverins and demi-culverins.

THE GALLEON

As already described, the large sailing warships of the early years of the sixteenth century were of the 'carrack' type with a high stern superstructure and even higher forecastle projecting out over the bows. The rounded hull form had a length to breadth proportion, on the water-line, of about $2\frac{1}{2}$ to 1.

Although improvements in rig had taken place, this form of hull left much to be desired in sailing qualities and by the middle of the century alterations in hull design had been introduced for, at first, the smaller warships. These alterations included a greater length to breadth proportion and the huge projecting forecastle was replaced by a lower erection set back from the bows, with a lightly built beak projecting from the stem.

Some of the smaller warships illustrated in the English 'Roll of the Navy' of 1546 show a stage in this development.

This new type of warship became known as the galleon. The derivation of this name is uncertain, but it undoubtedly originated in the Mediterranean, possibly in relation to a ship of different type. It was being applied to northern sailing ships by 1550. The projecting beak and the relative slimness of the new vessel perhaps brought to mind the galley and the consequent application of a somewhat similar name.

England led the way in the development of the galleon, and the knowledge and experience gained from long exploratory, privateering and trading voyages was rapidly incorporated into the design and rig of warships.

The surviving draughts of warships made by an English master-shipwright, Matthew Baker, in about 1585, show that by this date the English galleons were designed with good underwater lines. One of the draughts shows the hull of a vessel compared with the body of a fish showing an appreciation of some of the qualities required to provide the hull of a fast sailing vessel.

Matthew Baker's draughts do not show any particular named ships of the period, but the proportions of the vessels are so close to those recorded for warships in other documents that the plans can be accepted as representing the usual practice of the time. By using the combined information from these contemporary draughts, which include elevations, cross-sections and a sail plan, it is possible to reconstruct very accurate representations of Elizabethan warships.

As an example, a galleon of medium size—about 600 tons burden—would have been 150 feet long with a breadth of 38 feet and a depth in hold of 18 feet. The hull was divided longitudinally by three principal decks extending over much of the length of the vessel. The shipwrights still avoided cutting gunports through the wales and consequently the decks were not flush but, as in the earlier warships, were broken up by short sections placed two or three feet up or down as required. From the upper profile of the ship, known as the 'sheer', it is obvious that these steps were usually necessary at the extremities of the deck.

In the hold, on top of the ballast—principally stones—the bulk of the provisions were stowed: flour, salted meat and fish, and barrels of fresh water.

Immediately above the hold, at or a little below the water-line, the lowest deck was fitted. Known as the 'orlop', this deck was also a storage area. Above the orlop, the lower gun-deck carried the heaviest part of the armament, perhaps sixteen culverins mounted seven a side, with two as stern-chasers. On the upper gun-deck or main-deck, open in the waist, but surmounted by the forecastle at the bows and the half-deck and poop at the stern, medium-size cannon were carried, perhaps about fourteen demi-culverins and sakers. Between the upper gun-deck and the half deck was the 'great cabin' and the officers' quarters.

The rest of the complement, about 340 sailors, 40 gunners and 120 soldiers, slept where they could on the decks. Hammocks were not used in English warships until the very end of the sixteenth century.

In some vessels the half-deck was shortened to become the quarter-deck, a name which has survived until the present day.

Across the stern, on the outside, and extending some way along the quarters of the vessel, was an open gallery, forerunner of the elaborate stern-walks and quarter-galleries of the eighteenth century. This gallery was used as the officers' latrines.

The galley for cooking, consisting of a brick hearth and iron or copper boiler, was for most of the sixteenth century built on the ballast in the hold amidships. Towards the end of the century the galley, in some English warships, was moved to a much more satisfactory position in the forecastle, a position it continued to occupy in sailing warships until the nineteenth century.

The transfer of the galley was a gradual improvement and one which took place later in the warships of other nations. The Swedish warship *Wasa*, lost in 1628, had a galley in the older position in the hold.

On the Elizabethan galleon the forecastle and half-deck bulkheads were heavily built and provided with strong doors at access points so that in the event of the enemy gaining, by boarding, control of the waist of the vessel, these positions could be held as strong-points, with light guns mounted to fire through narrow slits to harass the enemy in the waist.

As ships became larger it was found that it was not possible to control the rudder by tiller only. Men hauling on ropes—known as relieving tackles—led through blocks on the tiller and at the sides of the vessel were used to assist the helmsman.

In the sixteenth century a device known as a whipstaff was employed. The whipstaff was a vertical lever, pivoted in the deck, with its lower end forked over the tiller. Two men moved the whipstaff, which in turn moved the tiller, which worked the rudder. The mechanism of the whipstaff was inefficient and only allowed about five degrees movement of the rudder on each side of the centre-line. The whipstaff can only have been used on straight courses and for manoeuvring the rudder must have been controlled by the relieving tackles already described.

Mariner's astrolabe, found at a place on the Irish coast where some of the Armada ships were wrecked.

Although most of the galleons were three-masted, with fore, main and mizen masts, some of the largest were fitted with a fourth mast, known as a bonaventure mizen. Three sails—course, topsail and topgallant—were carried on both the fore and main mast. The mizen and bonaventure mizen each supported a lateen sail, but were often without topsails as the lateen topsails carried on these masts earlier in the century were now seldom used. The only form of headsail employed was a spritsail under the bowsprit. In suitable weather conditions the spritsail, fore-course, main-course and lateen sails could be enlarged by attaching strips of canvas, called bonnets, to the lower edges of the sails. (The bonnet was not a new device; this method of enlarging a sail had been in use during the preceding two centuries.)

Until about 1580, the topmasts of ships were fixed permanently to the mast-heads of the lower masts, but after that date a method of fitting the topmast and topgallant mast was introduced which allowed these masts to be easily detached from the respective lower mastheads and lowered to the deck. This minor improvement was of some importance as it made possible the use of higher masts, and consequently a more lofty sail plan, which in very bad weather could be rapidly shortened.

From very early times the bows, sterns and the bulwarks of warships were painted in brilliant colours in order to give the vessel as martial an appearance as possible. In the tenth century coloured shields were slung along the outside of the gunwale and in the succeeding centuries somewhat similar shields—pavesses—bearing heraldic devices were placed along the rails of the forecastle, aftercastle and waist. Coloured strips of cloth were also used at various places on the hull, and round the fighting tops on the masts. Striped cloth awnings fitted over the upper decks of the forecastle and aftercastle were highly decorative as well as giving some protection from sun and rain.

The English galleon of about 1580 had a very distinct style of decoration. The upperworks at bow and stern were painted in contrasting colours—white, red, green, yellow and blue—in geometrical patterns of squares and triangles separated by bands of colour. Painted arches, pillars and panels also formed part of the decorative design. Similar panels with painted foliage instead of geometrical designs were used as decorations on galleons of other nations. At this date, with the exception of the figure-head, decorative carved work was almost entirely absent from English galleons but was more extensively used on Spanish, French and Italian galleons.

The design and armament of late sixteenth-century galleons was tested to the full in the series of actions which were fought in 1588 between the Armada assembled by Philip II of Spain and the English fleet of Queen Elizabeth I.

The Spanish Armada was a mixed fleet which included, when it arrived in the English Channel, four galleasses, twenty-four galleons designed and built as fighting ships, forty large merchant ships converted to warships, twenty-five store-ships and some thirty attendant small ships. Four galleys sailed with the Armada, but one was wrecked and the others were unable to complete the voyage to the English Channel, thus providing further evidence of the unsuit-ability of this type of warship for service in northern water conditions. The largest warships of the Armada were the *San Juan* of 1050 tons and the *San Martin* of 1000 tons. (The tonnage figures were calculated by the contemporary Spanish method, which gave a relatively higher figure than the corresponding English method.)

The available English vessels included thirty-four Royal ships ranging in size from the *Triumph* of 1100 tons and an armament which included seventeen culverins and eight demi-culverins, to the *Cygnet* of thirty tons armed with one minion and two small guns. In addition to the Royal ships over 150 merchant ships served with the fleet, but only about a third of these could be considered as formidable fighting ships.

In both fleets the average ships of most classes were about the same size, although the Spanish vessels looked larger because, in general, they were built with higher superstructures than the English vessels. With regard to performance,

The fireship attack on the Spanish Armada, 28th July 1588. Painting attributed to Aert van Antum.

Sir Francis Drake (1540–96), privateer and naval officer. Commander-in-Chief during the Armada actions. Died at sea off Nombre de Díos.

because of their lower build, and equally important, their better underwater lines, the English galleons were much faster and more easily manœuvred than the Spanish warships.

There was also a great difference in the armament of the two fleets. The Spanish fighting ships had a preponderance of medium- and short-range heavy guns—cannons, demi-cannons and periers—while in the English fleet long-range guns—culverins and demi-culverins—firing a lighter ball, formed the greater part of the main armament of the galleons.

These two factors—superior sailing qualities and the possession of a greater number of guns capable of inflicting damage at a greater range—together with the advantage of a much better local knowledge of weather and water conditions enabled squadrons of the English fleet, sailing more or less in line ahead, to get to windward of the roughly crescent formation of the Armada, which moved at the speed of the slowest ship, to impose the fighting distance and accordingly make a series of attacks to which the Spanish ships could make no effective reply. The Armada was thus harried along the English Channel and after more prolonged and severe engagements off Portland and the Isle of Wight eventually came to anchor off Calais.

Although during the passage along the Channel the Armada had suffered the loss of three larger ships and damage to many others, the English galleons, using their lighter-shotted, longer-range guns, were not able to break up the Armada's defensive formation and when the fleet came to anchor at Calais it was still in comparatively good order but seriously short of ammunition. However, the English launched a night attack by eight fireships, which caused panic and confusion. The Armada, forced from the anchorage, was broken up and the ships driven towards the Flemish coast.

Further actions occurred off Gravelines, in which the English, taking advantage of the shortage of ammunition in the Spanish ships, closed the range, inflicting much damage and further losses. The remnants of the scattered Armada were finally driven northwards to make the return voyage to Spain round Scotland and Ireland.

With the exception of the attacks by fireships the Armada actions were fought by gun-fire only. The older form of naval warfare, with 'boarding and entering' playing a principal part, so much desired by the Spanish whose ships carried large contingents of troops, was avoided by the English fleet. The Armada battles established the idea of naval tactics in which line-ahead attacks were made from the windward, but they showed that the long-range guns of the period were not powerful enough to destroy the heavily built galleons, and for the tactics to be fully successful it would be necessary to close in and use a broadside fired from a large number of guns firing a heavy ball.

THE EVOLUTION OF THE
THREE–DECKER

There are very few contemporary illustrations which give an accurate representation of the warships of the late sixteenth and early seventeenth centuries. From the rather meagre evidence it would seem that the largest galleons were three-deckers, that is, carried their heavy guns on three decks one above the other, but it is very doubtful that these decks extended the full length of the hull or that the gunports were in uninterrupted lines.

The Swedish warship *Mars* built at Kalmar in 1561–63, and the *Adler* built at Lübeck in 1565–66, are early examples of what should perhaps be called partial three-deckers.

A painting by a Dutch artist of the English 1200-ton warship *Prince Royal* built in 1610 provides an excellent example of a large galleon of the period. This vessel carried fifty-six guns on three decks. In design and construction the *Prince Royal* was apparently very similar to the large English galleons of the late sixteenth century, but elaborate carving and gilding had replaced the contrasting paintwork of the Tudor ships.

At the beginning of the seventeenth century the larger galleons were four-masted, but by 1618 with the square mizen topsail in general use it was found that additional sail area aft could be achieved more efficiently by increasing the size of the mizen-mast and the fourth mast, and the bonaventure mizen was finally discarded.

About 1600 a very small mast was first stepped on the forward end of the bowsprit of ships. This mast carried a square sail, known as a spritsail topsail, as an extra headsail. Although this mast, from its positions, could not be adequately provided with stays and was very liable to damage, it continued in use for more than a hundred years and—at least on paper—was considered part of the standard equipment of large English warships until the middle of the eighteenth century.

Early in the seventeenth century Dutch shipwrights in particular were well advanced in the art of shipbuilding and these shipwrights designed and built warships for other nations. In 1625–26 several warships were built in Holland for the French Navy and were used by French shipwrights as models for later vessels built in France.

The ill-fated Swedish sixty-four gun ship *Wasa* was designed by a Dutch shipwright and built in Stockholm in 1627–28. On 10th August 1628, the *Wasa*, while leaving Stockholm harbour on her maiden voyage, heeled over in a sudden gust of wind and sank.

The warship is stated to have been 203 feet long, figurehead to sternpost, with a beam of 38 feet, and to have carried forty-eight 24-pounder guns, eight 3-pounder, two 1-pounder and six mortars. Various attempts to salvage the *Wasa* were unsuccessful, although between 1664 and 1683 a number of the valuable guns were recovered. In 1956 the wreck of the warship was located in 105 feet of water and salvage operations followed which led, in 1961, to the recovery and final preservation in a specially constructed museum at Stockholm.

The *Wasa* thus provides a unique opportunity for naval archaeologists and historians to study the decorative and constructional details, internal economy, armament and fittings of an early seventeenth-century warship. It may even be possible to find out whether the loss of the *Wasa* was due to the bad design of the warship or to poor seamanship by the officers and crew.

An English warship, the *Sovereign of the Seas,* is depicted on an engraving published in 1638. This vessel, designed by the shipwright Phineas Pett and built at Woolwich in 1636–37, marked a further advance in the size and design of warships and is generally considered to be the first ship to carry three complete tiers of guns. The vessel was an enlarged version of the galleon type, but the beakhead was larger and stronger, the waist built higher and the quarter-galleries much larger and more elaborate. In addition to the three gun-decks there was a half-deck, quarter-deck and round-house, and of course the large forecastle deck at the bow. As first built the *Sovereign of the Seas* was 232 feet long overall, with a beam of 46 feet 6 inches, a depth in hold of 19 feet 2 inches and a tonnage burden of 1141 tons.

At this time the armament of the vessel consisted of 104 brass guns arranged as follows:

Lower gun-deck, twenty cannon drakes, with eight demi-cannon drakes as bow and stern chasers.
Middle gun-deck, twenty-four culverin drakes, with six culverins as bow and stern chasers.
Upper gun-deck, twenty-four demi-culverin drakes, with demi-culverins as bow and stern chasers.
Forecastle, eight demi-culverin drakes and two culverin drakes.
Half-deck, six demi-culverin drakes.
Quarter-deck, two demi-culverin drakes.

Externally *Sovereign of the Seas* was painted black with profuse decorations of gilded carved work. The cost of this extravagant decoration alone amounted to about a quarter of the total cost of the vessel. The rig of the *Sovereign of the Seas* also showed improvements over that of the earlier galleons. The fore and main masts carried topgallant sails and, in suitable wind conditions, royals were set on the fore and main masts and a topgallant sail on the mizen. At this date these latter sails were exceptional and royals did not come into general practice until many years later.

In 1651, in order to lighten the ship and so raise the level of the lower gun-deck ports, the upperwork of the *Sovereign of the Seas* was much reduced in height.

The *Prince Royal* arrives at Flushing in May 1613 with
Frederick V, Elector Palatine, and his consort Elizabeth,
daughter of James I of England, on board. Painting by
Hendrick Cornelisz von Vroom.

the round-house aft was removed and the half-deck shortened. The warship was again rebuilt in 1659–60 and in 1685. The *Sovereign of the Seas*, also named the *Sovereign* and the *Royal Sovereign*, was destroyed by an accidental fire in 1696.

The French warship *La Couronne*, launched in 1638, was nearly as large as the *Sovereign of the Seas* but carried seventy-two guns on two decks. For most of the seventeenth century the two-decked warship carrying sixty to ninety guns was the principal fighting vessel for most maritime nations.

During the century the designers and builders of warships began to study the scientific principles of naval architecture and in some cases their deliberations and conclusions were printed and published. 'Architectura Navalis' by J. Furttenbach, published in Ulm in 1629; 'Aeloude en hedendaagsche Scheepsbouw en Bestier' by N. Witsen, published in Amsterdam in 1671; 'L'Architecture Navale' by F. Dassie, published in Paris in 1677; and 'Skeppsbyggerij eller Adelig Ófning X' by Á. C. Rålamb, published in Stockholm in 1691, are examples of the study and thought applied, internationally, to naval architecture and shipbuilding.

An important English work of 1670, 'The Doctrine of Naval Architecture' by an eminent shipwright, Sir Anthony Deane, was not printed at the time, but an original manuscript copy is preserved. This work, which provides rules for arriving at the most suitable hull forms for warships, body plans of vessels of various sizes, sizes of timbers, lengths of masts and rigging, and a mass of other relevant information, was available to Admiralty officials and supplied the basic principles of English naval architecture for more than a hundred years.

During the later part of the seventeenth century a number of large three-decker warships were designed and built incorporating some of the scientific principles and practical ideas laid down in these treatises.

The *Prince* and the *Britannica* were typical examples of English 100-gun three-deckers. The *Prince* of 1395 tons was built in 1670 with a keel length of 131 feet and a beam of 44 feet 9 inches. The *Britannia* of 1708 tons, built in 1682, was 167 feet 5 inches long on the gun-deck and 47 feet 4 inches wide.

The first Swedish warship with three complete flush decks was the *Stora Kronan* of 124–128 guns, built at Stockholm in 1665–72, with a stem to sternpost length of 173 feet 10 inches and a beam of 39 feet.

The French *Royal Louis* of 1692 was a particularly well designed three-decker with excellent sailing qualities for a vessel of this type. The *Royal Louis* was of 2600 tons and 106 guns, with a stem to sternpost length of 176 feet and a beam of 48 feet.

The design of the first Danish three-decker, the *Fredericus Quartus* of 110 guns, launched in 1699, was based on that of the *Royal Louis*. The *Fredericus Quartus*, with a stem to sternpost length of 190 feet and a beam of 52 feet, is said to have been the largest ship afloat at that time.

All these late seventeenth-century capital ships were of modified galleon type. The midship transverse hull form, with the greatest width at about the water-line, was in general somewhat fuller than that of the earlier galleon. A much flatter bottom form was developed for the warships of such countries as Holland, Sweden and Denmark where the vessels were often employed in shallow waters. Due to a reduction in the height of the upper works there was less 'tumble home' at the bow and stern, but the greatly increased weight of the armament necessitated a fuller underwater form at these sections also, and the fine bow lines and long run aft shown in the contemporary draught of Elizabethan warships were no longer possible.

The long pointed beak of the galleon had been altered to a shorter, stronger and more curved structure set at a higher angle.

The open quarter-gallery of the earlier ship had developed into a very ornate tiered structure with glazed windows and a domed roof. At this period open stern galleries were fitted to the warships of Continental navies but in England, from about 1620 for a period of some seventy years, a closed stern with glazed windows was the fashion.

Experiments were made in methods of protecting the outside of the planking below water from the ravages of marine pests, and about 1670 sheet-lead sheathing was tried out for a period; this, however, proved ineffective because of corrosion caused by the electrolytic action set up between the lead and the iron fastenings of the hull.

The usual method of protection, at this period, was to coat the underwater hull with a compound of tar, sulphur and tallow, over which a sheathing of thin fir planks was nailed. Also the keel and lower part of the rudder were often protected by means of large-headed nails placed close together and strips of lead were sometimes nailed along the water-line.

The main constructional techniques were much the same for all European warships but differences occurred in the construction and positioning of individual parts of the hull structure.

In large ships the frames—which formed the ribs of the vessels—were too big to be cut from a single piece of wood and they were therefore made of several short lengths. The number and position of these pieces, known as floors, futtocks and top-timbers, which made up the frame, differed in various countries and at different periods.

In Continental warships the square, or transom, lower stern, first introduced about 1500, was continued well into the eighteenth century, but in English ships, from the early years of the seventeenth century, there was a gradual adoption of a form of stern construction, known as a 'round-tuck', in which the planking was curved round the quarters to the sternpost.

In England, at the beginning of the seventeenth century, the powerful navy built up during Queen Elizabeth's long reign was greatly reduced, with few large ships in service. However, Naval Commissions of 1608 and 1618 led to expansions which were continued in Charles I's reign, when special taxes were imposed to raise money for the purpose, and under the Commonwealth (1649–1660) when the navy was more than doubled in size. During the reign of Charles II (1660–85), the term 'Royal Navy' first came into use and much was done to augment the fleet, to improve its ships and to raise the status and conditions of both officers and men.

In 1677 Admiralty officers and Navy shipwrights prepared the first Shipbuilding Establishment. This Establishment laid down the principal dimensions of warships of each class. It was therefore the first attempt at standardisation for warships.

During the seventeenth century warships were first officially designated by the number of guns carried and from about 1626 the English fleet was divided into six groups called 'Rates'. 'First Rates' were ships with ninety or more guns, 'Second Rates' those with between eighty and ninety guns, 'Third Rates' fifty to eighty, 'Fourth Rates' thirty-eight to fifty, 'Fifth Rates' eighteen to thirty-eight and 'Sixth Rates' those with less than eighteen guns.

These classifications were in use until the nineteenth century although alterations occurred from time to time in the upper and lower limits of each division.

Very similar classifications were adopted for most navies. In France the divisions were known as the Premier to the Sixième Range, and corresponding terms were applied in other Continental navies.

In France under the direction of Jean-Baptiste Colbert (1619–83), a leading statesman in the administration of King Louis XIV, and Minister of the Marine from 1669, the French Navy, dockyards and personnel were reorganised and a naval construction programme undertaken which produced some of the finest warships of the period.

These French warships were wider in proportion to their length, carried few guns in relation to their size and were of less draught than their English counterparts. In consequence their lower-deck gunports were higher above the water, and the ships had greater stability, important factors when the vessels were in action.

In successfully copying the French 74-gun ship *Superbe* in 1672, English shipwrights repeated what had been done in 1487, when Henry VII directed that the French *Colombe* was to be copied, and were carrying out a policy which was to be

Stern of the French Warship *Le Soleil Royal*.

Jean-Baptiste Colbert (1619–83), French statesman. As Controller-General in Louis XIV's administration he reformed finance, subsidised shipbuilding and reorganised the French Navy.

continued throughout the eighteenth century when well-designed French warships were captured by the British Navy.

With regard to the tactics of naval warfare, for much of the seventeenth century the Continental navies still used, whenever possible, the boarding and hand-to-hand fighting tactics of the earlier period.

The English, however, with the outbreak of the first Dutch War in 1652, as a result of the experiences of the Armada actions and of subsequent hard-fought minor engagements which had proved that long-range gunnery was inaccurate and ineffective, adopted a close-range method of fighting which was to become the established gunnery practice of the British Navy until the end of the sailing warship.

With this method the fire of the broadside guns was directed against the hull of the enemy ship, with the design of so damaging the structure and killing and wounding so many of the crew that it was impossible for the vessel to continue the action.

In the French and other Continental navies a different gunnery policy was developed in which the fire of the guns, at a longer range, was directed principally against the masts, yards and rigging of the adversary.

For the English to make their gunnery tactics effective it was necessary to devise a method of manœuvring and controlling a large fleet so that individual ships could be brought into action at close range. The elementary 'line-ahead' formations—single-file formations is a better description—employed against the Spanish Armada and in the opening engagements of the Dutch Wars showed the way that this could be accomplished and led to the issue in 1653 of official 'Fighting Instructions' which laid down that 'line ahead' was the principal fighting formation. In 1665 the 'Fighting Instructions' were augmented and it was officially ordained that the distance between each warship forming the 'line' was to be 'half a cable', i.e. 100 yards.

By the end of the seventeenth century the Dutch and the French had also adopted the 'line-ahead' tactics but with less rigidity than the English.

At this period two major offensive stratagems were used in conjunction with 'line-ahead' tactics. One method was to attempt to double the enemy line—after sailing in line parallel to the enemy the leading ships passed round the end of the enemy column and formed a second line on the other side thus subjecting the enemy vessels to cross-fire. This manœuvre could be attempted from either the windward or leeward positions but was a difficult and dangerous proceeding. A later authority on naval tactics comments:

'The captains destined to double the enemy ought to be men of known ability as well as approved courage. They should not be ordered upon that expedition but in weather fit for sailing at the rate of three knots an hour (sic); and, for the greater promptitude and certainty of success, none but the best going ships are to be employed in that sort of manœuvre.'

'Doubling' movements were used with varied degrees of success at the battles of Solebay (1672), Beachy Head (1690) and Barfleur (1692).

The other major offensive stratagem employed with the 'line-ahead' tactics was to divide the enemy column by driving through it in 'line-ahead' formation, thus cutting off and throwing into disorder the enemy warship behind the break.

With the formal adoption of 'line ahead' as the order of battle it was necessary to insure that a much smaller and less powerful warship was not opposed by a stronger vessel, therefore the smaller Rates of warship were excluded from the line, which was made up from vessels with more than fifty guns, that is, normally, the First, Second and Third Rates only, and the vessels of these Rates became known as 'ships-of-the-line'.

The principal functions of the various Rates of the British Navy can be very briefly described as follows:

First, *Second* and *Third Rates*. Service as 'Ships-of-the-Line' in general fleet actions.

Fourth Rates. Guard duties with convoys of merchants ships, service as cruising ships in foreign waters and on expeditions of great distance.

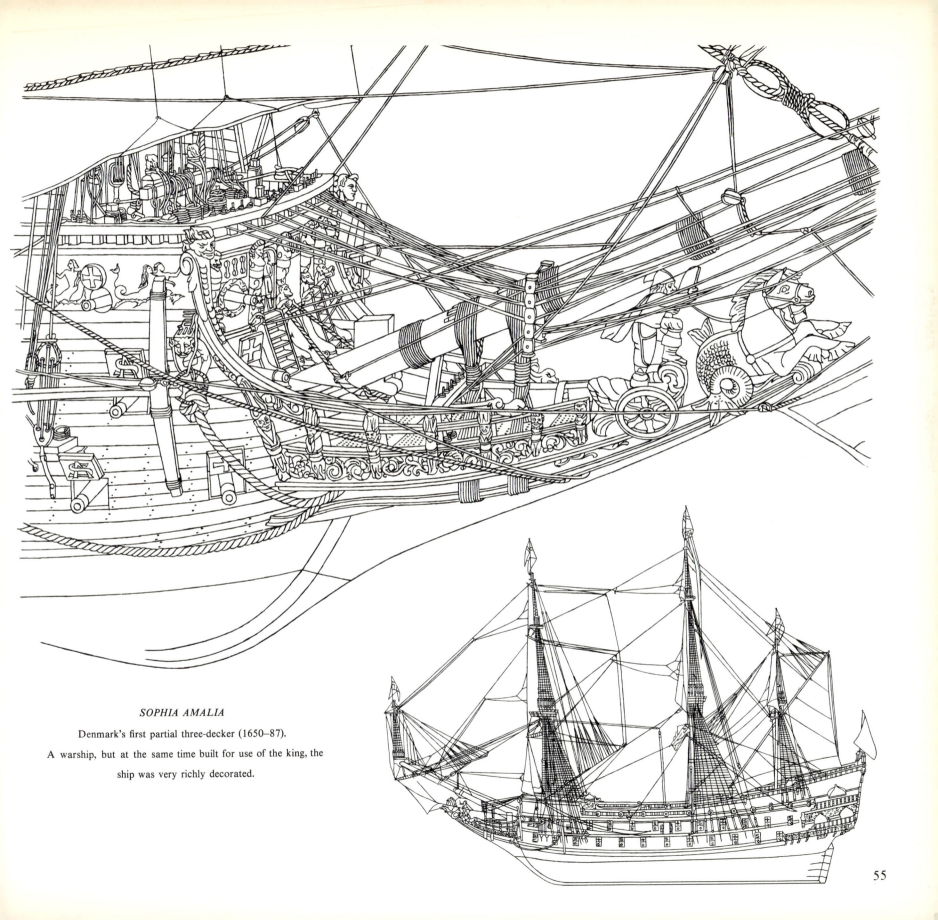

SOPHIA AMALIA

Denmark's first partial three-decker (1650–87).

A warship, but at the same time built for use of the king, the

ship was very richly decorated.

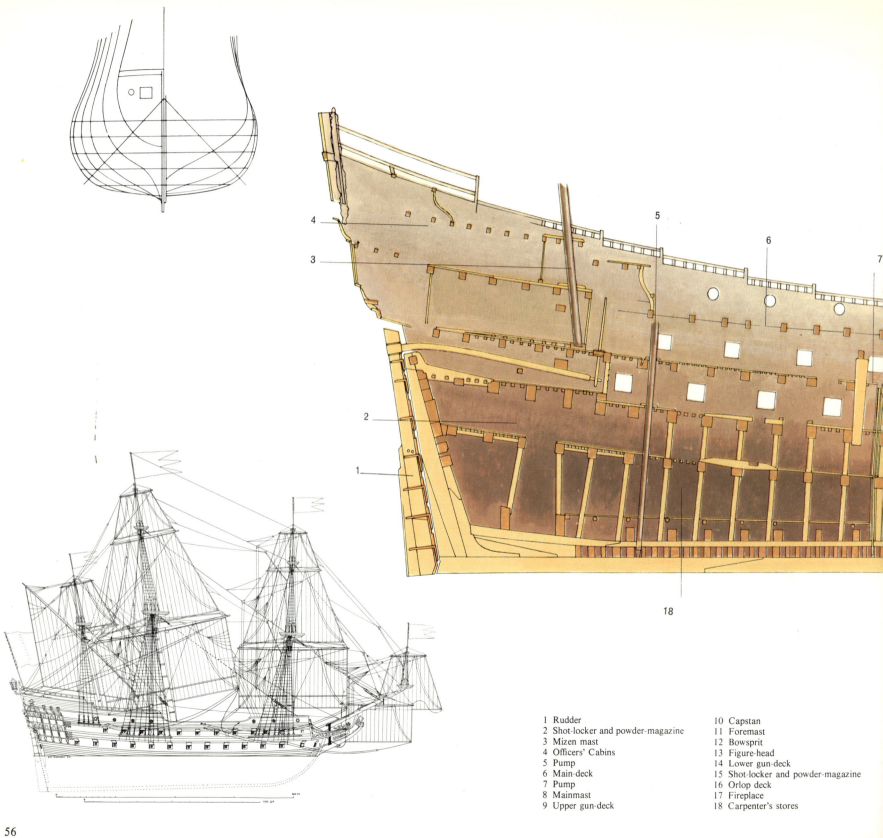

1 Rudder
2 Shot-locker and powder-magazine
3 Mizen mast
4 Officers' Cabins
5 Pump
6 Main-deck
7 Pump
8 Mainmast
9 Upper gun-deck

10 Capstan
11 Foremast
12 Bowsprit
13 Figure-head
14 Lower gun-deck
15 Shot-locker and powder-magazine
16 Orlop deck
17 Fireplace
18 Carpenter's stores

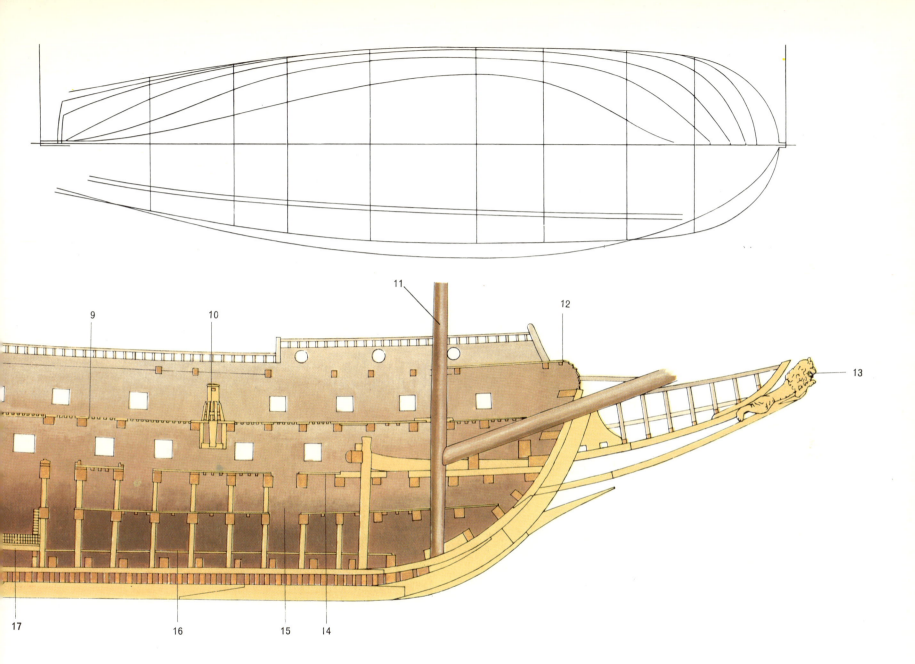

WASA

Longitudinal section
at the centre-line. This Swedish 64-gun warship capsized
in Stockholm Harbour in 1628.

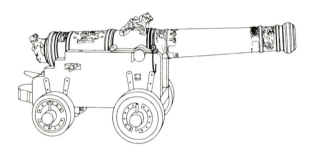

Find from the *Wasa*:
A sculpture showing a shield with a corn-sheaf—the coat of arms of the Vasa family—supported by two cherubs.

Model of one of the *Wasa*'s 24-pounder guns. These guns weighed about 3000 pounds and had a range of about 1600 yards.

Fifth Rates. Attached to squadrons of larger warships to act as scouts, to repeat signals and for operating against privateers or on short expeditions.
Sixth Rates. Coastal patrol duties.

The functions defined must be regarded as a general indication only, as the duties performed by individual vessels of the different Rates varied very considerably.

Later, during the eighteenth century, a large proportion of the warships with less than fifty guns were known by the various denominations of frigates. The name frigate, which originated in the Mediterranean, was applied to different types of ships at different periods. The best-known application was to the warship specially designed for fast sailing which carried its main armament on a single gun-deck. The name was very loosely applied in the seventeenth century; a shipbuilding contract of 1693 refers to 'one New Ship or Friggate to carry 80 guns'.

A 26-gun ship, the *Constant Warwick,* purchased for the Royal Navy in 1649 is said to have been the first real frigate built in England. This warship, built as a privateer in 1645, was designed on the same lines as those of very fast French privateers of the period. The *Constant Warwick* was of 305 tons, about 100 feet in length, stem to stern, with a beam of 26 feet and is said to have carried an armament consisting of eighteen demi-culverins on the main-deck, six sakers on what was virtually the quarter-deck, and on the roof of the chief officer's cabin, which formed a small poop, two minions were mounted.

The naval historian William James, writing in the nineteenth century, states: 'A ship of the size and armament of the *Constant Warwick*, well formed in her lower body, lightly but handsomely ornamented in her upper works and rigged according to the most approved plan of the day, did no discredit to the name of frigate, now first applied in England to any determinate form of vessel.' Later naval historians are more sceptical of the claim that the *Constant Warwick* was the first English frigate and regard the vessel as a small two-decker of the period.

Referring again to the late seventeenth-century three-decker First Rate ship, contemporary drawings are extant which show the internal arrangements of the vessel.

With a complement of over 700 men the crowded conditions which must have prevailed are apparent. Most of the crew now slept in hammocks slung between decks, but a manuscript of 1673 gives the establishment of cabins available to those whose office so entitled them:

Upon the poop for trumpeters—4
Round house for the eldest captain—1
Afore the round house on the starboard side for the second captain—1
Afore the second captain on the starboard side for the eldest lieutenant—1
Afore the round house on the larboard side for the secretary of an admiral—1
Afore the secretary on the larboard for the master—1
In the two bulkhead cabins upon the quarter-deck for the chief mate and judge advocate—2
Bulkead of the coach on the starboard side for the second lieutenant—1
On the larboard side for the commander of the land forces—1
Upper great cabin for the commander—1
In the lobby on the starboard side for the minister—1
On the larboard side (if no staircase) for a land officer—1
On the bulkhead of the forecastle on the starboard side for the carpenter—1
On the bulkhead of the forecastle on the larboard side for the boatswain—1
Within the forecastle on that side for his mate—1
The lower great cabin for the reformadoes (officers with rank but no command)
On the second deck, canvas cabins for mates, pilots, pursers, midshipmen and other officers, as the captain pleases to dispose of them—18
Pantries of wood for the commander's use—2
In the gunroom bulkhead for gunner and chirurgeon—2
In the gunroom, standing cabins for mates—2

Hanging cabins—6
Cockpit for the purser, steward and chirurgeons' mates—5
Steward room—1

The cooking arrangement for the crew was a galley with a fire-hearth and boiler situated on the middle-deck below the forecastle. Latrines for the officers were provided in the quarter-galleries at the stern, but for the men very primitive arrangements were made on the gratings in the bows, over the stem. This position was uncomfortable and also dangerous—an entry for the year 1694 in the diary of the seventeenth-century seaman Edward Barlow reads: 'Our cook, named William Cox, in the night rises out of his sleep and goes into the ship's head and either slips or falls over-board and was drownded.' To this day the latrines in British warships are known as the 'heads'.

The general working positions or 'action stations' of the crew of 780 men of a First Rate of 100 guns are given in a document of 1677, preserved at the Pepysian Library, Cambridge, as follows:

26 Cannon of 7	182 men	(to each 7 men)
28 Whole culverins	112 ,,	(,, ,, 4 ,,)
28 Sakers	84 ,,	(,, ,, 3 ,,)
14 Minions	42 ,,	(,, ,, 3 ,,)
4 Three-pounders	8 ,,	(,, ,, 2 ,,)
To carry powder for all the guns	34 ,,	
To fill and hand powder for all the guns	15 ,,	
Chirurgeon and crew in hold	10 ,,	
Carpenter and crew	8 ,,	
Purser and crew in hold	5 ,,	
Men for the small shot	110 ,,	
Men to stand by the sails	120 ,,	
Men for the boats and tops	50 ,,	

Among other improvements in the sails and rigging which occurred in the seventeenth century was the introduction of studding-sails. These light sails, which were used in moderate and steady breezes, were fitted as extensions on each side of a larger sail. Although said to have been invented by Sir Walter Raleigh in 1588, studding-sails seem to have been used about 1625 on the mainmast only by French and Dutch warships. By the end of the century these sails were in regular use for the topsails and lower courses of the fore and mainmast of all large warships.

Staysails, fore-and-aft sails suspended from the longitudinal stays of the masts, were introduced for warships about 1660. Reef-points were seen on the sails of the ships on the seals of Hastings and La Rochelle, as well as on the sails of the Hansa cog. They appeared till the beginning of the sixteenth century and then vanished for unknown reasons, to reappear in 1660.

About 1670 reef-bands with reef-points—short lengths of rope hanging on each side of the sail—were first used on topsails and made the reduction—or reefing—of these sails more simple and speedy.

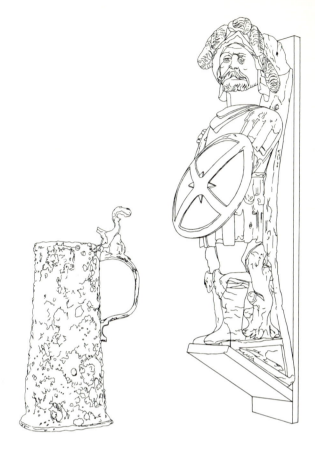

Finds from the *Wasa*:
Roman warrior from the port side of the lower quarter-deck.
Pewter tankard.

The Four Days' Fight, 1st to 4th June 1666, Second Dutch
War. In the foreground the *Zeven Provincien* with Admiral de
Ruyter on board. Painting by Abraham Storck.

Michiel Adriaanszoon de Ruyter, Dutch Admiral (1607–76).
In command of the Dutch naval forces during the Second and
Third Dutch Wars, responsible for the successful attack on the
Medway. He died in action from wounds received at the Battle
of Agosta.

At the beginning of the eighteenth century England possessed about one-third of the whole naval power of Europe; France and Holland together had about the same proportion and the other third consisted of the naval forces of other states.

Improvements in the design and a gradual increase in the size of warships continued throughout the eighteenth century.

In England, for the first fifty years of the century, this development was hindered by the system of shipbuilding Establishments which was imposed on the shipbuilders. After the original shipbuilding Establishment of 1677 further official regulations, laying down not only the standard dimensions of each class of warship, but also the sizes of the timbers used in their construction, were issued in 1691, 1706, 1719 and 1745, with additional proposals in 1733 and 1741. Although these successive rules steadily increased the size of ships, for instance a 100-gun ship built on the Establishment of 1745 was about 2 feet wider on the beam and some 11 feet longer on the gun-deck than a 100-gun ship of the 1677 Establishment, the rigid specification of the Establishments retarded the progress of English naval architecture and constrained the initiative of the shipwrights.

The greatest fault still attributed to British warships, even at this period, was that they were too small in relation to the number of guns they carried and therefore lay low in the water so that the lower-deck guns could not be used in rough weather and the ships 'sailed and worked heavily'.

Continental shipbuilders were free from the restraint of standardisation and were more easily able to incorporate in the design of warships the results of the current scientific investigation into the principles of naval architecture. In comparison with the British warships, Continental shipbuilders allowed a greater space between each gunport. This increased the length of vessel in relation to the number of guns carried, and the breadth of the vessel was increased in proportion. This of course gave a general increase in size and consequently in tonnage. The ship was more buoyant, the lower gun battery was higher above the water and with the guns arranged at greater intervals there was more room available for working them.

In France, following research into the resistance of solid bodies to water and the action of waves, particular attention was given to the design of the underwater hull form of warships. In consequence the French warships, in general, had better sailing qualities and were faster than English ships of a similar class. This fact was often demonstrated by the ability of the French fleet to break off from actions and, in the event of a chase, to outsail the English vessels.

The exact date of the introduction of that important feature, the steering wheel, is not known but in this the English perhaps led the way. In their ships of about 1700, tackles from the tiller, by which the rudder could be controlled, were led to a small windlass and by 1710 the steering wheel proper was in use, gradually to replace the cumbersome and inefficient whipstaff. The early steering wheels

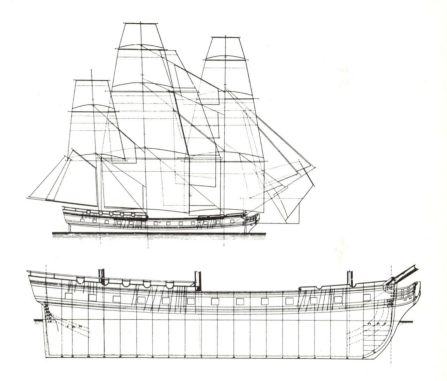

Danish 40-gun frigate *Havfruen*, 1789.

were of the single type, but later in the eighteenth century the double wheel which could be operated by a number of men was introduced for the larger ships.

Many warships of the Spanish Navy were particularly strongly built and, being larger than British vessels of the same Rate, possessed the advantage of greater stability and of being better able to withstand the effect of gunfire. In the second quarter of the eighteenth century a typical Spanish 70-gun ship was some 15 feet longer, 6 feet wider and 4 feet deeper in the hold than an English ship of the same armament. The Spanish vessel was of about 1700 tons compared with the 1250 tons of the English 70-gun ship.

In the same period the naval actions of the war between England and France, with her ally Spain, made very evident to the British Admiralty the inferiority of design and comparative size of the English warship. A particularly illuminating action took place in 1740 when a Spanish 70-gun ship, the *Princesa*, was only captured after a long and hard fight by three British men-of-war of equal rating.

In 1745 British master shipwrights from the various naval dockyards were ordered to produce a new set of standard dimensions for warships. Their efforts do not appear to have been altogether successful and this Establishment of 1745 was the last to be made. After about 1750 the individual ship-designer and shipwright was allowed more freedom to experiment and to produce larger and more successful warships.

Where possible 12-pounder guns were replaced by 18-pounders and 18-pounders by 24-pounder guns, but the importance of seaworthiness was more fully acknowledged and the ships designed for sixty and seventy guns were re-armed with fifty-eight and sixty-four guns respectively.

It is perhaps not generally realised how few First Rates with a hundred or more guns were built. For instance in the period 1750–90, despite the almost continuous naval warfare, only six 100-gun ships were built for the British Navy. These six vessels were: H.M.S. *Royal George* launched in 1756 (this vessel foundered at Spithead in 1782), H.M.S. *Britannia* launched in 1762, H.M.S. *Victory* launched in 1765, H.M.S. *Royal Sovereign* launched in 1786, another H.M.S. *Royal George* launched in 1788 and H.M.S. *Queen Charlotte* launched in 1790. In design the last of these eighteenth-century British 100-gun ships, the *Queen Charlotte*, differed little from the earlier examples, but the dimensions had been increased to give a gun-deck length of 190 feet, a beam of 52 feet 6 inches and a depth in hold of 22 feet 4 inches. The armament consisted of thirty 32-pounder guns on the lower gun-deck, twenty-eight 24-pounder guns on the middle gun-deck and thirty 18-pounder guns on the upper deck with ten 12-pounder guns on the quarter-deck and two on the forecastle.

In France, by this date, even larger ships had been built. The 118-gun ship *Commerce de Marseille*, built at Toulon in 1788, was for some years the largest vessel in the world. The *Commerce de Marseille* was 208 feet 4 inches long on the gun-deck, 54 feet 9 inches wide, with a depth in hold of 25 feet and of 2747 tons burden. The warship was captured by the British at Toulon in 1793, but was apparently poorly constructed and was broken up in 1802.

In 1757 an important new class of large two-decker 74-gun ships was introduced into the British Navy. The design of these vessels was taken from that of captured French 74-gun ships, such as the *Invincible* captured in 1747. As these 74-gun ships proved particularly successful and later in the eighteenth century this class of warship formed a large portion of the 'ships-of-the-line' of both French and British navies, a more detailed description of the vessels is appropriate

The typical 74-gun of the late eighteenth century was about 176 feet long on the gun-deck, had a beam of 49 feet and was of about 1800 tons, bigger in fact than the 100-gun ships of the late seventeenth century. The keel was made up from some seven pieces of oak scarphed together and was about 1 foot 6 inches wide and about the same depth. The thwartship frames, the ribs of the vessel, were 1 foot 4 inches wide and 1 foot deep, and were spaced about 1 foot apart. The keelson laying on the frames was 1 foot 6 inches square. The external planking, about 4 inches thick near the keel, gradually decreasing to a thickness of about

2 inches at the upper-deck bulwarks. The main wale, which provided longitudinal strength and extra protection at the water-line, was composed of planks about 8 inches thick. The hold, about 20 feet in depth, extended the whole length of the hull but was divided by bulkheads into the fore, main and after holds and other minor compartments.

At the bottom of the hold the ballast was disposed, about 70 tons of iron and 270 tons of shingle for a vessel of this size. (The correct weight and disposition of the ballast was an important factor in a sailing ship—too much ballast, placed too low, made the vessel roll badly and sail heavily. With too little ballast it was impossible to carry sail without risk of capsizing).

In the main hold, the fresh water and beer were stowed in casks on the ballast, together with other stores, provisions, etc.

The fore-hold contained the main magazine fitted with racks and drawers, etc., for the gunpowder. Just forward of the magazine was a small compartment known as the light-room, with double glass windows through which lanterns that were thus isolated from the gunpowder provided light for the magazine. A second magazine was located in the after-hold, which also contained the bread and spirit rooms.

Above the hold was the orlop deck of 3-inch thick planking resting on transverse beams 5 inches thick and 5 inches wide. Each beam was supported by a vertical oak pillar stepped on the keelson. Much of the orlop was used for stowing the coiled anchor cables (a ship of this size would carry at least seven cables 720 feet long, with a circumference of $20\frac{1}{2}$ inches and weighing over five tons) but cabins and stores for the purser, surgeon, boatswain, gunner and carpenter were also erected on this deck, together with store-rooms for the captain and lieutenant, and berths for the midshipmen.

Above the orlop the lower gun-deck consisting of 4-inch thick planking extended for the full length of the hull. In addition to the rows of 32-pounder guns arranged to port and starboard there were also attached to this deck the riding bitts with their cross-pieces to which the cables were secured when the vessel was at anchor. The cabins for their junior lieutenant and chaplain were erected on this deck with a gun-room as a mess for the midshipmen.

The upper deck immediately above was made of 3-inch planking and carried a battery of 24-pounder guns. On this deck the ward-room at the stern with the lieutenant's, master's and captain of marines' cabins were erected in such a manner that they could be easily taken down when the ship went into action. Forward on this deck just astern of the foremast was the galley with a fire-hearth.

On the quarter-deck, above the upper deck, was the captain's cabin at the stern, the steering wheel and a number of carronades to port and starboard. The forecastle deck at the bows also carried carronades while at the stern the roof of the captain's cabin, forming a short deck, was fitted with a skylight for the cabin below, and carried several light guns or carronades.

To provide extra protection while in action, the rolled hammocks of the crew were placed in nets, held by iron 'U' fittings, along the tops of the bulwarks. In the nineteenth century with the general adoption of solid bulwarks the nets were replaced by troughs made with planks.

It has been estimated that to build a 74-gun ship of this size nearly 4000 loads of timber were required. A mature oak tree of average size provided enough wood for one load.

The difficulty of protecting the underwater hull of a wooden ship from damage by marine pests has already been mentioned. In 1761 as an experiment, the English frigate *Alarm* was sheathed below the water-line with sheets of copper. After further tests on other vessels it was found that the iron fastenings of the hull were quickly corroded by the electrolytic action between the iron, the copper and the salt water. After about 1780, however, the iron bolts, etc., in the hull below the water-line were replaced by copper fastenings, and copper sheathing proved so successful that by the end of the century the underwater hulls of most large warships were protected in this manner. This sheathing was applied in the form of thin sheets, each about 4 feet long and 14 inches wide. Some 3300 such sheets and about one and a quarter tons of counter-sunk nails were required to sheath a 74-gun ship.

Alterations in the construction and ornamentation of the upper part of the hulls of warships also took place during the eighteenth century. From about 1750 the transverse 'square' beak-head bulkhead at the bows, always a source of weakness against both head seas and gun-fire, was replaced, first in small warships, by a much stronger round bow built up to the level of the forecastle deck. This round bow was next fitted to larger frigates, by the end of the century to two-deckers and finally to the largest warships.

Throughout the seventeenth and eighteenth centuries open walkways or galleries were fitted to the sterns of large warships of most Continental nations, although they were discarded for a time in English ships. In the warships of most navies, and in English warships after their re-introduction about 1680, it was the usual practice to fit two sternwalks to three-deckers and one to two-deckers. Large British warships built or rebuilt between about 1795 and 1813 were not fitted with open galleries. Frigates and other vessels with a single gun-deck rarely had sternwalks.

The extensive and elaborate carved and gilded ornamentation of the upper-works of late seventeenth-century warships gradually gave way during the eighteenth century to a more subdued form of decoration with less florid carvings at the stern, quarters and bow, and painted trophies of arms, foliage, etc., in the form of a frieze on a blue or black ground along the sheer of the quarter-deck and forecastle. For English ships it required a series of Admiralty orders to bring about this reduction in the decoration of warships. These orders finally specified the precise form, amount and cost of the carved work and became fully effective after about 1715.

Although occasionally the above-water hulls of eighteenth-century men-of-war were painted blue or red, the usual practice until late in the century was to 'pay' most of the hull with a mixture of turpentine and rosin and paint the wales black. For British ships the famous 'Nelson fashion' for warships, with black hulls and a yellow band along each line of gunports, was introduced in 1798 and lasted until about 1813.

Apart from the ships-of-the-line, from the middle of the eighteenth century, the ubiquitous frigates, with their main armament on one deck, formed increasingly important sub-divisions of the navies of the world, in which they were mainly employed in scouting, convoy duties and attacks on enemy merchant shipping. The frigates became progressively larger and by the end of the century the principal classes of these vessels consisted of frigates carrying forty-four, forty, thirty-eight, thirty-six, thirty-two, twenty-eight, twenty-four and twenty guns (most of the ship-rigged vessels carrying less than twenty guns were usually known as sloops-of-war in the British Navy and corvettes in the French fleet and in many other navies).

The increase in the size of frigates and in the weight of armament is well illustrated by the various classes of these vessels which were built for the British Navy in the second half of the eighteenth century.

In 1757 a class of 32-gun frigates was first introduced. These vessels were of about 670 tons and were 127 feet 9 inches long on the gun-deck, with a beam of 34 feet 4 inches. The armament consisted of twenty-six 12-pounder guns on the gun-deck, four 6-pounders on the quarter-deck and two 6-pounders on the forecastle. In 1780 the 38-gun frigate first appeared. These vessels were 141 feet long on the gun-deck, 39 feet wide and carried twenty-eight 18-pounder guns on the gun-deck, six 9-pounders on the quarter-deck and four on the forecastle. (The increase in the size of the gun-deck guns from 12-pounders to 18-pounders was a great improvement and a similar change took place in the armament of French frigates at about the same time.)

In 1797, 40-gun frigates were first built for the British Navy with a further increase in dimensions and armament. The *Cambrian*, launched in 1797, was typical of these frigates. In this frigate the gun-deck was 154 feet long and the

Figure-heads from Swedish warships *Försiktigheten*, 1784, and *Fäderneslandet*, 1783.

Death of Lord Nelson at Trafalgar, 21st October 1805. Painting by Denis Dighton shows Lord Nelson on the quarter-deck of *Victory* after being mortally wounded by a musket ball fired from the French ship *Redoutable*. He died with the knowledge of his great victory.

Horatio, Viscount Nelson (1758–1805), Vice-Admiral of the White. Was in command of the British fleets at the Battle of the Nile in 1798 and at Trafalgar.

beam 41 feet 3 inches. Twenty-eight 24-pounder guns formed the main armament with twelve 9-pounders on the quarter-deck and forecastle.

Similar increases in the sizes of frigates took place in other navies, and in the French fleet the classes of frigates often led the world in size and design.

British frigates were occasionally built to the French design, in some cases the design being further improved by the English designers and shipwrights. As an instance of this, the French 44-gun frigate *La Pomone*, captured in 1794, provided the basic design for the British frigate *Endymion* launched in 1797, but alterations to the design, including an increase of 8 inches in the hull width, produced a remarkably fine and fast-sailing frigate which remained in the British Navy until 1860. The *Endymion* was 159 feet 4 inches long on the gun-deck, 42 feet 7 inches beam and 1277 tons. The armament consisted of twenty-six 24-pounder guns on the gun-deck, fourteen 32-pounder carronades on the quarter-deck and two 9-pounder guns and four 32-pounder carronades on the forecastle.

During the whole of the eighteenth century a three-masted square-sail rig was standard practice throughout the navies of Europe for all warships from the frigate to the First Rate.

During the century the principal improvements in this three-masted rig were: the increase in the height of the mizen-mast by the addition of a topgallant mast; the development of the gaff spanker or driver sail from the lateen mizen sail; the lengthening of the bowsprit by the addition of a jibboom and flying jibboom, allowing the use of more fore and aft headsails; and the increased number of fore-and-aft staysails used between the masts.

For vessels below the Rate of frigate and for warships designed for special duties other rigs were often adopted. In the latter half of the eighteenth century most navies contained a number of brig-rigged vessels, and the very efficient and fast-sailing two-masted schooners developed for the merchant service in America and the West Indies were also used for naval purposes.

The bomb-vessel first used by the French at the end of the seventeenth century was a vessel specially designed and constructed to carry large calibre mortars to throw bombs into enemy fortresses and positions ashore. At the end of the eighteenth century the bomb-vessel was usually about 70 feet long and 200 tons burden. Two 10-inch mortars and a number of carronades were normally carried. The two-masted ketch rig, of main and mizen masts only, was particularly suitable for bomb-vessels as it allowed an almost uninterrupted forward field of fire for the mortars. However, in the latter half of the eighteenth century British bombs were ship-rigged. A three-masted lugger known as a 'Chasse-marée', which had been evolved from the eighteenth-century fishing luggers, was frequently used by French and British privateers during the Napoleonic wars. The large fore-and-aft lug-sails made these vessels very fast and enabled them to sail close to the wind.

The naval cutter, rigged with a large gaff mainsail, often also carried a square topsail and topgallant sail. Cutters were used for scouting and subsidiary services by the naval forces and particularly by the British Revenue service as coastal patrol vessels to counter smuggling activities.

EIGHTEENTH–CENTURY FIGHTING TACTICS

At the end of the seventeenth century the British Admiralty issued permanent 'Fighting Instructions'. Under this code the British fleet was required to fight in line-ahead formation, extending their line length for length with that of the enemy. Breaking the line in action was forbidden under the threat of courts-martial.

The British fleet usually tried to obtain the windward or 'attacking' position but the stultifying effect of the 'Fighting Instructions' was such that, for a period of about ninety years, the British fleet was unable to defeat decisively an enemy fleet in any major action.

Throughout this period the British admirals had adhered invariably to the established code of attack and endeavoured to obtain a windward position before engaging. Each warship steered directly to its opponent in the adverse line and

was positioned in a parallel position, to produce a general engagement from the van to the rear.

In 1782 an event occurred which was to bring about a complete change in British naval tactics, and as a writer of the period states, 'a new era has been fixed in the history of our naval transactions'. During the course of a battle, near the Isles of Les Saintes in the West Indies, between large fleets of British and French ships-of-the-line, the British admiral, Sir George Rodney, deliberately broke the 'parallel line' doctrine and led part of his line, from the leeward position, through the enemy column. As a consequence of this operation, which was to become known as 'cutting the enemy line', the rear of the French fleet was driven to leeward and severely damaged by raking gunfire. The van and centre of the French fleet escaped in different directions. The English fleet, instead of concentrating its attack on the disorganised and damaged French rear division, was ordered to chase the enemy van and did in fact succeed in capturing five ships-of-the-line.

After this action the 'cutting the line' manœuvre was, with the exception of the battle of the Nile where the French fleet was at anchor, uniformly practised by British admirals with great success and no major engagement proved indecisive.

At Trafalgar in 1805, the last great open-sea battle of the age of sail, the British admiral, Lord Nelson, again used the cutting the enemy line manœuvre. In this engagement the British fleet was formed into two parallel columns, one of twelve ships-of-the-line and the other of fifteen. The combined French and Spanish fleets, consisting of thirty-three ships-of-the-line, formed into a somewhat irregular line-ahead formation with some of the vessels two or three abreast. The two British columns, sailing more or less at right-angles to the enemy, broke through their line in two places. The twelve ships of one division tackled the sixteen van and centre Allied ships while the other division dealt with the seventeen rearmost vessels. In the mêlée which resulted from the breaking of the Allied line the British captured eighteen of the enemy ships.

THE FINAL PHASE OF THE SAILING

WARSHIP

TWO- AND THREE-DECKERS

In the period of about forty years from the last decade of the eighteenth century, sailing warships of each class reached their greatest size.

The French two-decker *Sans Pareil*, carrying eighty guns, had a gun-deck 193 feet long and a beam of 51 feet 6 inches. This 80-gun ship, launched in 1793, was thus nearly as large as the British 100-gun ships built only a few years earlier. It is therefore perhaps not surprising that when in the same year the British re-introduced the 80-gun two-decker—a type of vessel which had not been built in England for nearly a hundred years—the dimensions of the warship were much less than those of the French *Sans Pareil*.

The first of these late eighteenth-century British 80-gun two-deckers was the *Caesar* with a gun-deck length of 181 feet and a beam of 51 feet 3 inches. The *Ville de Paris*, built at Chatham in 1795, was the first warship designed to carry 110 guns built for the British Navy. The *Hibernia* was launched in 1804 as a 110-gun ship, but was converted into a 120-gun ship during extensive repairs in 1819–25 and her stern was altered to the circular form, which had been introduced by Sir Robert Seppings. The *Hibernia* was 201 feet long on the gun-deck, but between 1808 and 1815 four 120-gun ships, the *Caledonia*, *Howe*, *Nelson* and *St. Vincent*, were built which nearly equalled in size the French *Commerce de Marseille* of 1788. The British 74-gun ship *Bulwark*, built at Portsmouth in 1807, was 182 feet long on the gun-deck compared with the 176 feet of the 74-gun ships built in the late eighteenth century.

The changes in design of sailing warships which took place during this period were principally alterations to the upper part of the hull. The gradual introduction of the round bow has already been described and from about 1790 French warships were built with high solid bulwarks to the forecastle, quarter-deck and poop. This improvement, which provided more shelter for the crew, was not adopted for the larger ships of the British Navy until about 1797 and even then only for the forecastle. It was not until about 1802 that the decks of the quarter-deck and poop of British warships were protected in the same way.

The next major improvement in the design of the larger warships was an alteration in the design and construction of the stern. The form and construction of the old square stern was weak and the field of fire of the few guns which could be brought to bear from the stern and quarters was very limited. In 1820 British warships were first fitted with a circular stern, designed by Sir Robert Seppings, Surveyor of the Navy. The construction of this new form of stern was much stronger and gave facilities for additional stern fire. Further improvements to the circular stern were introduced in 1827 when the shape of the stern was altered to an elliptical form. The elliptical stern, while retaining the advantages of constructional strength and extra gunports on the quarters, permitted the fitting of the projecting walkways so prized by senior naval officers.

The Battle of Navarino, 20th October 1827. In this battle the Turkish and Egyptian fleets were defeated by the combined British, French and Russian fleets. Painting by Thomas Luny.

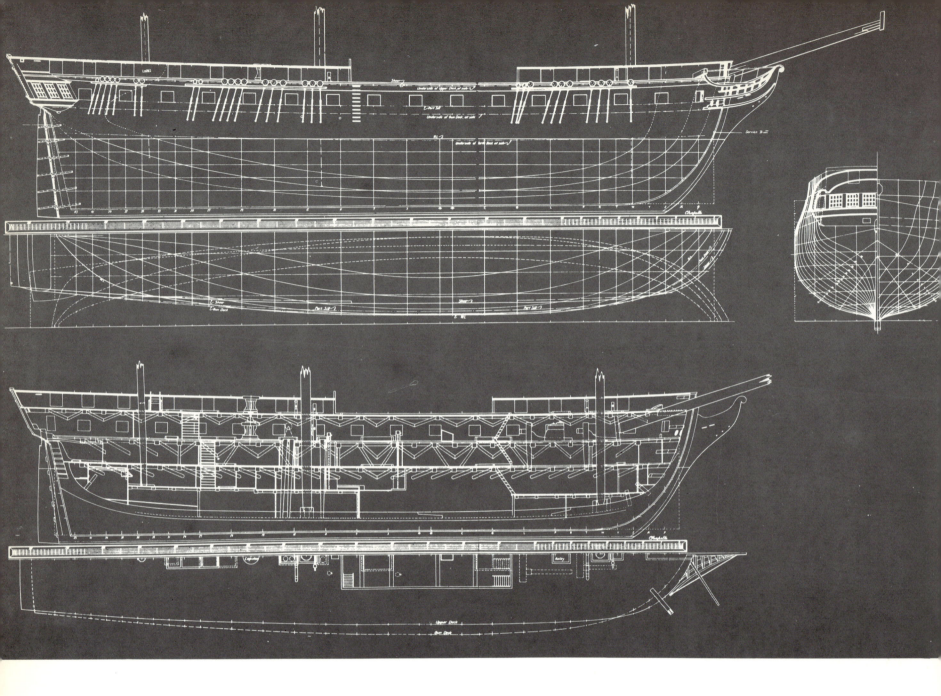

PRESIDENT

American 44-gun frigate. Redrawn from a British Admiralty plan

made after her capture.

With the great increase in the length of the larger warships new constructional methods were required to prevent the hull 'hogging', that is, for bow and stern to droop. A method had to be devised to strengthen the skeleton framework of transverse and longitudinal timbers.

As early as 1746 a French book describes a method of diagonal planking for the inside of the hold of a ship, and in 1768 the Swedish naval architect F. H. af Chapman published, in his famous work 'Architectura Navalis Mercatoria', plans which showed the use of diagonal ties to provide additional longitudinal strength. Further experiments with similar methods were made later in the eighteenth century and during the early years of the nineteenth century. By 1832 a 'trussed frame' form of construction had been established for British warships. This was accomplished by fitting to the hull, below the gun-deck, a complete system of internal diagonal timber ties and struts crossing the transverse frames at 45 degrees, with extra stiffening by additional longitudinal timbers. Further strength was given by fitting thick continuous longitudinal timbers above and below the junction of the deck beams with the sides of the ship.

The 92-gun ship *Rodney*, a two-decker designed by Sir Robert Seppings and launched in 1833, was constructed with a completely trussed framework. The *Rodney* was of 2626 tons burden, 205 feet 6 inches long on the gun-deck and later carried an armament of twenty-six 32-pounder guns and six 8-inch guns on the lower deck; thirty 32-pounders and four 8-inch guns on the main deck; and twenty-six 32-pounders on the quarter-deck. (The 8-inch gun was 9 feet long, weighed 65 cwt. and fired a 51-pound shell or 56-pound plugged hollow shot.) The unification of nearly all the main armament to 32-pounders made for a much more efficient supply service. Sir William Symonds, who was appointed Surveyor of the British Navy in 1832, designed vessels with a different underwater section, in order to increase the sailing speed of warships.

Warships built to Sir William Symonds' design were wide at the water-line, with rounded bilges and a 'V' section to the underwater body. Although certainly fast sailers, warships of this form had a tendency to roll and were therefore poor gun-platforms in bad weather conditions.

In the period of his surveyorship, Sir William Symonds was responsible for the building of nearly two hundred vessels for the British Navy, and his later designs combined with the stronger construction methods, which included the use of iron riders and knees, produced the most highly developed vessels in the history of the British sailing navy.

Notable examples of the larger warships built by Symonds were the 80-gun two-decker, *Vanguard*, launched in 1835, and the 110-gun, three-decker *Queen*, launched in 1839. The *Queen* had a particularly handsome stern with three tiers of windows and two open walkways, somewhat similar in general appearance to the old square stern, but at the level of the lower gun-deck a gunport was cut in each quarter. The unification of the armament continued in the *Queen*, which carried one hundred 32-pounder guns and ten 8-inch guns. In 1859 the *Queen* was converted to steam and screw propulsion.

The last two-decker sailing warships built for the British Navy were the *Albion*, launched in 1842, and the *Aboukir*, launched in 1848. Both these vessels were 90-gun ships designed by Sir William Symonds and, being nearly equal in size to the 120-gun ships of the *Caledonia* class, they were the largest sailing two-deckers built for the British Navy. Three other vessels of this class were laid down, but were altered for steam and screw propulsion before they were completed. In this context, it is interesting to note that the *Ganges*, an 84-gun ship built at Bombay in 1821, was, until paid off in 1861, the last sailing ship-of-the-line in active service in the British Navy.

In France, M. Sané, Inspecteur général du Génie Maritime, designed a number of sailing warships for the French Navy, including a class of three 120-gun ships, the *Montebello*, launched in 1812, the *Souverain*, launched in 1819, and the *Friedland*, launched in 1840. These vessels were 207 feet 4 inches long on the water-line with an overall breadth of 57 feet 5 inches and a displacement of 5005 tons.

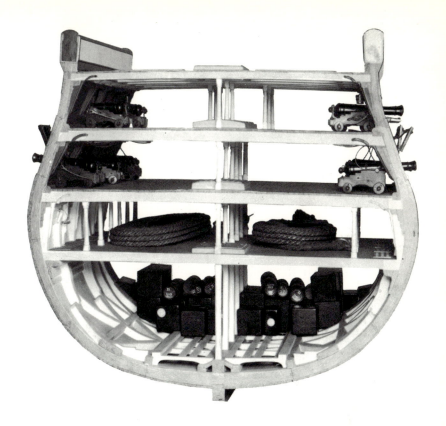

Midship section of H.M.S. *Rodney*. This 92-gun ship was launched at Pembroke in 1833.

Pages 70–71. French 120-gun ship *Le Valmy* built at Brest in 1838–47. The last three-decker sailing warship built for the French Navy. Water colour by F. Roux.

The *Hercule, Jemappes* and *Tage,* a somewhat smaller class of three-deckers, with a displacement of 4374 tons, were designed by a committee of five French naval architects and launched between 1836 and 1847.

The last three-decker sailing warship built for the French Navy was the *Valmy,* a 120-gun ship designed by M. Le Roux and launched at Brest in 1847.

The appearance of these French three-deckers was more impressive than that of the British warships of the same type. In the British three-deckers of the period, no guns were mounted on the deck which extended over the waist and connected the quarter-deck and forecastle. However, the French ships carried guns at this position and these weapons, with the quarter-deck and forecastle guns, formed a complete fourth tier of guns.

In general the French warships had higher and thicker masts than the ships of the British Navy and their topsails and topgallant sails were larger. This adversely effected the sailing qualities of the French vessels in strong wind conditions and particularly when the stability of the ship had been reduced by the loss of weight in the hold, due to the consumption of stores and provisions.

In 1832, squadrons composed of various classes of British and French warships sailed together, although under separate commands. In general the sailing performance of the French vessels was less satisfactory than that of the British ships and this led the French Minister of Marine to set up a Commission to investigate and report on the various differences of design, masting, etc., between the French and British warships and on the effect these differences had on the sailing qualities of the warships.

FRIGATES

In the nineteenth century the frigate continued to be a most important and useful unit of the sailing navies, and at the beginning of the century the British Navy alone had over two hundred frigates in commission.

In the last few years of the eighteenth century the government of the United States of America commenced a shipbuilding programme which was to have a great effect on the design of frigates. Between 1797 and 1800 three frigates were built which were larger and more heavily armed than frigates of any other nation. These vessels, the *Constitution,* the *President,* and *United States,* were 173 feet long on the gun-deck with an extreme breadth of 44 feet 4 inches. Although classed as 44-gun ships they carried a total of fifty-two guns and carronades. Thirty 24-pounder guns were mounted on the gun-deck and twenty-two 42-pounder—or 32-pounder—carronades on the forecastle, quarter-deck and on the deck over the waist amidships. Thus with two almost complete tiers of guns these vessels were the first 'double-banked' frigates.

At this date the largest frigate in the British Navy was the *Endymion,* classed as a 40-gun frigate, but in the method then adopted of calculating the rating all the carronades were not counted and the frigate actually carried a total of forty-six guns and carronades.

Consequently in 1812, when war broke out between Great Britain and the United States of America, the British frigates were outclassed by the larger American 'double-banked' frigates. As an immediate remedy the British Admiralty ordered three 74-gun ships, the *Goliath, Majestic* and *Saturn,* to be cut down and converted into 'razee' frigates. This was accomplished by removing the forecastles and quarter-decks of the 74s and leaving two complete tiers of guns. The idea of 'razee' warships was not new; a number of British and French vessels had been reduced in this manner during the eighteenth century.

In 1813, in addition to the 'razee' frigates, Britain built and launched two large frigates, the *Leander* and *Newcastle.* These warships were 174 feet long on the gun-deck and had a beam of 45 feet 1 inch. They were 'double-banked', with continuous solid bulwarks from bow to stern, and carried an armament of thirty-four 24-pounder guns and twenty-six 42-pounder carronades. The *Leander* and *Newcastle* were the first 60-gun frigates built for the British Navy. (The *Java,* a third British 60-gun frigate, was launched in 1815.)

To return to America, two further frigates of an improved *Constitution* class were built in 1813, the *Guerrière* and *Java*. These vessels were of about the same dimensions as the *Constitution* but although the deck from forecastle to quarter-deck was complete—this deck became known as the spar-deck in both British and American navies—because they had proved inconvenient in the earlier frigates, guns were not mounted on this spar-deck amidships. The armament of the *Guerrière* and *Java* consisted of thirty-three 24-pounder guns and twenty 42-pounder carronades.

The design of a group of five British 50-gun frigates built in 1813–14 shows the same return to the older gun layout on the spar-deck and completely 'double-banked' frigates did not occur again in the British sailing navy. The five British frigates were the *Glasgow*, *Liverpool*, *Severn*, *Liffey* and *Forth*, and they were armed with twenty-eight 24-pounder guns, two 9-pounder guns and sixteen 32-pounder carronades. These British frigates were built of pitch-pine, instead of the usual oak, and the average duration of these vessels was only about six and a half years.

Large frigates were of course built for other navies, and in France M. Sané in particular was responsible for some very fine warships of this type. The *Sirène*, built in 1823, one of a class of eight large frigates, designed by M. Hubert, was a typical example of a large French frigate. This vessel was 170 feet long at the water-line, had a beam of 44 feet and was armed with fifty-two guns. The *Sirène* was the French flagship at the battle of Navarino in 1827 when a combined force of British, French and Russian warships destroyed a Turco–Egyptian fleet.

Between 1834 and 1847 a class of five 60-gun frigates were built in France. These frigates, the *Belle Poule*, *Sémillante*, *Andromaque*, *Forte* and *Renommée*, were designed by M. Boucher and were 177 feet 1 inch long on the water-line with an extreme beam of 45 feet 11 inches.

In the British Navy the 50-gun frigate *Vernon*, launched in 1832, was an example of the earlier class of large frigates designed by Captain—later Sir William—Symonds. The *Vernon* was 176 feet long on the gun-deck, and with a beam of 52 feet 8 inches was, in common with other vessels designed by Symonds, wider on the water-line than other contemporary frigates, but Symonds' ships were also given finer underwater lines than was usual at that time and the *Vernon* was renowned for her sailing qualities. The frigate was fitted with an elliptical stern complete with projecting gallery and carried forty-four 32-pounder guns and six 8-inch guns.

The last 50-gun sailing frigates built for the British Navy were the *Arethusa* and *Octavia*, launched in 1849. Also designed by Sir William Symonds, these frigates were 180 feet long on the gun-deck, with a beam of 52 feet 9 inches and carried twenty-two 32-pounder 56-cwt. guns, eighteen 32-pounder 45-cwt. guns and ten 8-inch 65-cwt. guns. The *Arethusa* and *Octavia* were converted into screw-frigates in 1861. The *Constance*, built to the same design and launched in 1846, was altered in the same way in 1862 and two further vessels of the class, the *Sutlej* and *Liffey*, were made into screw steamers before they were launched in 1855 and 1856. All these large frigates had a complement of 500 men.

It is perhaps appropriate to close this account of the development of the sailing warship with a brief description of the sailing trials which took place in the last few years before the steam-powered vessel was generally introduced.

In the British Navy, from about 1820, experimental sailing took place occasionally so that the power of sailing and manœuvring abilities of individual ships could be tried in competition, in order to try and ascertain how to improve design.

Many classes of warship, from ships-of-the-line to cutters, competed in these trials. In 1844–45 an experimental squadron was formed with eight brigs as follows:

Name	Built	Length of gun-deck		Breadth		Tons	Guns	Designer
		ft.	ins.	ft.	ins.			
Cruizer	1828	100	0	31	0	384	18	Rule
Pantaloon	1831	92	0	29	5	323	10	Symonds
Waterwitch	1832	90	6	29	4	319	10	White
Daring	1844	104	0	31	5	426	12	White
Espiegle	1844	104	7	31	8	443	12	Chatfield, Creuze and Read
Flying Fish	1844	103	0	32	5	445	12	Symonds
Mutine	1844	112	0	32	0	428	12	Fincham
Osprey	1844	101	0	32	0	425	12	Blake

In the trials of 1844–45 observations were made and registered in each ship, in order to find the effect by both wind and sea. The observations noted the power and state of the wind, rate of sailing, points near the wind, angle of the main-yard with the keel, angle of leeway, common inclination, angle of pitching, position of helm, state of the sea, greatest roll to windward and quantity of sail set. The observations were made while the vessels were sailing with the wind on the beam or quarter, sailing before the wind and 'close-hauled'.

To sum up briefly the findings: In strong breezes the *Daring* was most successful with the *Flying Fish* and *Waterwitch* next. With the wind abeam the *Daring* and *Espiegle* were the faster ships while before the wind the *Flying Fish* and *Pantaloon* were best. On the whole the *Daring* was the superior vessel with *Flying Fish* next and the *Mutine* and *Osprey* were described as 'beaten vessels'.

Between July and December 1845 trials were made to determine the relative superiority of ships-of-the-line. The eight warships taking part in these trials were as follows:

Name	Built	Length of gun-deck		Breadth		Tons	Guns	Designer
		ft.	ins.	ft.	ins.			
Canopus	1796	193	9	51	7	2257	84	Captured French ship
St. Vincent	1815	205	0	53	7	2601	120	Seppings
Rodney	1833	205	6	54	6	2626	92	Seppings
Vanguard	1835	190	0	57	0	2609	80	Symonds
Queen	1839	204	3	60	0	3104	110	Symonds
Trafalgar	1841	206	0	54	7	2721	120	Symonds
Superb	1842	190	0	57	0	2583	80	Symonds
Albion	1842	204	0	60	0	3111	90	Symonds

In the first trials the *Queen* showed a marked superiority to any other ship in the squadron in working to windward. In sailing before the wind there was no marked difference in the performance of the ships. The *Vanguard* appeared to pitch deeply and heavily in a head sea and to roll deeply before the wind.

LA POMONE

A French 44-gun frigate captured by
the British in 1794. This frigate served
as a model for the British frigate *Endymion*
built in 1797.

The Confederate steam frigate *Merrimac* after destroying two
unarmoured Federal warships in Hampton Roads is engaged
by the Federal turret-ram *Monitor* in an indecisive battle.

THE ADVENT

OF THE STEAM AGE

The Battle of Trafalgar, though it was not the last major engagement of the age of sail, must be judged the great climax of war at sea during that epoch, in that it decided in favour of Great Britain the age-long rivalry between that country and France for supremacy at sea. In doing so it also wrecked Napoleon Bonaparte's ambitions to establish a European hegemony under his imperial rule. The sailing line-of-battle ships with which the battle was fought continued for another forty years to constitute the principal units of the world's fighting fleets. For almost as long, the smaller men-of-war retained masts and sails as their only means of propulsion. In 1827 the last big battle between sailing ships took place when a combined British, French and Russian fleet, under the command of Admiral Sir Edward Codrington, destroyed the Turkish and Egyptian fleet in Navarino Bay and thus secured Greek independence from Turkey.

But fifteen years earlier, while British and American sailing frigates were still fighting ferocious duels in the war of 1812, the first example had been made of a development which was to make such ships extinct. The versatile American Robert Fulton had designed and was building the first warship propelled by steam power.

This was by no means the first steam vessel, of course. In the late eighteenth century, experiments in the application of steam power had been made by the Frenchman Claude, marquis de Jouffroy d'Abbans in 1778 and 1783, the Americans James Rumsey and John Fitch in 1787 and the Scotsman Patrick Miller in 1788. The honour of producing the first steamer to be put to practical use, however, goes to the Scottish engineer William Symington, who in 1801 built the paddle tug *Charlotte Dundas* which proved itself by successfully towing two vessels through the Forth and Clyde Canal. Meanwhile Robert Fulton was experimenting in France and in 1803 successfully navigated a steamboat on the Seine. He thereafter returned to his native America and in 1807 the steamboat *Clermont*, which he devised, travelled (to the consternation of beholders of the flames and sparks belching from its funnel) from New York to Albany, some 120 miles, at a speed of 4 knots. On the outbreak of war in 1812, he turned his inventive mind to the production of the steam man-of-war mentioned above. The result, too late to take part in the war and completed after Fulton's death, was the steam frigate *Demologos*, a double vessel with a paddle-wheel between the two hulls. She was 156 feet long and armed with twenty-four 32-pounder guns. The *Demologos* was destroyed by an explosion of her magazine in 1829.

Fulton's ingenious concept, however, found no general favour with the navies of the world. The British Navy, though it soon adopted steam propulsion for such craft as tugs and dredgers, for a long time rejected steam power for any of its warships. The very idea, indeed, was looked upon with horror by the Board of Admiralty. A successful design of steam warship could make the whole British fleet obsolete overnight. As Lord Melville, First Lord of the Admiralty, wrote in 1828: 'Their Lordships feel it their bounden duty to discourage to the utmost of

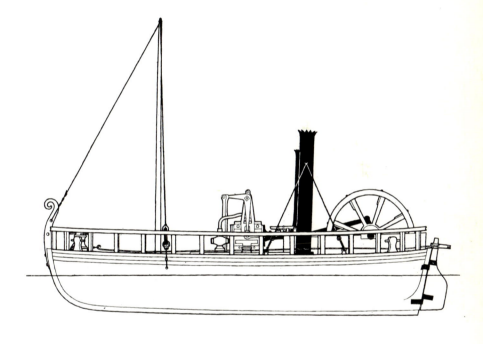

The first steamer put to practical use was the paddle tug *Charlotte Dundas*, built by William Symington in 1801.

their ability the employment of steam vessels, as they consider that the introduction of steam is calculated to strike a fatal blow at the naval supremacy of the empire.'

This ostrich-like attitude to the problem could not long be maintained. Across the Channel, the French, with far less to lose by a revolution in naval ship-design, were listening to the urgings of the brilliant artillery officer, General Paixhans, to start afresh with a steam navy. Stealing a march on the hesitant British, they might easily find themselves in a position to reverse the decision of Trafalgar.

Paixhans, indeed, was a man of vision far in advance of his time. As early as 1822 he was publicly foretelling the revolution in naval tactics which would come about with the adoption of steam propulsion and of explosive shells. He also advocated the adoption of a single calibre of gun—the largest possible—in warships, a concept which, rediscovered eighty years later, was to bring about the dreadnought revolution.

In the face of this threat, during the next ten years or so the British Admiralty accepted the proposition that, if possible, its warships should be given steam-engines. The change agreed in principle, its practical application came up against a seemingly insuperable difficulty in so far as the larger ships of the fleet were concerned. The only method of propelling a steamship which had been devised up to that time was by means of paddle-wheels. Except by employing Fulton's idea of a central paddle-wheel, which provided very poor manœuvrability and was never repeated, except in some Mississippi river gunboats during the American Civil War, these paddle-wheels protruded, one on each side, from the ship's hull. Not only were they extremely vulnerable to cannon fire, but their huge paddle boxes occupied the space required for a large proportion of the ship's own cannon. The broadside of tiers of heavy, smooth-bore cannon, firing solid shot, was still the armament of ships of war.

If half the armament had to be sacrificed to install so fragile a device as a paddle-wheel, the value of steam propulsion was doubtful, to say the least. It was restricted at first, therefore, to small ships employed as tugs and for other auxiliary functions. The first paddle-steamer built for the British Navy, the *Comet* of 238 tons, launched at Deptford in 1822, and several similar ships completed in the next few years, were not provided with guns until about 1830, when they first appeared in the List of the Navy and so entered the category of men-of-war.

The French Navy followed a similar course, their first steamer, the *Sphinx*, completed in 1830, being strictly only a despatch-vessel, rated as an *aviso*. She and her successors over the next decade were employed in the service of the Post Office or to transport supplies across the Mediterranean to French armies in Africa. The first real British steam warship was the sloop *Gorgon*, launched in 1837 and armed with a single cannon at bow and stern. A larger ship, classed as a steam frigate, was the *Firebrand*, launched in 1842.

By this time, however, inventive minds had been at work to adapt the steam-engine to drive a screw, a method of propulsion which had been appreciated since classical times, and used, on occasions, driven by manpower, but which had never before been harnessed to a machine. In 1825, when a prize was offered for the best method of propelling a ship without the use of paddles, Commander Samuel Brown, R.N., won it by fitting up a boat with a 12 horse-power steam-engine driving a two-bladed propeller on a shaft which projected from the bow. Though this device was successful, the project was not followed up. In 1826 and 1829 the Austrian engineer Joseph Ressel also made successful experiments with screw propulsion of the steamship *Civetta*. Ten years later, two engineers took out patents for rival screw-propulsion systems, Mr. Francis Pettit-Smith, an Englishman, in May 1836, and, in July of that year, Captain John Ericsson, a one-time Swedish Army officer, but at this time a civil engineer working in London.

Both made successful trials of their systems in small vessels; but whereas Smith's invention caught the attention of the British Admiralty and was soon afterwards adopted for ships of the Royal Navy, Ericsson found himself un-

appreciated in England. Encouraged by Mr. Francis Ogden, American consul at Liverpool, and an American naval officer, Captain Robert Stockton, Ericsson crossed the Atlantic to place his talents at the service of the United States Navy, an early consequence of which was the construction of the first steam-screw man-of-war, the U.S.S. *Princeton*.

In France, it was the shipbuilder Augustin Normand of Le Havre (1792–1871) and his English engineer collaborator Barnes who first applied screw propulsion to the despatch-vessel *Napoléon* (later re-named the *Corse*), which was launched in 1842 and achieved a speed of 12·4 knots. The screw they used was a development of a type patented by the Frenchman Frédéric Sauvage.

It was not without a convincing demonstration, however, that the overall superiority of the screw over the paddle was generally accepted. When arguments for and against both methods had reached deadlock in England, the British Admiralty staged a test which appealed to good sense and the public love of a sporting event. In May 1845 the steam-sloop *Rattler*, screw-driven, was put to compete with the paddle-sloop *Alecto*, of similar power and size.

Amidst great excitement the two ships first ran races in various weather conditions, which the *Rattler* won with ease. Crestfallen supporters of the paddle then fell back on assertions that at least for towing purposes it was superior. Thereupon the two ships were connected by a tow rope stern to stern, and a tug-of-war began. The *Alecto*'s paddles pounded the water bravely. Round the *Rattler*'s stern the sea boiled and foamed. But at first neither ship gained any way.

Then it was seen that the *Rattler* was inching forward. Her way slowly increased until finally the *Alecto*, her paddles still wildly thrashing the water, was being towed stern first at some $2\frac{1}{2}$ knots. The screw had conclusively won the day.

Now the last obstacle to an all-steam navy was seemingly overcome. Such an assumption, however, would ignore the overwhelming influence in that era of the great body of sea-going officers, brought up in sail, mistrustful of the reliability of the new-fangled steam-engine and dismayed at their dependence on frequent supplies of coal to keep functioning. They resented the smoke and dirt which befouled their spotless white decks and shining paint, and were contemptuous of the humble origins of the engineers whom they had to accept as fellow officers —though not for a long time as mess-mates. The thought of depending solely on such machines and men for mobility was abhorrent to them.

Thus the early steam warships with screw propulsion were essentially sailing ships with auxiliary engines. Funnels were lowered to the deck and propellers were jacked up out of the water when under sail. The first French screw frigate was the *Pomone*. Designed as a sailing ship, it was decided, while she was still on the slip, to give her a two-cylinder, horizontal engine of 22 horse-power driving an Ericsson propeller. Commissioned in 1845, she achieved 7 knots. Three years later the British Navy commissioned their first screw frigates, the *Dauntless* and *Arrogant*.

Screw propulsion was next applied to ships-of-the-line, the British launching their first in 1850, the *Agamemnon*, a 91-gun three-decker. Her engine was only looked upon as an auxiliary for use when entering or leaving harbour or when the wind was contrary. Sail drill was still a major preoccupation of her ship's company. 'Down funnel. Up screw. Make all plain sail' was the usual order on getting to sea. Nevertheless the soot-belching, oil-splashing machinery that her sailors so detested proved its worth when, in 1854, during the Crimean War, the *Agamemnon* and a sister ship were the only two ships of the British fleet bombarding Sevastopol which were in the slightest degree effective, by reason of their ability to move about freely regardless of the direction of the wind.

The French were less conservative in their adoption of screw propulsion. Two years earlier than the *Agamemnon*, the 90-gun ship-of-the-line *Napoléon* (not to be confused with the despatch-vessel of that name mentioned earlier), designed by Dupuy de Lôme, achieved a speed of nearly 14 knots under steam power alone and made successful, long sea passages under steam.

The various types of early marine engines are described separately elsewhere.

The steam paddle-boat invented by Claude François, Marquis de Jouffroy d'Abbans in 1783, on the Saône at Lyons. The earliest known successful steam vessel.

77

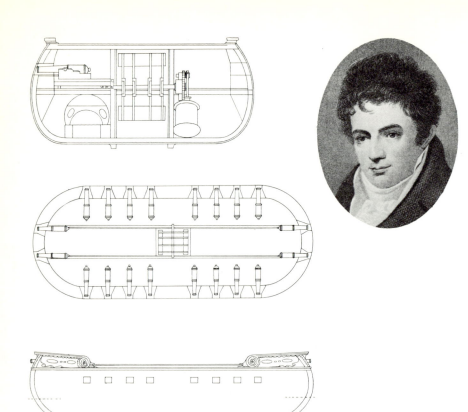

U.S.S. *Demologos*, designed and built by Robert Fulton in 1812, though not completed until after his death in 1815.

Robert Fulton (1765–1815), an American, was a prolific inventor whose most notable achievements were the successful, man-propelled submarine *Nautilus* in 1800 (see page 167) and early steam vessels from 1803. His paddle-driven *Demologos* was the world's first steam warship.

The other great innovations of the middle of the nineteenth century in their design of warships must now be considered—the introduction of armour protection, the development of the rifled, shell-firing gun and its mounting in revolving turrets, and the transition from wood to iron in ship construction. These developments are closely interlocked, the introduction of one giving rise to the necessity for another, each progressing to overcome the effect of the other in leap-frog fashion.

Armour protection for ships may be said to be as old as sea warfare, an example being the decorative Viking shields fixed along the bulwarks of their galleys. It is from the Far East, however, that the first record comes of a ship armoured, as we use the term, with iron plates—as long ago as the sixteenth century. At that time Korea and Japan were at war, and the Japanese efforts to invade Korea were being prevented by the Korean Navy led by a remarkable seaman, Yi-sun-sin. The Korean admiral was a tactician of masterly skill, and he also displayed great technical ingenuity by constructing what he called his 'Tortoise Boat'. This craft, with its domed deck of iron plates studded with spikes, was immune to the missiles of the day, and was impossible to capture by boarding.

In Europe the use in ship construction of heavy timbers of seasoned oak, to a great extent resistant to penetration by solid roundshot, made the complications of adding an iron skin not worth while. In the latter part of the eighteenth century both in France and England, experiments were, however, being made with explosive shells. Though this 'ungentlemanly' form of warfare soon became common on land, it did not at first commend itself to seamen, for several reasons. A spherical shell was not very effective against the solid oaken sides of ships, and it was difficult to load safely into the old muzzle-loading cannon. To be efficient in a sea-fight the shell had to be cylindrical and pointed, to give it penetrative power. But such a projectile fired from a smooth-bore gun turned somersaults as it flew through the air, so that it could be relied upon neither to land where it was aimed nor to hit nose-first when it arrived.

With such disadvantages to shell-fire, the school of thought which condemned such a form of warfare as 'inhuman' held the field for many years after enthusiasts such as the French General Paixhans had begun to press for change. By 1839, however, all navies were beginning to introduce a proportion of shell-firing guns into the armament of their ships. In a world at peace, no practical tests between the two forms of projectile were possible. Everything depended upon pure theory. Then in 1853, Russia and Turkey went to war. In November a Russian fleet, armed for the most part with Paixhans smooth-bore, shell-firing guns, attacked a squadron of Turkish ships in the harbour of Sinope. The odds against the Turks were overwhelming—the Russians had six ships-of-the-line, two frigates and three steamers against seven frigates, three corvettes and two steamers. The result would have been a foregone conclusion in any case, as the Turks had no shell-firing guns, but the speedy massacre which resulted was ascribed largely to the results of shell-fire upon the Turkish wooden ships.

The effect on naval opinion everywhere was to make the necessity for armour imperative. The day of the ironclad had dawned. Yet even now it was not primarily for the purpose of ship-to-ship fights that armour was introduced. Few occasions for this arose during the Crimean War. The function of the French and British fleets was to support their land forces; their task was to reduce forts on the shore.

It had long been an established truism of naval strategy that ships could not successfully engage forts; but now, for a short period of history when the development of guns was at a standstill prior to the introduction of the rifled barrel, this principle no longer held good so long as the ships were armoured.

The French were the first to react to the lessons of Sinope. By 1855 they had constructed and brought to the Black Sea three armoured floating batteries. Flat-bottomed for operation in shallow water, they were bad sea-boats, had a speed of only 2 to 3 knots, and could not in any way be considered as ships-of-the-line. They were, in fact, towed out to the Black Sea by paddle frigates. Steam-driven

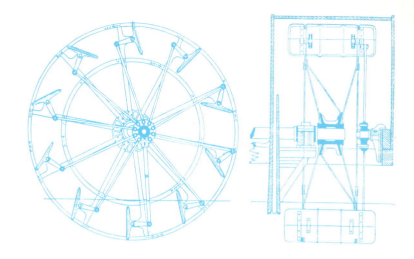

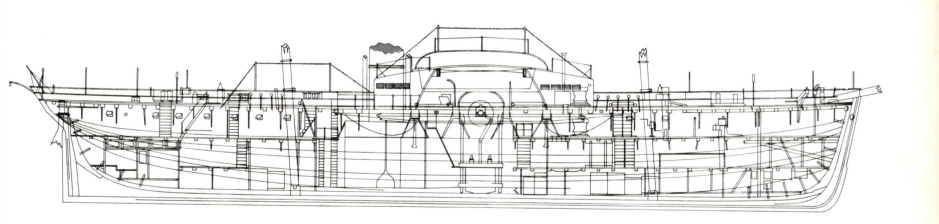

Top left: The *Sphinx*, first steam vessel acquired by the French Navy (1830).

Top right: A 'feathering' paddle-wheel introduced around 1840 to obviate the disadvantages resulting from the oblique action of the floats of the radial paddle-wheels.

Bottom: The *Bulldog*, one of the British Navy's first steam warships.

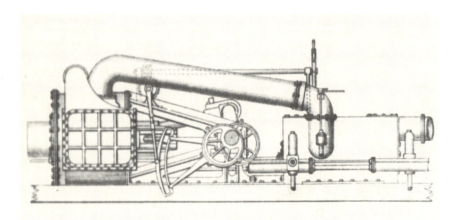

To decide the relative efficiency of paddle and screw propulsion, the British Admiralty staged in 1845 a tug-of-war between the screw-sloop *Rattler* and the paddle-sloop *Alecto*. It was won spectacularly by the former.

Penn trunk-engine as fitted in screw-frigate H.M.S. *Arrogant*.

and of wooden construction, their armour consisted of $4\frac{1}{2}$-inch iron plates backed by 17 inches of wood.

On 17th October 1855 these ships, *Dévastation*, *Lave* and *Tonnante*, went into action as part of a combined Anglo-French squadron entrusted with the task of reducing the Russian fort at Kinburn at the mouth of the Dnieper. While the old-fashioned wooden ships gave supporting fire and engaged some outlying batteries, the ironclads stationed themselves some thousand yards from the fort, and opened fire.

Within four hours, during which the Russians hurled solid shot as well as shells at the French ships, the fort was forced to surrender after losing 45 men killed and 130 wounded, while the three floating batteries had suffered only trifling damage and casualties. The Russian roundshot, bouncing off the iron plates, and the shells exploding harmlessly on impact, made it clear, once and for all, that armour had come to stay. The British Navy was not slow to follow the French example. Its first four ironclads were frank copies of the French ships, but they were followed by four more ships, *Thunderbolt*, *Terror*, *Aetna* and *Erebus*, which, though they were not in any way ships-of-the-line, took a further important step towards the development of the modern battleship; for they were constructed throughout of iron and were thus the first ships to combine iron hulls, armour and steam propulsion.

The fighting navies had been very slow to take this step. As far back as 1832, despite a storm of criticism, the English engineer Brunel had designed and built the first large iron transatlantic liner, the *Great Britain*.

But governments dependent upon an annual parliamentary vote for every penny they spent on the navy had to persuade a body of uninformed members of the rightness of any such revolutionary ideas as the change from wood to iron. In 1843 the British Admiralty proposed to lay down a flotilla of iron frigates, but opposition was so fierce and so prolonged that the Admiralty was forced to cancel the order.

It was the lessons of the Crimean War which finally broke down all opposition. Steam propulsion, armour and shell-firing guns had been shown to be essential features of any warship. The increasing size and weight of the whirling, cumbrous engines of those days was becoming too much for wooden hulls to support. The increasing thickness of the armour required to withstand the growing destructiveness of shells was too great a burden for the wooden side-planking to which it was secured. Finally, the weight and shock of the big pivot shell guns which were being introduced were setting up stresses and strains which only an iron hull could absorb. The time was at last ripe for the emergence of the first iron-built battleship.

Yet even now it required one final incentive before the British Admiralty took the decisive step. In 1859 the French launched the 5600-ton *Gloire*, the first of a class of large, wooden, armoured warships designed by Dupuy de Lôme. The *Gloire* incorporated a number of new features in her design, but the most significant was the concentration of her armament in a single tier of powerful guns. The weight thus saved was put into an armoured belt, $4 \cdot 7$ inches thick. Originally given only pole-mast she was later full-rigged for sail, but a single-screw steam-engine gave her a speed of $13\frac{1}{2}$ knots.

Her armament consisted of thirty-six guns of a new model, 66-pounder, shell-firing, rifled breech-loader, thirty-four of them on the broadside and two on pivot mountings. Three sister ships were built, one of which, the *Couronne*, was of iron hull, and ten more of an improved type, the *Provence* class. Two more ships, basically similar in design, though mounting two tiers of guns and fitted with a ram, the *Magenta* and *Solferino*, were added, so that by 1865 the French Navy could boast the most powerful, homogeneous and mobile squadron in the world.

To maintain her supremacy, Britain was bound to provide an answer. Thus it was that in 1860 the famous *Warrior* was launched, the first all-iron battleship-of-the-line to take to the water, though the *Couronne*, launched four months later, had been the first to be laid down.

The *Warrior* and her sister ship *Black Prince* were very large ships for their

H.M.S. *ARROGANT*

One of the earliest British screw-frigates.

The three-decker *Agamemnon*, first British ship-of-the-line to be steam-driven. Here seen when employed laying the trans-atlantic cable, when elaborate protection for the propeller was provided.

day, displacing 9210 tons. Their armour was $4\frac{1}{2}$ inches thick. Their gun batteries, though initially composed of smooth-bore cannons on conventional gun-carriages, were most formidable and, with the development of rifled guns, were altered from time to time to keep them up to date. The *Warrior* had a top speed of $14\frac{1}{2}$ knots, and although by this time a warship's engines were recognised as the primary means of propulsion, men-of-war still retained the masts, yards and sails of full-rigged ships.

This may seem surprising and be contemptuously ascribed to obstinate conservatism on the part of naval officers, particularly as, across the Atlantic, Ericsson's new design of steam warship, the U.S.S. *Monitor*, with no masts and sails, was about to make history in the American Civil War. But it must be remembered that the *Monitor* could hardly qualify as an ocean-going ship, whereas ships like the *Warrior* and *Gloire* were designed to fulfil the world-wide commitments of the navies of that age. In every ocean of the world it was warships of the major navies which played the principal and often the solitary part of policeman and law-enforcer. Such ships needed to be capable of long voyages and extended cruises in areas where coaling-stations were few and far between. It was not surprising, therefore, that naval officers of the 'Up funnel, down screw' days were reluctant to discard the well-tried and sure methods which had served their fathers, in favour of engines which might break down and boilers requiring fuel which might not be available at the vital moment.

Coaling-stations were established throughout the world, and machinery gained steadily in reliability, until these arguments were no longer valid. However, it was not until the increase in armament and armour reduced the stability of warships to such an extent that they could no longer safely carry the top-weight involved in masts and yards, or take the heeling moment of a spread of canvas, that sails were at last abandoned. A tragic disaster, which is described later, hastened the decision.

The other major development which the *Warrior* and *Gloire* lacked, and which had to come before the modern man-of-war could be said to have been born, was the replacement of the broadside of fixed guns by a centre-line battery of pivot guns or revolving turrets. In the natural sequence of events, this would have had to await the advent of the iron ship, which alone could support the monstrous weight of the armour, the big guns and the revolving machinery. It is true that the first ship to be equipped with a gun turret, the *Monitor*, was in fact of basically wooden construction. But the heavy timbers, to give her the necessary strength, and the weight of armour plate had the result of making her barely seaworthy.

In 1862, the U.S. Navy launched a ship similar in design to the *Warrior*, which was subjected to the test of battle. This was the *New Ironsides* which, when engaging the Confederate Fort Sumter, survived some sixty or seventy hits on her 4-inch side armour without serious damage. Later in the Civil War the spar torpedo of a Confederate 'David' torpedo boat was exploded against her hull and, though leaks and internal damage were caused, she remained afloat.

While the idea of mounting a few large guns in turrets, instead of the broadside of smaller guns, was coming to the fore, important developments in the design of the guns themselves were also taking place. As noted before, the early supporters of explosive shells were disappointed with their inaccuracy and lack of penetrative power. The system of giving gun-barrels twisted internal grooves or rifling had long been understood and used in small-arms to give the bullet the spinning flight which so greatly increased its accuracy. A round bullet from such a gun, however, lost much of its range, so the next step was to make an elongated, pointed bullet. Rifles then achieved a performance which finally abolished the smooth-bore musket.

A similar process began to be applied to the cannon in 1846 when Major Cavalli, a Sardinian artillery officer, and Baron Wahrendorff, a Swedish ironmaster, each constructed a gun with spiral grooves machined on the inside of its barrel. Into these fitted spiral projections on the cylindrical projectiles. As this rifling complicated the process of loading the shell into the gun from the muzzle, the guns were given a system of breech-loading in which the breech was closed by means of a wedge held in place by a 'culot' or false breech. Both of these guns produced good results on trial, but neither reached sufficient perfection for them to be adopted by navies of any of the major powers and it was not until 1856 that a rifled gun was introduced which gained acceptance by the British Navy.

This was the gun devised by Mr. W. G. Armstrong (later Lord Armstrong and head of the famous armaments firm of that name). The Armstrong gun was what was known as a built-up gun, consisting of a barrel on to which a number of coils or jackets were shrunk by being heated, passed along the barrel into position and allowed to cool. The gun was thus given progressively greater strength from muzzle to breech. The barrel was rifled on the polygroove system (i.e. with a large number of shallow grooves). To provide for breech-loading, the breech-piece, a solid forging of wrought iron, bored and screw-threaded, was shrunk on to the rear end of the barrel. A slot drilled through it and the coil above allowed a wedge to be inserted which closed the rear end of the barrel, sealing the mouth by means of gas rings, and was held in place by a hollow screw through which the gun had been previously loaded. The cylindrical, pointed projectiles were cased in lead so as to bite into the multiple grooves of the rifling. The gun was fired by means of a vent drilled down through the wedge.

Guns of this type, commonly known as screw-guns, were introduced into the British Navy in 1860, but a serious drawback was soon revealed in that there was nothing to prevent the gun being fired before the breech was properly closed, and that unless great care was exercised the wedge was often believed to be screwed close home when, in fact, it was not. A serious accident could then occur, and when a number of these took place in the British flagship *Euryalus* during the bombardment of Kagoshima, Japan, in 1862, the admiral's unfavourable report caused the larger Armstrong breech-loading guns to be withdrawn. As guns of that period, employing quick-burning black powder as propellant, were short in the barrel, making muzzle-loading possible, though inconvenient, even with rifled guns, the British Royal Navy reverted to muzzle-loading, the studded shells being awkwardly eased down the grooves of the rifling. Meanwhile on the Continent other types of breech mechanism were being invented.

The originator of the interrupted-screw breech block, which was to become the prototype of most breech mechanisms for big guns, was an American mechanic, Ben Chambers, who patented a form of slotted screw in 1849. Four years later a U.S. patent for a similar device was issued jointly to J. P. Schenkl and A. S. Saroni, the rights of which were then bought by Mr. Arthur Eastman. It was subsequently introduced into France by General Treuille de Beaulieu, who played a leading part in its adoption by the French Navy in 1858 after modification of the crude original design. In this type of mechanism the breech block has four sections of interrupted screw threads. The operating lever first swings the block into the breech, then rotates it one-eighth of a turn to engage its screw threads with corresponding ones in the wall of the breech and finally locks the breech block in place.

Another type of breech mechanism, like Armstrong's employing a wedge, was devised by the German gun manufacturer Krupp, originally for army field guns, but later applied to naval guns also. This did not suffer from the same defect as the Armstrong breech, however, and, like the interrupted-screw breech system, was a success from the start. French and German ships were thus invariably equipped with breech-loading guns from this time onwards. The British, on the other hand, in spite of the advantages of breech-loading, did not revert to it until 1881. Changes followed so fast on one another's heels during this period that navies were far from homogeneous, comprising ships ranging from old-fashioned, full-rigged wooden ships-of-the-line little different from those of Nelson's days, with broadsides of muzzle-loaders, to steam propelled ironclads with, perhaps, mixed armaments of broadside and pivot guns, smooth-bore and rifled barrels, muzzle-loading and breech-loading.

The next major development in the design of the man-of-war came about as a result of the continual increase in the size of the guns of their main armament, a

Stanislas Dupuy de Lôme (1816–85). Designed the steam ship-of-the-line, the 90-gun *Napoléon*, in 1848. Converted a number of sailing ships to steam and, in 1858–59, superintended the building of the world's first sea-going ironclad *Gloire*.

John Ericsson (1803–89). Swedish engineer who, after thirteen years in England, where he experimented successfully with screw propulsion, moved to the U.S.A. where he designed the *Monitor* (page 74) and her successors.

few large rifled, shell guns coming to be preferred to a large number of smaller pieces.

In order to enable these few large guns to cover as wide an arc of fire as the more numerous smaller guns of a battery, the idea was born of enclosing them in armoured turrets which could revolve with the guns, leaving only the gun muzzles exposed. Three men of inventive genius applied their minds at about the same time to giving the idea practical effect—John Ericsson in the United States, Captain Cowper Coles, R.N., in Great Britain and Dupuy de Lôme in France. Ericsson was first in the field, however, with a turret ship, the *Monitor*, built to his design in 1862, his concept coming into being as the result of the quickening effect of war, in this case the Civil War between the United States of America and the seceding Confederate States. When the latter, with considerable ingenuity, provided themselves with the only armoured ship on either side, it was to Ericsson that the United States Navy turned to devise something with which to even the odds.

At the opening of the war in 1861, the dividing line between Northern and Southern territory on the east coast ran through the broad estuary of Hampton Roads. On the south side was the Confederate naval base of Norfolk, with fortifications on the southern shore of the Roads. The far side was in Federal hands, and ships of the Northern navy could therefore lie in safety close inshore under the protection of batteries.

At this time the United States Navy was a small force composed largely of obsolete wooden sailing ships with a few steam-and-sail ships, most of which were on foreign stations. None of its ships was armoured. The Confederates, however, were even worse off, and they possessed a much smaller shipbuilding capacity, especially in iron. The Federal ships stationed at Newport News to guard against any excursion by Confederate warships up Chesapeake Bay and the Potomac against the capital city of Washington seemed therefore in no great danger of attack.

But across the water, work was going on which was to alter the situation. A wooden frigate of the United States Navy, the *Merrimac*, had been burnt and scuttled at Norfolk when the naval base was occupied by the Confederate forces. The hull had been raised and found to be little damaged, while the engines also were capable of repair. Ingenious hands had at once set to work to convert her into the first armoured American ship and the first warship completely to discard masts and sails.

The hull was cut down, and a heavy timber deck laid over the existing berth deck. On this was erected a casemate with sides sloping inwards to support a strong flat deck 20 feet wide. The walls were of 12-inch timbers covered by oak planks, 4 inches thick and armoured with two layers of iron plates, each layer 2 inches thick. These walls projected down and out over the sides of the hull, like the eaves of a house, to protect the hull.

Through ports in the casemate walls on each side grinned the muzzles of three 9-inch, smooth-bore guns and a 6-inch, rifled pivot-gun, all firing explosive shells, while fore and aft were two 7-inch, rifled guns which could be trained on the keel-line or on to either beam. As a final weapon of offence, a cast-iron ram was bolted to the prow, projecting a distance of 2 feet below the water-line.

Though the ingenious adapters of the *Merrimac* (renamed the *Virginia*) took the bold step forward of relying solely on steam-engines to propel her, it is unlikely that they ever envisaged her as a sea-going craft. Her reconditioned engines were incapable of driving her at more than 2 or 3 knots.

News of this Confederate naval activity soon reached the United States Navy Department. The old-fashioned wooden ships in Hampton Roads guarding the capital would never be able to stand up to such a ship as the *Merrimac*. In great haste, John Ericsson was commissioned to design and build a ship which could do so.

Ericsson was an early supporter of the turret idea, and so the ship which he designed, the *Monitor*, was naturally built round such a mounting. Like the *Merrimac*, she relied solely upon a steam-engine driving a screw. This gave her a speed of some 5 knots. Her low wooden hull was armoured down to the water-line with five layers of 1-inch iron plate, projecting out from the hull as protection against being rammed. But there the similarity to the *Merrimac* ended.

On her heavily timbered and iron-shod deck was mounted a single revolving turret containing two 11-inch, muzzle-loading smooth-bore guns firing solid shot weighing 170–180 pounds. To re-load them they were hauled back inside the turret, which was made of eight layers of 1-inch iron. The turret was 20 feet inside diameter and 9 feet high. Except for her two low funnels and ventilating tubes, which could be unshipped for battle, the only other projection above the *Monitor*'s deck was a pilot house or conning tower made of 9-inch iron logs and built in the manner of a log cabin, with $\frac{5}{8}$-inch eye-slits for captain and helmsman.

With a freeboard of barely one foot, the *Monitor* resembled nothing so much as a Camembert cheese box on a steam-driven raft, and it was not surprising that her sea-keeping qualities were low. But the threat which she was built to meet was one which was likely to deploy only in the sheltered waters of rivers and estuaries as the navies of North and South brought support to their land forces. There was no possibility of blue-water fights between the opposing fleets. Furthermore, the threat was an urgent one. Speed in completion of the *Monitor* was paramount if the *Merrimac* were not to achieve a domination of the Chesapeake Bay area and menace the capital.

Owing to bureaucratic delay, it was not until October 1861 that the contract with Ericsson was finally signed, but from that moment the work of construction was pressed with feverish energy. The hull was launched on 30th January. On 6th March 1862, the *Monitor* sailed from New York for the south, in tow of a tug.

It was none too soon; for even as the *Monitor* was experiencing her first alarming encounter with the open sea, final preparations for the *Merrimac*'s first sortie were being made at Norfolk. At noon on 8th March she emerged from the Elizabeth River and attacked the Federal warships anchored along the north shore of Hampton Road, all of which were of wooden construction. The sailing frigate *Congress* and the sloop-of-war *Cumberland* were quickly destroyed (the latter by ramming), their own broadsides bouncing harmlessly off the *Merrimac*'s iron sides. The three remaining ships ran themselves ashore where the *Merrimac* with her deep draught could not reach them. Well satisfied, the *Merrimac* returned to Norfolk for the night.

By the following morning, however, after a hazardous journey in rough seas, the *Monitor* had arrived, and when the *Merrimac* steamed out into Hampton Roads a duel began between these two strange craft in which neither was able to inflict fatal damage upon the other in spite of the prolonged bombardment each endured at point-blank range, and in spite of efforts to sink each other by ramming. At the end of the day the *Merrimac* returned to Norfolk intending to renew the battle as soon as she had patched up her injuries. When she came out to fight on two later occasions, however, the *Monitor* refused action on strict orders from Congress, where it was feared that damage to her might leave the way open for the *Merrimac* to steam up the Potomac to Washington.

The drawn battle of Hampton Roads was nevertheless to have a great influence on naval construction and tactics throughout the world. The imperviousness of armour to both shot and shell of the day, whether fired from smooth-bore or rifled guns, gave a strong impetus to the search for improved weapons, and hastened the retirement of wooden men-of-war everywhere.

Perhaps the most noteworthy result of the battle was the emergence of a belief in the importance of the ram, which was to dominate the tactics followed in the famous sea-fight of Lissa four years later. Given the short effective range of the guns of the 1860s and the difficulty of inflicting serious damage on armoured ships with them, the tactics of ramming were to prove sound when put to the test on that occasion.

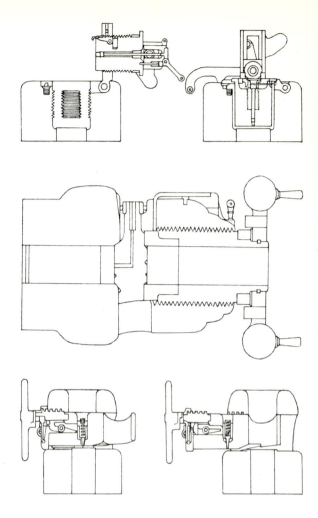

Early breech mechanisms.

Top: The interrupted-screw type was developed by the French from an American invention in 1858.

Centre: The Armstrong breech proved liable to accident and was abandoned. The British Navy reverted to muzzle-loading until 1881 when they adopted the interrupted-screw type.

Bottom: German naval guns adopted the wedge type developed by the armaments firm of Krupp.

H.M.S. *WARRIOR*

The first iron-hulled
armoured warship to be launched (1860). Like the smaller
French *Gloire*, to which she was a reply, she was classed as a 'steam-frigate'
owing to her single gun-deck.

Right: Transverse section of *Warrior*.

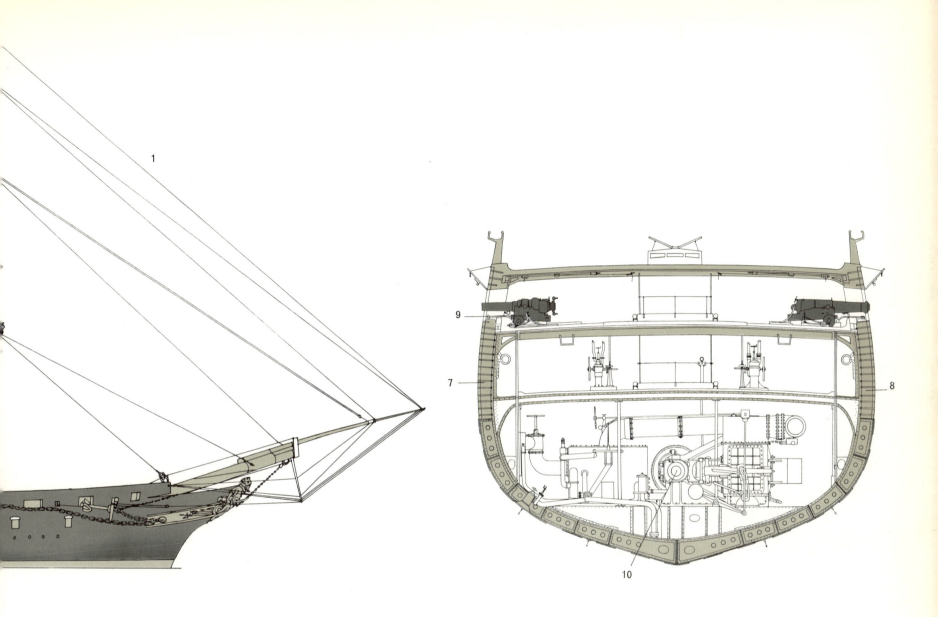

1 Three-masted full-rigged ship
2 Propeller
3 Captain's cabin
4 Gunports
5 Lifeboats
6 Funnels
7 Armour: $4\frac{1}{2}$ inches wrought iron, backed by 18 inches of teak
8 Iron hull
9 Guns: smooth-bore cannons, muzzle-loader (right); later altered to rifled breech-loader (left)
10 Steam engines: horizontal (trunk) engines, top speed $14\frac{1}{2}$ knots

H.M.S. *GORGON*

One of the earliest British steam warships, armed with

a single cannon at bow and stern.

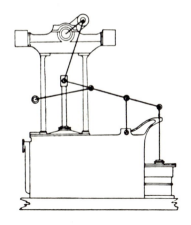

The first paddle-steamers adopted the simple beam-engine in use ashore in which motion was transmitted to the paddles by means of an overhead beam. To save vertical space, however, this was soon modified into the side-lever engine, and this powered all steamships up to the year 1837. In that year a type of direct-acting engine, with the cylinder directly beneath the crank and with a short connecting rod, was invented by John Seaward of the Millwall firm of Seaward and Capel, and installed in the paddle-sloop H.M.S. *Gorgon*. The piston-rod end was guided by a parallel-motion system and this type of engine came to be known as a 'Gorgon' engine. Two years later the Lambeth firm of Joseph Maudslay and Field, which up to this time had had a virtual monopoly of supplying the side-lever engines for naval steamers, patented the twin-cylinder engine. In order to obtain a long stroke in the limited height available, these engines had two pairs of cylinders, each pair having a common connecting rod. They became known as 'Siamese' engines, after the Siamese twins who were at that time on exhibition in England. The next type of engine devised for paddle-wheel steamers and one which came into universal use was the oscillating engine, which obviated the use of a connecting rod, the first being fitted in British men-of-war in 1843.

By this time screw propulsion was coming into favour. A number of inventors had been experimenting with this, but the two who achieved the most success and recognition were Francis Pettit-Smith in England and John Ericsson in America. Their screws were of quite different construction. Ericsson's design was, in fact, a pair of contra-rotating wheels with blades round their circumference. The rear 'screw' was driven by the main propeller shaft, which ran inside a sleeve which, rotated by toothed gearing, drove the forward 'screw' in an opposite direction. This propulsion was fitted in the first screw man-of-war, the U.S.S. *Princeton*, in 1844. Smith's screw was more like the propeller of today, though it had only two blades instead of the more usual four which came later into favour.

The first screw-propelled warship in the British Navy, the sloop *Rattler*, was fitted with Smith's screw, which was driven by a Maudslay 'Siamese' engine through gearing. At this stage of marine engineering, engines were too slow to drive a screw effectively, and gearing was necessary to increase the speed of the propeller shaft. The first French screw-propelled warship, the despatch-vessel *Corse* (ex-*Napoléon*), initially employed a screw developed from that designed by the Frenchman Frédéric Sauvage, and improved upon by Normand and Barnes.

Higher-speed engines capable of driving the propeller shaft directly began to take the place of the geared engine in the 1850s, a development which was contemporaneous with and dependent upon that of boilers to provide higher-pressure steam. An early example was the French frigate *Pomone*, launched in 1845, in which an Ericsson type of screw was driven at 40 r.p.m. by a directly coupled engine. This engine, the first to be constructed in France for a screw-driven ship, was the product of the Mazeline workshops at Le Havre. Between 1854 and 1884, the working steam pressure was gradually raised from 25 pounds per square inch

Seaward's direct-acting engine as fitted in H.M.S. *Gorgon*. Distinguished by the parallel-motion system of guiding the piston rod, shown diagrammatically above.

Screw/sail ship-of-the-line *Napoléon* of 92 guns, constructed by Dupuy de Lôme, was launched 18 May 1850. Her speed of 13·86 knots astonished the world in her day.

to more than 110 pounds. To produce this, the design of marine boilers advanced from the early rectangular flue boiler to the rectangular multitubular or 'box' boiler, one of the first of which was that fitted in the *Pomone*, and finally to the cylindrical multitubular boiler.

In the pursuit of higher speeds, Maudslay's produced the double piston-rod engine while Penn, who had probably done most to perfect the oscillating engine for paddle-steamers, devised his 'trunk-engine'. At first these were single-cylinder or two-cylinder simple expansion engines. The next development was that of the compound engine, in which the steam was first admitted at full pressure to one or more high-pressure cylinders. The residual pressure on leaving this cylinder was then applied to a larger, low-pressure cylinder, thereby using up more of the energy contained in the steam pressure.

Such engines having proved successful in merchant ships since 1853, the French Navy ordered a set from their English inventors, Charles Randolph and John Elder, for the sloop *Actif*, which ran her trials in 1862. This engine consisted of two groups, each of one high-pressure and two low-pressure cylinders, disposed in V-form. A similar type of engine was tried out in the British frigate *Constance* in 1863, but did not prove a great success. It was not until 1866 that an efficient compound engine was fitted to a British man-of-war. This was the armoured frigate *Pallas* for which the firm of Humphreys, Tennant and Company constructed a horizontal two-crank engine with tandem cylinders.

Meanwhile the French Navy, under the influence of their great constructor Dupuy de Lôme, had developed a type of horizontal compound engine in which three cylinders of equal diameter (one H.P., two L.P.) were used, the steam being reheated after leaving the H.P. cylinder, an idea first put forward by the young Benjamin Normand in 1860. Following successful trials of this type of engine in the naval transport *Loiret* in 1863, they became standard for nearly all French naval vessels. Horizontal compound engines reached their peak of perfection in 1878 in the fast, twin-screw despatch-ships *Iris* and *Mercury* of the British Navy, which attained the record speed of $18\frac{1}{2}$ knots.

In the meantime the type of engine which was eventually to be universally adopted had been under development for many years. This was the triple-expansion or quadruple-expansion engine, the pioneer in the application of which was the French engineer Benjamin Normand (1830–88), elder brother of the eminent naval constructor Jacques-Augustin Normand (1839–1906). At the same time vertical engines with the cylinders inverted had been gaining favour. A number of merchant ships had been supplied with such engines, but it was not until 1886 that the first triple-expansion engines were fitted in warships, the little torpedo gunboat *Destructor* of 386 tons built for the Spanish Navy by the Clyde-bank firm of Thomson Bros., later John Brown, which achieved the remarkable speed of $22\frac{1}{2}$ knots, and the Italian cruiser *Dogali*, the engines for which were designed by the English engineer F. C. Marshall of the firm of Hawthorn, Leslie and Company. Four cylindrical boilers supplied steam to two triple-expansion engines in the *Dogali* for alternative use on a single-propeller shaft. Developing 7197 horse-power, these engines gave her a full speed of 19·7 knots and proved most reliable over many years of service on foreign stations. The first British battleship to have triple-expansion engines was the *Victoria*, launched in 1887. The vertical arrangement of engines was not at first favoured for men-of-war as their height made it impossible to give them the protection of being below the water-line. The French cruiser *Dupuy de Lôme*, laid down in 1887, had horizontal triple-expansion engines driving her two outer shafts, a vertical engine to drive the central shaft. The armour belt for cruisers was largely introduced to give protection to vertical engines, the first large British man-of-war to be so designed being the armoured cruiser *Shannon*, launched in 1875.

As ever higher steam pressures were sought in the cause of economy of fuel and reduction in the weight of machinery, the water-tube boiler was developed and, after a long controversy lasting more than a decade, finally superseded the cylindrical fire-tube boilers. In the latter the combustion gases passed through large tubes surrounded by water and the steam gathered in the upper part of the

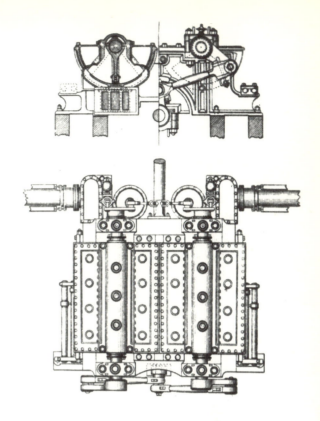

Pendulum engine of the U.S.S. *Princeton*, the first screw-frigate. She was propelled by the type of screw invented by John Ericsson, also shown here.

Top left and bottom: The 'Scotch' boiler, most commonly found fire-tube boiler in the early days of steam, in which the furnace gases passed through tubes surrounded by water.

Right: A 'water-tube' boiler in which the water was heated in the tubes by furnace gases flowing round them, the steam being collected in a steam-drum at the top.

cylinder. In the water-tube boiler the reverse process was employed, with the water being heated in a large number of pipes by the combustion gases flowing round them, the resultant steam being gathered in a steam-drum. A number of different types of such boilers were devised, some having large-gauge and some small-gauge water tubes. The first to be adopted for the larger British men-of-war was originally a French invention, the vertical, large-tube, Belleville type.

For smaller ships, such as torpedo boats, however, and eventually for all men-of-war the small-tube type, in which steam could be raised in a fraction of the time required in large-tube boilers, was more suitable. Invented in 1873 by Commander F. du Temple of the French Navy, the type was improved upon by British and French shipbuilders such as Thornycroft and Yarrow and the Frenchman Normand, until each was producing virtually original designs. In America Nathaniel Herreshoff designed a somewhat different type though owing much to the du Temple conception. In the course of time the three-drum, small-tube boiler became the universal type for warships.

With the adoption of triple-expansion, vertical engines, working under high steam pressure provided by water-tube boilers, the main machinery of men-of-war had reached the limit of efficiency of steam reciprocating engines. Only in size and horse-power could they further advance and here, too, they soon came up against a limit owing to the immense strains applied to the ships' structures and to the fixed portions of the machinery by the huge masses of metal of the moving parts. How this was overcome by the steam turbine and the diesel internal-combustion engine, is described later.

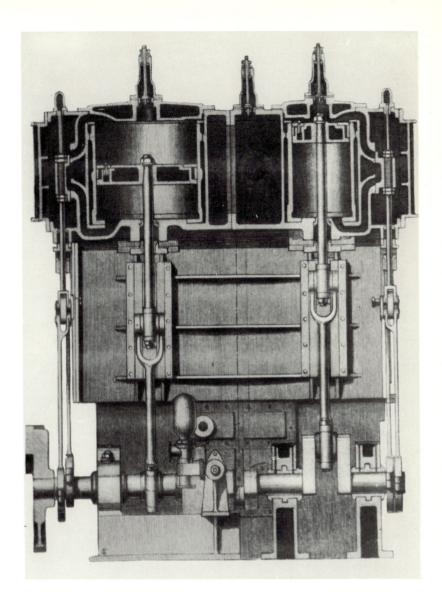

An early compound engine. As higher steam pressures became available, compound engines were devised in which the residual pressure after use in the first, high-pressure cylinder was expanded in a second, low-pressure cylinder.

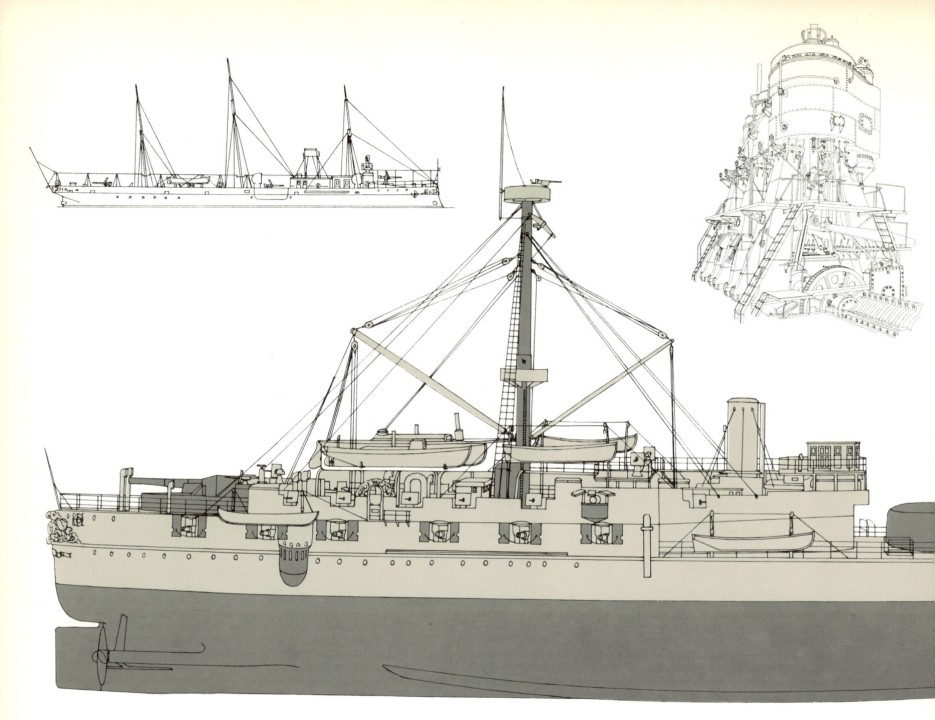

DESTRUCTOR/DOGALI

Top right: A triple-expansion reciprocating engine.

a type which superseded the compound engine. The Spanish torpedo gunboat *Destructor* (*top left*)

and the Italian cruiser *Dogali* (*page 95*), both built in England in 1886,

were the first warships to have such engines,

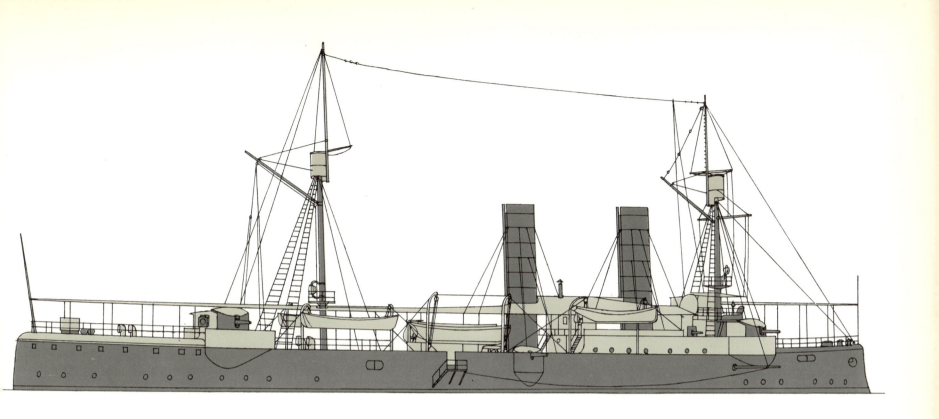

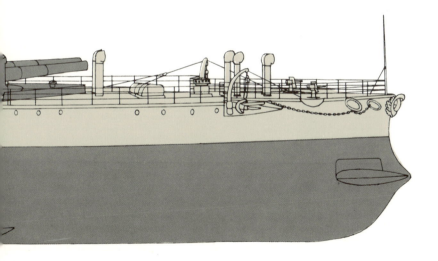

H.M.S. *VICTORIA*

The first British battleship to have
triple-expansion engines.

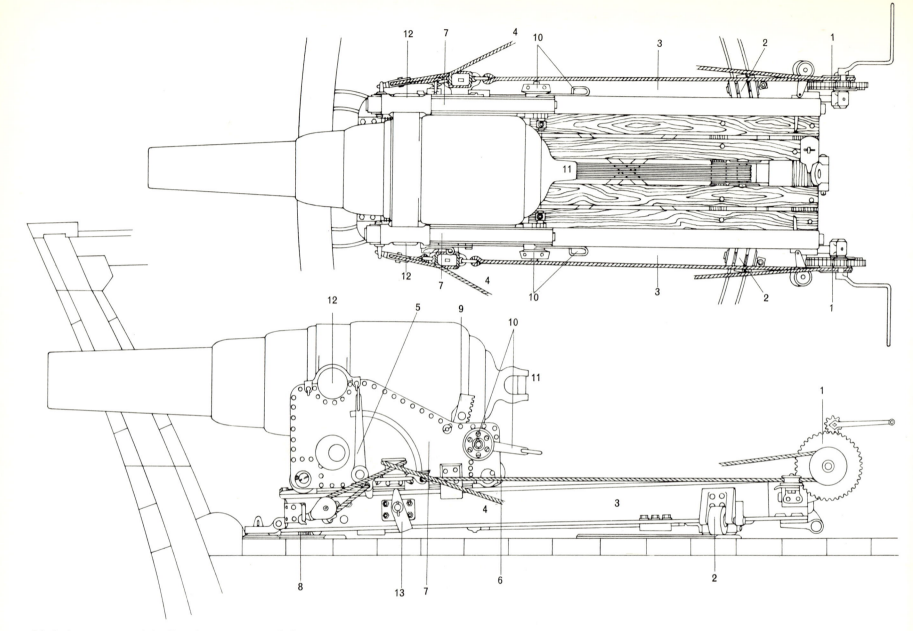

7-inch Armstrong muzzle-loading pivot-gun on wrought-iron
carriage and slide as supplied to a number of navies in the late
nineteenth century.

1 Running-in winch   8 Pivot
2 Rollers of slide   9 Segmental arc for elevating
3 Slide   10 Elevating drum and lever
4 Side rope for running-out   11 Breech
5 Adjusting lever for compressor 12 Trunnions
6 Trucks   13 Compressor plate
7 Carriage

When the French Navy, in 1855, constructed the first armoured vessels, the *batteries flottantes*, *Dévastation*, *Lave* and *Tonnante*, for the purpose of engaging the Russian ports at Kinburn, an unending competition was initiated between the penetrative power of gun projectiles and the resistant capability of armour plate. As guns of large calibre and higher muzzle velocities were successively developed, ever thicker and tougher armour was given to warships in reply.

This first armour plate, made by the firm of Schneider's of Le Creusot, was of wrought iron, $4\frac{1}{2}$ inches thick, backed by 18 inches of teak, as fitted to the first French sea-going ironclad, *Gloire*, and was proof against the 68-pounder, smooth-bore guns of the day. The British reply to the *Gloire*, the *Warrior*, was similarly armoured. Inevitably the gun manufacturers were then inspired to produce guns and ammunition which would penetrate this armour. The development of rifled guns, described elsewhere, culminated in 1860 with the production of the Armstrong gun with multi-grooved rifling which fired a pointed—or strictly an ogival—projectile of chilled iron coated with lead into which the rifling bit as it passed down the barrel to give it spinning flight. The lead was later replaced by a copper driving band on the base of the shell.

By 1868 battleships were being clad with 9 inches of wrought iron; three years later H.M.S. *Devastation* had 12 inches; while the British *Dreadnought* and the French *Redoutable* of 1875–76 had 14 inches. Iron armour reached its practical limit in the British *Inflexible*, where, against the threat of the monstrous 100-ton guns being supplied by Armstrong to foreign navies, 24 inches of armour on a sandwich system of two 12-inch plates, each with a layer of teak backing, was applied. The contemporary French *Amiral Duperré* had single plates of 22-inch thickness.

The time had come to seek a material of greater resistant capability than mere iron. Steel was the obvious choice and the pioneers in the manufacture of steel armour plates was again Schneider's. Such plates were found to offer greater resistance than iron; but they were also found to be excessively brittle. In 1876, to decide what armour should be given to the projected Italian battleships *Duilio* and *Dandolo*, Schneider steel plates 22 inches thick were tested at Spezia against wrought-iron plates of similar thickness, made by Cammell's and Brown's of Sheffield and Marrel Frères of Marseilles, each with a 19-inch teak backing. Both materials resisted penetration by shells from 10-inch and 11-inch guns. When a 17·7-inch (100-ton) gun was fired, however, the iron armour was perforated whereas the steel plate was shattered to pieces.

The Italians decided to fit 22-inch steel armour plates. Meanwhile both Cammell and Co. and John Brown and Co. of Sheffield had evolved a compound armour, in which a steel face was welded on to iron. This proved so successful in trials both in England and in France that for the next ten years the armour of nearly all battleships was of this type. In France, the steel works of St. Chamond, St. Étienne, Firminy and Rive de Gier all took up the manufacture of compound

French battleship *Amiral Duperré* (1879). The extreme 'tumble-home' was a feature of French ships of the period and permitted guns mounted in sponsons a clear field of fire ahead or astern.

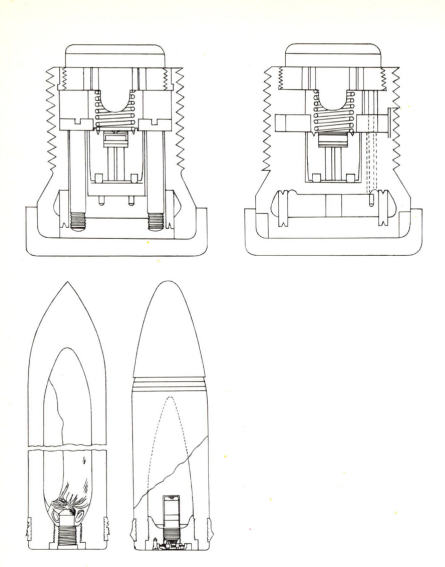

Top: Base fuses of Armstrong armour-piercing shells.

Bottom: Armour-piercing shells. An early type (*left*). The 'capped' shell (*right*) was a development to improve penetration, the cap taking the first impact and protecting the sharp, hardened point under it.

armour; but Schneider's, convinced that homogeneous steel would eventually prove superior, refused all orders for compound armour and pressed on with research, finally achieving success with a method of oil tempering after forging. In December 1881, 20-inch steel armour plate for the French battleship *Terrible* was successfully tested. During the next two years a series of comparative tests was held in Italy between compound plates manufactured by Cammell's and Brown's, and Schneider steel plates of similar thickness in which chilled-iron projectiles from the 17·7-inch Armstrong gun were fired. The Schneider plates proved incomparably better.

From this time homogeneous steel replaced compound as the preferred armour in French and Italian warships. Under the influence of the Italian constructor Benedetto Brin, who played an energetic part in the financial organisation, the great Terni steel works and the firm of Vickers-Terni were founded at Spezia, equipped by Schneider for the manufacture of steel plates and, in combination with the Orlando and Odero shipbuilding and engineering firms at Genoa and the Armstrong gun factory at Pozzuoli, enabling Italy to build, arm and equip warships complete. The French Navy continued for a time to employ compound armour until other steel manufacturers could adapt their equipment to manufacture Schneider steel, Schneider's themselves being unable to satisfy all the demands.

The U.S. Navy decided in 1887 to adopt Schneider steel armour and in 1890 competitive trials were held in the United States and in Russia to compare the various types of armour. In the American trials three plates, $10\frac{1}{2}$ inches thick, were compared; one was of plain Schneider steel, one of Schneider nickel steel with a 5 per cent nickel content, and one of compound armour. Fired at by 6-inch and 8-inch guns, the compound armour was both penetrated and broken; the plain steel plate resisted penetration by either projectile but broke up; the nickel steel was penetrated by the 8-inch projectile but remained free of any cracks. In the Russian trials the plain steel proved rather better than the nickel steel in which there was 3 per cent of nickel. From this time 5 per cent nickel was accepted as the best material for armour plate. Though the plain-steel plate used in the Russian trials was manufactured by Vickers, British steel manufacturers had dropped far behind their Continental competitors. Being still unable to produce steel plates of the size and thickness necessary for the armour belt of a battleship, and as the British Admiralty was loth to turn to their French naval rivals for them, compound armour continued in use in the British Navy as late as 1892, the whole of the *Royal Sovereign* class being so fitted.

There now came a swing of the pendulum in favour of the gun owing to the introduction of steel projectiles. Cast-steel shot had been in production since 1881 and a type known as a 'Compound Armour Piercer' with a hardened point on a 'soft' body was patented by Hadfield's in 1885. A 'Sheathed Projectile' with a hard envelope and a soft core was developed in 1887, while the French firm of Holtzer produced a chrome-steel shell. Armour piercers of forged steel were manufactured by Firth's and Vickers and this material came to supersede cast steel, the manufacture and treatment of which were particularly intricate and difficult.

This period, during which the gun was the master of armour, lasted only a few years; for, in the meantime, research had been going on to improve steel armour plate and, in 1891, the American engineer H. A. Harvey perfected a method of face-hardening by the application of carbon at very high temperatures for a long time, followed by water tempering. The resultant face-chilled carburised nickel steel, or 'Harveyed' steel as it came to be known, proved greatly superior to anything which had gone before, the hardened face tending to shatter the projectile, the plate neither cracking nor flaking. Twelve to fourteen inches of Harvey nickel steel was found to give better protection than the 24 inches of wrought iron applied to the *Inflexible*. Manufacture was begun in that year by the Bethlehem Iron and Steel Works and was taken up in England by the leading steel-plate manufacturers, Cammell's, Brown's and Vickers, who applied the process to plain steel without any nickel content, and the French firms of St. Chamond, Chatillon Commentry and Marrel Frères. Harvey steel became the universal armour used

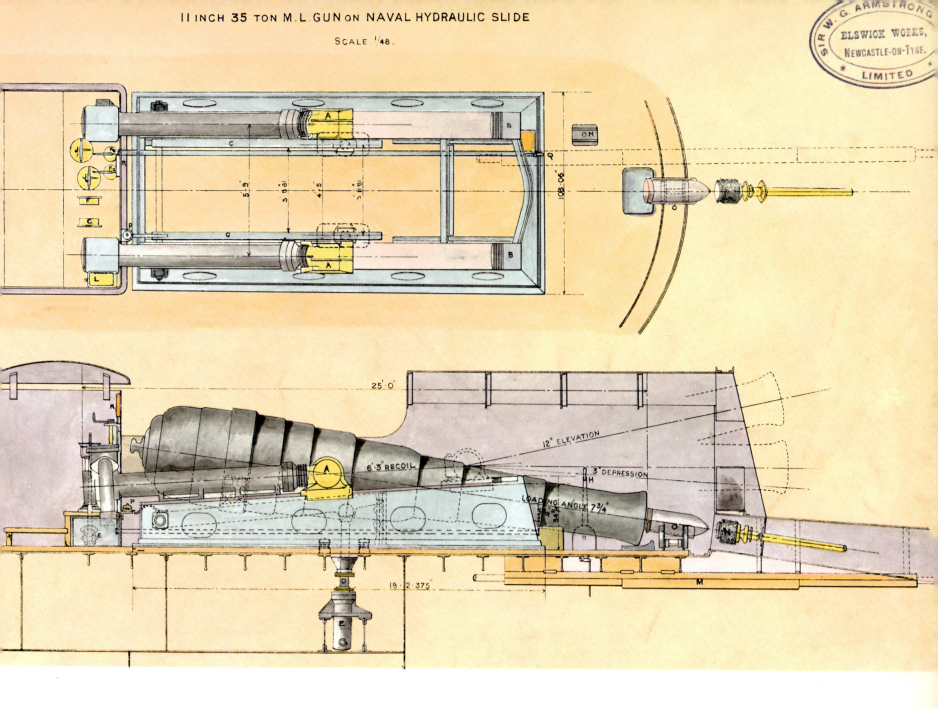

11 INCH 35 TON M.L.GUN ON NAVAL HYDRAULIC SLIDE

SCALE 1/48.

SIR W.G. ARMSTRONG
ELSWICK WORKS,
NEWCASTLE-ON-TYNE.
LIMITED

12° ELEVATION

6'3" RECOIL

3° DEPRESSION

LOADING ANGLE 7¾°

25·0"

18·2·375

Turret mounting for an 11-inch muzzle-loading gun, showing
the loading arrangements.

Italian naval engineer and administrator Benedetto Brin (1833–98). Designer of the battleships *Duilio* (pages 101 and 163), *Dandolo*, *Italia* and *Lepanto* (page 118). Brin served as Minister of Marine and Foreign Minister in the Italian government.

in warships, until the Harvey method was superseded by that devised in 1894 by the great German armament firm of Krupp's and taken up soon afterwards by Schneider's of Le Creusot. By 1897 the British manufacturers had acquired the right to use Krupp's process and had taken tardily to the incorporation of nickel in their steel. The gas process used by Krupp and Schneider, or similar processes, were soon adopted by the American Bethlehem and Carnegie steel companies and by the Terni works in Italy, and Krupp armour plate came to be universally applied to warships. A further development in the manufacture of armour plate was the addition of a proportion of chromium to the metal, first introduced in 1892 by the St. Chamond Company in France, the product being known as nickel-chrome steel.

Face-hardened steel proving impervious to the ordinary forged steel shells, efforts were now renewed to devise an armour-piercing projectile. Experiments turned in the direction of giving the shells caps. The idea had been tested in England as early as 1878 when a 9-inch shell with a wrought-iron cap passed through a 13-inch plate of compound armour, remaining unbroken. The idea was not followed up, however, by the British, and, although it was revived in Russia in 1890 by Admiral Makaroff, it was not until 1894 that successful tests of a capped chrome-steel shell made by Firth's in England and of a capped Holtzer shell in Russia led to its general adoption. The American government carried out a series of tests from 1894 to 1896 with various types of projectiles fitted with caps of soft steel. On the result of these trials, the U.S. Navy in 1896 acquired the right to use the Johnson Patent and introduced the capped shell into service.

France and Russia also adopted the capped shell; but in England, though manufacturers, particularly Vickers, continued to advocate caps, it was not until 1904 that they were generally admitted into the British Navy. These shells with their solid, soft-steel caps quickly abolished the supremacy established by face-hardened steel armour so that the procedure of giving warships successively heavier and heavier armour began again. The superiority of the armour-piercing shell was still further increased when, in 1908, Firth's devised the 'Hollow Cap', being closely followed by the firm of Hadfield's with their own version. These were so successful that the hollow cap soon became universal not only in England but in other navies also.

Up to 1894, the armour-piercing shell was looked upon as a projectile purely and simply for perforating armour. It was not expected to carry a destructive bursting charge through the plate, though a very small cavity was provided filled with a small amount of powder, hardly enough to burst the body of the projectile. In 1895, however, the Wheeler-Stirling Company of America produced a 'semi-armour-piercing' shell which carried a bursting charge of 5 per cent capacity which could carry its charge through a Harvey plate two-thirds of its calibre in thickness. This was further developed by the Firth-Stirling Company in 1903 into a fully armour-piercing type with a $2\frac{1}{2}$ per cent capacity capable of perforating a plate of its own calibre in thickness.

By the beginning of the First World War, semi-armour-piercing shells were given a $6\frac{3}{4}$ per cent capacity while the capacity of the armour-piercing shell proper had been increased until, with $2\frac{3}{4}$ per cent of high-explosive filling, it possessed a high degree of destructive power after perforating a considerable thickness of armour plate.

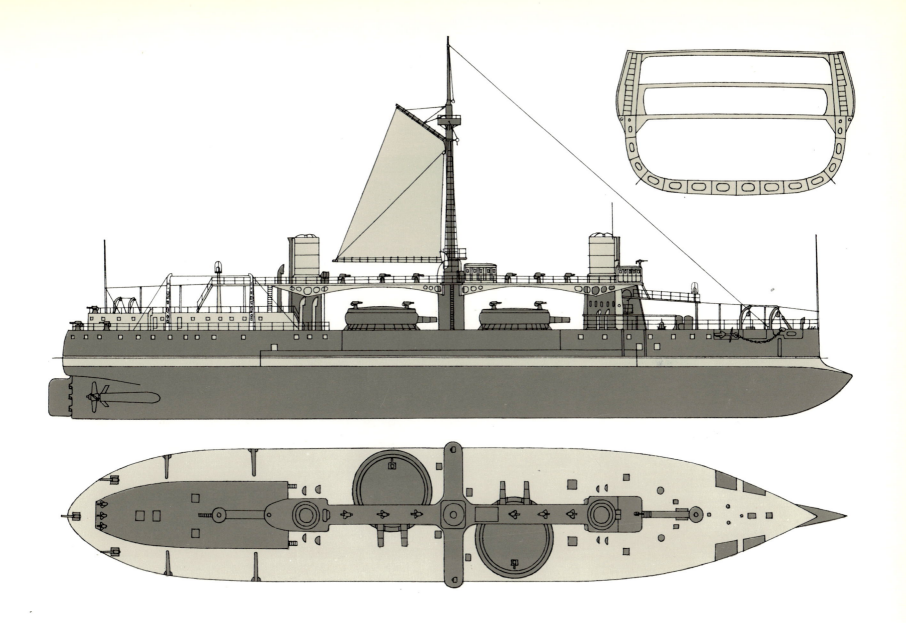

DUILIO (1876)

An Italian battleship designed by Benedetto Brin.

The first to incorporate diagonally sited turrets for huge (17·7-inch) guns in

a central citadel.

Left: Russian circular coast-defence battleship *Novgorod*. She and a similar ship, the *Vice-Admiral Popov*, were designed to provide a steady gun platform on a shallow draught for inshore operations.

Right: Early British turret ships, H.M.S. *Glatton* and *Hotspur*, were developments of the monitor type for coast-defence service.

H.M.S. *CAPTAIN*

H.M.S. *Captain*, which combined turrets and a full rig of
sails, capsized and sank in 1871.

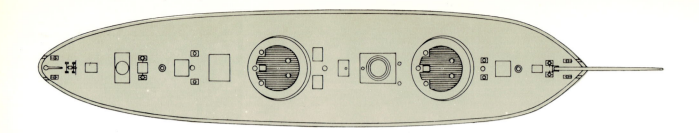

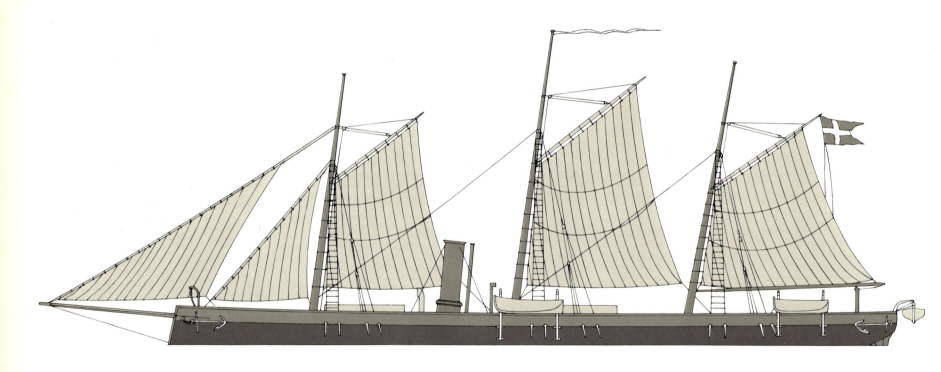

ROLF KRAKE

Turret ship designed for the Danish Navy by Captain Coles,

who designed the ill-fated *Captain*.

THE COMING

OF THE BIG GUN

While the coastal nature of the naval operations in the American Civil War was resulting in the development of the Ericsson type of low freeboard, mastless turret ship, generically classed as 'monitors', across the Atlantic the man-of-war was evolving mainly on different lines. A few ships of the *Monitor* type were acquired by European navies for coast-defence duties. Ericsson's rival turret enthusiast, Captain Cowper Coles, R.N., designed one for the Danish Navy, the *Rolf Krake*, built by Napier's of Glasgow in 1863 with two turrets in which were mounted 8-inch guns. A similar ship, the *Arminius*, was built by Samuda Brothers of London and was bought in 1865 for the Prussian Navy. The turret was first introduced into the French Navy in 1865 when the *Cerbère*, designed by Dupuy de Lôme, was laid down. She was followed by the *Tonnerre* class with two $12\frac{1}{2}$-inch breech-loading guns worked by hydraulic power, as was the revolving turret. These ships had a maximum speed of 14 knots as compared to the 12 knots of their British equivalents such as the *Glatton*, which mounted a pair of 12-inch guns in a turret, and the *Hotspur* which had a fixed turret with a single gun revolving inside it on a turntable. Another ship of this general type was the *Affondatore* built for the Italian Navy at the Millwall Iron Works on the Thames in 1866.

It is perhaps necessary here, in view of the different meaning which later attached to the word, to point out that the original turret was simply an armoured gun-house which revolved on the ship's deck. A system of mounting the big guns on turntables on the top of armoured towers or 'barbettes' grew up alongside the turret system and eventually the two combined with the armoured gun-house superimposed on the barbette. Called at first 'turret-barbettes', these later usurped the name of 'turret', which is apt to cause some confusion when ships of the mid-nineteenth century are being considered.

These ships were furnished with a massive iron ram projecting as much as 12 feet from the stem and they were generally classed as 'turret-rams'. The adoption of the ram, which of course had been a notable feature of warships in the age of galleys, had been advocated in 1840 by the French Admiral Labrousse and some convincing trials of its effectiveness had been carried out by the French Navy in 1844. The first major warships to be designed with a ram, however, were Dupuy de Lôme's *Magenta* and *Solferino*, laid down in 1859. The ram, indeed, was a feature of most ironclads of this epoch.

With regard to the coast-defence type of ship, mention must be made of some remarkable coast-defence battleships built for the Russian Navy. These were the circular armoured ships *Novgorod* and *Vice-Admiral Popov*. With the object of obtaining a great displacement with only a moderate draught, as well as providing a steady gun platform, these ships were given flat circular hulls, much the shape of a frying pan, with their rudders mounted on a protuberance. Three sets of engines drove six propellers to give a maximum speed of $8\frac{1}{2}$ knots. Two guns—11-inch, 28-ton guns in the *Novgorod*, 12-inch, 40-ton guns in the *Popov*—were mounted in the centre on a revolving platform, protected by a fixed, open-top

Early French breech-loading gun and crew.

On pages 106–107 is shown a painting of the sinking of the Italian battleship *Ré d'Italia* at the Battle of Lissa, rammed by the Austrian ship *Erzherzog Ferdinand Max*, an event which did much to encourage belief in the ram in naval warfare. Painting by C. Frederik Sörensen.

tower, or barbette, over the top of which the gun fired. Such an arrangement was to be found in a number of ships of this period, particularly French men-of-war. Its chief advantage over the turret was its comparative lightness. Thus for the same weight the gun could be mounted higher, giving the gun's crew an improved line of sight and avoiding the washing down in a seaway which was one of the shortcomings of the turret ship with its necessarily low freeboard. Furthermore it allowed the crew to work in the fresh air instead of in the choking smoke of the turret's atmosphere. It had two disadvantages: it made reloading of a muzzle-loader difficult to arrange and it exposed the crew to enemy fire while reloading. Both these disadvantages were eventually overcome by means of a hydraulically operated disappearing mounting on which the gun sank behind the armour of the barbette to be reloaded; this arrangement was later fitted to the *Popov*. Up to a point, these circular ships did provide a steady gun platform in seas which would set a normal ship rolling; but, as can be imagined, the flat dish-shaped bottom was subjected to severe buffeting by the waves, while the deck was almost permanently awash when under way.

With regard to fully sea-going men-of-war, the decade from 1860 to 1870 witnessed a controversy between the two schools of thought. On the one hand were the advocates of some form of revolving mounting for the main armament, either the turret, as mounted in the *Monitor*, or the barbette, as favoured by the French Navy; on the other side were those who continued to pin their faith to the broadside principle, though as guns increased in size, the latter was modified to become the 'central battery' with a few guns concentrated within an armoured citadel or casemate amidships. The revolving turret, as has been seen, was adopted for coast-defence monitors. But the central battery of guns firing mostly on the broadside continued in favour so long as a full rig of sail was retained as well as steam power; in such ships the maze of standing rigging made the turret or barbette system of little advantage. The first example of the central battery ship was the *Bellerophon* designed for the British Navy by the most distinguished naval architect of the day, E. J. Reed, later Chief Constructor of the Navy. Launched in 1865, she was fitted with a ram bow, armoured with 6 inches of iron and mounted ten 9-inch guns in the central battery, two 7-inch guns in an armoured bow battery and three other 7-inch guns unprotected. This arrangement, however, permitted only two 7-inch guns to fire forward.

In 1866, before broadside ships passed from the scene, two fleets composed of such ships were to meet in a battle which was to emphasise the requirement for a forward field of fire. Italy, as an ally of Prussia, had joined in the war of 1866 against Austria–Hungary. On the 20th July, when the Italian fleet under Admiral Count Carlo di Persano was covering a convoy of troopships assaulting the island of Lissa in the Adriatic, the Austrian fleet under Admiral von Tegetthoff was sighted bearing down to the attack. Both fleets were composed of broadside ships with the exception of the new Italian turret-ram *Affondatore* mounting two 9·75-inch rifled guns, but which, fresh from her English shipyard where she had been hastily commissioned, was not fully prepared for battle. Having, in spite of this, shifted his flag to her at the last moment from the *Ré d'Italia*, a fact which was not realised by some of his ships, Persano formed ten of his armoured ships into a somewhat extended line ahead with the *Affondatore* acting independently abreast of the centre division. Tegetthoff's fleet, though numerically superior, was composed partly of unarmoured screw-propelled ships. His armoured squadron contained two new ships, his flagship, the *Erzherzog Ferdinand Max*, and the *Habsburg*, but the big Krupp breech-loading rifles which they were designed to mount had not been delivered when war broke out, and the Prussians had naturally withheld them from the enemy. In their place the Austrian ships had to make do with an old-fashioned broadside of 56-pounder, smooth-bore cannon, almost useless against armour. The remainder of the squadron consisted of five smaller broadside ships with a mixed armament of Krupp 64-pounder, breech-loading rifles and 56-pounder smooth-bores. The Austrian was thus much out-gunned by his opponent, whose ships all had broadsides of rifled guns, and he

107

The first major warships to incorporate a ram in their design were the French ships *Magenta* and *Solferino* above, designed by Dupuy de Lôme and launched in 1861.

decided to make up for this inferiority by making use of the ram. Forming his ships into three arrowhead formations with his armoured squadron of seven ships leading, he steered directly for the enemy line. Amidst the billowing clouds of thick black smoke from the funnels of the mass of coal-burning ships, his armoured squadron unwittingly passed through a gap in the Italian line. Three of his ships swung around to engage the Italian centre on the far side on opposite course. Tegetthoff himself, seeing the leading Italian division haul round to port to attack the Austrian wooden ships in the rear, turned back with his flagship and the *Kaiser, Salamander* and *Habsburg* to counter this move.

On completion of his turn, however, Tegetthoff found himself abreast the *Ré d'Italia* and *Palestro*. Charging into the fray he made two attempts to ram with the *Ferdinand Max* but succeeded in delivering only glancing blows to the Italian ships. As he drew off for a further attempt, a shell from an Austrian ship struck home in the stern of the *Palestro*, starting a raging fire and forcing her to quit the line, finally to blow up. At the same time the steering gear of the *Ré d'Italia* was damaged and she swung round out of control. As she did so, her captain, Count Faa di Bruno, saw an Austrian armoured ship across his path through the smoke pall ahead of him. On his beam was the *Ferdinand Max* steering straight for him.

What passed through di Bruno's head at this moment will never be known. It would seem that he was not conditioned to an instinctive use of the ram when opportunity offered, and shrank from collision with the ship ahead of him. He rang his engines to go astern, and brought his ship to a standstill. As she lay motionless, a stationary target, the *Ferdinand Max*, moving at a speed of $11\frac{1}{2}$ knots, drove her stem with a destructive crash into the Italian's engine-room on the port side, rolling her far over to starboard.

The *Ferdinand Max* backed away, and as the *Ré d'Italia* rolled back again to port, the water poured into her gaping wound and she sank like a stone with 381 out of her crew of 549.

Elsewhere in the battle there was wild confusion. Where armoured ship met armoured ship, neither was able to inflict much damage on the other. Persano, who had placed much faith in the *Affondatore*, had been steaming aimlessly through the mêlée and had found no opportunity to use her formidable ram. But in the rear of the Italian line the Austrian wooden ships had been boldly attacking the Italian armoured division.

In the *Kaiser*, an old-fashioned screw-driven two-decker, Commodore Petz, well imbued with his admiral's offensive spirit, had gone fearlessly in to ram the *Ré di Portogallo*. Striking at an acute angle, the Austrian tore away the Italian's boats and gun-port lids and displaced some 60 feet of her armour; but, as the *Kaiser* lay close alongside, the full broadside of the *Ré di Portogallo* crashed into her, setting her on fire and bringing down her bowsprit and foremast in a tangle of wreckage across her funnel. The *Kaiser* managed to withdraw with steam pressure for her engines failing.

While Commodore Petz was in this unhappy state, the *Affondatore* loomed out of the smoke. Persano gave the order to ram, but in two successive attempts her captain failed to do so. The ram was not proving so simple a weapon as had been expected. At the third attempt the Italian had more success, and the *Kaiser* lay athwart his bows at his mercy. But at the last moment Persano, out of chivalry, turned deliberately away. The two fleets now disengaged and, after they had manœuvred for a time in sight of one another, Persano withdrew, leaving the Austrians well entitled to claim a victory. The biggest of the Italian ships had been sunk; another, the *Palestro*, had blown up.

The Battle of Lissa, fought for reasons of prestige when the war was virtually over, was not a decisive battle; nor was it important except from the point of view of its effect on warship design and naval tactics. The sinking of the *Ré d'Italia*, pictured with varying degrees of accuracy and dramatic effort in illustrated journals, advertised the effectiveness of the ram at a time when armour had won an ascendancy over the gun. The success of the ram, and the head-on approach it necessitated, emphasised the importance of a clear field of fire directly ahead for the main armament. An effort to achieve this was made in the design of the British ship *Hercules*, launched in 1868, which was given a central battery of eight 10-inch, 18-ton guns, four of which were on turntables at the corners of the citadel, allowing them to fire over an arc from the bow to the quarter, as well as two 9-inch and four 7-inch guns, half firing ahead and half astern. Ships of similar type were built for all the principal navies of the world during the next decade, varying chiefly in the size and type of the guns of their main armament, some following the British in mounting muzzle-loaders, others adopting the breech-loading designs developed by the French arsenals or Krupp in Germany.

Meanwhile, however, the ideas of those who favoured the mounting of a few big guns in turrets were gaining ground. Ericsson's *Monitor*, described earlier, was not intended to be an ocean-going ship. His contemporary, the British Captain Cowper Coles, on the other hand, had designed a turret ship which he believed to be not only fully seaworthy but with an armament and armour which would make her greatly superior to any broadside ship. Coles' reputation as an inventor and ship designer stood so high that, in spite of some strong expert criticism, the British Admiralty gave their blessing and financial support to the construction of his ship, the *Captain*, by Laird's of Birkenhead.

The conception of a sea-going, sail-rigged turret ship was not peculiarly Captain Coles'. The Admiralty, indeed, had already laid down their own version of such a ship, the *Monarch*, at about the same time. Where Coles' design differed was in the absence of any forecastle or poop, permitting his centre-line turrets to fire directly fore and aft, and in the use of tripod masts which, requiring no standing rigging, left a clear field of fire for the turret guns on the broadside. The *Monarch*, in comparison, having a normal forecastle and poop blanking fore and aft fire and the usual maze of standing rigging restricting the training of her turrets, had few, if any, advantages over a central battery ship.

The tragic story of Coles' *Captain* must now be told. His scheme to do without forecastle and poop was condemned by Laird's, who had learned from experience with coast-defence turret ships built for other navies that without such super-structure the turret guns would be awash in a seaway and could not be worked. Reluctantly, Coles bowed to this decision. Worse was to follow. A sick man, Coles was unable to give personal supervision to the ship's construction. No official check of the weights going into her was made. A multiplicity of small excesses in the weight of the myriad items that go to make up a ship raised her displacement from the designed 6963 tons to one of 7767 tons. The consequence was that her freeboard, intended to be 8½ feet, was only 6½ feet when completed. Towering over this low-lying hull were three tripod masts and the yards of her full set of sails, their rigging coming down to a flying deck from which the sails were worked.

In spite of this, everyone except a few head-shaking experts, including Chief Naval Constructor Reed, had confidence in the *Captain*. True, her constructors, Laird's of Birkenhead, were somewhat uneasy about her after her trials, and recommended that the Admiralty should give her an inclining test for stability. The test showed her to be reasonably stable; but, disturbed by her abnormally low freeboard, the Royal Corps of Naval Constructors set calculations afoot. These, when completed, raised serious doubts as to her safety, not so much on the score of straightforward stability as on account of the fact that a heel of more than 14 degrees put her lee deck under water. There seemed a danger, therefore, that with the leeway induced by a press of sail, the resistance of this water might increase the capsizing force of a beam wind and sea.

These calculations took some time. The conclusions had not been confirmed when the *Captain* joined the fleet under the command of Captain H. T. Burgoyne, an officer with the reputation of a fine seaman. In her first two cruises with the Channel Fleet the ship won golden opinions from all who sailed in her or watched her performance under sail or steam.

Admiral Symonds, after seeing her make good shooting in heavy weather, reported: 'She is a most formidable vessel and could, I believe, by her superior armament, destroy all the broadside ships of the squadron in detail.'

French battleship *Marengo*, launched in 1869. Designed by Dupuy de Lôme.

The doubts of the Naval Constructors were, however, to be tragically confirmed. On 6th September 1871 a sudden furious squall caught the *Captain* with her three topsails set but double-reefed. She heeled so far and so suddenly that the watch on deck were thrown from their footholds and were unable to obey the orders to let go the topsail sheets and lower the topsails. Her list rapidly increased until she capsized, taking with her, as she sank, her designer Captain Coles, Captain Burgoyne and all but eighteen men of her crew of 500.

Nevertheless Coles' ill-fated experiment did not discredit the turret concept, the brief career of the *Captain* only serving to show that though turret mountings were superior to the broadside arrangements, turret ships could not also be given sailing rig. If either turrets or sails had to go, it had to be the latter. So in 1873, the *Devastation*, a battleship with twin turrets fore and aft, screw-driven, massively armoured, but with a solitary signal mast only, joined the British fleet. Coles' conception of a low freeboard forward and aft was adhered to, giving a clear arc of fire from right ahead or right astern to either beam for the forward and after turret, respectively. Universally criticised by a conservative Navy when she joined the fleet, and certainly excessively wet, which later necessitated a raising of the freeboard, she was otherwise a great success and set a pattern which would eventually be followed in the design of most battleships for the next thirty years.

Nevertheless the British Admiralty was not yet entirely convinced of the obsolescence of sailing rig or of the broadside, central battery arrangement. As late as 1877 the *Alexandra* was added to the fleet, a full-rigged ironclad with a central battery of twelve guns on two decks. In the upper battery a 25-ton, 11-inch gun at each forward corner could fire from ahead to the beam and an 18-ton gun at each after corner covered the arc from astern to either beam. On the deck below, three 18-ton, 10-inch guns on each side could fire on the beam and one on each bow could fire from right ahead to either beam. In the same year the *Téméraire* was completed with yet another arrangement. On a lower deck in a divided battery were two 11-inch and four 10-inch guns firing on the beam. On the upper deck two 25-ton guns were mounted in the fashion favoured by the French, on the top of fixed barbettes, but with disappearing mountings, as described earlier in connection with the circular Russian coast-defence ships. Without this type of mounting, of course, reloading of barbette-mounted muzzle-loaders, which were still the standard weapons in the British Navy, was virtually impossible. This was one reason for the early favouring of the turret system by the British Navy, as compared to the French Navy, where breech-loading had been early introduced.

Nevertheless, in spite of the early criticisms of the *Devastation* voiced in the fleet, another mastless turret ship, the *Thunderer*, followed her, a sister ship except for the fact that the guns in her forward turret were of 12·5-inch calibre and were hydraulically operated, while the turrets themselves were rotated by steam power, as opposed to the hand-worked mountings in the *Devastation*. A feature of these ships was the flying deck necessitated by the low freeboard and the constant washing down of the upper deck in a seaway mentioned above. The next mastless, turret ship, the *Dreadnought*, launched in 1875, was given greater freeboard, her sides rising up to the height of the turret deck. Finally the *Inflexible*, launched in 1876 and having her two turrets sited diagonally at opposite corners of a central citadel, was given a freeboard of 20 feet and was able to dispense with the flying deck altogether. Her four 80-ton, 16-inch muzzle-loading guns as well as the turrets themselves were hydraulically powered, as all turrets in the British Navy were to be thereafter.

The idea of a central citadel which now became generally fashionable amongst naval designers, as well as the diagonal siting of the turrets, had been first put into practice by the Italian naval constructor Benedetto Brin in his revolutionary battleships *Duilio* and *Dandolo* to which the *Inflexible* was a somewhat imitative reply. The Italians seemed to have stolen a march over the British by obtaining from the Elswick Gunworks four 100-ton, 17·7-inch muzzle-loading guns for the *Duilio*, making her the most powerfully armed battleship in the world. The British,

dependent upon the Royal Ordnance Factory, Woolwich, could only install 80-ton, 16-inch guns. In fact these monstrous, clumsy weapons, at a time when adequate machinery for loading and manipulating them had not yet been devised, had such a slow rate of fire that they were less effective than the 12-inch guns which later became the standard battleship main armament in all navies.

It was their introduction, however, which made the central armoured citadel seem necessary. Ever-thicker armour was required to protect a ship against them. As there was a limit to the weight of armour that a ship could carry, it became necessary to concentrate it to cover the vital areas in the centre of the ship and sacrifice the side armour before and abaft it. To compensate for the lack of armour at the extremities, the fore and aft portions of the ship were minutely subdivided and some of the compartments were filled with cork, thus, it was hoped, permitting these parts of the ship to be battered in action without destroying the integrity or stability of the ship.

An alternative conception by which the armoured belt was discarded in favour of this cellular system of minute subdivision, combined with a high speed, materialised in the next battleships designed by Benedetto Brin—the *Italia* and *Lepanto*—which are discussed later.

No sooner had the idea of the central citadel with a few very big guns become the accepted pattern for battleships than, about 1880, the advent of a new opponent caused a fresh look to be taken at warship design. This was the torpedo boat, firing the locomotive torpedo, which made it necessary to redesign the big ships' armament to include a number of small, quick-firing guns which had to be carried on the broadside. The immediate result in the British Navy was a class of ship, named after distinguished admirals, launched between 1882 and 1885 in which the citadel was elongated to enclose a battery of 6-inch guns, of the new breech-loading type, varying from three to five on either side, while on the superstructure above were mounted twenty-two 6-pounder and 3-pounder quick-firers. The laying down of these ships coincided with the advance in gun design consequent on the introduction of brown powder, mentioned elsewhere, which led to the British gun manufacturers finally abandoning muzzle-loading. Thus this class had the distinction of being the first British battleships to have breech-loading guns for their main armament. This, in turn, allowed the guns to be mounted in barbettes, one at each end of the citadel, in each of which were either two guns, varying in size between 12-inch in the first of the class, the *Collingwood*, 13·5-inch in the *Anson*, *Howe*, *Rodney* and *Camperdown*, or, in the *Benbow*, single 16·25-inch guns. Barbette mountings enabled the guns to be sited 5 feet higher than in any previous battleships, so commanding a much better field of fire. Nevertheless, barbettes had not yet entirely superseded turrets and the next two battleships launched for the British Navy in 1887, the *Sans Pareil* and the *Victoria*, were given single turrets forward, each mounting two huge 110-ton, 16·25-inch breech-loaders, a last expression of the concept of the school which believed in the superiority of a few massive blows over the sustained fire of smaller, more manageable and quicker-firing guns. From this time onwards for the next thirty years, gun calibres were to be limited to a maximum of 13·5 inches.

This is perhaps a suitable place to consider the advances in gun design which led to these developments, the means whereby the ever-larger guns had been mounted and served, and finally the developments which ended the cult of the monster gun.

The failure of the Armstrong breech-loading system and the reversion to muzzle-loaders by the British and other navies which relied upon Armstrong's for their armament has been mentioned. With the introduction of turrets, it may be wondered how these guns could be loaded. At the beginning of the turret period, however, this was not a problem, the guns being so short that there was room to reload them from inside the turret when run in. As the guns grew in muzzle length, this was no longer possible. For the 12·5-inch guns of H.M.S. *Thunderer*, therefore, a system was devised whereby the turret was rotated so that the muzzle of the gun to be loaded, run in and fully depressed, came in line with one of two

SCALE ⅟₂₅.

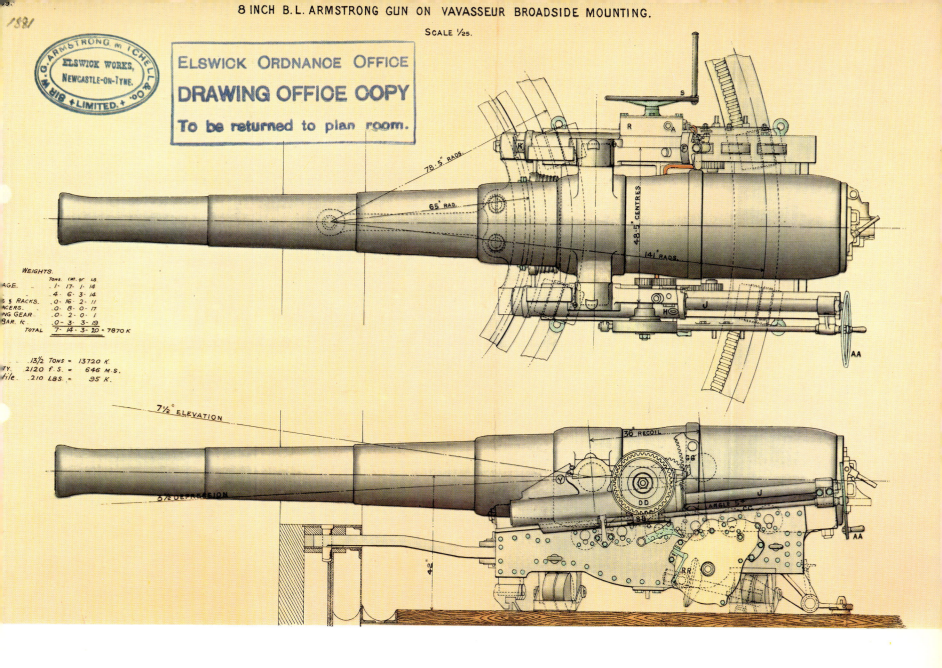

8-inch breech-loading broadside gun on Vavasseur mounting.

French battleship *Redoutable* (1876). The first armoured ship to employ steel frames and steel armour. More effectively sub-divided than earlier ships by means of watertight double-bottom and longitudinal and transverse bulkheads.

loading tubes leading obliquely up from the deck below into the turret. Hydraulic pressure then forced the rammer, projectile and cartridge up the tube and into the gun. For the much bigger and longer guns of the *Inflexible*, loading had to be done with the gun muzzles protruding from the turret. To enable this to be done from under cover, the edge of the armour deck around the turret was raised and inclined upwards to form a glacis. When the gun muzzles were depressed they came under this glacis and the turret was rotated to bring them in line with one of the loading tubes which passed through the face of the glacis.

Breech-loading guns did not require such arrangements; their ammunition could be brought up inside the turret from the magazine below. Or, where they were mounted on barbettes, the ammunition could be brought up inside the barbette towers by hydraulic hoists. Both the French and the Germans, who early developed a reliable breech-loading system, took advantage of this and avoided the low freeboard and poor arc of fire of the British turret ships.

A serious drawback to muzzle-loading revealed itself by the disastrous explosion of one of H.M.S. *Thunderer*'s 12-inch guns on 2nd January 1879 in which eleven men were killed and thirty-five others injured. The cause of it, as decided by a committee of investigation, was that, following a misfire, the gun was inadvertently loaded with a second charge and second shell, an error which could not have been made with a breech-loading gun. Nevertheless both French and Germans had their share of burst guns, a hazard which was finally overcome by the mastery of the technique of using steel for gun-barrels in place of wrought iron. One advantage breech-loading might have been expected to enjoy was a higher rate of fire than with muzzle-loading. This does not seem to have resulted, however, with big naval guns, so long as the design of the gun mountings restricted loading to a single fixed position in elevation and training. Comparative figures as between the British and French battleships of this period, indeed, show that the muzzle-loaders in the former could get off three or four rounds in two minutes, the breech-loaders of the latter only one. Not until almost the end of the nineteenth century, when a means of turret loading on any bearing was devised and the chain rammer was introduced, enabling the guns to be loaded at any elevation, did the advantage in rate of fire of breech-loading take full effect.

It was not only in size that guns were increasing in so spectacular a fashion during the latter half of the nineteenth century, but also in accuracy, hitting power and range, all of which were dependent upon muzzle velocity. To increase this it was first necessary to arrange for the propellant force of the powder charge to act upon the projectile for as long a period as possible. The small-grained black powder used in the old smooth-bored guns expended all its energy immediately on ignition. The first step taken when rifled guns were introduced was, therefore, to make up the gunpowder in larger grains or pebbles and later into small six-sided cakes, called prismatic powder. A further means of reducing the initial pressure in the gun barrel was then taken by providing an enlarged cartridge 'chamber'. This achieved considerable improvement and all guns were thereafter 'chambered'; but it was found that the powder was not all consumed before the projectile left the muzzle and quantities of burning powder followed it out. Guns had therefore to be made longer, a development which was undesirable so long as they were muzzle-loaders, and led to the universal adoption of breech-loading. With the restriction on length of barrel now removed, the way was open for using an even slower-burning powder which was obtained by decreasing the proportion of sulphur and increasing those of saltpetre and charcoal. The result was a brown powder commonly called 'cocoa powder'. With all these developments the muzzle velocity of a 13·5-inch gun, for example, was raised from 1600 feet per second to more than 2000 feet per second. Meanwhile research had been going on to develop a propellant which would obviate the dense clouds of smoke given off by a gunpowder charge, and towards the end of the nineteenth century a smokeless powder composed of a mixture of nitro-glycerine and gun-cotton was introduced. Made up in charges of long thin tubes it was given the name 'cordite'.

Cordite generated much greater energy than gunpowder and so permitted the use of smaller charges. This in turn assisted the development of quick-firing guns

The Spanish frigate *Numancia*, built at Toulon, which was the first armoured ship to circumnavigate the world (1865–67). Water-colour by Rafael Monleon.

PREUSSEN

One of the first warships to be built in a German yard (Stettin, 1876).

Top: After modernisation in 1890.

Bottom: As originally completed.

up to 6-inch in size in which the charges were encased in brass cartridge cases, and, in the case of smaller guns, the cartridge and shell were joined together, enabling the whole round to be inserted in the breech in one motion.

Until about 1887, guns known as 'quick-firers' had all been of the smallest calibre, the best known being the Hotchkiss and Nordenfelt 3-pounders and 6-pounders. These had breech mechanisms which made use of a sliding wedge, similar to that of the Krupp system. Now, however, Armstrong's in Britain and Canet in France, at about the same time, evolved a modification of their interrupted screw breech mechanism for larger guns which enabled a single motion, instead of several, both to revolve the breech block to unlock (or lock) it and to swing it open (or shut).

This was achieved by making the breech block coned instead of cylindrical, so that it could be swung away on its hinges without having first to be withdrawn. The recoil of the guns themselves was so arranged that the gun-layer could continue to control and aim the gun during the discharge, which also contributed to a higher rate of aimed fire.

The first Armstrong quick-firer was of 4·7-inch calibre, firing a projectile of forty-five pounds weight with which a rate of fire of fourteen rounds per minute could be kept up, as compared to an ordinary 5-inch breech-loader which could not achieve a higher rate than two rounds a minute. This quick-firing system eventually became standard for most guns of 4·7-inch calibre or larger, those in which brass cartridge cases were used being classified as 'quick-firers', the remainder simply 'breech-loaders'.

A later development in quick-firing guns of the smaller sizes was that which utilised the motion of recoil to open the breech and eject the cartridge case automatically, such guns being designated 'semi-automatic'.

The 'Admiral' class had been much criticised as deficient in armour protection, the belt of 8 to 18 inches of compound armour covering only half the ships' length, so that in the next two battleships to be built for the British Navy, the *Nile* and the *Trafalgar*, the thickness of the armour belt was not only increased at the water-line to 16 to 20 inches, but it was carried forward and aft to cover two-thirds of the whole length. Similarly a more extensive armoured citadel protected the base of the two turrets in which the four 67-ton, 13·5-inch guns were mounted. Above this, six 4·7-inch of the new quick-firing type (later replaced by 6-inch) were in an armoured upper battery. It will be noted that the designers again specified the turret in place of the barbette. Fashion was to change yet again, however. The turret system continued to be criticised on the grounds that it entailed a low freeboard and placed the guns too low down over the water, hampering their operation in heavy weather. Thus when the eight battleships of the *Royal Sovereign* class were begun in 1889, all except one of them, the *Hood*, mounted their four 67-ton, 13·5-inch guns in open barbettes constructed of 17-inch armour plate. With a displacement of 14,000 tons, these ships were bigger than any previous ships of the British Navy. A belt of 8- to 18-inch armour on the water-line covered two-thirds of the length and a secondary armament of ten 6-inch guns was mounted on two decks. The lower-deck guns were mounted in armoured casemates while those on the upper deck were fitted with individual shields which revolved with the guns. These ships were an unqualified success with the exception of the *Hood*, where the turrets showed up unfavourably compared to the barbettes in the remainder.

Though the *Royal Sovereign* was in many ways the prototype of what was to become known as the 'pre-dreadnought' battleship, subsequent classes were now to enjoy the benefit of the invention of Harvey steel plate. An armour belt of only 6 to 8 inches could be substituted for the 8 to 18 inches of the *Royal Sovereign* with a consequent large saving in weight.

The final step in the development of the typical pre-dreadnought battleship came when the *Majestic* class, launched between 1895 and 1896, were given revolving gun-houses on top of the fixed barbettes, an arrangement that was to become standard practice in all navies. Called at first 'barbette-turrets', these

Netherlands armoured ship *Buffel* (1868).

H.M.S. *Majestic* (1895). Prototype of the 'pre-dreadnought' battleship with twin 12-inch barbette-turrets fore and aft and a secondary armament of smaller guns in armoured casemates.

mountings gradually came to be designated simply 'turrets'. With the *Majestic* class and similar ships built for all the principal navies of the world, mounting four 12-inch breech-loading guns in barbette-turrets and a secondary armament of smaller guns in armoured casemates, battleships had reached the final stage in their development prior to the sudden forward leap in design which produced the *Dreadnought* in 1905.

While the British Navy was thus advancing in the short space of forty years from the wooden-hulled, three-decker sailing ship-of-the-line to the steel mastodons driven or powered by steam and electricity of the twentieth century, other navies were making similar progress but with variations in armour plan and armament according to the fancy of their naval constructors.

The French Navy, for example, was more reluctant than the British to discard masts and sails and continued to equip their sea-going ironclads with them for many years after the emergence of H.M.S. *Devastation*. This entailed providing them with a high freeboard, as the disaster to the *Captain* illustrated, and the French ability to use barbette mountings for their breech-loaders facilitated such a design.

The first French battleship of the central battery period was the *Richelieu* of 8651 tons, launched in 1873 and followed during the next two years by the similar *Colbert*, *Friedland* and *Trident*, though each differed from the others in the arrangement of their armament. The *Richelieu* mounted six $10\frac{1}{4}$-inch guns in the central main-deck battery with a $9\frac{1}{2}$-inch gun at each corner of the battery, *en barbette*, and another in the bow. She could thus fire three heavy guns right ahead, five on either beam and two right astern. The *Colbert*, in comparison, substituted an armoured redoubt forward, containing two $10\frac{1}{4}$-inch guns, and another aft with a single $9\frac{1}{2}$-inch, while the *Friedland* mounted eight $10\frac{1}{4}$-inch guns only, of which six were in the battery and two up on the spar deck for fore and aft fire.

Following this class of ship came the *Redoutable*, launched in 1876, which had the distinction of being the first armoured ship to employ steel framing in her construction. Her armour, too, was of steel, while her iron hull was given a comprehensive watertight subdivision by means of a double-bottom and watertight longitudinal and transverse bulkheads. This was the last French ship to incorporate a central redoubt. Next came the *Dévastation* and *Courbet* (ex-*Foudroyant*) which, on a displacement of 10,800 tons, mounted four of the new French 13·4-inch and four 10·5-inch guns and were protected by an armoured belt 15 inches thick.

A feature peculiar to French battleships of this time was the marked 'tumble-home' (the inward-curving slope of the sides from the water-line upwards), which enabled the guns in the citadel to fire fore and aft without obstruction. It was present also in the next battleship to join the French fleet, the *Amiral Duperré*, in which the 'tumble-home' was so acute that the width of the upper deck was 7 feet 9 inches less than that of the gun-deck. The *Amiral Duperré*, like her predecessors, was a full-rigged sailing ship in spite of her twin screws driven by triple-expansion reciprocating engines which gave her a speed of 14 knots. She carried two of her four 13·5-inch, 48-ton breech-loading guns mounted in barbette towers protruding sponson-fashion beyond the ship's side, port and starboard, allowing them a clear field of fire ahead. The other two guns, also *en barbette*, were on the centre-line with the mizen mast rising between them. No doubt it was as much from foresight of the growth of the importance of the torpedo boat as because close-range fighting, broadside to broadside, was still visualised by all navies, that the French designers never neglected to provide a secondary battery of smaller guns, in this case fourteen 5·5-inch quick-firers, seven on each side, as well as numerous 3-pounders.

The sponson arrangement for barbettes was abandoned in the next French battleships to be built, the *Amiral Baudin* and *Formidable*, each of which had three 14·5-inch guns on the centre-line. This allowed only one heavy gun to fire ahead and one astern so that in the next class, *Hoche*, *Marceau*, *Magenta* and *Neptune*, the sponson arrangement was reverted to for the two midship heavy guns, with two more mounted on the centre-line. This allowed three guns to fire

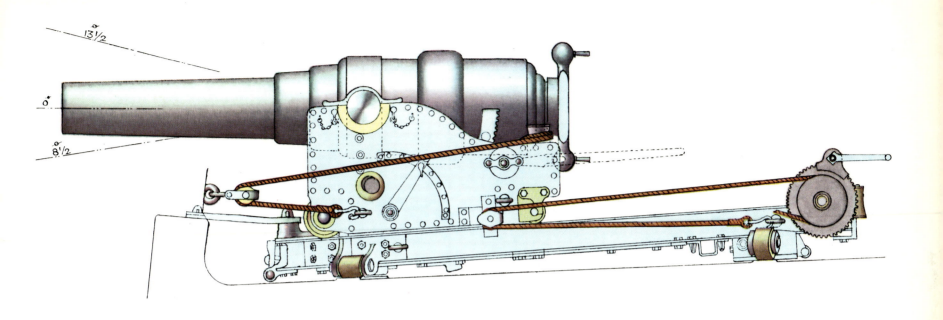

13½

8½

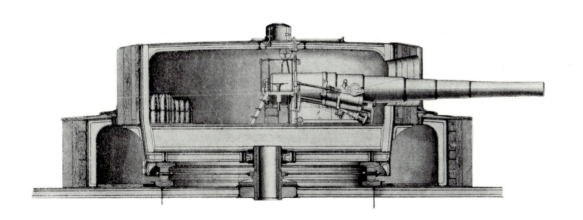

Top: 7-inch naval breech-loading 'screw-gun' on sliding carriage.

Bottom: 10-inch breech-loading gun in a turret of H.M.S. *Thunderer* after her modernisation in 1892.

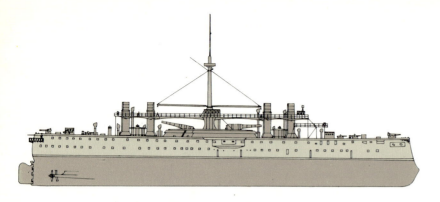

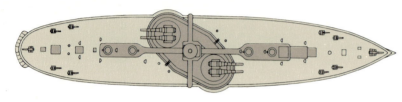

Top: Italian battleship *Lepanto* (1883). Sacrifice of armour protection for high speed (18 knots) made her and her sister ship *Italia* forerunners of the battle-cruiser.

Bottom: Japanese cruiser *Naniwa* (1885).

ahead or astern, an arrangement particularly favoured at a time when close action and the use of the ram, as at Lissa, was visualised. A similar arrangement was to be found in the *Jauréguiberry* class, which joined the French fleet at the end of the nineteenth century. These five ships of similar arrangement and weight of armament but widely differing silhouettes marked the adoption by the French Navy of turrets, as opposed to barbettes. Devised by Canet's armament works, these hydraulically operated turrets were mounted over a central ammunition hoist which rotated with the turntable. Similar turrets were mounted at that time in several Swedish and Danish coast-defence ships.

Between the *Neptune* and *Jauréguiberry* classes, an interesting ship added to the French Navy was the *Brennus*, the first to mount turrets as described above and also the first to incorporate a belt of light armour above the main belt as a protection against the newly invented quick-firing guns, an arrangement which was thereafter to be found in all battleships. The *Brennus* incorporated yet another innovation in that she had her secondary armament under armour in turrets or casemates. Not until the *Charlemagne* class, launched in 1895–96, did the French finally follow the British arrangement of mounting the big guns in pairs in barbette-turrets, a system which had been adopted by most other navies by this time.

The Russian Navy had quickly accepted the revolution in battleship design represented by the British *Devastation*. They had been early supporters of the turret concept, but their first turret ship the *Kniaz Minin* had been designed with tripod-mast sail rigging in Captain Coles' system and, following the disaster of the *Captain*, she had been converted to a broadside ship. In 1874, however, they launched the *Piotr Veliki* at Cronstadt, a mastless ship with two turrets, mounting four 12-inch breech-loading guns. Though three powerful battleships with six 12-inch guns on disappearing mountings on turntables, the *Catherine II*, *Sinope* and *Tchesmé*, were launched in 1887, the Russians later reverted to the standard pre-dreadnought layout of four 12-inch guns in two turrets on the centre-line and a secondary armament of smaller guns.

By the turn of the century the Russians possessed fairly homogeneous squadrons of such ships with a displacement of between 11,000 and 13,000 tons, in which between twenty and thirty water-tube boilers of the Belleville or Niclausse type supplied steam to triple-expansion engines to give top speeds of 18 knots. Two of these ships were built in foreign yards, the *Retvisan* at Cramp's of Philadelphia, and the *Tsarevitch* in France at Les Forges et Chantiers de la Mediterranée at La Seyne.

It was not until 1864 that the Prussian (later the German) Navy began to grow from a heterogeneous collection of minor war-vessels for coastal operations into a sea-going fleet, the first steps taken being the ordering of a few armoured vessels from England and France such as the broadside ship *König Wilhelm* and the purchase of the coast-defence ship *Arminius*. In 1873, after the Franco-Prussian War, it was decided to acquire a squadron of 'armoured frigates', as battleships of that era were called. The first two, designed by E. J. Reed, the foremost British constructor, and built in England, the *Kaiser* and *Deutschland*, were of conservative design with an armoured casemate amidships overhanging the sides, housing a battery of ten $10\frac{1}{4}$-inch Krupp breech-loading guns. As well as twin screws driven by the already old-fashioned two-cylinder, horizontal steam-engines which gave them a top speed of $14\frac{1}{2}$ knots, both ships were full-rigged for sail.

At about the same time the first three major warships to be built in German yards were completed—the *Grosser Kurfürst*, the *Friedrich der Grosse*, and the *Preussen*. Though these had their four $10\frac{1}{4}$-inch Krupp guns mounted in two turrets, surrounded by an armoured casemate, they retained their full rig of sails. Following these came the *Sachsen* class of ships, launched in 1877, which mounted, inside an armoured citadel, six $10\frac{1}{4}$-inch Krupp breech-loading guns, two at the forward end of it and four at the corners of a battery at the after end, all arranged to fire *en barbette*. These were the first German ships to adopt the principle of concentrating the armour protection to form a central redoubt or citadel and an armoured or 'protected' deck, leaving the ends of the ship

12-inch gun turrets for H.M.S. *Cornwallis* being assembled in the famous Elswick gun factory of Armstrong's in 1901.

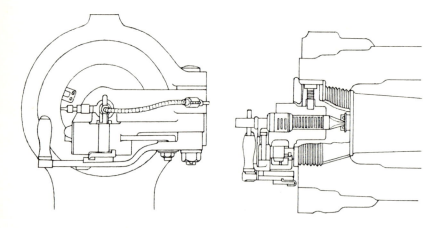

The single-motion breech mechanism introduced by Armstrong about 1887 which converted the ordinary breech-loading gun into a quick-firer (Q.F.).

unprotected, except for cork-filled compartments with coal bunkers behind them, a system first adopted by the British for cruisers and then extended to battleships by the Italians in the *Duilio* and by the British in the *Inflexible*.

The German Navy, in comparison to others, mounted smaller guns tor the main armament of their ships, the weight saved being applied to better armour protection. The *Brandenburg* class which followed the *Sachsen*'s mounted six 11-inch guns in pairs on barbettes; but the following class—*Kaiser Friedrich III*—laid down between 1895 and 1898 had four 9·4-inch backed up by a secondary armament of eighteen 5·9-inch quick-firers.

Within the next classes—ten battleships all of very similar design laid down between 1901 and 1905—German battleships assumed the typical pre-dreadnought shape and layout, but with two twin turrets of 11-inch guns as compared to the 12-inch in contemporary ships of other navies, backed by a secondary armament of fourteen 6·7-inch; no further ships were built prior to the transformation of battleship design which took place with the opening of the dreadnought era.

Although Italy joined the ranks of naval powers soon after her unification, she relied at first upon foreign shipyards and designers for her men-of-war. All the Italian ships at the Battle of Lissa in 1866 were foreign built. When she decided to rely upon her own resources to effect a naval renaissance in 1872, however, she discovered a rich vein of native talent in the art of ship design in which she was to establish herself at once amongst the leaders. Her first famous naval constructor was Benedetto Brin, whose initial major undertakings were the 12,000-ton battleships *Duilio* and *Dandolo*, in which he exercised his great ingenuity to try to retain an adequate degree of armour protection while mounting guns bigger than any previously at sea. Originally intending to mount four 12·5-inch guns, which would have permitted him to provide the conventional complete armour belt, when Armstrong's offered first 15-inch guns and later 17·7-inch monsters, Brin decided to incorporate them into his design at the expense of armour protection. This was limited to a steel belt on the water-line amidships, 147 feet in length, the maximum thickness of which was 21·6 inches. Above this was a shorter redoubt of 16·9-inch armour from which rose the two twin turrets in echelon, an arrangement which was to be copied in the British *Inflexible*. The result, prestigious in that it gave the young Italian Navy the most powerful ships afloat, but less satisfactory from the point of view of battle-worthiness, has been discussed previously when considering the *Inflexible*, constructed in answer to the *Duilio*.

An interesting feature of the *Duilio* was the big compartment on the water-line aft, closed by massive watertight doors in the stern, through which a torpedo boat housed there could be launched. Two other torpedo boats were carried on the upper deck.

In his next two ships, the *Italia* and *Lepanto*, Brin again mounted four 17·7-inch guns, this time at the complete sacrifice of any armoured belt. Only the bases of the two turrets, the ammunition hoists and the base of the funnels were armoured. In compensation the cellular system of protection by numerous small compartments filled with cork or coal was extended over the entire length of the ships. The resultant saving in weight allowed these ships to attain the remarkable speed for their day of 18 knots. This important feature, inspired by the Italian Minister of Marine, Admiral di Saint Bon, at a time when the Italian Navy was liable to find itself fighting the numerically superior French Navy as a result of the dispute over the French occupation of Tunis, permits these two ships to be looked upon as the forerunners of the battle-cruisers of the dreadnought age.

The *Italia* design was not persisted with, however, battleship design reverting to the *Duilio* type in the *Andrea Doria* class of three ships laid down in 1885, a design that had in the meantime been outmoded by the British 'Admiral' class, which had signalled the end of the cult of the monster gun. It was not until the *Benedetto Brin* was laid down in 1900 with a complete belt of 2 to 6 inches of Terni steel armour and a main armament of four 12-inch guns that the Italian Navy fell into line with others in producing typical pre-dreadnought battleships.

An impression by the Japanese artist Kokunimasa of the Battle of the Yalu River (1894) in which the Japanese Navy defeated the Chinese. Japanese sailors (in white) are shown boarding a Chinese ship. Woodcut.

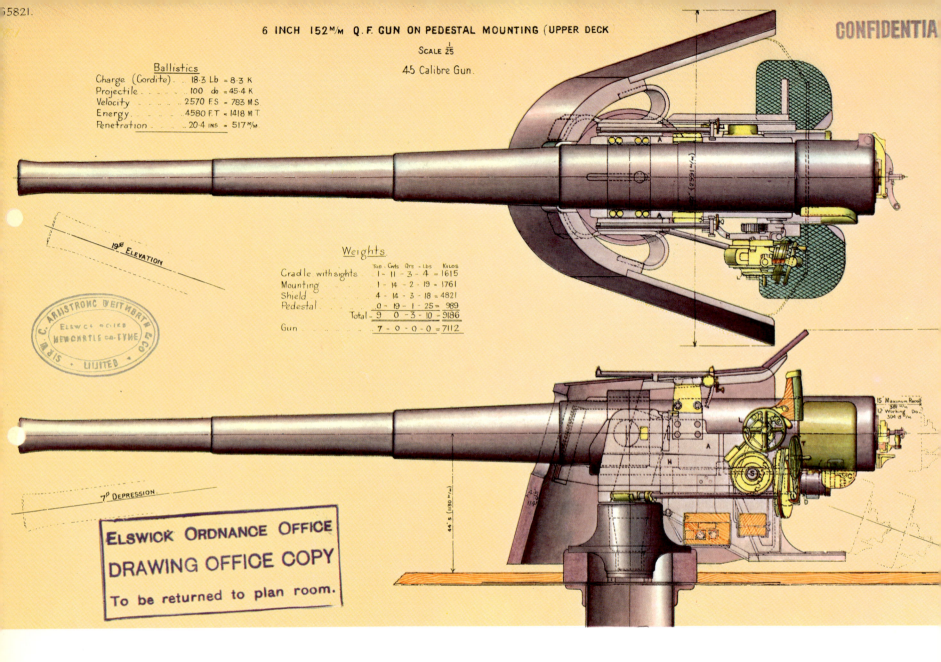

6 INCH 152ᴹ/ᴹ Q.F. GUN ON PEDESTAL MOUNTING (UPPER DECK

SCALE $\frac{1}{25}$

45 Calibre Gun.

CONFIDENTIA

Ballistics

Charge (Cordite)	18·3 Lb	= 8·3 K
Projectile	100 do	= 45·4 K
Velocity	2570 F.S.	= 783 M.S.
Energy	4580 F.T	= 1418 M.T
Penetration	20·4 ins	= 517 ᴹ/ᴹ

19° ELEVATION

7° DEPRESSION.

Weights

	Ton - Cwts - Qrs - Lbs	Kilos
Cradle with sights	1 - 11 - 3 - 4	= 1615
Mounting	1 - 14 - 2 - 19	= 1761
Shield	4 - 14 - 3 - 18	= 4821
Pedestal	0 - 19 - 1 - 25	= 989
Total	9 - 0 - 3 - 10	= 9186
Gun	7 - 0 - 0 - 0	= 7112

6-inch quick-firing gun on a pedestal mounting.

The early developments of the man-of-war during the age of steam were given the test of battle on which the next step in progress was based. Thus steam propulsion was tested during the Crimean War in 1854, and, together with the application of iron armour and the use of explosive shells, made the old wooden sailing ships which had ruled the seas for three centuries totally obsolete. The arrangement of guns in large numbers on the broadside, limited in their arcs of training, was outmoded by that of a few, large rotatable pieces following the example of Ericsson's monitors during the American Civil War and by the tactics of ramming at Lissa in 1866 which seemed to indicate the need for forward-firing guns.

During the next thirty years the only skirmish between men-of-war from which any lessons could be learnt with regard to armament or armour protection was that, mentioned elsewhere, between the *Shah* and *Huascar* in 1877. The one thing demonstrated in this inconclusive fight was the inability of the medium-calibre guns mounted in the British cruiser, with the low muzzle velocity induced by the black gunpowder still customary at that time, to penetrate the $4\frac{1}{2}$ inches of wrought-iron armour of the Peruvian ship, even when fired at short range. The result was to confirm the practice of mounting ever-larger guns in the hope of being able to master the ever-thicker armour being fitted, culminating in the monstrous, 100-ton guns of the Italian battleship *Duilio* and the 24 inches of armour on the side of the British *Inflexible*.

The trend was halted and, at first, reversed by the introduction, on the one hand, of smaller guns, but with the higher muzzle velocities made possible by improved propellant powders; on the other hand the invention of tougher armour through the use of steel and steel alloys.

None of these things had been seriously tested before the turn of the century. In 1894 a Chinese and a Japanese fleet had met in battle off the mouth of the Yalu River. The former, centred on two German-built battleships of 1882 vintage, and handled on the tactical principle of the head-on approach made popular by Tegetthoff at Lissa, was opposed by a nominally weaker Japanese fleet, but one which contained a 'flying squadron' of the comparatively new-fangled, fast, protected cruisers and mounting a great many 6-inch and 4·7-inch quick-firing guns. The relative effectiveness of the two sides was obscured by the incompetence of the Chinese crews and defects in their ammunition on the one hand, as opposed to the high state of efficiency and discipline of the Japanese on the other.

This action, which resulted in a notable victory for the Japanese, was, nevertheless, studied with great interest by the naval experts of every nation. Controversy raged furiously as to the lessons to be learnt from it. Supporters of the fast, multi-gun ship claimed that their views had been justified by the Japanese victory. Too much weight was being put into armour, they insisted, which would be better allocated to guns. Their opponents objected that the test had not been a fair one owing to the faulty tactics of the Chinese admiral and the incompetence of the Chinese gunners. The fire of the Japanese quick-firers had annihilated the Chinese cruisers, but had failed to inflict any vital damage on their two armoured ships. On the other hand, only three hits—on the unarmoured Japanese flagship from the big guns of the Chinese ships—one of them a solid shot which passed straight through the ship, doing little damage, and another a shot which broke up on impact, spewing cement instead of a bursting charge—had been sufficient to put her out of action.

Any conclusions to be drawn from the Battle of the Yalu had, in any case, to be studied in the light of the rapid advances taking place in the quality of armour plate and the range, hitting power and speed of loading of all guns in that epoch. When American and Spanish fleets met in battle during the war of 1898, the engagements were too one-sided to shed much light on the matter. Rightly or wrongly, the two principal types of ship designs adopted by most navies subsequently were, firstly, battleships similar to the British *Majestic* class, mounting four 12-inch guns in hydraulically operated turret-barbette mountings, with a secondary armament of numerous 6-inch or 8-inch guns and a belt of nickel or chrome steel varying between 9 inches and 12 inches in thickness, the type that would later be generally designated 'pre-dreadnoughts'; and secondly, armoured cruisers such as the Russian *Rossia*, mounting four 8-inch breech-loaders and sixteen 6-inch quick-firers, the Japanese *Idzumo* class or the United States *California* class with similar armaments.

The French Navy, in particular, under the influence of Admiral Aube and his followers of the 'Jeune École', who believed the day of the battleship was over, favoured this latter type, the design of which they had greatly advanced with the *Dupuy de Lôme* in 1890 and her successors.

When the Russo-Japanese War broke out in 1904, it was mainly these two types of ships, supported by the uncertain but much-feared potentialities of the recently developed torpedo boats and destroyers, that were to be pitted against each other. The striking power of their high-velocity guns was impressive even against the modern chrome-steel armour of their opponents. The ability to take advantage of it at anything but a very short range, however, was doubtful, the weapons having outstripped the means of control and direction which were still confined to small rangefinders and simple telescopic sights on the guns.

Although the French fleet had instituted battle practice at ranges of more than 5500 yards as early as 1896 and was developing simple fire-control systems, in the

Painting by the Japanese artist Eizo Okusei of the Japanese attempt to block the entrance to Port Arthur by sinking blockships across the channel.

British fleet firing practice was still confined to shooting at moored targets at a range of a couple of thousand yards with each gun independently controlled and aimed. Indeed, the problem of spotting the fall of shot from the mixed, unco-ordinated armaments of the larger ships at anything above point-blank range was insoluble and made longer-range shooting of doubtful effectiveness. The generally held concept of a naval action was still that of ships pounding one another from a distance of two or three thousand yards with every gun that could be brought to bear.

Gunnery enthusiasts such as Captain Percy Scott in the British Navy and Lieutenant-Commander W. S. Sims in the United States Navy had been advocating more ambitious fighting ranges and devising improved methods of training gunlayers and of controlling gunfire. It was another concept, however, which was to make their ideas feasible.

In Italy, the brilliant naval designer Vittorio Cuniberti had been advocating the advantages of a battleship armed only with big guns all of the same calibre which, by facilitating the spotting of the fall of shot, would permit effective fire at the great ranges of which the modern big guns were capable. Cuniberti's design for such a ship, which was rejected by the Italian Admiralty, was published and undoubtedly influenced the thinking of the British admiral who was to bring it into being. Sir John Fisher, while Commander-in-Chief of the Mediterranean Fleet in 1898, set the Chief Constructor of Malta Dockyard, Mr. W. H. Gard, to work on designs for two such ships, a battleship which he called the *Untakeable*, and an armoured cruiser, the *Unapproachable*. The former was the embryo of the design of the revolutionary *Dreadnought*, the latter of the first battle-cruiser *Inflexible*.

Meanwhile, two pre-dreadnought navies were about to test in battle the men-of-war which had evolved in the ninety years since Fulton gave steam propulsion to the *Demologos*. Of the craft developed since first-class navies last fought each other, the first to see action were the 30-knot destroyers built by Thornycroft and Yarrow in 1899 for the Japanese Navy—ten little ships, each of some 300 tons displacement, with two tubes for 18-inch Whitehead torpedoes, one 12-pounder and five 6-pounder quick-firing guns. Before any formal declaration of war had been made, they were sent in to deliver a clandestine attack under cover of darkness on the Russian fleet at Port Arthur. Destroyers had been expressly designed for such attacks and the fear of them had led to the development and mounting of large numbers of quick-firing guns aboard all major warships.

The Russian fleet lay at anchor in the Roads outside Port Arthur with steam available only for running such auxiliary engines as pumps and dynamos and with no precautions against surprise attack except their 'crinoline' torpedo-nets spread around them, two ships detailed to maintain a searchlight guard and two destroyers on picket duty twenty miles to seaward. The Japanese flotilla, in spite of falling into some confusion in the black of the night and through running foul of the unsuspecting Russian destroyer patrol, pressed their attack closely, firing nineteen torpedoes at the stationary Russian battleships and cruisers at ranges varying between 700 and 1600 yards. Only three torpedoes scored against these easy targets, two Russian battleships and a cruiser each taking one hit but not suffering fatal damage. On the other hand, though all but the leading Japanese division, by which the three hits were scored, were caught in the Russian search-lights and hotly engaged by the many quick-firing guns, they suffered only minor damage and returned safely to harbour. The disappointing results of this first massed attack by torpedo craft in circumstances ideal for them, and an even more complete fiasco on another occasion when forty Japanese torpedo boats and destroyers failed to score a single torpedo hit, did little to minimise the sinister threat of the locomotive torpedo launched from surface warships, all of which at that time mounted torpedo tubes either on deck or below the water-line. Indeed, as the performance of torpedoes improved, they were to come to have a dominating influence on naval tactics.

It was on the inevitable clash between the opposing squadrons of armoured warships, however, that the eyes of naval experts were expectantly turned as the

Russian pre-dreadnought *Pobieda* of the Port Arthur squadron which took part in the Battle of 10th August 1904.

Japanese gun-crew serving a quick-firing gun.

Russo-Japanese War developed. The first of such encounters took place on the morning after the initial torpedo attack, 9th February 1904, when the Japanese C.-in-C. Admiral Togo, led his fleet into the Port Arthur Roads in the hope of catching the Russians in confusion and disarray. In this he was unsuccessful and the two fleets passed, cannonading one another, on opposite courses, 7000 yards apart. The Japanese line was led by the six battleships forming the First Division, *Mikasa* (Togo's flagship), *Asahi, Fuji, Yashima, Shikishima* and *Hatsuse*, typical pre-dreadnoughts, each mounting four 12-inch guns in twin turret-barbettes and fourteen 6-inch in broadside casemates. Following the battleships came the homogeneous squadron of armoured cruisers *Idzumo, Adzumo, Yakumo, Tokiwa* and *Iwate*, each mounting four 8-inch guns in twin barbettes and twelve or fourteen 6-inch guns. Bringing up the rear came a squadron of four protected cruisers, three of them with two 8-inch and ten 4·7 inch quick-firers, the fourth with four 6-inch and eight 4·7-inch quick-firers. The Russians, with two of their battleships and a cruiser out of action as a result of the earlier torpedo attack, opposed with five battleships led by the flagship, *Petropavlovsk*, and of similar armament to those under Togo, and a mixed cruiser squadron comprising the armoured cruiser *Bayan*, mounting two 8-inch and eight 6-inch guns, three protected cruisers each with eight or twelve 6-inch quick-firers and two light cruisers with 4·7-inch quick-firing guns.

Such a massive confrontation of artillery at a range of less than 8000 yards might have been expected to wreak decisive damage on one side or the other. But the shortcomings of the pre-dreadnought types of ship were at once revealed, with their mixed batteries of heavy guns confusing the spotting of the fall of shot and hampering the primitive fire-control arrangements. This, in turn, by limiting action to a comparatively short range, imposed a flat trajectory on the projectiles so that those which hit an enemy ship did so on the side armour and failed to penetrate.

When the two fleets drew apart and disengaged, the Russian cruisers, which, being nearest the enemy, had drawn most of the Japanese fire, had received a number of hits but none had been put out of action. The Russian battleships, too, had been repeatedly hit—one of them, the *Pobieda*, fifteen times—but many of these had been from the Japanese secondary armament and not a shell had penetrated their armour or inflicted serious damage. Total Russian casualties were 21 killed and 101 wounded. The Japanese battleships likewise suffered hits on four of their number, the *Mikasa* being hit three times by heavy shells, but suffering only superficial damage, and their casualties were even lighter than those of the Russians. The theories of Cuniberti and Sims were thus early confirmed by the test of war.

They were to be further strengthened when the two fleets met in the open sea on 10th August 1904. On this occasion, long-range gunfire, by 12-inch guns alone, proved itself to be much more effective than indiscriminate fire at shorter range by guns of many different calibres. Furthermore it was demonstrated that, in battle between armoured ships, only the big 12-inch shells really counted, 8-inch and 6-inch shells failing to do any serious damage. Thus while the *Mikasa* early in the action suffered heavy damage and a great many casualties from two hits by Russian 12-inch shells, when the Japanese later had an opportunity to bring all their guns from 6-inch upwards to bear on the enemy, the Russians emerged virtually unharmed from the forest of shell splashes that surrounded them. After several hours of cannonading, in which the *Mikasa* had been repeatedly hit, with mounting damage and casualties, when the battle seemed about to end in favour of the Russians, it was the explosion of two 12-inch shells aboard the Russian flagship, throwing her out of control and the line into confusion, that reversed the fortunes of the day, the Russians being forced into ignominious flight.

In the best known and decisive, final sea battle of the war fought in the Straits of Tsu-shima on 27th May 1905, when the Japanese fleet annihilated the Russian Baltic fleet, it was again the 12-inch guns, firing at long range, which dominated the action.

Japanese pre-dreadnought *Mikasa*, flagship of Admiral Togo throughout the Russo-Japanese War, 1904–05. Heavily damaged at the Battle of 10th August, she was repaired and flew Togo's flag at the decisive victory of Tsu-shima, 1905.

Admiral Heichahiro Togo, Japanese C.-in-C. during the Russo-Japanese War.

KNIAZ SOUVAROFF

Russian pre-dreadnought *Kniaz Souvaroff*, flagship of

Admiral Rodjestvensky.

The Battle of Tsu-shima and its less decisive but more evenly matched predecessor of 10th August 1904 were naturally seized upon for study by naval experts the world over. Tactical lessons were drawn from them and fiercely propounded. Technical details of the ships involved were closely studied to explain the relative performance of the two sides. Yet in fact almost every form of equipment in the battleships of either fleet was about to be made obsolete, the tactical conclusions thereby being given doubtful validity.

Only the revelation of the ineffectiveness of the smaller guns against armoured ships was to be of consequence. The mixed gun armament, compelling a decisive range of only 3000 to 5000 yards, the system—or lack of it— of fire control, the propelling machinery, so fallible when driven at full power, all were about to be superseded to make a new revolution in battleship design.

Ever since the previous revolution occasioned by the introduction of steam propulsion and the use of armour, warships and their armament had been designed simply to be more powerful and better protected than those being added to rival navies. If the French Navy built a battleship with, say, four 10-inch guns and ten 6-inch with an armoured belt 8 inches thick, the answer by the British Navy might be a ship with four 12-inch guns or a secondary battery of 8-inch weapons and perhaps thicker armour, on the assumption that these two ships or two lines of such ships might fight it out at short range, 'hammer and tongs', until one or the other was reduced to a wreck or sunk—as indeed was the case at Tsu-shima.

The inability to hit a target at the long range of which the bigger guns were capable of firing made such an idea not unrealistic. As late as 1903, the fighting range of battleships was considered to be in the region of 3000 yards. At such ranges the whole of the large mixed battery of guns, mounted wherever space could be found for them, could be brought into action. The range once found, a high percentage of hits could be obtained by gun-layers using quite simple sights.

Not only were gunnery experts devising means of training gun crews to load their guns rapidly and aim them accurately, they were also turning their inventive talents to designing systems of fire control by which spotting of fall of shot was done from a central position and corrections passed to all the guns. Such a system called for the simultaneous firing of all the guns in salvoes; this, in turn, facilitated spotting even at long range as it was at once apparent whether all the shell splashes were beyond the target (in which case a 'down' range correction had to be applied), short (in which case an 'up' range correction was made), or 'straddling' (which meant that the range was correct). Using such a method, guns could be controlled at much longer ranges.

This method, however, required that all the guns of a salvo should be of the same calibre, their projectiles thus having the same time of flight, that at least four guns should be fired in each salvo and to make a straddle identifiable, that the rate of fire should be fast enough for the range to be not greatly altered between salvoes by an alteration of course by the target. To achieve the necessary rate of

fire and for other reasons, the guns of a turret were fired alternately, in the British Navy at least, so at least eight guns had to be mounted in twin turrets. On the other hand this arrangement enabled accurate fire to be directed at ranges beyond that of all but the biggest guns on board, making the smaller sizes useless: the latter could therefore be dispensed with, their weight and space being allocated to providing a greater number of big guns. So the idea of the all-big-gun man-of-war was born. As mentioned before, first mooted by the Italian Vittorio Cuniberti, it was taken up by both the British and United States navies. Plans by the latter suffered delays, however, and it was the British Admiralty under the influence of Admiral Fisher which acted first. A number of alternatives were considered before one was decided upon which, on a displacement of 18,000 tons, called for a main armament of ten 12-inch guns in twin turrets and an anti-torpedo-boat battery of twenty-seven 12-pounder, 3-inch quick-firers. Five 18-inch torpedo tubes, four of which fired on the broadside and one astern, were installed in compartments below the water-line.

There was more in Fisher's mind, however, than a rearrangement of the gun armament. In order to catch an unwilling enemy and then to choose the range at which to fight, superior speed was necessary. Speed, then, higher than anything so far attained by a battleship, must be sought, and furthermore a capability of *sustained* high speed. Already reciprocating engines were reaching the limit of power and speed possible in the space available in a warship. Unlike the engines of a passenger liner, which, unlimited in height, could have a very long piston stroke and could so develop considerable power at moderate revolutions, a battleship's engines, cramped underneath the armoured deck, had to whirl at a tremendous pace. The wear and tear at high speed was therefore much greater.

The scene in the engine-room of a pre-dreadnought battleship at speed was like an inferno. As the great piston-rods leapt wildly up and down and the connecting rods whirled the massive cranks round, hot oil and water spurted everywhere. Seawater from hoses playing on hot bearings sloshed in the bilges. In an atmosphere murky with steam from dozens of small steam leaks, the engineer officers would stand on the greasy deck plates, oilskins buttoned to the neck, their faces black and their clothes soaked in oil and water. Over all would be a noise so deafening that telephones could not be used. Breakdowns from overheated bearings or broken steam joints were common, and were always expected. After any prolonged period of high-speed running there would be work for the dockyard engineers.

Thus at the battle of 10th August 1904, Togo had been reluctant to order a battle speed of 15 knots, though the slowest ship in the Japanese battle squadron had a top speed of 18. But coming now to the aid of the ship-designers was the steam turbine, in which all the moving parts rotated. Instead of the shock and strain involved in reversing the direction of motion of huge pistons, piston-rods

The Battle of Tsu-shima, 27th May 1905, as portrayed by the Japanese artist Shotaro Tojo. Admiral Togo's First Squadron, led by his flagship *Mikasa*, is seen. In this battle, in which the Russian fleet was annihilated, the primacy of the turret-mounted big gun in naval battle was demonstrated and this encouraged the development of the all-big-gun battleship, the first of which was the *Dreadnought* (1906).

131

Japanese destroyer *Ikazuchi* of the type which attacked the Russian fleet off Port Arthur at the beginning of the war of 1904–05.

and connecting rods with every revolution of the shaft, power flowed smoothly from the high-pressure steam on to the blades of the turbine rotor.

The marine steam turbine was applied first to the propulsion of destroyers. The next warships to be so fitted were the British cruiser *Amethyst* and the German *Lübeck* laid down in 1903, both powered by Parsons' turbines. When the trans-Atlantic liners *Lusitania* and *Mauretania* proved an unqualified success powered by turbines, it could no longer be doubted that the day of the reciprocating engine for fast ships was over. Parsons' turbines developing 23,000 horse-power to drive four propeller shafts were incorporated in the design of the new battleship which was to be named *Dreadnought*. When she sailed for trials she registered a speed of 21 knots on the measured mile; but even more impressive was the reliability of her main machinery at sustained high speed when, after a month's steaming and calibrating trials in the West Indies, she made the return trip of 7000 miles at $17\frac{1}{2}$ knots without a single defect, a performance unimaginable with reciprocating engines.

The *Dreadnought* had two significant but not vital imperfections. Her anti-torpedo armament of 3-inch guns was to prove inadequate, being replaced in later classes by 4-inch; and the unhappy arrangement of her fore tripod-mast immediately abaft her forward funnel made the control top unapproachable at times owing to the heating up of the tripod and uninhabitable at other times on account of smoke. Nevertheless her performance and design were so successful and revolutionary that, at one stroke, all other battleships afloat were made obsolete.

The effect of this thunderclap in the world of warship design was felt most severely across the North Sea, where, since 1898, under the influence of Admiral von Tirpitz, Secretary of State for Naval Affairs, Germany had embarked upon a programme of shipbuilding aimed at destroying Britain's long-unchallenged naval supremacy. In 1898, the Reichstag passed the first of a series of Navy Acts authorising the construction of a modern fleet, the backbone of which would be a squadron of nineteen battleships, to be completed by 1903. In 1900, however, this Act was replaced by another providing for a battle fleet of two fleet flagships, four squadrons of eight battleships each and appropriate numbers of cruisers and torpedo craft.

Thus it was upon a world in which the battleship strength of the major naval powers was a political question of the utmost importance that the *Dreadnought* burst with such impact. The German Navy realised at once that dreadnoughts must supersede all earlier types. All battleship construction was held up while new designs were brought out. In March 1908 the first German dreadnought, the *Nassau*, was launched. At the same time, the Germans not only constructed dry-docks large enough to accommodate the biggest dreadnoughts likely to be built—a step which was to give them a big advantage over British designers, limited by their existing dry-docks—they also set to work with feverish energy to enlarge the Kiel Canal and its locks to permit dreadnoughts to pass between the Baltic and the North Sea without having to make the long and difficult passage through the Sound between Denmark and Sweden, the Kattegat and the Skagerrak.

Meanwhile the naval armaments race between Britain and Germany began again as soon as the lessons of the *Dreadnought* had been absorbed. The German Navy Law of 1900 was amended in 1906 and again in 1908, until it was calculated that by 1920 a German Navy would exist far stronger than anything which Great Britain had so far possessed.

For a time Britain held aloof from an armaments race. In 1905 she had laid down four battleships to Germany's two. The next year each had laid down three. In 1907 Britain further reduced her programme to two, while Germany increased hers to four. In one of his speeches, the Kaiser styled himself 'Admiral of the Atlantic'.

British fears were at last fully roused. In the face of great public agitation both political parties in Britain came to agree in the necessity to keep ahead of German naval construction.

'Two keels to one' became the popular cry in Britain, so that in August 1914, when war at last came, the Royal Navy found itself with twenty dreadnought-battleships to Germany's fourteen, and nine battle-cruisers against four. Even so, only by concentrating them all in home waters could a numerical superiority be assured over the German fleet, which could choose its own moment to come out at full strength.

Though the British Navy inaugurated the dreadnought era, the *Dreadnought* herself being followed by the three ships of the *Bellerophon* class, and three of the *St. Vincent* class, completed in 1909 and 1910, other navies soon followed suit. The United States Navy, indeed, had produced designs in 1904 for two all-big-gun battleships of 16,000 tons, the *Michigan* and *South Carolina*, and in the following year construction was authorised by Congress. These ships, which were not completed until September 1909, failed like the early German dread-noughts to incorporate turbine propulsion. The American ships, however, made an extremely important contribution to the design of warships by adopting the system of superfiring for the main armament, one turret firing over the top of another. Prior to this innovation, not only were a proportion of the guns re-stricted in their arcs of fire by the obstruction of the superstructure and of other turrets so that only a part of the armament could fire on either side, but mountings and magazines were dispersed around the ship, causing the maximum incon-venience in the layout of machinery spaces. Now the whole main armament could be situated on the centre-line, permitting all guns to fire on either side over an arc of some 160 degrees from right ahead or right astern.

This arrangement had been considered when designs for the *Dreadnought* were under consideration; it had been discarded on account of the blast effect upon the lower of the two turrets. The American designers had overcome this by doing away with sighting hoods on the tops of turrets, replacing them by screened sights projecting from the side walls of the turrets. From this time onwards super-imposed turrets on the centre-line became the standard arrangement.

Following the *South Carolina* and *Michigan*, the Americans laid down towards the end of 1906 two 20,000-ton ships, *Delaware* and *North Dakota*, the former with reciprocating triple-expansion engines of 16,500 horse-power, the latter with Curtis turbines (later replaced by Parsons' turbines). Both ships mounted ten 12-inch guns and fourteen 5-inch and achieved a speed of 22 knots. The very similar *Utah* and *Florida*, laid down in 1909, were powered by Parsons' geared turbines, as were the *Arkansas* and *Wyoming*, laid down in the following year, which mounted six superimposed twin 12-inch turrets.

The first British dreadnought to adopt superfiring was the *Neptune*, completed in 1911, which had a superimposed turret aft, though she and two later British ships, *Colossus* and *Hercules*, retained their midship turrets mounted in echelon.

The advent of the all-big-gun capital ship led to great improvements in the systems of control, enabling these guns to fire effectively at the great ranges—ten miles or more—of which they were capable. The first steps were simple enough, comprising the fittings of a rangefinder in a 'fighting top' high up the fore-mast, and a system of voice pipes to the gun positions through which ranges were passed to be set on the individual gun sights. A fire-control officer in the top gave the order to all the guns to fire simultaneously, thus achieving salvo firing. Studying the fall of shot, he could then pass simultaneous corrections to the range settings.

Next, communications were electrified; a sight or gun director was fitted in the fighting top, the movements of which, by means of electrical indicators at the guns, enabled all guns to fire exactly on the same bearing and with the same elevation. Bigger and more accurate rangefinders were fitted, the German Navy excelling in this equipment by means of a stereoscopic system.

The next step, inevitably, was to increase the size of the guns and of the thick-ness of armour protection and consequently the size of the ships themselves. In November 1909 the British laid down the *Orion*, first of the so-called super-dreadnoughts, with a displacement of 22,500 tons (2500 tons more than the *Colossus*), mounting ten 13·5-inch guns in twin, superfiring, centre-line turrets

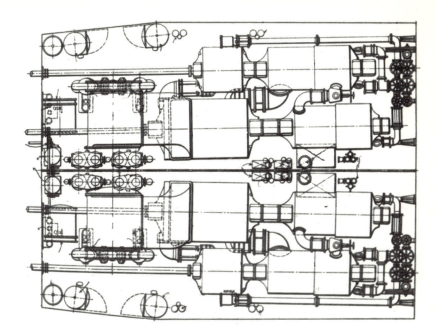

Layout of the engine room of a turbine-driven dreadnought battleship.

The Austrian super-dreadnought *Viribus Unitis*, laid down in 1910, mounting two superfiring triple turrets fore and aft. Was sunk in Pola harbour by Italian Lieutenant Paolucci and Major Rossetti, who penetrated the harbour using an early form of human torpedo. Painting by August Ramberg shows *Viribus Unitus* at the head of the Austrian fleet (1912).

Inflexible, the first battle-cruiser in which were combined the all-big-gun principle with high speed at the sacrifice of armour protection.

and with a 12-inch armour belt as compared with 11 inches in the *Colossus.* Four ships of this class were completed in 1912, being followed in the next year by the four ships of the *King George V* class and in 1914 by four *Iron Duke*'s, all of which mounted ten 13·5-inch guns.

The German Navy meanwhile retained 12-inch guns (though firing a heavier shell than British 12-inch) in their capital ships while, on the other hand, incorporating much greater armour protection than that in British ships. This they were able to do because the British constructors were handicapped by limitations in the beam they could give their ships if they were to be able to use the existing British dry-docks.

Besides other advantages, the additional beam available to German designers enabled them to incorporate a system of anti-torpedo protection which had been first devised by the French constructor Émile Bertin. As long ago as 1899 he had designed the small battleship *Henri IV,* of 9000 tons, with an internal, longitudinal curved bulkhead, sometimes referred to as an 'elastic bulkhead', to absorb the shock of a torpedo warhead explosion. A similar system adopted by German designers was to make their ships remarkably invulnerable to underwater explosions during the First World War. The *Nassau* class, their first dreadnoughts, completed in 1909 and displacing 18,602 tons, mounted twelve 11-inch guns in six twin turrets, two pairs of which were sited on the beam abreast the superstructure, which allowed a broadside of eight guns. They were followed by the four ships of the *Ostfriesland* class of 22,448 tons displacement with a similar turret arrangement, but substituting 12-inch guns. The next class, the five super-dreadnoughts of the *Kaiser* class, carried only ten 12-inch; but the after pair of turrets being superimposed on the centre-line, the two midship turrets placed diagonally and the fore turret on the centre-line, these ships could still produce a broadside of eight guns. The weight saved by the discarded turret, and an increased displacement of some 2000 tons to a total of 24,325, allowed heavier armour. The belt, at 13·8 inches maximum, was 2 inches thicker and other armour was in proportion.

The *Kaiser* class were the first German battleships to have turbine drive, giving them a horse-power of more than 55,000 and a speed of 22·3 knots. Approaching completion when the First World War broke out were the four ships of the *König* class in which superfiring was adopted fore and aft, allowing all five twin 12-inch turrets to fire on either beam.

The United States Navy can be said to have joined the trend towards the super-dreadnought in 1911 when they laid down the 27,000-ton *New York* and *Texas,* mounting ten 14-inch guns in pairs of superimposed turrets fore and aft and a fifth turret forward of the after mast. Partly owing to a dispute with the builders of turbines in the United States and partly in pursuit of fuel economy and increased operational range, these ships and a successor, *Oklahoma,* laid down in 1912, reverted to reciprocating engines for their propulsion. The *Oklahoma*'s sister ship *Nevada,* however, was given Curtis geared turbines. These two ships incorporated the triple turret, their fore and aft triple turrets each having a twin turret superimposed, thus giving a broadside of ten 14-inch guns.

These ships were noteworthy for a reversion by U.S. designers to the principle of devoting all the armour to protection of the ship's vitals. Firing trials had seemed to show that light armour was useless in battleships. The secondary armament of fourteen 5-inch guns was therefore left unprotected. The main deck was left without the customary belt of medium armour, the weight saved being devoted to an increase to $13\frac{1}{2}$ inches of the thickness of the main belt over the middle and lower decks for 400 feet of the 537 feet on the water-line, with 8 inches of armour covering the length further aft as far as the rudder head. Barbettes were made $13\frac{1}{2}$ inches thick, while the turrets had 18 inches of armour on their faces, 16 inches on their sides and 10-inch roofs. The funnel uptakes were also protected by $13\frac{1}{2}$ inches of armour. This adoption of the 'all or nothing' principle was eventually to be copied by the British, French, Japanese and Italian navies in battleships of the post-First World War period.

The trend towards ever-bigger ships continued with the laying down of the two ships of the 31,400-ton *Pennsylvania* class, the three *New Mexico* class of 32,000 tons and the *California* and *Tennessee* of 32,300 tons, between 1913 and 1917, all of which mounted twelve 14-inch guns in triple turrets. An innovation in the *New Mexico* which was to become standard practice in American capital ships was the introduction of electric drive, her General Electric Company turbines driving two generators from which power was delivered to four propelling motors.

Other principal navies lagged behind the British, German and American in adopting the dreadnought concept. The first Japanese dreadnought, the *Kawachi*, and her sister ship *Settsu*, of 21,420 tons, were laid down in January 1909 mounting twelve 12-inch guns in single twin turrets fore and aft and two twin turrets on each beam.

Succeeding Japanese battleships, of which the first were the 30,600-ton *Fuso* launched in 1914 and her sister ship *Yamashiro* the following year, were super-dreadnoughts, taking advantage of the superfiring arrangements to mount twelve 14-inch guns in twin turrets all in the centre-line. These two ships were followed by the *Ise* and *Hyuga* of 31,260 tons in which a more compact turret arrangement was achieved by mounting their twelve 14-inch guns in three pairs of twin, superimposed turrets. A secondary battery of ten 5·5-inch guns on each side was mounted below the forward superstructure.

Though the Italian Navy did not lay down their first dreadnought, the *Dante Alighieri*, until 1909, this ship, designed by the Italian Chief Constructor, General Masdea, was the first to incorporate triple turrets which gave her the powerful armament of twelve 12-inch guns on the comparatively small displacement of 20,500 tons. In the absence of any superfiring arrangements, however, this only permitted ahead or astern fire by three guns. This shortcoming was eliminated in the next Italian battleships of the *Giulio Cesare* class, laid down in 1910, by having twin turrets superimposed on the forward and after triple turrets, and a triple turret amidships, giving ahead and astern fire of five guns and a broadside of thirteen.

An even more concentrated arrangement was adopted by the Austro-Hungarian Navy for their first dreadnoughts of the *Viribus Unitis* class, laid down in 1910, in which two superfiring triple 12-inch turrets fore and aft gave ahead and astern fire of six guns and a broadside of twelve.

Triple turrets were also adopted by the Russians for their first dreadnoughts, four ships of the *Gangut* class laid down in 1909, mounting twelve 12-inch guns on a displacement of 23,000 tons. The design, as finally accepted by the Russians, was a combination of ideas from a number of sources, notably John Brown's of Clydebank who also supervised their building in Russian yards, and of the Italian Cuniberti. It was on the latter's recommendation that the triple turret was adopted and it was probably the influence of his Mediterranean-orientated mind that led to the low freeboard and flush deck of these ships intended for operation in another enclosed sea, the Baltic. Russian contributions to the design included a specially strengthened bow for ice-breaking and a 16-foot-wide complete armour belt of Krupp steel which compensated for its unusual expanse by being only 8·8 inches thick at its maximum.

Four more dreadnoughts of the *Imperatritsa Maria* class of similar design and the same armament for the Russian Black Sea fleet were launched shortly before the outbreak of the First World War. Another, of some 27,000 tons, was launched in 1916 but was never completed.

The French Navy, finally discarding the small-ship theories of the 'Jeune École', were the last of the major navies to build dreadnoughts. The six turbine-driven battleships of the *Danton* class laid down in 1907 were pre-dreadnoughts with a mixed armament of four 12-inch guns and twelve 9·4-inch. The first French dreadnoughts, the four ships of the *Jean Bart* class, were laid down in 1910 and 1911. Displacing 23,120 tons, they mounted twelve 12-inch guns in superimposed twin turrets fore and aft and a single twin turret on either beam. Parsons' turbines of 28,000 horse-power gave them a full speed of 21–22 knots. These ships were followed a year later by the three super-dreadnoughts of the *Bretagne* class of about the same size but mounting ten 13·4-inch guns.

The epoch-making battleship *Dreadnought*, the first all-big-gun battleship.

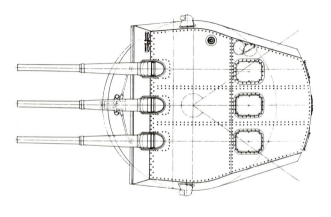

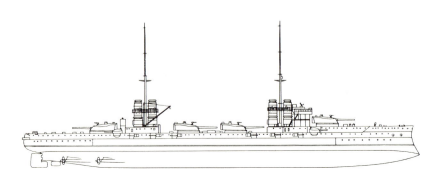

NEW YORK/DANTE ALIGHIERI

Dreadnoughts of the U.S. and Italian navies.
the *New York* (*top*) and the *Dante Alighieri* (*bottom*). The U.S. Navy introduced
the superimposed turret system, the outstanding feature of the so-called
'super-dreadnought', subsequently adopted by all navies.

The triple turret, permitting greater gunpower from the available
space, was first introduced by the Italian and Austrian navies.

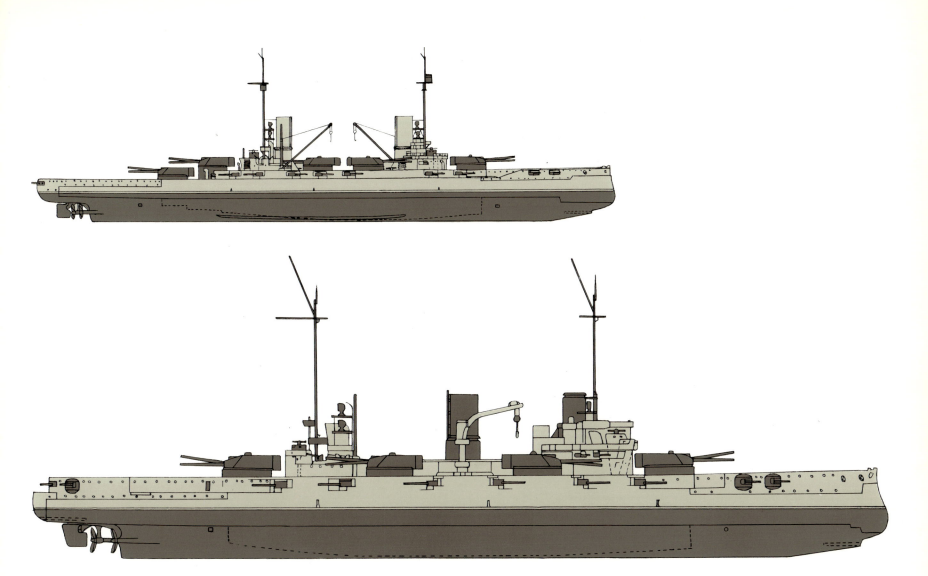

Grand Admiral Alfred von Tirpitz, founder of the German Navy and advocate of a large High Sea fleet to challenge the sea power of Britain.

NASSAU/KAISER

German dreadnoughts. The *Nassau* (*bottom*), mounting twelve 11-inch guns in twin turrets, was the first German dreadnought to be completed. The *Kaiser* class ship (*top*) with ten 12-inch guns and superimposed turrets was a super-dreadnought.

French dreadnought *Courbet*, completed in 1913, one of the
four *Jean Bart* class, mounting twelve 12-inch guns in twin
turrets.

While the epoch-making transformation in the design of the battleship represented by the *Dreadnought* was taking place, similar consideration was being given to the design of cruisers. That even the biggest armoured cruisers were unfit to take their place in the battle line was appreciated even before the conclusive demonstration in the naval engagements of the Russo-Japanese War. At the same time they were too slow to fulfil the cruiser's traditional functions of scouting and commerce protection.

This had been appreciated for some time. In England, Admiral Fisher had poured scorn on the armoured cruiser, which, he said, could neither fight nor run away. In France, Émile Bertin and the Minister of Marine Lockroy had put forward the idea in 1896 of what they called a *cuirassé croiseur* or 'battleship-cruiser' as opposed to the *croiseur cuirassé* or 'armoured cruiser'. By sacrificing armour protection, on a displacement of 14,500 tons they were to have mounted two single 12-inch and fourteen 6·4-inch guns and would have been 2 knots faster than contemporary battleships. In 1899, they again advocated a ship of this type with four 12-inch guns, sixteen 6·4-inch and a speed of 21 knots.

Only the Japanese and Italians, however, brought this concept into being by constructing ships mounting battleship armaments in cruiser hulls.

The former built the *Ikoma* and *Tsukuba* of 13,000 tons laid down in 1904, mounting four 12-inch guns in twin turrets, twelve 6-inch, twelve 4-inch and twelve 3-inch, with an armoured belt of from 7 inches to 4 inches and achieving a speed of 21 knots. These ships, ingenious though their design was, were basically, however, small pre-dreadnought battleships. So, too, were the Italian cruisers designed by Vittorio Cuniberti, the first of which, the *Regina Elena*, was laid down in 1901. But with their powerful armament of two 12-inch and twelve 8-inch guns mounted in a ship of only 12,500 tons and with a speed of 22 knots they were an added incentive for the British Navy to apply the dreadnought principle to the construction of its new cruisers.

As in the case of the *Dreadnought* the two essential features of the battle-cruiser were the elimination of the intermediate-sized guns in favour of more of the biggest calibre and the provision of high and reliable top speed by turbine drive. The latter, in accordance with Admiral Fisher's dictum that speed was a ship's best protection, was to be provided by Parsons' turbines of 41,000 horse-power driving four screws to give a speed of 25 knots, at the expense of side armour protection. The result was the *Inflexible*, laid down on the Clyde in February 1906 and followed soon afterwards by the *Indomitable* and *Invincible*—armoured cruisers (soon to be reclassified as battle-cruisers) of 17,250 tons, mounting eight 12-inch guns in twin turrets and sixteen 4-inch quick-firers.

Impressive as these ships were, with an armament permitting them to engage battleships, they possessed an Achilles heel in their light armour protection, which was only 6 inches thick amidships tapering to 4 inches at the bow with no belt abaft the after turret. When the German Navy built its first battle-cruiser, the *Von der Tann*, laid down in 1907, by giving her eight 11-inch guns as compared to the 12-inch of the *Inflexible* and a displacement of 19,000 tons, it was possible to apply a complete armoured belt of $9\frac{3}{4}$ inches amidships, tapering to 4 inches at bow and stern. With this, and a speed of more than 25 knots provided by her Parsons' turbines, the *Von der Tann* was to prove greatly superior to contemporary British battle-cruisers. The three ships of the *Inflexible* class were followed in 1911 and 1912 by the *Indefatigable* and *New Zealand*, of similar size and armament.

The Germans followed the *Von der Tann* with the *Moltke*, completed in 1911, of 22,635 tons displacement, and the *Seydlitz* in the following year, displacing 24,605 tons. Restricting their main armament to 11-inch guns, of which each mounted ten in twin turrets, German designers were able to give them an armour belt with a thickness of 12 inches maximum as compared to the 7 inches of contemporary British battle-cruisers. The same applied to the last German battle-cruiser built to be completed before the outbreak of the First World War, the *Derfflinger*. Mounting eight 12-inch guns as compared to the eight 13·5-inch of the *Lion* class, she was given much heavier and more complete protection.

Of the other major navies, only the Japanese adopted the battle-cruiser design in the years prior to the First World War. In order to profit by the experience gained by the British in the design of such ships, they ordered their first battle-cruiser in January 1911 from Vickers for delivery two and a half years later. This ship, the *Kongo*, launched in May 1912, displaced 27,500 tons and mounted eight 14-inch and sixteen 6-inch guns and eight 21-inch submerged torpedo tubes. Parsons' turbines of 70,000 horse-power and Yarrow water-tube boilers gave her a speed of 28 knots. In the arrangement of her turrets and in general appearance and size she was very similar to the British *Tiger* launched nineteen months after her. Three sister ships, *Hiyei*, *Kirishima* and *Haruna*, were built in Japanese yards and completed in 1914.

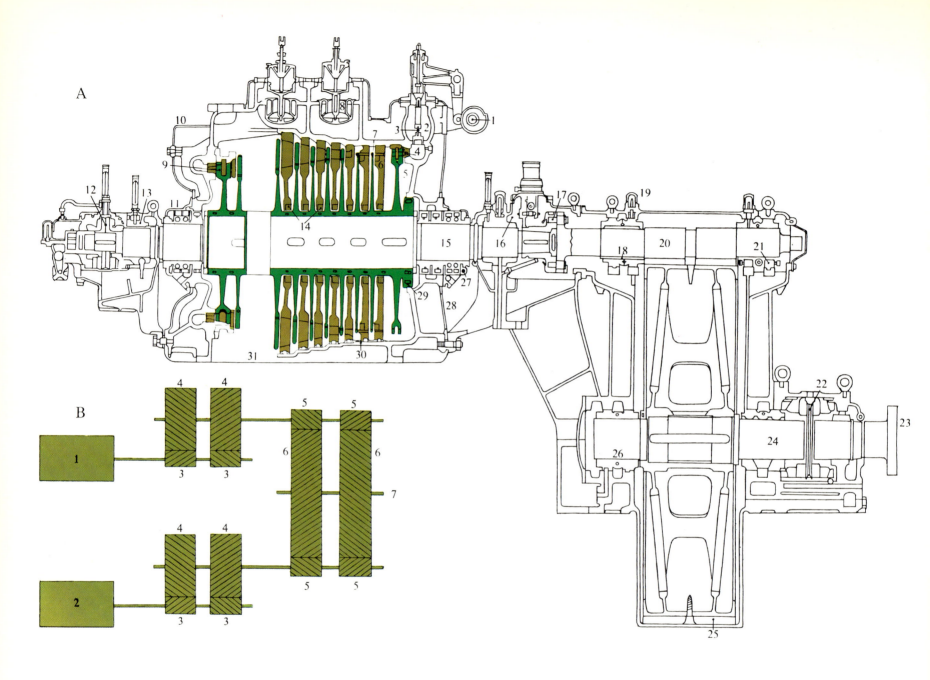

A

B

A *Minesweeper turbine*

1 Cam shaft
2 Steam inlet
3 Nozzle control valve or
   throttle valve
4 Nozzle block
5 Velocity stage (Curtis)
6 Diaphragm
7 Wheel
8 By-pass valve
9 Astern turbine
   elements

10 Shield
11 Steam-sealed packing
12 Thrust bearing
13 Bearing
14 Shaft packings
15 Turbine shaft
16 Bearing
17 Coupling
18 Bearing
19 Sight glass
20 Pinion

21 Gear
22 Thrust bearing
23 Line-shaft flange
24 Shaft
25 Gear
26 Bearing
27 Turbine gland
28 Shield
29 Shaft packing
30 Casing
31 Foundation

B *Double-reduction gear*

1 H.P. turbine
2 L.P. turbine
3 1st reduction pinion
4 1st reduction gear
5 2nd reduction pinion
6 2nd reduction gear
   (main gear)
7 To propeller shaft

THE TURBINE

Engineering developments following the invention of the steam reciprocating engine called for ever more power. This entailed larger engines turning at higher speeds, the movement of heavy metal masses being reversed hundreds of times a minute. The strain on the engines themselves as well as on their foundations, and so on the ship's structure, was approaching the bearable limit. Some other way of utilising steam power to rotate propeller shafts was clearly needed.

The solution was obviously to turn a wheel or a cylinder by blowing a jet of steam against blades attached to it. Several such devices had been invented, but had not been developed into practical machines, when the Hon. Charles Parsons, head of an engineering firm at Gateshead-on-Tyne, in 1884 patented his first compound steam turbine.

Steam turbines may be of the impulse type in which steam passes through stationary, divergent nozzles against a single ring of vanes mounted on the periphery of a revolving wheel; in this case, the expansion of the steam taking place entirely in the nozzles, the potential energy of the steam is turned into kinetic energy and it emerges from the nozzles at a very high velocity. Such a turbine revolves at extremely high speed and is unsuitable for driving a ship's propeller shaft except through gearing providing a high degree of reduction.

To overcome this difficulty, Parsons devised an engine composed of a number of successive turbines of increasing diameter allowing a more gradual expansion of the steam as it passed through alternate rows of fixed and moving blades, the former acting as nozzles to direct the steam on to the next set of moving blades on the periphery of the turbine rotor.

The first turbine to be installed in a ship was of this type, the ship being the *Turbinia*, a small high-speed craft constructed in 1897 in which year it was demonstrated at the Fleet Review in Spithead, where she steamed up and down between the lines of assembled warships at some 34 knots. So impressed were the British Admiralty that the first turbine-driven destroyer, the *Viper*, was built in 1899 at the shipyard of Hawthorn, Leslie and Company on the Tyne. She achieved the record speed of 36·58 knots.

Parsons' turbines were now more and more in demand for ships of all kinds, the first light cruisers to receive them being the British *Amethyst* and the German *Lübeck*, laid down in 1903. In 1905 one of the most revolutionary features of the epoch-making *Dreadnought* was her Parsons' turbines, driving her smoothly and reliably at 21 knots. For many years Parsons' turbines held a virtual monopoly; but eventually rival types were developed, notably the American Curtis which combined the features of the impulse turbine with those of Parsons' compound type by expanding the steam in several stages, one wheel being provided for each stage. Other types which were adopted for warships were the French Rateau and the German Zoelly and Schulz.

For all its manifest advantages over the reciprocating engine, the direct-acting turbine was uneconomical when run at low or moderate speeds. To obviate this,

The Hon. Charles Parsons (1854–1931), inventor of the reaction steam turbine and adapter of it to marine propulsion (1897), when it was first demonstrated in his high-speed vessel *Turbinia*.

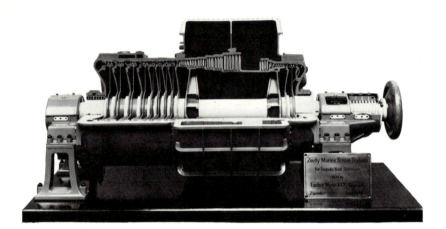

An early marine turbine engine.

the next development was inevitably to insert reduction gearing between the turbine and the propeller shaft, so getting the greatest efficiency out of both turbine and propeller. This was first introduced experimentally in the British Navy with the H.P. turbines of the destroyers *Badger* and *Beaver* in 1911. This was followed in 1914 by the application of reduction gearing to all the turbines of the destroyers *Leonidas* and *Lucifer*, in which double helical gears with involute teeth were arranged to give a single reduction. This system proved surprisingly free of vibration and had an acceptable degree of noise. Furthermore the life of the teeth exceeded all expectations. It was therefore adopted in all types of British men-of-war and was generally followed elsewhere. A notable exception was the U.S. Navy, in whose later super-dreadnoughts similar results were achieved by means of electric drive, partly on account of a dearth of gear-cutting capacity in the United States.

Electric drive was first tried out in the U.S. Navy in 1913 in the collier *Jupiter* (which was subsequently converted into the U.S. Navy's first aircraft carrier). So successful was it that electric drive was incorporated in the battleship *New Mexico*, laid down in October 1915, and in all subsequent U.S. battleships and battle-cruisers built or projected until 1937, when the U.S. Navy fell into line with all others by adopting geared turbines for the fast battleships laid down in that year.

Electric drive had certain advantages. The propelling machinery could be electrically controlled by switches which could be sited in any convenient part of the ship; full power was available for going astern; turbines operated at constant speed as in a shore power station so that high temperatures of super-heat could be readily adopted with a resultant gain in steaming economy. On the other hand it inserted an additional link in the chain of power transmission, a link which was highly vulnerable, a fact demonstrated during the Battle of Jutland when switches were thrown out and circuits broken in several British ships under the shock of explosions. Furthermore, reduction gearing induced a lower transmission loss and was very much cheaper to manufacture and install.

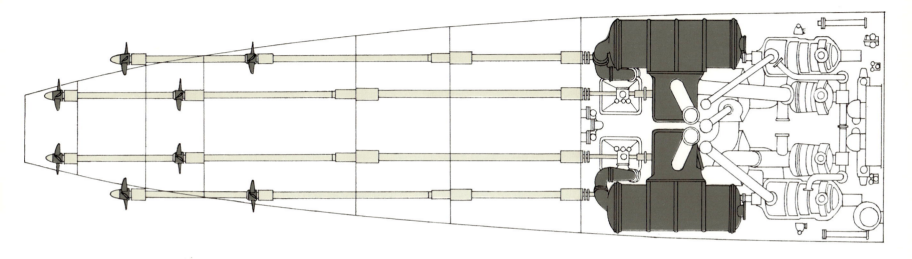

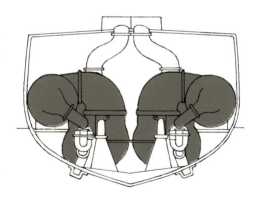

Diagram of the layout of the machinery of the first turbine-driven destroyer, H.M.S. *Viper* (1899).

H.M.S. *Shah* (1873), a slow, unarmoured but heavily armed cruiser whose failure to subdue the piratical Peruvian monitor *Huascar* in 1877 demonstrated the defects of such a design.

So far, consideration has been confined mainly to the effect of the advent of the age of steam and steel on the major warships of the world's navies, the capital ships as they came to be eventually called, and to some extent to the 'boats'— submarines and torpedo boats. Between these two extremes was developing at the same time the wide variety of ships which, descended from the frigates, corvettes and sloops of the days of sail, were at first collectively designated 'cruising vessels'.

The nomenclature of the mid-nineteenth century is confusing to the student of today. The first armoured and steam-driven warships such as the *Gloire* and the *Warrior* were classed as frigates owing to their single tier of guns, though they were more than a match for any existing ship-of-the-line. During the following decade, steam-driven ships of some 6000 tons displacement like the *Shah* and the *Inconstant* in the British Navy were also classed as steam frigates, although they mounted 10-inch and 9-inch guns, while ships of between 2000 and 4000 tons such as the French *Alma* class, which displaced 3700 tons, and the *Sané* class of 2000 tons, which had a speed of 14 knots, were classed as corvettes.

In 1887 the frigates and corvettes of the British Navy were reclassed as cruisers, and, as design progressed, were subdivided into 'belted', 'protected', and 'armoured' cruisers. For clarity, in this book, all intermediate warships between battleships on the one hand and torpedo craft, sloops and gunboats on the other, during the nineteenth century, will be called cruisers and their development will be examined together. Ideally, their characteristics included a fairly high speed, relatively moderate displacement and gun calibre, and an extended radius of action. This qualified them to carry out the policing and 'flag-showing' duties on foreign stations during peace, to act as scouts for the main fleets and to patrol the trade routes during war. On account of their peace-time functions they retained their sailing rig longer than battleships, the first 'mastless' British cruiser being H.M.S. *Blake*, launched in 1889. Impetus towards the construction of large cruisers with a fair turn of speed, for the British Navy, was given by the impressive performance attributed to the *Wampanoag* class of cruisers built for the U.S. Navy about 1863. These wooden ships were intended for commerce raiding and designed by the Engineer-in-Chief, Benjamin Franklin Isherwood. The *Wampanoag* achieved the record speed of 17½ knots on trials and, with an armament of ten 8-inch smooth-bore guns, two 100-pounders, two 24-pounder howitzers and one 60-pounder rifled pivot-gun, could catch any ship she wished and escape from any that outgunned her.

Though others of this class, with machinery of a different design from Isherwood's, were much slower, the *Wampanoag*'s performance made a considerable impression on British naval opinion and resulted in the first British ships that can be classed as cruisers in the modern idiom, the *Inconstant* and the *Shah*, launched in 1868 and 1873. Constructed of iron, their hulls were sheathed in wood and coppered to combine additional strength with protection from marine growth and teredo worm, major considerations for ships intended for prolonged commissions on foreign and tropical stations. Sheathing and coppering remained a feature of cruisers long after iron hulls were replaced by steel. These two ships were heavily armed, the *Shah* having no less than twenty-eight guns of which two were 10-inch and sixteen were 6-inch, while the *Inconstant* mounted ten 9-inch and six 6-inch. They were amongst the first ships to be equipped to launch Whitehead torpedoes. They proved to be too large and clumsy, their armament too large and slow-firing for their function as cruisers. When the *Shah* engaged the piratical Peruvian monitor *Huascar* in 1877 off the Bay of Ilo, the limitations of the British ship became evident. During the engagement, which was carried on for some three hours at a range of between 1500 and 2500 yards, the *Huascar* was repeatedly hit but neither her 4½-inch side armour nor her turret was penetrated even by the *Shah*'s 10-inch guns. One British projectile which pierced the *Huascar*'s port quarter, where the armour was only 2¼ to 3 inches thick, did not explode. The *Huascar*, whose shooting was, fortunately for the unarmoured *Shah*, wild and ineffective, finally escaped by making for shallow water along the coast where the cruiser could not follow her. During the action a Whitehead torpedo was launched from the *Shah*, but the *Huascar* altered course at that moment and the torpedo failed to hit.

In the twenty years following the launching of the *Inconstant*, a great variety of unarmoured 'cruising vessels' was built by all navies. They mostly lacked the speed necessary for their duties with the fleet and, being virtually unprotected, had little value except as gunboats on foreign stations, for which purpose they mounted an unnecessarily large amount of heavy, slow-shooting guns. Typical of such ships were the American cruiser *Chicago*, with a speed of 18 knots, mounting two 8-inch and six 6-inch guns on a displacement of 4500 tons, and the smaller British cruisers of the *Archer* class which carried six 6-inch guns on a displacement of 1770 tons.

French cruisers of that period were the *Tourville* and *Duquesne* which, with a displacement of 5500 tons, a speed of 17 knots and an armament of 7·6-inch and 5·5-inch guns, were designated first-class cruisers; the second-class cruiser *Duguay-Trouin* of 3200 tons and 16 knots; and the *Villars* class and the *Éclaireur* of 2250 tons and 1650 tons, respectively, which were third-class cruisers.

The desirability of cruisers having some degree of armour protection for their vitals led finally to the development of the armoured deck, ships so fitted being called 'protected cruisers'. A protective deck was first incorporated in the British warship *Shannon* as early as 1875, and the *Nelson* and *Northampton* which followed her. But these ships of nearly 6000 tons, carrying also an armour belt on the water-line, and so really the first example of an 'armoured cruiser', were designated as second-class battleships. With a speed of only 14 knots, and a broadside armament, however, they were satisfactory neither as battleships nor as cruisers.

147

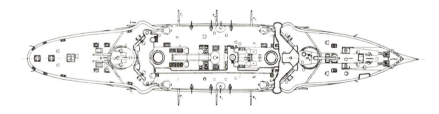

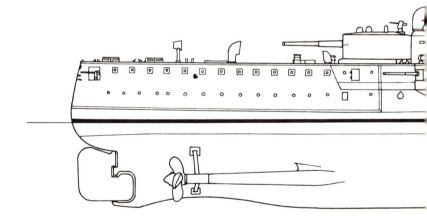

WAMPANOAG

American cruiser *Wampanoag* (1867)

which, with a speed of $16\frac{3}{4}$ knots, was the fastest ship in

the world of her day.

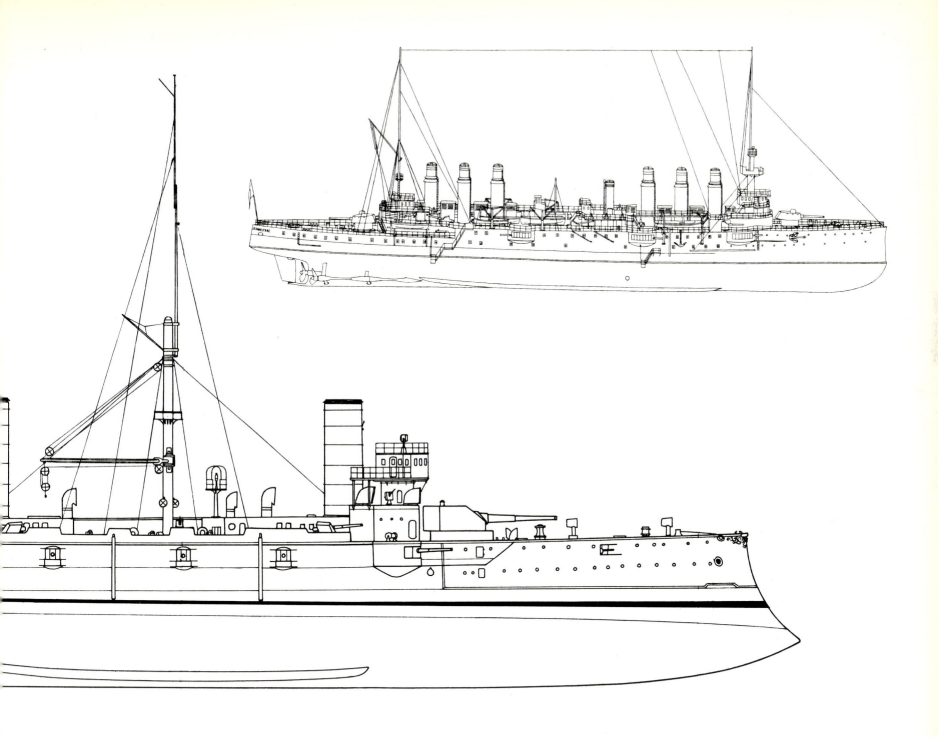

GIUSEPPE GARIBALDI

Italian armoured cruiser *Giuseppe Garibaldi*,
designed by General Masdea, one of a most powerful class built for several navies
from 1893 onwards. (*Above and page 148*, deck longitudinal.)

JEANNE D'ARC

French armoured cruiser *Jeanne d'Arc* (1899), a type which came to
supersede the protected cruiser.

Soon afterwards the French Navy constructed similar scaled-down battleships (*cuirassés de croisière* or *cuirassés de station*) of the *Dueguesclin* class of which the *Bayard* served as the flagship of Admiral Courbet in the war with China in 1884–85. Such ships were of some 6000 tons, were protected by an armoured belt 6½ inches to 10 inches thick and mounted four to six 9·4-inch and six 5·5-inch guns. Russian ships of a similar type were the *Vladimir Monomach* and *Dmitri Donskoi*.

The first true cruisers to be given the protected deck were the British *Comus* class of 2200 tons in 1878, which were followed by the four ships of the *Leander* class of 4300 tons. The chief French naval constructor at this time, the celebrated Émile Bertin, had for some years been advocating the *tranche cellulaire* system of protection—a cellular layer of small compartments sometimes filled with cork over a protected deck. The first French protected cruiser built to his design was the *Sfax*, launched in 1882. She had this cellular system which had also been incorporated by Benedetto Brin in the Italian battleships *Italia* and *Lepanto* described on page 120. The *Sfax*, with a speed of 16·7 knots and an armament of six 6·4-inch and two 5·5-inch guns, was a very successful cruiser.

The protected cruiser really came into its own, however, when in 1883 the Elswick yard of Sir William Armstrong, where Mr. William White was Chief Constructor, launched the *Esmeralda*, built for the Chilean Navy to Armstrong's design. She had an armoured deck, 1 inch thick, with sloping sides extending below the water-line. With a displacement of 2950 tons and a speed of 18·3 knots, she had the ideal characteristics for a cruiser, except for the inclusion of two heavy 10-inch guns in her armament. She was the first cruiser to discard masts and yards.

So successful was the *Esmeralda* that all navies aspired to possess similar ships. From the Elswick yard Argentina bought several, while Italy, which had bought the *Giovanni Bausan* from Armstrong's in 1885, went on to build three similar cruisers of the *Etna* class. The type was also copied by the Austrian Navy in the *Kaiser Franz Joseph I* and the *Kaiserin Elisabeth*. The similar *Naniwa* of the Japanese Navy and the *Irene* and *Prinzess Wilhelm* of the German Navy were also built between 1885 and 1887.

In the British Navy the new trend led to the construction in 1885 of the *Mersey* class of 4050 tons, mounting two 8-inch guns and ten 6-inch, the *Medea* class of 2800 tons with six 6-inch in 1888 and finally the *Blake* in 1890, a ship of 9000 tons, mounting two 9·2-inch and ten 6-inch guns, with a speed of 20 knots.

American protected cruisers of this period were the *Charleston* of 3370 tons, a speed of some 18 knots and a mixed armament of 8-inch and 6-inch breech-loaders, and the similar, though slightly larger, *Baltimore*, *Philadelphia*, *San Francisco* and *Newark*. All these ships depended for their main armament on heavy, unwieldy breech-loading guns with too slow a rate of fire for the cruiser's tasks in peace and war.

A new development with this type of ship came about, therefore, with the introduction of quick-firing guns in which the breech could be opened by a single movement of the breech lever. Protected cruisers were given an armament of a large number of such weapons, 6-inch or smaller, instead of the fewer, heavier breech-loaders of their predecessors. The successful prototype of this class of ship, the *Dogali*, was again built by the Elswick firm, this time for the Italian Navy, in 1888. With a complete protective deck of 2 inches of armour on the sloping sides and 1 inch on the horizontal portion and a speed of 19·6 knots, the *Dogali* mounted a main armament of six 6-inch quick-firing guns in addition to a number of smaller guns and four torpedo tubes on a displacement of 2088 tons.

A year later the Italian Navy took delivery of another Armstrong cruiser, the *Piemonte*, designed by Sir Philip Watts, later famous as designer of H.M.S. *Dreadnought*, which, on a displacement of 2640 tons, incorporated a 3-inch protective deck and a battery of six 4·7-inch quick-firers as well as a main armament of six 6-inch. The *Piemonte*'s speed was more than 22 knots. Both the *Dogali* and the *Piemonte* gave satisfactory service over many years, the latter

remaining in service until 1920, the former ten years more, as flagship of the Uruguayan Navy, thus maintaining the high reputation of the Elswick cruisers.

The quick-firing gun was now adopted by most other navies for their protected cruisers, though the British Navy continued to build a number of larger ships carrying heavy breech-loading guns as well as a great many cruisers of medium or small size with an armament of quick-firers. Of the former there were the ships of the *Edgar* class completed in 1891, mounting two 9·2-inch guns and ten 6-inch on a displacement of 7350 tons, and the *Crescent* class of 7700 tons, mounting one 9·2-inch and twelve 6-inch guns. These had a speed of 18 knots and a protective deck of 5 inches of armour. Designated first-class protected cruisers, this type of ship increased in size over the years reaching a maximum with the 14,200-ton *Powerful* and *Terrible* in 1895 which mounted two 9·2-inch guns in turrets, sixteen 6-inch guns and sixteen 3-inch. They had a 6-inch protective deck and a speed of 22 knots. Second-class protected cruisers were those with a main armament of 6-inch guns, typical of these being the *Astraea* class of 4360 tons, a speed of 20 knots and an armament of two 6-inch and eight 4·7-inch guns, built in 1893, and the *Dido* class of 1895–96, 5600 tons displacement, mounting eleven 6-inch quick-firing guns and nine 3-inch. Smaller cruisers with a displacement between 1580 tons, such as the *Barrosa* class of 1889 which mounted six 4·7-inch quick-firers, and the 2200 tons of the *Pelorus* class of 1896–99 with eight 4-inch guns, were designated third-class protected cruisers.

Other navies restricted themselves partly to the smaller types of protected cruisers. Typical examples were the Italian *Lombardia* class of 2730 tons, mounting four 6-inch and six 4·7-inch quick-firers, a development of the original Armstrong design. With a top speed of 17 to 18 knots and a radius of action of 4000 miles at 10 knots, they were designed expressly for service on distant stations, in which employment they proved very successful. Other cruisers of the period were the Japanese *Kasagi* and *Chitose* of 4760 tons, built in the United States and carrying two 8-inch breech-loaders and ten 4·4-inch quick firers; the six ships of the German *Bussard* class of 1890–95, mounting eight 4·1-inch quick-firers, the *Gazelle* of 1900, followed by the *Niobe* class with a displacement of 2360 tons and a battery of ten 4·1-inch guns; the United States Navy's second-class protected cruisers of the *Cleveland* class which mounted ten 5-inch quick-firers on a displacement of 3200 tons.

The French Navy similarly restricted themselves to a moderate tonnage for their protected cruisers, the *Jean Bart*, *Cassard* and *Descartes* classes of some 4000 tons being intended for scouting duties, while smaller, third-class cruisers of around 2000 tons were also built. For employment on foreign stations was commissioned the 8000-ton *D'Entrecasteaux* with a speed of 19½ knots, while the faster *Chateau Renault* and *Guichen* of a similar size but with a speed of 23 knots were designed to operate as commerce raiders in the *guerre-de-course* which French policy at the end of the nineteenth century envisaged under the influence of Admiral Aube and the 'Jeune École'.

It was the great improvement in armour plate brought about by the Harvey, Krupp and Schneider methods of treating steel and the increasing effectiveness of quick-firing guns and high-explosive shells which led to the next development, that of the armoured cruiser. The destructive power of the new guns and ammunition, as demonstrated in trials by the French Navy, using the old armoured corvette *Belliqueuse* as a target, was such that the protective deck was no longer considered adequate. The sides of the ship had also to be armoured. Up to now this had not been possible owing to the great weight of armour required to be effective.

But from Harvey and Krupp steel armour of only 6 inches thickness could now be made capable of resisting penetration by all but the largest guns, which allowed ships of moderate tonnage to be given an armour belt without too great a sacrifice in operational range and speed. The first ship to take advantage of this was the French cruiser *Dupuy de Lôme*, launched in 1890.

Along the whole length of the ship ran an armoured belt of 4 inches of Harvey steel, to the lower edge of which was joined a domed protective deck of

$1\frac{1}{2}$ inches. Below this deck, covering the machinery spaces, was a splinter deck, the space between the two decks being filled with coal as an additional protection. The space behind the armoured belt was occupied by a watertight structure $3\frac{1}{4}$ feet wide, divided into small compartments and filled with cellulose. This system of 'defence in depth' was an innovation which, in one form or another, was to be extensively used in other armoured ships, notably the British *Majestic* class of battleships. The *Dupuy de Lôme* made use of three propellers, one central and one on each side, a feature thereafter to be found in all French cruisers. Her hull was also characteristic of French construction of that period, with a considerable 'tumble-home' and a projecting ram bow so pronounced that it did away with the normal forecastle. The poop was similarly cut away aft. She was followed, between 1892 and 1895, by the four armoured cruisers of the *Admiral Charner* class and the *Pothuau*, all of similar construction.

The French Navy at this time was strongly influenced by the theories of Admiral Aube and the 'Jeune École', which condemned the battleship as obsolete. Mounting the new, quick-firing guns, firing shells filled with the new powerful explosives, armoured cruisers, they believed, would be able to destroy the unprotected areas of battleships, thus affecting the stability of these 'easily capsizable' types.

It was not until the French Navy in 1896 laid down the *Jeanne d'Arc* of 11,270 tons displacement, a speed of 23 knots and an armament of two 7·6-inch guns in turrets and fourteen 5·5-inch quick-firers, with a complete armoured belt of 5·9-inch steel armour as well as a protective deck, that the British Navy followed suit with the *Cressy* class. These 21-knot ships, on a displacement of 12,000 tons, mounted two 9·2-inch guns in turrets and twelve 6-inch quick-firers and had a 6-inch armoured belt.

The Russian Navy's *Rossia*, launched in 1896, was of similar type, though she and the somewhat larger (13,220 tons) *Gromoboi* mounted no less than twenty-two 6-inch guns as well as four 8-inch.

These ships and the *Rurik*, completed four years earlier, were given the very large coal capacity of 2500 tons, enabling them to steam 19,000 miles at 10 knots —from the Baltic to the Pacific—without refuelling.

From this time onwards the armoured cruiser was to be found in all the major navies, superseding the protected cruiser. One of the most successful designs was that of the Italian *Garibaldi* class, designed by General Masdea under the influence of Brin, the first two of which were laid down in 1893.

On a displacement of 7350 tons, they mounted a main armament of either one 10-inch gun forward and aft, one 10-inch forward and two 8-inch aft, or two 8-inch forward and aft. The secondary armament of the first four consisted of five 6-inch and three 4·7-inch each side; later versions had seven 6-inch and five 3-inch each side. Masdea had adopted Brin's suggestion that 25 per cent of the weight should be devoted to protection, 15 per cent to the armament and 20 per cent to the machinery. This gave the *Garibaldi*'s a horse-power of 14,000, a top speed of 20 knots, a complete armoured belt of 6 inches of nickel steel tapering to 3·2 inches at the ends and a protective deck of 1·2 to 1·9 inches. In addition the barbettes were of 6-inch armour, while the deck above the gun battery was of $1\frac{1}{2}$ inches.

So much admired were these ships that, of the first eight to be laid down, four were bought by Argentina and one by Spain, the other three joining the Italian Navy as the *Giuseppe Garibaldi*, *Varese* and *Francesco Ferrucio*. Two others were built for Argentina later but were bought by the Japanese in time to play a notable part in the Russo–Japanese War as the *Kasuga* and *Nisshin*.

The Italian Navy went on to lay down two 23-knot, 10,000-ton armoured cruisers, the *Pisa* and *Amalfi*, in 1905, following them with the *San Marco* and *San Giorgio*, in the former of which Parsons' turbines replaced the reciprocating engines. Not commissioned until 1909, however, these ships, with their mixed main armament of 10-inch and 7·5-inch guns, had already been made obsolete by the advent of the all-big-gun battle-cruiser.

Across the Atlantic, the U.S. Navy had also taken advantage of the advent of

French second-class cruiser *Duguay-Trouin* (1877).

German armoured cruiser *Fürst Bismarck* (1897) portrayed in Hong Kong in 1909 by the painter Alexander Kircher.

Harvey steel to build its first armoured cruiser, the *New York*, in 1891, displacing 8200 tons and armed with six 8-inch guns and twelve 4-inch quick-firers. Only one other such ship was added, however, the *Brooklyn* in 1895, before the naval expansion which began in 1902 when six ships of the *Colorado* class of 13,800 tons, mounting four 8-inch, fourteen 6-inch and eighteen 3-inch guns, were laid down. They were followed by four ships, the even bigger *Tennessee* class launched between 1903 and 1905 which mounted the formidable mixed armament of four 10-inch, sixteen 6-inch and twenty-two 3-inch guns on a displacement of 14,500 tons and had a complete belt of 3 to 5 inches of Krupp armour.

The French and British were, however, the principal builders of armoured cruisers, each class being of greater displacement than the last, rising to the 13,780 tons of the French *Edgar Quinet*, launched in 1907, which mounted fourteen 7·6-inch guns in turrets or casemates, and the 1906 British *Minotaur* class of 14,600 tons with a mixed armament of four 9·2-inch guns in twin turrets fore and aft, and ten 7·5-inch in single turrets on the beam.

Meanwhile the Germans, as part of their programme of naval expansion in rivalry with the British, had developed a similar type of ship, starting with the *Fürst Bismarck* of 1897 of 10,650 tons which had a belt of Krupp steel with a thickness of 8 inches maximum and mounted four 9·4-inch guns in twin turrets, six 5·9-inch in single turrets and six more in casemates. Five other ships of around 9000 tons followed between 1900 and 1903 before the famous *Scharnhorst* and *Gneisenau* were launched in 1906.

The age of the armoured cruiser with a mixed armament was now over, superseded in its turn by the all-big-gun battle-cruiser which, as the *Dreadnought* had done with battleships, made all its cruiser predecessors obsolete. The German Navy's last orthodox armoured cruisers were the *Scharnhorst* and *Gneisenau*, mounting eight 8·2-inch guns and six 5·9-inch on a displacement of 11,420 tons, which gained fame by their victory at the Battle of Coronel over the outdated British cruisers *Good Hope* and *Monmouth*, only themselves to be similarly overwhelmed when brought to action off the Falkland Islands by the battle-cruisers *Inflexible* and *Invincible*.

At first misunderstanding the revolution in cruiser design brought about by the dreadnought concept, the Germans, before adopting the battle-cruiser design with the *Von der Tann*, followed the *Scharnhorst* and *Gneisenau* with a hybrid type, the *Blücher*, completed in 1908. With a displacement of 15,500 tons and the remarkable speed of 25·8 knots provided by three sets of triple-expansion reciprocating engines, enabling her to keep up with battle-cruisers, the *Blücher* was out of her class when employed with them owing to her 8·2-inch guns and comparatively light armour protection. In the running fight off the Dogger Bank in 1915 she was able to do little but accept the hammering from the British battle-cruisers' 13·5- and 12-inch guns which sent her to the bottom.

Although with the coming of the armoured cruiser, protected cruisers ceased to be built, a requirement remained for small, fast warships to reconnoitre for the fleets, mounting an armament of light, quick-firing guns to engage their enemy equivalents or torpedo craft and relying upon their speed to avoid action with heavy enemy ships. Early examples of this sort of ship were the 'torpedo cruisers' built for the French and Italian navies between 1885 and 1890, ships of less than 1000 tons displacement, unarmoured, carrying half a dozen small quick-firers.

The French ships of this type, such as the *Wattignies* and *Condor*, had a speed of 18 knots. Italian equivalents were the *Tripoli*, launched in 1886, followed by the *Goito* and *Partenope* classes, all of around 850 tons and having a speed of 20 knots. In 1899 the Italians built two larger and faster torpedo cruisers, the *Coatit* and *Agordat* of 1313 tons and a speed of 23 knots, which mounted twelve 3-inch and eight 6-pounder quick-firers. These two ships can be said to have been the forerunners of the type which was to be known as the 'light cruiser' in the dreadnought era. For the Russian Navy, the German Schichau yard built the 3000-ton *Novik*, completed in 1900, which made a notable name for herself during the Russo-Japanese War. She carried an armament of six 4·7-inch guns and six

above-water torpedo tubes. Three sets of four-cylinder, triple-expansion engines and twelve water-tube boilers of the Thornycroft type gave her a speed of 25 knots. Three similar but slower cruisers were built at other yards, one of them by Burmeister & Wain, Copenhagen.

At about the same time the French built the larger, fast cruiser *Jurien de la Gravière* of 5500 tons, a speed of 23 knots and an armament of eight 6·4-inch guns, intended for scouting duties; but they did not persist with this type, nor did they take to the smaller type of 'Scout' which the British Navy began to build in 1903.

Eight ships of this type, the first of which was the *Sentinel*, were built between 1903 and 1904 with a displacement of 2900 tons, an armament of nine 4-inch guns and two 18-inch torpedo tubes and a speed of 25 knots. Subsequent classes were designated light cruisers, the size increasing, first to the 3300 tons of the *Bellona* and *Blanche* classes, then to the 5000 tons of the 'Town' class, launched between 1909 and 1914.

At about this time the Italian Navy launched their first light cruisers, three ships of some 3500 tons, *Quarto*, *Nino Bixio* and *Marsala*, mounting six 4·7-inch and six 3-inch guns, but which, by adopting oil fuel and destroyer-type machinery, achieved a speed of 29 knots. The German Navy, too, after building cruisers roughly equivalent to the British types, such as the *Königsberg* class of 3396 tons and the *Cöln* of 4280 tons, mounting ten and twelve 4·1-inch guns respectively, launched the first of the *Breslau* class in 1911, which, though coal-fired, achieved 28 knots.

British light cruisers of the 1912–13 programme of the *Arethusa* class were therefore oil-fired and designed, by means of fast-running, destroyer-type machinery, for 30 knots, though only 29 knots was achieved in practice. The last light cruisers to be laid down before the outbreak of the First World War comprised twelve ships of the *Calliope* class of similar size and speed, but incorporating for the first time the new geared turbine.

Of smaller types of warship, the torpedo boat, the destroyer and the submarine are examined in sections devoted to them in particular.

During the latter part of the nineteenth century and the first forty years of the twentieth, however, the colonial era it may be called, navies of the great powers had need of types of warship other than those which formed their main fleets. As European and American commercial interests spread through Asia, Africa and South America, the need arose to support and protect the trading communities which had taken up residence amongst sometimes unruly and sometimes hostile people and to protect merchant shipping from piratical attacks. For these purposes, besides the foreign station cruisers, small ships of a number of different types were built and maintained in distant parts. They were known to the world at large as 'gunboats', but were more correctly divided into types such as 'sloops', 'gunboats', 'river monitors' and 'river gunboats' in the British Navy, and equivalent names in other navies.

Typical of British 'sloops' at the turn of the century were four ships of the *Espiegle* class of some 1070 tons, wood-sheathed and coppered for service in waters where docking facilities were scarce, driven by twin sets of triple-expansion steam-engines at the modest top speed of 13 knots, mounting six 4-inch guns and rigged for sail. French equivalents were the *Kersaint* of 1243 tons and the three ships of the *Zélée* class of 646 tons. The German Navy built six ships of the *Eber* and *Jaguar* classes of some 900 tons, while the United States Navy had gunboats such as the *Helena* of 1397 tons, built in 1895, and the *Dubuque* of 1085 tons, in 1904.

As European traders penetrated inland in Asia and Africa up the great waterways such as the Yangtse-kiang in China, the need arose for river gunboats, flat-bottomed craft which would come to no great harm from grounding on the ever-shifting sandbanks, and of sufficiently light draught to navigate the shallow stretches of the rivers. The French began as early as 1884 to build a number of ships such as the *Bobillot* of 120 tons and a draught of less than 2 feet and the

Berthe de Villers of 180 tons and a draught of 2 feet 4 inches, both driven by stern paddle-wheels at about 9 knots.

During the 1890s a number of such shallow-draught boats were built for service in China, on the River Congo, on Lake Chad, on waterways in Dahomey and on the rivers of Indo-China, some propelled by stern paddle-wheels, some by screws. Most were built in sections and could be transported overland. One such boat, the *Faidherbe*, was carried by African porters from Lake Chad to the upper reaches of the Nile in the famous expedition of Captain (later General) Marchand which caused friction between England and France when he occupied Fashoda, leading to a dispute between France and Britain with regard to the Sudan.*

The British Navy first acquired river gunboats for service in China in 1897 when two 150-ton flat-bottomed boats, *Woodcock* and *Woodlark*, with a draught of only 2 feet were built by Thornycroft's on the Thames and four smaller, 85-ton boats of a similar type were built by Yarrow's. Two Thornycroft boats, *Vigilante* and *Argus*, were also built for the French Navy in 1900. Three years later the Japanese bought, for the same purpose, a Thornycroft boat, the *Sumida*, and from Yarrow's acquired the *Fushimi* of 180 tons and a draught of 2 feet 4 inches. Constructed in sections and erected where required, their twin-screws worked in tunnels to save them from damage on the numerous occasions of grounding, giving a speed of 13 knots to the Thornycroft boats, 9 knots to the smaller, Yarrow boats. The main armament of both types consisted of two 6-pounders. Boats of this type were to be a familiar feature of the river scene on the Yangtse and Pearl Rivers for the next thirty years.

Although, in point of time, it is taking us ahead of our story, the later river gunboats built for the British Navy are contained in this section. They were of two classes and both were built early in the First World War primarily for service on the River Tigris during the campaign in Mesopotamia against the Turks.

The 'Fly' class, built by Yarrow's in sections and transported to Abadan for erection in 1915 and 1916, were of 98 tons displacement, 126 feet in length and 2-foot draught. Their single screws, working in tunnels, gave a speed of $9\frac{1}{2}$ knots. Their armament was one 4-inch, one 3-inch, one 6-pounder, one 3-pounder and a 2-pounder 'pom-pom', automatic gun.

A larger type, the 'Insect' class, was ordered at about the same time, initially for an intended expedition on the River Danube which, in the event, did not take place. In the interests of secrecy these boats were designated 'China gunboats' while building, though their first employment, as with the 'Fly' class, was on the Tigris in support of the British Army. Of 625 tons displacement and with an armament of two 6-inch and two 3-inch guns, their flat-bottomed design gave them a draught of only 4 feet. Triple-expansion reciprocating engines of 2000 horse-power drove them at a top speed of 14 knots.

After the war these boats did, in fact, become China gunboats, being towed out to Hong Kong and Shanghai for service on the Pearl River and the Yangtse-kiang where they remained until the outbreak of the Second World War.

The American, German and Japanese navies also stationed gunboats on the Yangtse-kiang after the end of the First World War. The first two American boats to be built were the 190-ton vessels *Monocacy* and *Palos* which had a draught of 2 feet 4 inches and 13 knots. A peculiar feature of these ships was that their boilers were designed to burn wood and no coal was carried, on the mistaken belief that the former was plentiful up the Yangtse and the latter scarce, whereas the opposite was in fact the case.

Germany's first two river gunboats were the *Tsingtau* and the *Vaterland* of 220 tons and 13 knots with a draught of 3 feet, stationed in 1904 on the Pearl River and the Yangtse-kiang respectively. An improved version, the *Otter*, with a speed of 15 knots, followed in 1910. This ship and the *Vaterland* were taken over by the Chinese and were used by them during the Second World War against the Japanese.

* Similar types of boat were used by the British in Africa, such as the *Mosquito*, built in 1890 for service on the Zambesi River.

Top: China gunboat H.M.S. *Heron* (1897), a shallow-draught vessel for operation on the Yangtse-kiang and Pearl River.

Bottom: French river gunboat *Moulun* (1884), one of several built for operation in Indo-China.

American gunboat *Monocacy* (1910).

156

THE DEVELOPMENT OF TORPEDOES,

TORPEDO BOATS AND DESTROYERS

The first torpedoes were not the self-propelled miniature submarines which came to have such a commanding influence on sea warfare in the two world wars. The name torpedo was first given to sea mines; then to explosive charges attached to the end of long spars. These were extended forward from the bows of picket-boats or other small, fast craft and detonated by being rammed against the side of the target ship. Another type was towed, the tow rope being carried out at an angle by a device similar to the trawler fisherman's 'otter' board. Neither of these devices was of practical use against a ship under way or with adequate gun defences and alert to the threat, though the French Admiral Courbet successfully employed the spar torpedo to defeat the Chinese Navy in the Min River in 1884. It was not until a locomotive torpedo was invented which was submersible and self-propelled that such weapons began seriously to affect the armament, design or tactics of the man-of-war. Credit for the first steps in this direction must go to the Austrian, Captain Luppis, though he did not himself go further than to devise a self-propelled, boat-shaped craft, guided by lines attached to its rudder. When his invention was rejected as too crude by the Austrian government, Luppis turned for advice to Mr. Robert Whitehead, the English manager of a marine engine factory at Fiume. The result, after two years' experiment, was the first Luppis-Whitehead torpedo in 1867 in which, by means of a compressed-air engine, a charge of eighteen pounds of dynamite in its head was driven at 6 knots to a range of a few hundred yards.

The Austrian government being unwilling to finance the development even of this improved weapon, Whitehead offered it to other powers and in 1869, after British naval officers from the Mediterranean Fleet reported favourably on a demonstration given to them, Whitehead was invited to bring two torpedoes and a discharging apparatus to England. After experiments there at the end of 1870, the British government bought the right of manufacture for £15,000. Similar rights were subsequently bought by many countries, including France, Germany, Austria, Italy, Russia and Sweden.

Launching gear for Whitehead torpedoes, either from a position on deck or, later, from submerged tubes, soon became a regular feature of all major warships. In 1877 the first locomotive torpedo was launched in action from the British cruiser *Shah* in her fight with the Peruvian monitor *Huascar*, described elsewhere. The attack failed, as did the first attempt to use the Whitehead torpedoes by the Russians in their war with Turkey in the same year. In January 1878, however, history was made when a torpedo launched from the Russian steamer *Constantine* off Batoum hit and sank a Turkish steamer.

Over the years the performance of the locomotive torpedo, developed on different, though not dissimilar lines by the various navies, steadily improved. By the turn of the century the torpedo in general use was a weapon $16\frac{1}{2}$ feet in length, 18 inches diameter, weighing some 1200 pounds, with a top speed of 30 knots and a range of 800 yards. In 1898 the torpedo's accuracy was greatly improved by the introduction of an automatic steering device controlled by a gyroscope (invented by the Austrian engineer Obry), while during the first decade of the twentieth century speed and range were much increased by burning fuel in the compressed air and so driving the engine by a mixture of hot gas and air and, later, by introducing steam to the mixture.

The advent of the Whitehead torpedo resulted in an upsurge of interest in developing the torpedo boat, which, up to now armed only with the spar or towed torpedo, had exerted only a limited influence. Successful operation of such boats by both sides during the American Civil War, however, had encouraged the minor maritime powers to acquire similar craft for coastal-defence purposes and a number had been built between 1873 and 1875, the first (*Rap*) for Norway, followed by a sister ship for Sweden and others for Denmark, Austria and Argentina, by the Thames-side yards of Thornycroft and Yarrow. These were all small vessels of some 7 or 8 tons displacement, 55 feet long, with a speed of 15 knots.

The French Navy can justly claim to have first introduced a torpedo boat equipped to launch the locomotive torpedo. This Torpedo Boat No. 1 with a displacement of 101 tons, built in 1877 by the Claparède yard on the Seine at St. Denis, near Paris, had two axial underwater tubes, one forward and one aft between the twin screws which were driven by two compound, three-cylinder reciprocating engines. Although, with a speed of only 14·25 knots, she was not a great success, she was a conception much in advance of her time and can be looked upon as the prototype of the sea-going torpedo boat which was to come into fashion some years later.

In England, meanwhile, Thornycroft had launched, in 1876, a 19-ton craft, the *Lightning*, whose single screw gave her a speed of 18 knots. When she was fitted with torpedo launching gear in the bow, her success was such as to lead the British Admiralty to order twelve similar boats from various firms and one of them, built by Yarrow, achieved the unprecedented speed of 21·9 knots.

The French also decided to acquire a few Thornycroft and Yarrow boats and to build similar craft themselves in their own yards. The Thornycroft boats were of about 13 tons displacement with a speed of 14 knots, while the Yarrow type was of 27 tons displacement and 17 knots speed. Both types could launch two Whitehead torpedoes. It was originally envisaged that such craft should be hoisted aboard battleships and operated from them. This never eventuated except in the case of the Italian battleship *Duilio* which incorporated a special compartment on the water-line aft in which was housed a torpedo boat. Certain ships, however, such as the Danish cruiser *Valkyrien* and the armoured coast-defence vessels *Tordenskjold* and *Ivar Hvitfeld*, each carried two second-class torpedo boats, while the British and French navies each operated for a time in the 1890s a ship specially designed to carry torpedo boats, the *Vulcan* (British) and the *Foudre* (French).

These early torpedo boats were soon to be designated second-class torpedo

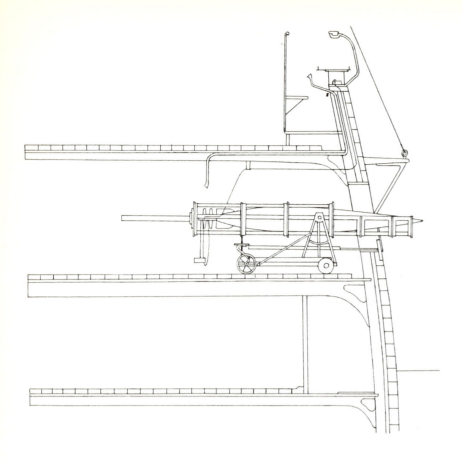

Torpedo-launching system for early type of Whitehead torpedoes in British cruisers.

boats; for Yarrow now moved on to construct for the Russian Navy the first successful sea-going or first-class torpedo boat, the *Batoum*, 100 feet long, with a horse-power of 500, a speed of 22 knots, and a displacement of 40 tons.

By 1884 the first-class torpedo boat had become an important element of all the major navies of the world, Russia leading with one hundred and fifteen of them, France having fifty, Holland twenty-two, Britain nineteen, Italy eighteen and Austria seventeen. The British Admiralty, as can be seen from these figures, did not share in the enthusiasm for these craft, which they looked on as more suitable for minor naval powers who would need them to counter the close blockade of their coasts, a tactic still considered the classic way of exercising sea power.

For the same reason, France, her navy somewhat in decline, favoured them. During the Franco-Prussian War of 1870 little active employment had been found for her navy and there had been much public speculation as to whether the large sums spent on it were worth while. At the same time, under the influence of Admiral Aube, a 'Jeune École' had grown up in the French Navy which believed that the era of the battleship had passed, and that it should be replaced by a large number of fast, light craft for coastal defence and fast, light cruisers for attack on the enemy's commerce, the classic *guerre de course* to which the weaker naval power must inevitably resort.

To such a school of thought, the torpedo boat appealed strongly, and when Admiral Aube became Minister of Marine in 1886, he immediately suspended the construction of battleships, laying down instead fourteen cruisers and ordering no less than thirty-four new torpedo boats. He also established a Torpedo School, inspiring a rapid development of the mobile torpedo as well as encouraging the development of submarines, giving the French Navy a clear lead in those craft.

The multiplication of torpedo boats across the narrow waters of the Channel by France, which was then still regarded as the traditional enemy of Britain's sea power, now began to preoccupy the British Admiralty. Seeking an antidote, they built in 1886 their first 'torpedo gunboats' or 'torpedo catchers' of the *Grasshopper* class. They were followed by further small ships of the *Spanker* class in 1889 and the *Jason* class three years later. With a speed of less than 20 knots, these ships of 700 to 800 tons were too slow and unmanœuvrable to catch torpedo boats, particularly in the sneak night attacks for which the latter were best suited. Similar ships, *avisos-torpilleurs*, built for the French Navy at about the same time, such as the *Bombe* class of 1885–86 and the *Lévrier* in 1891, were equally unsatisfactory.

Prototype of the ultimate antidote was the 386-ton *Destructor* (Destroyer) built for the Spanish Navy by Thompson's of Clydebank (today John Brown's) in 1884 to suggestions made by Captain Villamil. The first warship to be driven by twin triple-expansion engines, she achieved a speed of $22\frac{1}{2}$ knots in trials.

The speed of torpedo boats was mounting all the time, however, and the *Destructor* was soon outmoded. Nevertheless it was not until 1893 that anything better was achieved. In this case it was Yarrow who produced the first torpedo-boat destroyer, H.M.S. *Havock*. In essence she was simply a larger torpedo boat mounting a battery of quick-firing guns (one 3-inch, 12-pounder and three 6-pounders) as well as three torpedo-launching tubes. However, the additional space for boilers and engines (triple-expansion reciprocating) made available by her 240 tons displacement gave her a speed of 27 knots.

The success of the first four destroyers, the *Havock* and *Hornet* built by Yarrow, the *Daring* and *Decoy* by Thornycroft, led to thirty-six more boats of similar performance being ordered. In the meantime, however, Normand's yard at Le Havre produced in 1895 the first-class torpedo boat *Forban* for the French Navy, while Yarrow's built the destroyer *Sokol* for the Russians, both of which achieved 31 knots. The British at once decided that they, too, must build faster boats, the result being the type known as '30-knotters', though few of them actually achieved 30 knots in loaded condition.

The majority of these boats of some 300 to 400 tons, with low, turtle-back forecastles which made them extremely wet and uncomfortable in any seaway, were driven by reciprocating engines, the very high piston speeds of which resulted in frequent breakages. Among them, however, were the *Viper*, the first turbine-driven warship, which achieved 36·58 knots, and the *Cobra*, which also had Parsons' turbines and was only a knot slower.

This epoch-making development had been under way since 1891 when the British engineer, the Hon. Charles Parsons, who had since 1884 been a manufacturer of steam turbines as a means of driving electric dynamos, decided to adapt them to ship propulsion. Six years later, his little 44-ton ship *Turbinia* made a great impression as she steamed up and down at high speed between the long lines of warships assembled in 1897 at Spithead for a royal review. In 1899, the shipyard of Hawthorn Leslie and Company, on the Tyne, built H.M.S. *Viper* for the Parsons Steam Turbine Company.

Destroyers now became an essential feature of all navies. Their function in company with the fleets was to counter and drive off enemy torpedo craft and to deliver torpedo attacks themselves.

To achieve their high speeds, the British '30-knotters', including the *Viper* and *Cobra*, were built with extremely light scantlings and with side plating only $\frac{1}{4}$ inch thick and, though high tensile steel was used in their construction, their hulls were dangerously weak for operation in a seaway. The loss of the *Cobra*, which broke her back and foundered when on passage from her building yard to receive her armament, caused a reaction against turbines and high speed, so that the next type of destroyer built for the British Navy between 1903 and 1905, the *River* class, were larger (550 tons), more strongly built and had the high, flared forecastle which became standard for British destroyers from that time. Driven by reciprocating engines of 7000 horse-power, except for one boat, the *Eden*, which had turbines, they had only the moderate top speed of $25\frac{1}{2}$ knots. On the other hand they were able to mount four 3-inch guns as against the single 3-inch and five 6-pounders of the '30-knotters'.

Up to the turn of the century the French Navy remained content to build torpedo boats, the largest of which did not exceed 190 tons displacement. They watched and profited by the experience of their British rivals, however, and in 1899 their first destroyer, the 300-ton *Durandal*, designed and built by Normand, achieved a reliable $27\frac{1}{2}$ knots. A feature of this ship and the large number of French destroyers for which she became the model was her raised flying-deck from which better control of the armament was possible compared to the wave-swept decks of British destroyers prior to the 'River' class. Later destroyers of this class achieved more than 31 knots and, though they all relied upon reciprocating engine propulsion, attained a reliability which their British contemporaries lacked.

Experiments with different types of turbines in three torpedo boats built during 1902 were followed in 1906 by the laying-down of the 440-ton *Chasseur* class of destroyers in which various types of machinery were tried. The results convinced the French Navy of the superiority of the turbine and of oil-burning over coal and in 1909 the 700-ton *Casque* class of destroyer was laid down, incorporating both these developments and having the raised forecastle similar to the British 'River' class. The *Casque* and her sister *Bouclier* achieved record speeds of 34·9 and 35·33 knots respectively. These ships, indeed, were the first prototypes in the French Navy of the modern destroyer and in 1912 were classed as fleet torpedo boats (*torpilleurs d'éscadre*) as opposed to their predecessors which were torpedo-boat destroyers (*contre-torpilleurs*), a designation abandoned by the French Navy at this time. Displacing 700 tons, they mounted two 3·9-inch and four 9-pounder guns and four 18-inch torpedo tubes.

Destroyers of all navies were now to join in the sudden advance in warship design signalised by the launching of the *Dreadnought*. The naval arms race between Britain and Germany was in full progress. Both navies needed ocean-going torpedo craft to accompany their battle squadrons to deliver torpedo attacks during fleet actions and to drive off the attacks of their opponents. With battle-cruisers capable of 25 knots being built, destroyers able to maintain a reliable speed well in excess of that were essential. This called for a reversion to turbine

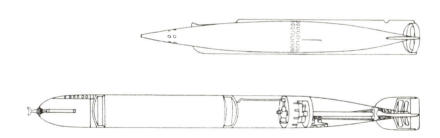

Robert Whitehead (1823–1905), English engineer and inventor of the locomotive torpedo in 1866. Manufacturing rights were bought by all navies, but Whitehead torpedoes continued to be manufactured at his factory at Fiume and later at Weymouth from 1890.

The first Whitehead torpedo is shown above. Below it the torpedo as it was later developed.

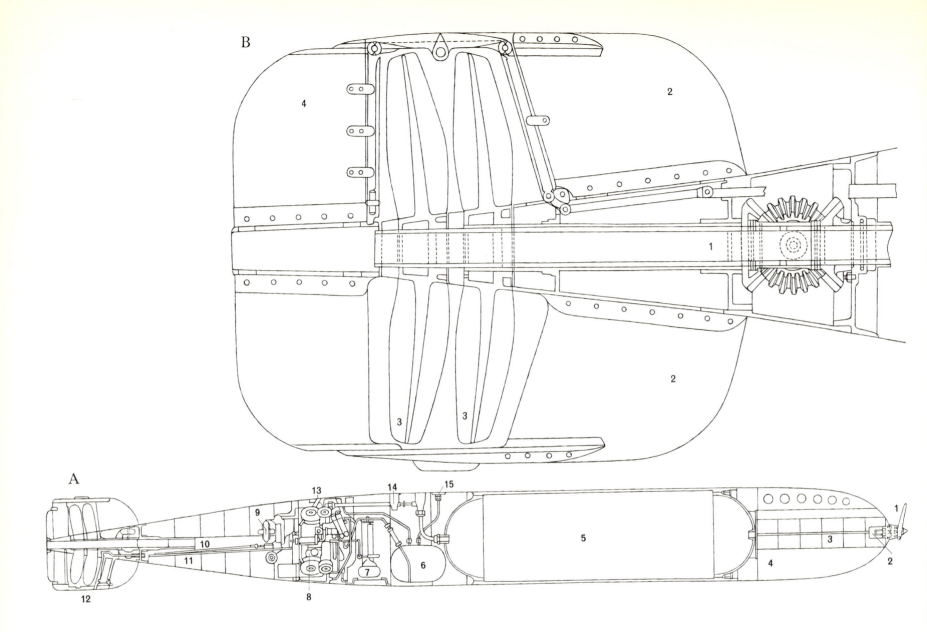

B

A

2

4

2

3   3

13   14   15

9

10

11

12   8

5

6

7

1

3

4

2

A   *Diagrammatic section of*
    a torpedo

1 Horn
2 Primer
3 Explosive charge
4 Warhead
5 Air flask, air vessel
6 Fuel and water tanks
7 Depth gear
8 Steam-engine
9 Gyro-servomotor
10 Propeller shafts

11 After body
12 Tail section
13 Air lever
14 Air-charging valve
15 Fuel (water) charging valve

B   *Tail assembly of a torpedo*

1 Propeller shafts
2 Fins
3 Contra-rotating propellers
4 Rudder
5 Horizontal rudders

drive. At the same time, after years of experiment by all navies, oil-firing for boilers had been perfected and made more efficient than coal-burning.

In the British Navy, therefore, the 'River' class were followed in 1907–09 by a number of turbine-driven, oil-fired boats known collectively as the 'Tribal' class from their names, though, in fact, they differed widely from each other in size and armament.

In performance, however, they were similar, having speeds of between 33 and 35 knots, while their armament was either five 3-inch guns and two 18-inch torpedo tubes or two 4-inch guns and two torpedo tubes.

As in other navies, German destroyers developed from torpedo boats, and, indeed, in the German Navy they continued to be called torpedo boats up to the end of the First World War. Each year from 1887 a few more boats were added, rising in size from about 300 tons to some 600 tons in 1909. They all mounted three 18-inch torpedo tubes and, up to 1906, a gun armament of a few 4-pounder guns only. In that year 3·5-inch guns began to be incorporated and the first boat to have Parsons turbines—the *G. 137*—was completed. Earlier boats, driven by reciprocating engines, had achieved 30 knots. *G. 137* had a speed of 33·9 knots and all subsequent boats had either Parsons, Curtis or Zoelly turbines.

Each year saw the completion of up to a score of destroyers for the British and German navies. The former sought robustness and a powerful gun armament, while the latter preferred higher speeds and a sacrifice of gun armament in favour of a greater number of torpedo tubes. Thus by 1913, the standard British destroyer with a displacement of 1200 tons and a speed of 27 to 29 knots mounted three 4-inch guns and four 21-inch torpedo tubes; whereas the contemporary German boat of 700 tons mounted only two or three 3·5-inch guns but four or six 19·7-inch torpedo tubes, and had a speed of 32 to 34 knots.

While Germany and Britain were engaged in their naval arms race, other navies built fewer destroyers, though they, of course, adopted the mechanical and constructive improvements made possible by the great engineering advances of the twentieth century. The Russian Navy, for example, adopted turbines built by Vulkan of Stettin in 1911 for its first large, modern destroyer, the *Novik*, which achieved the remarkable speed of 37 knots. Italy, which up to 1909 continued to build small (400-ton) boats with reciprocating engines and speeds of 29 to 30 knots, now installed Zoelly turbines in their new 30-knot destroyers, though they followed the German example in restricting the size of these boats to 590 tons.

Japan similarly adopted turbine drive, in her case Parsons turbines, in 1909 for her 790-ton and 1150-ton destroyers which had speeds of 33 and 35 knots respectively. In the United States, where a naval renaissance was taking place, the new era saw some twenty-six new destroyers of 700 to 740 tons join the fleet between 1909 and 1912, all turbine driven, with speeds of about 30 knots and an armament of five 3-inch guns and six 18-inch torpedo tubes.

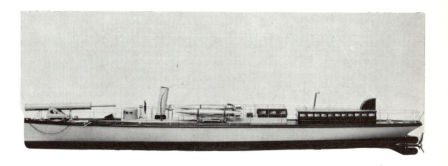

Top: The *Lightning* (1876), the first British torpedo boat to be armed with a Whitehead torpedo.

Bottom: Russian destroyer *Sokol* (1895).

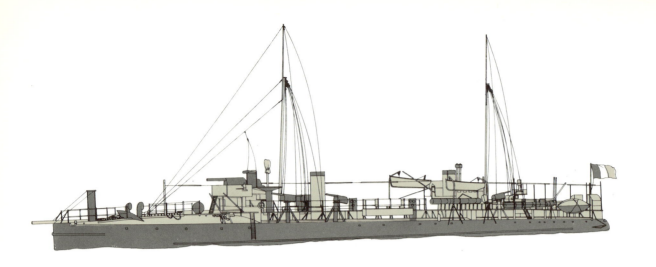

DURANDAL/NEMBO

Top: The *Durandal*, the first French destroyer (1899) built by Normand.

Bottom: Italian destroyer *Nembo* (1901).

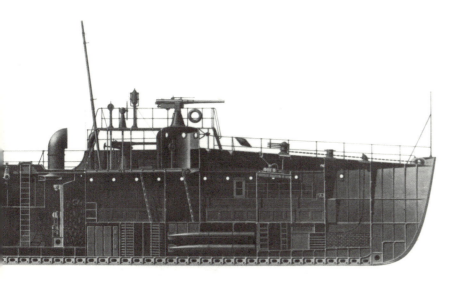

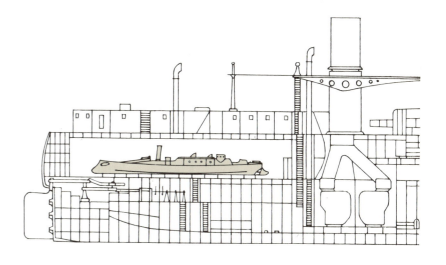

H.M.S. *HAVOCK*

The first torpedo-boat destroyer, built by Yarrow in 1892.

Right: Section of the Italian battleship *Duilio*

(*see also page 101*) showing the hangar in which a second-class

torpedo boat was housed.

Wilhelm Bauer's second submersible *Le Diable Marin*, built in
Russia in 1855, could carry a crew of fourteen to eighteen and
dive successfully. Picture shows *Le Diable Marin*, 6th
September 1856, during the coronation festivities for Alexander
II when four musicians played the national anthem while
submerged.

While wooden sailing ships mounting tiers of smooth-bore cannon firing solid shot were still the proud rulers of the sea, the type of craft which was eventually to challenge the pre-eminence of their monstrous steel, turreted successors in the super-dreadnought age—the submarine—was already the subject of promising experiments. These, indeed, are reputed to have begun as long ago as 1578 when William Bourne, an Englishman, described a craft with internal leather ballast tanks open to the sea, with screw presses which, on being unscrewed, permitted water to enter and fill the tanks, upon which the boat sank lower in the water and finally submerged. On screwing up the presses again, the water was ejected and the boat regained its buoyancy. Whether such a craft was ever successful is not recorded. The next recorded experiments were made by a Dutch physician, Cornelis Drebbel, whose craft is credited with making a voyage under water from Westminster to Greenwich, in 1620, being propelled while just awash by oars passing through the hull, the openings being kept watertight by leather joints.

In 1650 a Frenchman, de Son, constructed at Rotterdam what was undoubtedly the first mechanically propelled submersible, a spindle-shaped craft which could be ballasted down so as to leave only a small platform above the surface and driven by an internal clockwork paddle. Whether this arrangement was dynamically sound or not was not tested, for when the day of trial came, the mechanism proved too weak to drive the paddle. De Son had run up against the difficulty which was to hold back the submarine as a practical vessel long after the problem of submerging had been solved—the provision of a suitable engine.

The next recorded attempt to construct a submarine, in 1776, reverted to the use of human motive power and, considering the state of mechanical knowledge of that time, and that it achieved such a large degree of success, must be accounted one of the most ingenious inventions of maritime history. Its author was a young American, David Bushnell, his inspiration the bitter war being fought by his countrymen to gain their independence from British rule, his target the flagship of the British fleet lying in New York harbour, the 64-gun H.M.S. *Eagle*.

The hull of Bushnell's boat was roughly the shape of two tortoise shells placed hollow to hollow against each other (from which it took its name, *Turtle*), with a short cylindrical conning tower pierced by a glass window. At the bottom were a foot-operated valve to admit water to submerge the boat and two hand-pumps to eject it in order to surface. A horizontal screw to drive the boat through the water, a vertical screw to take it up or down and a rudder to steer it were all operated by cranks projecting inside, where the one-man crew could operate them. A compass guided his course and a water-gauge indicated his depth. Finally, attached to the outside was an explosive charge connected to an external screw designed to be driven into the hull of a ship from underneath by means of yet another internal crank. In spite of the multiplicity of controls to be operated by one man, Bushnell's submarine was manoeuvred by an army sergeant, Ezra Lee, under cover of darkness to alongside the *Eagle* where Lee submerged and

brought the craft up under the warship's bottom exactly as planned. There he wound the handle to drive the attachment screw into the ship's bottom, only to find it would not penetrate, presumably because it had been overlooked that the ship's bottom was copper-sheathed. A second attempt in another position similarly failed. Then the boat was surfaced by mistake alongside the ship. Day was by this time breaking, and the gallant Lee had no choice but to try to escape before being discovered. With the aid of the tide and his horizontal screw he made good progress, but the little conning tower was sighted by look-outs on Governor's Island. A boat set out in chase, but by slipping the explosive charge, which presently blew up, Lee distracted his pursuers and escaped to safety. Though the problem of giving the boat motive power had been so ingeniously overcome, this early submarine failed as a warship for lack of the other essential, a suitable weapon.

The next inventor to undertake construction of a submarine was the American Robert Fulton, who has been mentioned elsewhere as the first man to apply steam propulsion to a man-of-war. He had gone to live in France in 1797 and there, as early as 1800, he launched on the Seine at Paris the *Nautilus*, a submarine driven by a hand-worked two-bladed propeller, submerged by water ballast and controlled by vertical and horizontal rudders. For manoeuvring on the surface the *Nautilus* was provided with a mast and sail which could be laid horizontally on the top of the boat when it was desired to submerge. Its weapon was a towed container of explosive, the tow line of which passed through a hole in a spike which had first to be driven into the target's bottom as the submarine passed under it. The craft was most successful and on trials was driven submerged by its crew of three for upwards of an hour at a speed of 2 to 3 knots. But when Fulton offered to use it on behalf of the French against the British with whom the French were then at war the idea was rejected with horror by the Minister of Marine as a barbarous invention. A similar reception greeted Fulton when he transferred himself to England in 1804. A committee appointed by the prime minister, William Pitt, to examine his proposals were equally appalled by them, while the First Lord of the Admiralty, Earl St. Vincent, considered that 'Pitt was the greatest fool that ever existed to encourage a mode of warfare which those who commanded the seas did not want and which, if successful, would deprive them of it'. Thus discouraged, Fulton returned to America where, as recounted earlier, he reverted to earlier experiments in the application of steam propulsion to ships, with notable success. An indication of Fulton's farseeing inventive genius is given by the fact that the proposal for a submarine made by him to the British Admiralty envisaged an interior and an exterior hull with ballast tanks occupying the space between them, an arrangement which was to make the submarine for the first time into a seaworthy vessel a hundred years later.

The next inventor to apply himself to the construction of submarines was the Bavarian Wilhelm Bauer. His *Brandtaucher*, built at Kiel in 1850, worked on principles similar to those of the *Nautilus*.

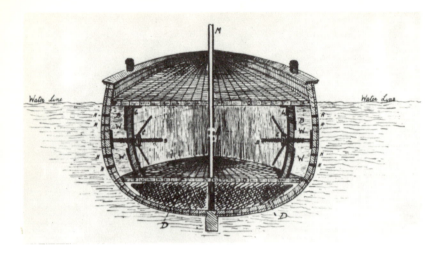

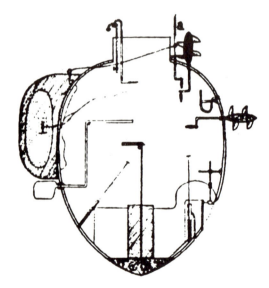

Top: Bourne's submersible boat (1578), an experimental craft launched on the Thames at London.

Bottom: Bushnell's *Turtle* (1776). With this craft the British flagship *Eagle* was attacked during the American War of Independence.

Though it was fundamentally sound and made successful trial runs, it was finally lost during one of these through going too deep and so causing the hull to collapse under the pressure of water. Nevertheless he and his crew of two escaped by a method which was later to become standard, namely by admitting water into the hull until the pressure inside equalled that outside, permitting the hatch to be opened, whereupon the three men came to the surface in the bubble of air.

This catastrophe lost Bauer the confidence of his Prussian patrons, however, and he left to offer his services first to the Austrians and then to the British; but it was not until he finally entered the service of the Russians in 1855 that he received sufficient backing to enable him to build another successful submarine, called unofficially *Le Diable Marin*. With her, Bauer made more than a hundred successful trials and gained considerable fame when, during the coronation of the Tsar Alexander II in September 1858, he took musicians under water whence they could be heard playing the national anthem.

The French were the next to experiment with a submarine, a craft of 435 tons designed by Captain (later Admiral) Bourgois and constructed in collaboration with the French naval constructor Charles Brun. Named *Le Plongeur*, it was launched at Rochefort in April 1863. It marked a great advance in that it was driven, submerged, by a compressed-air engine: but, although it was provided with horizontal rudders, the problem of maintaining a level depth was never satisfactorily solved, and, as no offensive weapon other than the spar torpedo yet existed, development was stopped after a series of trials.

While these experiments were under way in France, others were taking place in American waters where the Civil War was in progress. From plans furnished by Horace L. Hunley and two others, a craft had been constructed by Confederate engineers from a cylindrical iron boiler with tapered ends added. Some 40 feet long, driven by a crew of eight men working a hand-cranked propeller at a speed of about $2\frac{1}{2}$ knots, the *H. L. Hunley*, as she was called, was enabled to dive by means of ballast tanks and could then proceed totally submerged or with the tops of two breathing pipes above the surface.

Dogged with ill-luck, the *Hunley*, having twice foundered—on the second occasion with the loss of the whole crew, including Hunley himself—and twice salved, it was in the awash condition and armed with a spar torpedo in the bow that she at last achieved success by sinking the Federal warship *Housatonic* off Charleston on 17th February 1864, only to be herself sunk with all hands by the same explosion.

Up to this time, all efforts to produce an effective submarine man-of-war had foundered from the lack of two essentials—an engine to drive it when submerged and a practical offensive weapon which could be used without danger to the user. The time was now approaching when these two difficulties would be overcome, the first by means of the electric motor, the latter by the locomotive torpedo. Nevertheless steam was still to provide the motive power in the next two submarines to be built. The first of these was the invention of a Mr. Garrett, by profession a priest of the Church of England. After experimenting with a small, man-powered boat in the docks at Liverpool, he had a larger, 45-foot boat with a steam-engine built towards the end of 1879, which he called the *Resurgam*. Using water ballast to destroy all but a small reserve of buoyancy, he relied upon hydroplanes to take the craft under water. The engine was on the principle of Lamm's fireless locomotive in which, steam having been raised in a boiler while on the surface, the latent heat obtained from it was stored in hot-water tanks, which gave sufficient energy to work the engine for four or five hours, giving a speed of 2 or 3 knots. Before the effectiveness of the *Resurgam* could be tested, she was lost while making deep-sea experiments.

Garrett's idea, however, was taken up by Nordenfelt, the gun expert, who had a boat of 60 tons displacement, 64 feet in length, built at Stockholm in 1885. A steam-engine of a similar type to Garrett's was installed. Like the *Resurgam* too, a reserve of buoyancy was retained when submerged, but to assist in diving, two vertical propellers were driven by a 6 horse-power steam-engine which was automatically shut off by a simple form of hydrostatic valve at a selected depth. For the first time a submarine carried a locomotive torpedo, a Whitehead torpedo being carried in a discharging tube placed outside the hull in the bow. This first Nordenfelt boat was sufficiently successful to induce the Greek government to buy it in 1886. Two larger boats of 160 tons and carrying two torpedoes were sold to Turkey the following year. Nordenfelt then built an improved boat at Barrow-in-Furness in which an engine of 1300 horse-power was installed to give it a surface speed of 14 knots and a submerged speed of 5 knots for 20 miles. The spindle shape of his earlier boats was abandoned for a more normal boat shape in an effort to improve level depth-keeping. A conning tower at each end, topped by a stout glass dome, was provided, from which the captain and a look-out could navigate the boat when awash. Finally the two Whitehead torpedoes were now carried in internal discharge tubes. This submarine, after an impressive demonstration at the Naval Review of 1887 at Spithead, was sold to the Russian Navy, but became a total loss when wrecked on the coast of Jutland on passage to Russia.

Nordenfelt's craft came near to fulfilling all the requirements for an effective submarine man-of-war; but it had two serious shortcomings. Its system of depth-keeping by means of vertical screws failed to achieve fore-and-aft stability when submerged. On the surface or when awash, the boat functioned well, but once submerged it oscillated wildly in depth. Secondly, coal-fired steam power was basically unsuitable, it being almost impossible to prevent fumes from the furnace entering the boat and gassing the crew. A Spaniard and a Frenchman share the distinction of being the first to take advantage of the development of the electric motor powered by storage batteries for submerged propulsion. The submarine boat designed by the Spaniard Isaac Peral and launched in September 1888 was driven by two 30 horse-power electric motors taking their power from 420 electric cells, with auxiliary motors to drive ballast pumps and vertical diving screws on Nordenfelt's principle. It proved so successful that the Spanish government awarded Peral a large money prize.

An interesting feature of Peral's submarine was the 'optical tower' rising some 6 feet from the centre of the hull, inside which the controller could stand and, so long as the top of the tower was kept above the surface of the sea, navigate the craft through glass portholes, an arrangement which may perhaps be looked on as a forerunner of the periscope. Peral's boat, however, suffered from fore-and-aft instability in the same way as Nordenfelt's. The Spanish Navy lost interest in submarines after this one example.

Not so the French, who now took a world lead in developing them. It was while Nordenfelt was experimenting with his steam-powered boats that M. Goubet, in 1886, constructed his first craft, a tiny two-man contraption only $16\frac{1}{2}$ feet in length and weighing 10 tons, but powered by an electric motor. His idea was that it should be hoisted aboard a battleship and operated in the same way as a second-class torpedo boat, with the inestimable extra advantage of being able to attack unseen. This concept naturally won it the encouragement of Admiral Aube, at that time Minister of Marine, and of the 'Jeune École' of the French Navy referred to in the chapter on torpedo boats. Goubet's method of attaining fore-and-aft stability was by means of a pendulum which, on being displaced by any divergence of the boat from the horizontal, switched on a small rotary pump to transfer water ballast from one tank to another. A similar system was incorporated in a larger 26-foot *Goubet II*. Nevertheless, fore-and-aft control was still unsatisfactory and, until it could be solved, little future for the submarine could be envisaged. It was in the next French submarine, the *Gymnote*, conceived by the great Dupuy de Lôme and built in conjunction with him by another celebrated naval constructor, Gustave Zédé, that the incorporation of hydroplanes at last, after numerous initial difficulties, provided the solution which was to become standard in all subsequent submarines.

The *Gymnote*, 60 feet in length and displacing 31 tons, could have been inspired by the locomotive torpedo which Whitehead had invented some years earlier and which was virtually a miniature version of the cigar-shaped *Gymnote*. Launched in September 1888, the submarine, driven by a battery-powered electric motor,

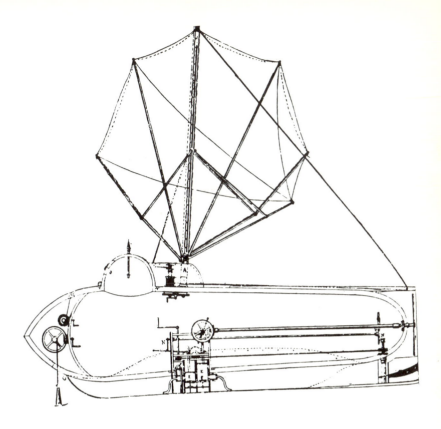

Fulton's *Nautilus* (1800). The first really manœuvrable man-propelled submersible.

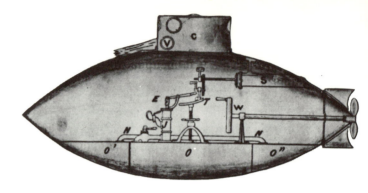

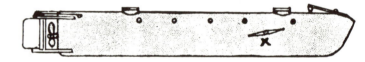

Top: Garrett's submersible boat *Resurgam* of 1879 and his first submersible of 1878 *(right).*

Right: Submersible boat *Hunley* mounting a spar torpedo operated by the Confederates in the American Civil War.

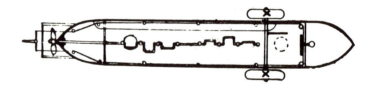

achieved 7 knots on the surface and 5 knots submerged. She proved a great success, making some two thousand successful dives during her existence.

The *Gymnote*, nevertheless, was essentially an experimental boat only. A much larger version, 148 feet long and displacing 266 tons, was launched on 1st July 1893, and, in honour of the famous constructor who had died while the boat was being built, she was named the *Gustave Zédé*. After early difficulties owing to excessive weight and poor design of her electric batteries which had 720 cells arranged in two tiers, and after additional hydroplanes had been fitted to improve fore-and-aft control, the *Zédé* proved an unqualified success. With a surface speed of 12 knots, a submerged speed of $9\frac{1}{2}$ knots and a radius of action of 175 miles at 5 knots, she made more than 2500 dives without accident. Carrying three torpedoes, one in the launching tube in the bow and two spares, she achieved such impressive triumphs in dummy attacks on battleships, the first torpedo launchings from a submarine, that the advent of the submarine as an effective man-of-war was finally established. In 1899 a smaller boat, of similar type, the *Morse* designed by M. Romazzotti, who had also been responsible for the *Zédé*, was launched and proved equally successful.

Successful as these boats were, they suffered, of course, from the handicap of a very short endurance, limited by the capacity of their electric storage batteries. The next step was to incorporate an engine for propelling the boat on the surface and to drive a dynamo in order to recharge the electric storage batteries. As a result of an open competition sponsored by the French government in 1896 for the best design for a new submarine, the plans of the naval constructor Maxime Laubeuf were accepted and on 21st October 1899 the 200-ton submarine *Narval* was launched at Cherbourg.

Laubeuf's thoughts had been directed not so much towards designing an improved version of earlier submarines as towards producing an improved torpedo boat—one which could submerge to make its attack or to avoid detection, but which could at other times be at least as seaworthy as the ordinary torpedo boat. His solution was not only revolutionary but epoch-making in that it led the way to making the submarine a really sea-going man-of-war.

It comprised giving the boat a double hull. The strongly constructed inner, cigar-shaped hull contained all the vital equipment. The outer hull, built of thin plates, had the lines of a torpedo boat. Together with the ballast tanks, situated in the space between the two hulls, this gave the vessel a 42 per cent coefficient of buoyancy as compared to the 2 per cent or 3 per cent of the 'pure submarines' so far constructed which proceeded more or less awash when on the surface. The *Narval*, which Laubeuf called a 'submersible', had all the characteristics and sea-keeping qualities of a torpedo boat when fully surfaced. Though Robert Fulton had imagined a craft of this type a hundred years earlier when making his proposals to the British Admiralty, Laubeuf had no knowledge of the fact, which was not made public until after the *Narval*'s trials. The *Narval*'s armament consisted of four sets of outboard torpedo-launching gear of a type invented by the Russian engineer Drzewiecki.

Laubeuf's other innovation was the provision of a 250 horse-power triple-expansion engine, driven by steam from an oil-fired Adolphe-Seigle tubular boiler, for surface operation and for battery charging, which gave the submarine a range of 500 miles at $6\frac{1}{2}$ knots and a maximum speed of 10 knots on the surface. Her electric motors gave her a top submerged speed of $6\frac{1}{2}$ knots. With a fixed conning tower, rising from the centre of the flat upper surface of the hull, and a periscope, the first submarine to be so fitted, the *Narval* had the appearance which was to become common to all submarines from this time onwards, except for the smoke-funnel abaft the conning tower.

This, indeed, was the outward sign of the one feature which had still to be supplanted to make a truly satisfactory, sea-going submarine man-of-war. Time for the boiler to cool down and to blow off steam was needed before diving—in the case of the *Narval* as much as twenty-one minutes at first, though this was later reduced to twelve. In all other aspects, her trials, which took place during 1900, proved a complete success.

Top: Bourgois' and Brun's submarine *Le Plongeur* driven by compressed air (1863).

Bottom: Isaac Peral's submarine built for the Spanish Navy (1888).

French submarine *Anguille*, one of twenty similar craft built between 1903 and 1904 with electric propulsion motors receiving power from an internal combustion motor generator on the surface and storage batteries when submerged.

Amongst the designs which gained awards in the competition in which Laubeuf secured the first prize were those of Romazzotti for the 140-ton *Morse*, which was already nearing completion, and of Maugas for an all-electric type, the 184-ton *Farfadet* class, of which four were built between 1899 and 1901. Two other boats of the same type as the *Morse*, the *Français* and *Algérien*, were also launched during 1900 and 1901. All these boats were of the single-hull type with buoyancies of only 4·5 to 7 per cent, and were designed and laid down before the success of the *Narval* established the superiority of the 'submersible' over the 'pure submarine'.

The double-hull type did not entirely supersede the other, however. The former, with its good sea-keeping qualities and long radius of action, was accepted as an 'offensive' type, a submersible version of the first-class torpedo boat; the latter, suitable only for operation in sheltered waters, took its place amongst the 'defensive' second-class torpedo boats.

The naval programme approved by the French Parliament in 1900 included no less than thirty-eight underwater craft, of which twenty were to be of a defensive type designed by Romazzotti. The remainder included the *Narval* herself and four improved *Narval*'s of the 157-ton *Sirène* class and thirteen of a new design by Laubeuf. With the coming to power of a new Minister of Marine, Pelletan, however, though the *Sirène* class and the defensive, 68-ton *Naiade* class were completed, only two of Laubeuf's new design were laid down.

The *Naiade*'s are chiefly of interest on account of their form of propulsion. While submerged this was by means of an electric motor drawing its power in the usual way from storage batteries. For surface propulsion, the internal-combustion benzol engine drove a generator, the power from which drove the electric motor, the first example of this form of electric drive which was later to be much employed.

It was the two newly designed Laubeuf boats, of 175 tons, the *Aigrette* and *Cicogne*, with a buoyancy of 29 per cent, which finally set the pattern on which submarines were now to be developed by all navies. For in these two boats, for the first time, were installed the new type of heavy-oil internal-combustion engine which is known by the name of its German inventor, Rudolf Diesel. This type of engine had been invented as long ago as 1892, but only now had it reached the stage of development which made it reliable and powerful enough to drive a craft of this size. Successful as Laubeuf's steam-driven submarines were, such a system had obvious disadvantages; but at the time of their construction internal-combustion engines were either insufficiently powerful for his purpose or they burnt petrol, with all the danger inherent in the use of so volatile and inflammable a fuel, entailing risks which the French prudently preferred not to accept.

The genius of Bourgois, Brun, Dupuy de Lôme, Zédé, Romazzotti, and, above all, Laubeuf, had given the French Navy an effective submarine arm years in advance of its rivals. Elsewhere, however, experiments on a smaller scale were being made. Nordenfelt's early efforts have been mentioned. Though ingenious in conception, they had a basic defect in their system of depth control and never reached the stage of development when they could be counted as practical warships.

In the United States, as early as 1893, the Navy Department had invited inventors to submit plans for a submarine torpedo boat. The result was seen in the construction of three boats, one by the Detroit Dry Dock Company for a Mr. Baker, another by the Columbia Ironworks at Baltimore for Mr. Lake and a third for Mr. Holland by his own company.

The principal feature of Baker's little 40-foot, cigar-shaped, two-man boat was its use of two propellers, one on each side amidships, which could be swivelled so as to give vertical as well as horizontal motion and so control its depth-keeping. This proved to be its downfall, as it failed to provide efficient fore-and-aft control. The Lake boat, on the other hand, though driven in the normal way by a propeller while on the surface, on submerging was allowed to sink to the bottom, where the petrol engine, supplied with air through a hose attached to a float on the surface, was connected to a pair of driving wheels on which the boat progressed

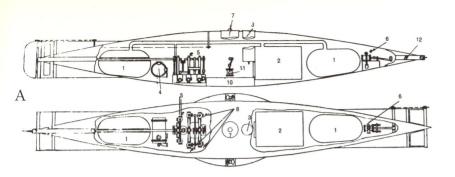

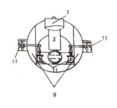

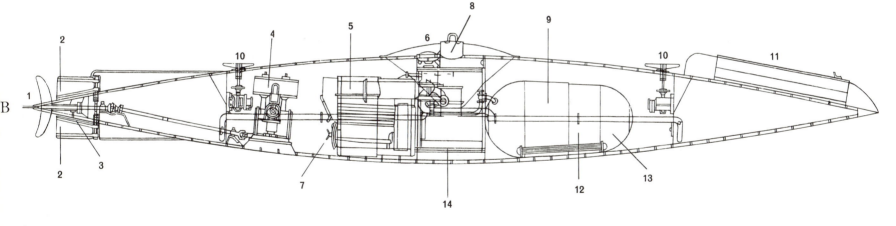

A

1 Hot-water cisterns
2 Boiler
3 Funnel
4 Condenser
5 Compound engine
6 Engine for working
   horizontal rudders
7 Conning tower
8a, b, c Pumps
9 Water tanks
10 Buoyancy tank
11 Engine for working
   vertical screws
12 External torpedo tube

B

1 Propeller
2 Vertical rudders
3 Movable joint into
   propeller shaft
4 Steam engine
5 Boiler
6 Orifice for funnel
7 Furnace door
8 Conning tower
9 Hot-water cistern
10 Vertical screws for
   diving
11 Torpedo tubes
12 Radiator
13 Valve
14 Buoyancy tank

Top left: Nordenfelt's first steam-powered submersible (1885).

Top right: Photo of Nordenfelt's first submersible during trials at Landskrona, Sweden.

Bottom: Nordenfelt submarine built for the Turkish Navy (1887).

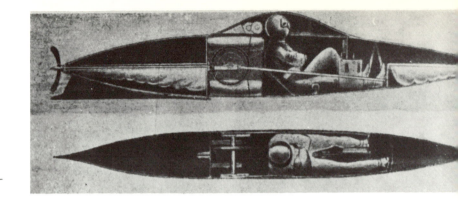

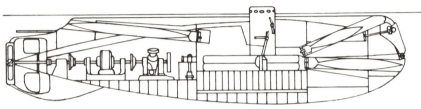

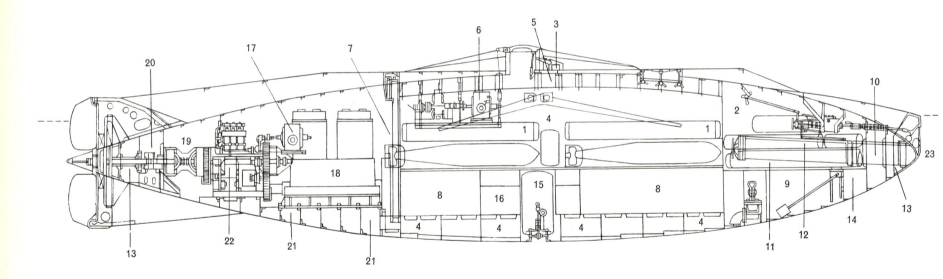

Development of the Holland submarine
from 1875 (*top right*) to 1901. No. 8 (1899—*top left*) was
the first submarine acquired by the U.S. Navy, No. 9 (*bottom*) becoming the prototype
for a class of seven similar boats.

1 2000-pound air flask	13 Fore trimming tank and after trimming tank
2 Compensating tank for torpedo	
3 Compass	14 Water round torpedo tank
4 Main ballast tank	15 Circular buoyancy tank
5 Vents to main ballast tank	16 Auxiliary ballast tank
6 Auxiliary motor bilge pump	17 Main bilge pump
7 Ventilator	18 Four-cylinder gasolene engine
8 Electric storage batteries	19 Clutch
9 Gasolene tank	20 Thrust bearing
10 Torpedo tube	21 Water/ballast tank
11 Torpedo compensating tank	22 Electric motor
12 2000-pound air flask	23 Bow cap

along the sea bed. Though Lake later constructed successful submarines which could navigate at varying depths as well as along the sea bed, it was Holland's boat which first fulfilled the requirements of the U.S. Navy Department. Holland had been experimenting with submarine boats since 1875 when he had built the *Holland No. 1*, a little craft 16 feet long driven by its single operator by means of pedals connected to a screw. Over the ensuing years Holland built a number of experimental submarines and it was a design for a *Holland No. 7* which was submitted to the Navy Department in 1894. A contract was given in March 1895, but owing to various administrative delays construction did not begin until June of the following year. In the interval Holland had been directed by the Navy Department to abandon his plan to install a petrol engine for surface operation, which he had successfully embodied in an earlier model, in favour of two sets of triple-expansion steam reciprocating engines and oil-fired boilers, giving the boat 1500 horse-power.

As Holland warned, this, besides entailing a lengthy process of blowing off steam before diving, made the interior of the boat unbearably hot when submerged. Foreseeing the inevitable failure of the *Plunger No. 7*, as it was called, he privately built a *Holland No. 8*, 53 feet long, 75 tons displacement with a 50 horse-power petrol engine. Ballast tanks were filled to submerge and the water was blown out by compressed air to surface again, while small trimming tanks right forward and right aft, the contents of which were also adjustable by compressed air, in combination with horizontal rudders or hydroplanes gave fore-and-aft control. The boat, though virtually only a miniature, was a success. The *Plunger* was abandoned, the *Holland No. 8* was accepted in its place. A slightly larger version, *No. 9*, became the prototype of seven Holland boats built for the U.S. Navy.

These boats, which were $63\frac{1}{3}$ feet in length, had a surface displacement of 104 tons; submerged, 120 tons. The single propeller was driven on the surface by a four-cylinder, 160 horse-power petrol engine; when submerged, by a 70 horse-power electric motor powered by a storage battery. This motor could also be driven by the petrol engine as a dynamo to recharge the battery. A single bow torpedo tube was incorporated with spare torpedoes stowed in trolleys on top of the battery tank. A crew of seven was carried. To dive the boat, water ballast was taken in until the reserve buoyancy was reduced to about 300 pounds, the petrol engine was disconnected, the motor connected up to the propeller shaft and the boat driven ahead, when water pressure on the hydroplanes took her below the surface and controlled her there until it was desired to surface.

Though these early Holland boats incorporated most of the features which were to comprise the submarine man-of-war, their small size, engine-power and coefficient of buoyancy (12 per cent) placed them among the defensive type of boat of which the French Navy already possessed a number and which, after long experiment, had reached a higher degree of reliability. Nevertheless the British Admiralty, which up to this time had shown little interest in submarines, now signed a contract for five similar boats to be built by Vickers Sons and Maxim in their shipyard at Barrow-in-Furness.

Whether because, as has been suggested, the wrong plans were forwarded to Vickers, or because the prototype was more primitive than had been realised, the British version had to be largely redesigned and, even so, was too under-powered and unseaworthy for the stormy seas round the British Isles. It was not until a British-designed boat on similar lines, the 180-ton *A.1*, was launched at Barrow in 1902, incorporating a 500 horse-power Wolseley petrol engine, which gave speeds of $11\frac{1}{2}$ knots on the surface, 8 knots submerged, that the British Navy had a successful and moderately seaworthy submarine. Development then went ahead at an increased tempo under the encouragement of Admiral Fisher, the dynamic First Sea Lord who was responsible for the dreadnought revolution taking place amongst surface ships. Thirteen *A* class boats were followed between 1904 and 1906 by twelve larger *B* class which had a 13-knot surface speed, and thirty-eight similar *C* class between 1906 and 1910. All these boats had petrol engines for surface propulsion and battery charging and it was not until 1911 that diesel

Italian submarine *Glauco* (1905) designed by Laurenti and making use of Laubeuf's double-hull principle.

propulsion was adopted in the *D* class. With this class, a design was finally achieved in which, by means of a partial double-hull arrangement in the form of ballast tanks exterior to the pressure hull, sufficient buoyancy was attained to make British submarines really effective, ocean-going craft.

In the U.S. Navy, progress during those years was much slower, the first seven Holland boats comprising the whole submarine force until the Electric Boat Company began a long history of submarine construction with three small 170-ton boats in 1906, following these with small classes of successively larger boats, *C*, *D*, *E*, *F*, *H* and *K*, the last of which, completed in 1912, had a displacement of 390 tons surfaced, 520 tons submerged.

Meanwhile other navies had also been building or acquiring submarines. The Russian engineer Drzewiecki had begun experimenting as early as 1876 with small pedal-driven boats and later with electrically propelled boats. They proved too small and too slow for practical acceptance, however. But in 1896 Drzewiecki entered a design in the open competition organised by the French government which resulted in the construction of the *Narval*. Drzewiecki's design for a steam- and electric-propelled boat only gained second prize and was never built. In 1901 Lieutenants Kolbasieff and Kuteinoff designed an electric boat, the *Piotr Koschka*, which had a limited success; but it was not until 1903 that a boat of the Holland type with a petrol engine for surface propulsion, the 175-ton *Delfin*, was built by Bubnov.

Five further boats of similar type were built in 1904 before the Russians turned to Krupp's Germania yard where three 200-ton boats for the Black Sea Fleet, *Karp*, *Karass* and *Kambala*, were designed and built between 1905 and 1907. By 1913 the Russians were building for themselves a few boats of the *Tyulen* class designed by Bubnov, which had a 650 to 800-ton displacement and incorporated nine 18-inch torpedo tubes. They also built the first submarine minelayer, the *Krab*, which operated successfully in the Black Sea during the First World War.

In Sweden, which had seen the birth of Nordenfelt's first successful boat, an engineer named Enroth had soon afterwards designed an improved version of it. But Sweden's first practical submarine man-of-war was a boat on the Holland pattern, the *Hajen*, which was launched at Stockholm in 1904. Japan, too, was impressed by the success of Holland's design and, during the Russo-Japanese War of 1904–05, five Hollands were built at Quincey Point, Massachussetts, and shipped to Yokohama in sections. There they were put together and successfully operated, but they were not completed in time to take part in the war.

Two other navies had interested themselves in submarines at an early date— the Italian and the German. The Italian engineer Pullino had constructed a small experimental boat named after himself, similar in design to the French *Gymnote*, in 1892. Results were sufficiently encouraging to lead to a larger boat, the *Delfino*, to his design, in 1896. Using the Nordenfelt system of vertical screws for submerging and having only electric propulsion, the *Delfino* achieved little success, however, even when reconstructed some years later.

The most notable Italian submarine designer was Luigi Laurenti, whose boats, the 160-ton *Glauco* and *Squalo*, launched in 1905 and 1906 and followed by three more, made use of the double-hull arrangement first seen in Laubeuf's *Narval*, though Laurenti's design was by no means a mere copy. Laurenti boats were subsequently built for Britain by Scott's of Greenock and others for Sweden, Denmark, Portugal, Brazil and Spain were built in Italy. The Swedish Laurenti boat *Hvalen* created a world record in 1909 by proceeding from her building yard at La Spezia to Stockholm unescorted.

Italian boats continued to rely upon petrol engines (FIAT) for surface propulsion until the *Medusa* class, completed in 1913, which incorporated diesel drive.

The German Navy had built two Nordenfelt submarines as far back as 1890, the shortcomings of which did not encourage the construction of any more. In 1902 a little electric boat was built at Kiel. But it was the design of a Spanish citizen, M. d'Equevilley, a Frenchman by birth, that set the German Navy truly on the path of submarine construction. After working for some years as a constructor with a French shipyard, he had joined Krupp's Germania yard at Kiel where he had designed a small 17-ton electric submarine, the *Forelle*, which was subsequently bought by the Russian Navy in 1903.

D'Equevilley, who had made a study of Laubeuf's design principles, went on to design a large submersible of 235 tons, similar to the French *Sirène*, but employing a petrol engine for surface propulsion and battery charging. Launched in August 1905 as *U.1*, this boat was a success and became the first of a long line of 'U-boats' which were to play a vital role in two world wars.

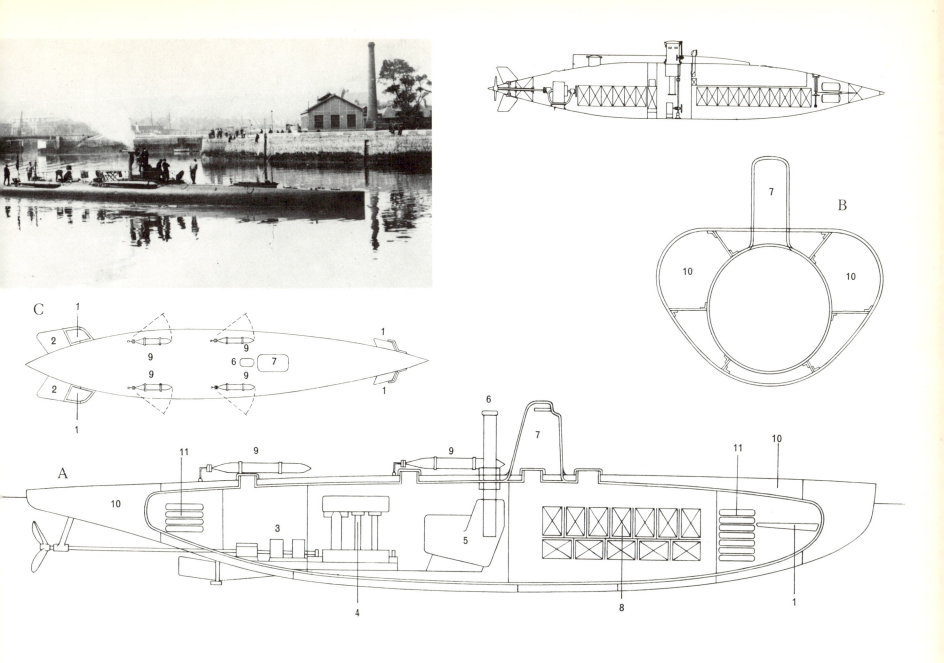

PLAN OF NARVAL

A Longitudinal section
B Transverse section
C Plan

1 Hydroplanes
2 Fixed horizontal planes
3 Electric motor
4 Steam engine
5 Boiler
6 Collapsible funnel
7 Conning tower
8 Electric batteries
9 Torpedo tubes
10 Water-ballast tanks

Top right: French submarine *Gymnote* (1888), the result of a collaboration between Dupuy de Lôme and Gustave Zédé. The first to make use of hydroplanes for fore and after control.

Top left, centre and bottom: Laubeuf's *Narval* (1899), prototype of the modern submarine, an ocean-going submersible torpedo boat making use of external ballast tanks and enjoying, for the first time, a high coefficient of buoyancy ($42\frac{1}{2}$ per cent).

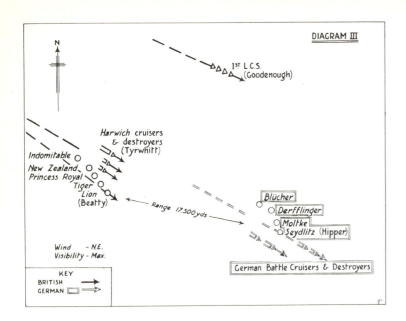

DIAGRAM III

1ST L.C.S.
(Goodenough)

Harwich cruisers
& destroyers
(Tyrwhitt)

Indomitable
New Zealand
Princess Royal
Tiger
Lion (Beatty)

Range 17,500 yds

Blücher
Derfflinger
Moltke
Seydlitz (Hipper)

German Battle Cruisers & Destroyers

Wind – N.E.
Visibility – Max.

KEY
BRITISH
GERMAN

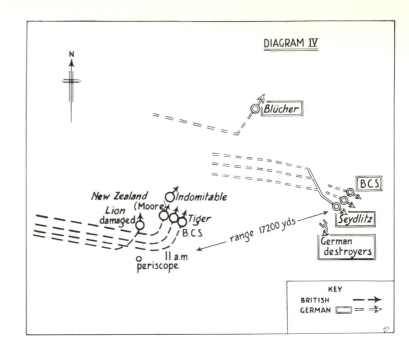

DIAGRAM IV

Blücher

New Zealand
Indomitable
Lion (Moore)
damaged
Tiger
B.C.S.

range 17200 yds

B.C.S.

Seydlitz

German
destroyers

11 a.m.
periscope

KEY
BRITISH
GERMAN

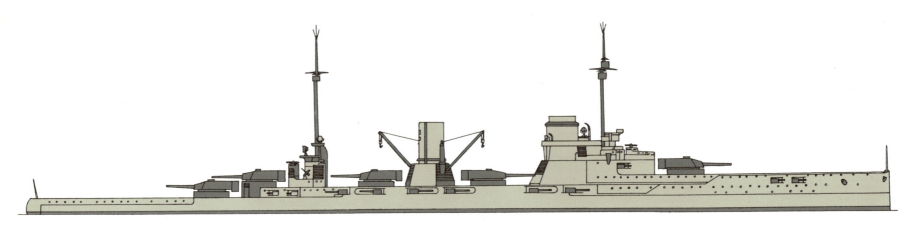

SEYDLITZ

The battle-cruiser *Seydlitz*, 24,605 tons.

Hipper's flagship at the Dogger Bank, escaped destruction at Jutland only as a result

of her effective armour protection and compartmentation.

Track charts of the Battle of the Dogger Bank:

Situation at 9.25 a.m., 24th January 1915.
Situation at 11.4 a.m., 24th January 1915.

Rear-Admiral Franz Hipper, commander of the German battle-cruiser force at the Dogger Bank and again, later, at Jutland.

Just as the warships of the pre-dreadnought era came to be tested in battle during the Russo–Japanese War at the very time that obsolescence was overtaking them, so the dreadnought and super-dreadnought battleships and battle-cruisers of the two largest and most up-to-date navies were to meet in combat during the First World War at a time when their sovereignty over the oceans was being threatened by the submarine, and their eventual supplanter, the aircraft carrier, had already been conceived. The sea fights between the previously untested types of ship of the British and German navies between 1914 and 1916 became the subject for heated controversy over the comparative qualities of design.

In the first major clash of the war, the old British armoured cruisers *Monmouth* and *Good Hope* were destroyed off Coronel on the coast of Chile in November 1914 by the seven-year-old armoured cruisers *Scharnhorst* and *Gneisenau*. The one-sided battle served to show the superiority of the modern armoured cruisers over the cruisers acquired in large numbers by the British Navy at the turn of the century, ships which Admiral Fisher had so rightly described as being able neither to fight nor to run away. When the *Scharnhorst* and *Gneisenau*, in their turn, succumbed in the Battle of the Falkland Isles on 8th December 1914 a more significant fact was established; for it was by their contemporaries in age, but their successors in point of development, the dreadnought-type battle-cruisers *Invincible* and *Inflexible* that they were annihilated, thus demonstrating the passing from the scene of the armoured cruiser of the pre-dreadnought age as a unit of the battle fleet.

That the lesson was learnt by neither side was to be seen in the fate of the German armoured cruiser *Blücher* at the Battle of the Dogger Bank in 1915 and of the British *Defence* and *Warrior* in the Battle of Jutland in 1916. It was out of the clash between similar ships of the dreadnought type, however, that the principal lessons affecting the development of major ships-of-war were to emerge.

The first of these was the Battle of the Dogger Bank on 24th January 1915 when the German battle-cruisers *Seydlitz* (flagship of Rear-Admiral Hipper), *Moltke* and *Derfflinger* accompanied by the armoured cruiser *Blücher*, in the course of a 'tip-and-run' raid, were intercepted by the British battle-cruisers *Lion* (flagship of Vice-Admiral Beatty), *Tiger*, *Princess Royal*, *New Zealand* and *Indomitable*. In the face of this superior force Hipper fled and the encounter developed into a long stern chase. In the early stages of the running fight the rear German ship, *Blücher*, and the leading British ship, the *Lion*, bore the brunt of the exchange of fire. The former soon suffered hits and began to lag behind her consorts, while the British ship was hit once without serious consequences.

The *Lion* now shifted her fire on to the *Seydlitz* and scored two hits, the second of which exposed a weakness in the German arrangements for handling ammunition between the magazines and turrets. A 13·5-inch shell pierced right through the 9·8-inch armour of the *Seydlitz*'s after turret, bursting in the reloading space where charges waiting to be loaded into the guns caught fire. Flames roared up into the turret, killing the gun crews, and downwards through the shell hoist into the ammunition chamber. There the men tried to escape through a connecting door into the ammunition chamber of the adjoining turret, only to be followed by the flames which now reached that turret also, with the same appalling consequences. More than a hundred men were killed. Hipper's flagship was saved from destruction only by the heroism of three of the *Seydlitz*'s crew, who, grasping the red-hot valve wheels, succeeded in flooding the after magazines.

Fortunes now reversed as the German ships, indistinctly visible behind their own smoke, remained almost unscathed (except for the *Blücher*, which was being hammered to destruction). The *Lion* began to suffer under repeated heavy blows. When one engine was put out of action and her speed reduced from 26 to 15 knots, tactical command passed to Beatty's subordinate Rear-Admiral Sir Archibald Moore, who concentrated the British ships against the doomed *Blücher*, allowing the remainder to escape.

A lesson of the utmost importance had been given to the Germans by the calamitous fire in the *Seydlitz*. Neither side took steps at this time, however, to obviate a recurrence by fitting anti-flash arrangements whereby flash or fire in one space of the turret-magazine complex could be prevented from spreading to the next. The British, in particular, were to pay heavily for the omission later.

The consequence of the lighter armour protection of the British battle-cruisers as a result partly of the limitations in beam imposed by the size of British dry-docks and partly of the desire for speed at the expense of armour, had not yet made themselves evident. Their margin on speed, indeed, had enabled them to bring the enemy to action at the Dogger Bank. But with a maximum thickness of armour of 9 inches in the *Lion* class and only 6 inches in earlier ships, as compared to 11 inches in the *Seydlitz* and *Moltke*, the British ships were to find themselves at a grave disadvantage in a straight fight seventeen months later.

By the summer of 1916 both the British Grand Fleet and the German High Sea Fleet had received reinforcements of new dreadnoughts. The latter had brought its dreadnought battleship strength to a total of sixteen by the addition of the four *König* class which joined the fleet during 1914 and its battle-cruiser strength from four to five when they commissioned the *Derfflinger*'s sister ship *Lützow* in August 1915.

The Grand Fleet had received a considerably larger reinforcement. Besides three dreadnoughts which had been under construction for foreign navies and were taken over on the outbreak of war, five ships of the remarkable *Queen Elizabeth* class had been commissioned.

Of the former, the most interesting was the *Agincourt*, which, laid down at Armstrong's Elswick yard in September 1911 for the Brazilian Navy, as the *Rio de Janeiro*, was sold by the Brazilians while still uncompleted to the Turkish government early in 1914 and renamed the *Sultan Osman I*. In August 1914, this ship was commandeered for the Royal Navy and renamed *Agincourt*.

Designed by Armstrong's Chief Constructor, Mr. Perrett, who had been responsible for some famous Elswick cruisers, the *Agincourt* mounted no less than seven twin 12-inch turrets, all on the centre-line on a displacement of 27,500 tons. To accommodate so many turrets she was the longest battleship of her time (632 feet), though her beam was only 89 feet, and the weight left available for armour restricted her to a belt of only 9 inches maximum, to 9 inches for her end barbettes between decks and only 3 inches for the remainder. She was, nevertheless, a valuable accretion of strength to the British battle line.

Also built at Elswick was the *Canada*, which, laid down for Chile in December 1911 as the *Almirante Latorre*, was one of the two ships ordered by that country in response to Brazil's ordering of the *Rio de Janeiro*. A more conventional super-dreadnought, resembling the British *Iron Duke*, she mounted ten 14-inch guns in twin, centre-line turrets on a displacement of 28,000 tons.

The third ship was the Turkish *Reshadieh*, laid down in 1911 in Vickers' yard at Barrow. She, too, was a conventional super-dreadnought with ten 13·5-inch guns in twin turrets on a displacement of 23,000 tons. Taken over by the British she was renamed *Erin*.

The most important addition to the British fleet, however, had been the five fast battleships of the *Queen Elizabeth* class, the laying down of which in 1912 and 1913 had been a notable step forward in the design of battleships. The inevitable growth of capital ships in size and gunpower as well as the bitter armaments race between Britain and Germany had led to the former deciding that the battleships of the 1912 programme should have 15-inch guns. Normally the introduction of guns of a new calibre would have entailed delays in completion of the ships while the mountings were designed and a trial gun built for proving.

To avoid this, a design of mounting was hastily prepared by the Ordnance Board which Armstrong's undertook to execute, while the guns themselves were to be accepted straight from the drawing board, though arrangements were made for one of them to be hurried on four months ahead of the remainder so that essential trials for range and accuracy might be made.

In the meantime study of the likely composition of the German High Sea Fleet as it would be in 1914 and 1915 indicated that a speed of 25 knots would be required to contain it and bring it to action. Such a speed could only be attained by the use of oil-fired boilers; and so the long controversy between the advocates of coal and oil was finally resolved in the British Navy in favour of the latter; from this time onwards no more coal-burning capital ships, cruisers or destroyers were ordered for the British Navy.

The advent of the fast *Queen Elizabeth* class of ships sounded the knell of the lightly armoured battle-cruiser. The cost of the latter ships had risen until it was nearly double that of a contemporary battleship and, as the First Lord of the Admiralty, Mr. Churchill, argued, it would be better to give them the heaviest armour as well as high speed and powerful guns. 'To put the value of a first-class battleship into a vessel which cannot stand the pounding of a heavy action is false policy,' he wrote prophetically. 'The battle-cruiser, in other words, should be superseded by the fast battleship.'

The return of Admiral Fisher, progenitor of the battle-cruiser, as First Sea Lord in 1914 was to lead to a temporary reversal of this policy, resulting in the battle-cruisers *Repulse* and *Renown*, described later; and, though outmoded battleships, heavily armoured, comparatively slow mastodons, were yet to be built by all the major navies, the capital ship of the future was the fast battleship.

To achieve the speed of 25 knots, the 29,150-ton *Queen Elizabeth*'s required an increase of 150 per cent in horse-power as compared to the 30,000 horse-power of the 21-knot *Iron Duke*'s. Mounting eight 15-inch guns, their armour was only fractionally less than that of the *Iron Duke*'s.

In May 1916 the comparative capital-ship strengths of the rival fleets facing one another across the North Sea were: British—twenty-four dreadnought battleships, nine battle-cruisers; German—sixteen dreadnought and six pre-dreadnought battleships, five battle-cruisers. The great superiority of the former made a direct challenge by the latter out of the question.

The Battle of Jutland, in which the qualities of the British and German dreadnoughts were to be tested, came about as a result of the attempt by the Commander-in-Chief of the German High Sea Fleet to bring about a situation in which the portion of the British fleet based on Rosyth (Beatty's six battle-cruisers and the Fifth Battle Squadron composed of four *Queen Elizabeth* class fast battleships) could be brought to action before the main Grand Fleet, coming from its more distant base at Scapa Flow, could intervene.

Unfortunately for Scheer's plan, the British Admiralty, by monitoring German naval radio traffic, was able to know well in advance of any German sortie. Consequently when the High Sea Fleet sailed in the early hours of 31st May 1916, the Grand Fleet had already been at sea for some hours and was steering for a rendezvous off the Jutland Bank between its two portions under Admiral Jellicoe from Scapa and Beatty from Rosyth.

Nevertheless, Jellicoe and Beatty were still some sixty-five miles apart when the latter encountered Hipper's battle-cruisers. Hipper, outnumbered and outgunned, steered to lure Beatty towards Scheer's battle fleet, still beyond the southern horizon. A gun battle on roughly parallel courses and at ranges varying between 16,500 yards and 13,000 yards ensued between Beatty's six battle-cruisers and Hipper's five. The outcome was clearly in favour of the latter, two of Beatty's ships, the *Queen Mary* and *Indefatigable*, blowing up and sinking, whether as a result of inadequate armour protection to the magazines or through lack of anti-flash precautions will never be certainly known; the flagship, *Lion*, was only saved from a similar fate by flooding the magazine and shell room of her centre turret. Two other ships, the *Princess Royal* and *Tiger*, were also heavily damaged.

In spite of poor shooting by Beatty's ships in the early stages, Hipper did not escape hits and these became very heavy and damaging when the four *Queen Elizabeth*'s, left behind when the battle-cruisers turned south, at last brought their 15-inch guns accurately into action. On the other hand, none of Hipper's ships was sunk or put out of action, a comparative immunity which owed much to the better armour protection and watertight subdivision of the German battle-cruisers, though another factor was the poor design of British armour-piercing shells. The *Seydlitz* was also hit by a torpedo fired by a British destroyer during this phase of the battle; but the anti-torpedo bulkhead which German ships, with their greater beam, were able to incorporate, minimised the damage and the *Seydlitz* kept her place in the line.

At this point the German battle fleet was sighted coming up over the southern horizon. Beatty promptly turned about and now the situation was reversed, with the German fleet being lured towards a totally unexpected encounter with the greatly superior Grand Fleet. It was while reversing course, however, that the design of the *Queen Elizabeth* class came under its severest test.

As each ship swung ponderously round in the wake of the next ahead, it plunged into a veritable forest of shell splashes. Both the *Barham* and the *Valiant* were hit and suffered casualties. As the *Malaya*, the rear ship of the squadron, reached the turning-point, salvoes fell round her at ten-second intervals. A 12-inch shell burst in her starboard 6-inch battery, setting the ready-use ammunition ablaze and causing more than a hundred casualties. Another hit the roof of one of her after turrets, but the armour kept it out and it did no serious damage. When her seemingly interminable ordeal was over and she steadied her course in the wake of the squadron, *Malaya* miraculously emerged with her main armament undamaged and speed unimpaired.

And as the 5th Battle Squadron steamed northwards it was able to demonstrate also the great offensive superiority of the *Queen Elizabeth* class. Two of them, *Barham* and *Valiant*, engaged Hipper's battle-cruisers, scoring hits on *Lützow* and *Derfflinger* and heavily damaging the *Seydlitz*. Hipper's men, who had been somewhat contemptuous of the British battle-cruisers' gunnery, paid a grim

H.M.S. *Iron Duke*, super-dreadnought, Admiral Jellicoe's flagship in the British Grand Fleet 1914–16. Mounted ten 13·5–inch guns in twin turrets.

From left to right:

Admiral of the Fleet Lord Fisher, the great administrator and innovator who introduced the dreadnought era and shook the British Navy out of its unjustified complacency at the turn of the century.

Admiral Sir David Beatty, commander of the British Battle-cruiser Fleet 1914–16 and of the Grand Fleet to the end of the war.

Admiral Sir John Jellicoe, commander of the British Grand Fleet 1914–16, including the Battle of Jutland.

179

tribute to that of the Fifth Battle Squadron. *Warspite* and *Malaya* meanwhile engaged the leading German battleships and, in spite of the increasingly difficult light, got hits home on to the *Grosser Kurfürst* and *Markgraf*.

As the battle ran northwards, Beatty's ships gradually drew away from the slower German battle fleet and the firing died away. Ahead, unknown to Scheer, was the whole strength of the Grand Fleet which, in the nick of time, was to be deployed across his bows, forming a gigantic trap into which the German line was to run headlong. How Scheer succeeded in extricating himself and, during the night, working his way across the rear of the unsuspecting Jellicoe's massed battleships is too long a story to give here in detail. Only the incidents in which the characteristics of warships on either side were tested need concern us.

The first of these occurred when a squadron of British armoured cruisers, scouting ahead of the Grand Fleet, lumbered out of the smoke-laden haze between the two fleets to come under fire from Hipper's battle-cruisers. The cruel lesson of the Falklands battle was repeated as the *Defence* and *Warrior* were quickly set ablaze, the former to blow up and sink, the latter to stagger out of the battle so heavily damaged that she had to be abandoned and scuttled.

When the *Warspite* of the 5th Battle Squadron, engaging Scheer's battleships, suffered a jammed rudder and circled helplessly for a while under the concentrated fire of the whole German van, and was hit over and over again by 12-inch shells, she escaped vital damage. At about the same time, on the other side of the far-flung battle, the British *Invincible*, one of the first of the too lightly armoured battle-cruisers, hotly engaged with the *Lützow* and *Derfflinger* and punishing them savagely with her 12-inch guns, was herself hit by a single salvo of shells which penetrated to her vitals. A violent explosion tore her in half, and by the time her two consorts swept by, only her bow and stern standing up out of the water remained. The contrast between these two incidents served to demonstrate very clearly the passing of the lightly protected battle-cruiser from the scene in favour of the fast battleship, of which the *Queen Elizabeth* was the prototype.

No further encounters between the two fleets took place during the First World War; so it was on the lessons learnt from Jutland that future development of warships was to be based. While naval experts wrangled over these matters, the two types of warship which were to dethrone the battleship from its position of pre-eminence, the submarine and the aircraft carrier, were advancing from unreliable auxiliaries to major elements of the fleet. They are given separate sections of this book to themselves.

H.M.S. *Lion*, battle-cruiser, flagship of Vice-Admiral Beatty commanding the Battle-cruiser Fleet. Mounted eight 13·5-inch guns as compared to 12-inch in contemporary German ships, but at the expense of armour protection.

The battle of Jutland provided the opportunity to compare the design, construction and armament of the opposing ships. In this, the most outstanding feature was the rapid destruction of three British battle-cruisers by a small number of hits from 11-inch and 12-inch shells, compared to the capacity of similar German ships to survive when pounded by 13·5-inch and 15-inch shells, the *Lützow* and *Seydlitz* receiving twenty-four hits by heavy shell and the *Derfflinger* twenty. Various explanations were put forward. Opponents of the battle-cruiser concept saw in it a condemnation of the Fisher theory that speed and hitting power were the best protection and the battle-cruiser concept began to go out of fashion soon afterwards; on the other hand subsequent investigation showed that the German ships, though they had considerably heavier side armour than their British opponents, were penetrated again and again but with less fatal consequences. Insufficient deck armour to withstand the plunging trajectory of shells at the great ranges (for that date) at which the action was fought was also blamed; but in this respect the German ships were little better equipped than the British.

Reports that British shells were defective, either breaking up on impact or failing to explode correctly, led to the subsequent issue of improved ammunition; yet the German armour was penetrated more often than was the British, and the German battle-cruisers suffered heavily from fires caused by shells which penetrated their turrets. Both the *Derfflinger* and the *Seydlitz* had two turrets burnt out, the *Von der Tann* and *Lützow* each had a cartridge fire in one of their turrets.

The crucial point is that in the German ships the damage was not so immediately fatal; whereas the *Queen Mary, Indefatigable* and *Invincible* had disintegrated in cataclysmic explosions, a fate which the *Lion* only escaped by the timely flooding of a magazine.

German ships were not only more heavily armoured; they were also more minutely subdivided than their British counterparts, which made them virtually unsinkable by gunfire, a characteristic which was to be found again in their battleships of the Second World War period twenty-four years later. No British ship had to suffer the repeated hits by 13·5-inch and 15-inch shells received by the German battle-cruisers, and if they had, it is doubtful if they would have survived such punishment. The *Lützow*, on the other hand, though completely disabled, had to be torpedoed by her own destroyers before she would sink; the *Seydlitz*, hit by a torpedo as well as twenty-four times by heavy shells, with her forecastle awash, reached harbour going astern and aided by two salvage pump steamers. The *Derfflinger*, with damage almost as severe, also reached harbour under her own steam.

Following the Battle of Jutland the British took steps to profit from the lessons learnt. Ships under construction and those which came into dockyard hands for refit or repair were given increased armour protection over their magazines, while arrangements to guard against the spread of fires in turrets and ammunition-handling rooms were fitted.

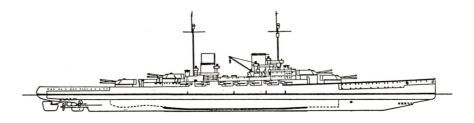

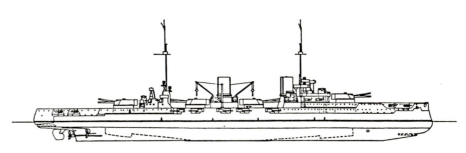

Top: German battle-cruiser *Lützow*, laid down 1912, Hipper's flagship at the Battle of Jutland in which she was destroyed. Sister ship to the *Derfflinger*, which survived a severe pounding in the battle.

Bottom: German battle-cruiser *Von der Tann*, laid down 1908, took part in the Dogger Bank and Jutland battles. Better armoured than contemporary British battle-cruisers, she survived a heavy battering in the latter battle.

As it happened, British and German capital ships were never again to meet in battle during the First World War. Several new ships were added to both fleets, however, before the war ended. Each navy had laid down in 1913 and 1914 a class of battleships of remarkably similar size and gunpower, the *Revenge* class by the British, the *Bayern* class by the Germans. Up to this time, comparison between contemporary British and German capital ships had shown the former devoting more of the available tonnage to offensive power at the expense of defensive characteristics than the latter. German ships had mounted 11-inch guns when their opponents had 12-inch; by the time the British had progressed to 13·5-inch, the Germans were still relying upon 12-inch and were consequently able to give their ships heavier armour protection.

With the *Bayern* class, however, the German designers took a double step in the direction of greater fire-power, providing eight 15-inch in four twin turrets. As a consequence, the contemporary *Revenge* class of similar displacement (28,000 tons) devoted almost exactly the same percentage of it to armour (31·7 per cent) as did the *Bayern* (31·6 per cent). The principal difference between the two types lay in the additional beam of the German ships, an advantage conferred by the bigger dry-docks available to them, which permitted more effective anti-torpedo protection. The longitudinal anti-torpedo bulkhead of 2-inch armour was inset 13 feet from the outer hull and, as the fuel was coal, it was reinforced by bunkers 6 feet wide.

The question of protection against the ever-increasing effectiveness of the torpedo had been under study by British designers, who had been able to give partial torpedo bulkheads to their super-dreadnought classes, and in the *Queen Elizabeth* class this had been increased to a 2-inch bulkhead covering nearly the whole length of the hull. Nevertheless with a beam 8 or 9 feet less than contemporary German ships this could not be made so effective. Experiments with the old battleship *Hood* in 1914 had shown that additional safety against underwater explosion might be given to existing as well as projected ships by fitting some form of outside protection in the form of a 'bulge' or 'blister'. The *Ramillies*, last of the *Revenge* class, completed in September 1917, was provided with this new form of protection and thereafter all large British ships had a 'bulge' incorporated in their designs. The loss of speed in the *Ramillies* was found to be less than one knot.

A number of small ships built or adapted to mount heavy guns for shore-bombardment purposes during the First World War, called 'monitors', were fitted with very wide bulges, the effectiveness of which was demonstrated when three of them were torpedoed and all reached harbour.

When Admiral Fisher returned to the Admiralty in 1914, his belief in the lightly armoured battle-cruiser had prevailed. His advocacy of it had soon been backed by the success of the *Invincible* and *Inflexible* at the Battle of the Falkland Isles and he had obtained permission for two battleships of the 1914 programme to be redesigned as very fast battle-cruisers, *Repulse* and *Renown*.

Fisher insisted on 15-inch guns for them and, as only six twin 15-inch turrets could be made available within the fifteen-month limit he set for completion of the ships, they had to be content with three turrets each. As with the later ships of the *Courageous* class, products of Fisher's unorthodox ideas, this ran counter to one of the main requirements of the all-big-gun capital ship, salvoes of not less than four guns. Fisher's dictum that speed and hitting power were a ship's best protection was followed to its practical limit, in the *Renown* a speed of $32\frac{1}{2}$ knots being provided by Brown-Curtis turbines of 120,000 horse-power driving four screws with steam from no less than forty-two large-tube boilers. Armour was limited to a narrow belt of 6 inches maximum thickness extending only 2 feet 2 inches below the water-line—protection equal to that of the *Indefatigable* which was to prove so inadequate at Jutland. So far as side armour was concerned, little could be done to profit from the lessons of that battle, but additional horizontal armour over the magazines was installed during construction. For underwater protection these two ships were the first large ships to incorporate the 'bulge' as an integral part of their hull.

Only one other battle-cruiser was to be completed by any navy during the war—the German *Hindenburg*, a sister to the *Lützow*, which, though laid down in 1913, did not join the High Sea Fleet until 1917. A large programme of German battle-cruisers had, however, been projected. Four ships of 31,000 tons and a speed of 28 knots mounting eight 14-inch guns in four twin turrets were laid down, and two of these, the *Mackensen* and the *Graf Spee*, were launched in 1917. Three more ships of 33,500 tons which were to have mounted eight 15-inch guns were also begun; none of these ships was ever completed.

Meanwhile in England, with the retirement from the scene of Admiral Fisher, in May 1915, the concept of the very fast, lightly armoured battle-cruiser had gone out of favour. Four such ships had been ordered in April 1916; but experience gained from the Battle of Jutland led to considerable changes in the design, the armour protection being very greatly increased at the expense of some 4000 tons added displacement and a slight reduction of speed. None had been completed at the end of the war, when work was stopped and the contracts cancelled on all but one, the *Hood*, which was finally completed in 1920.

This beautiful ship of 42,100 tons displacement, a speed of 31 knots, an armament of eight 15-inch guns and protected by an armoured belt 12 inches thick, was the first example of a man-of-war combining the characteristics of the battleship and the battle-cruiser, the prototype of the fast battleship which was conceived first to form the backbone of the modern fleet and, later, when the aircraft carrier achieved its dominating position, to be an essential element of the fast carrier task force.

The *Hood* was a ship far in advance of her time and a failure to perceive the future role of the battleship led to ships of an older type being built for some years after her arrival on the scene. Nevertheless, though in her day the deck protection over her magazines was greater than anything previously incorporated, she lacked the massive armour protection of her vitals which would have been available if the 'all-or-nothing' system of protection as inaugurated by the *Nevada* class of the U.S. Navy had been adopted. Modernisation, which was applied to most battleships during the inter-war years, passed her by, with the consequence that when the test of war came twenty-one years later, the Achilles heel of inadequate protection of her magazines was found by a shell from the German *Bismarck* and, in a devastating explosion, she disintegrated and sank.

Beyond the two main naval protagonists of the First World War, the construction of new capital ships came largely to a halt. The French Navy had followed its first dreadnoughts of the *Jean Bart* class with three super-dreadnoughts of the *Bretagne* class. With a displacement of 23,000 tons, they mounted ten 13·4-inch guns in twin centre-line turrets. Five further ships of the *Normandie* class of 25,230 tons, which were to have mounted twelve 13·4-inch guns in quadruple turrets, were laid down during 1913 and 1914, but work was stopped on them soon after the outbreak of the war and they were never completed.

Four interesting ships laid down for the Russian Navy in the Baltic were likewise abandoned before completion. These were the *Borodino* class of 32,500 tons which were designed originally to mount twelve 14-inch guns in centre-line triple turrets, though this was subsequently altered to 12-inch. Their comparatively light, though extensive armour protection, the principal feature of which was a complete lower belt of 9·4-inch Krupp steel with a 4-inch belt above it, put them in the battle-cruiser class; but their designed speed of 26·5 knots was more that of fast battleships.

Laid down in 1912, they were not launched until 1915 and 1916, and none had been completed when the revolution brought construction to an end.

The Italian Navy had provided for the construction of the four battleships of the *Francesco Caracciolo* class. On a displacement of 34,000 tons they were to have had eight 15-inch guns. With a projected speed of 28 knots and fairly heavily armoured, these ships, designed by the Italian constructor Masdea, would have been very advanced ships for their day. Only the *Caracciolo* was ever laid down, however, and she was never completed. The Italian Navy was thus left with the

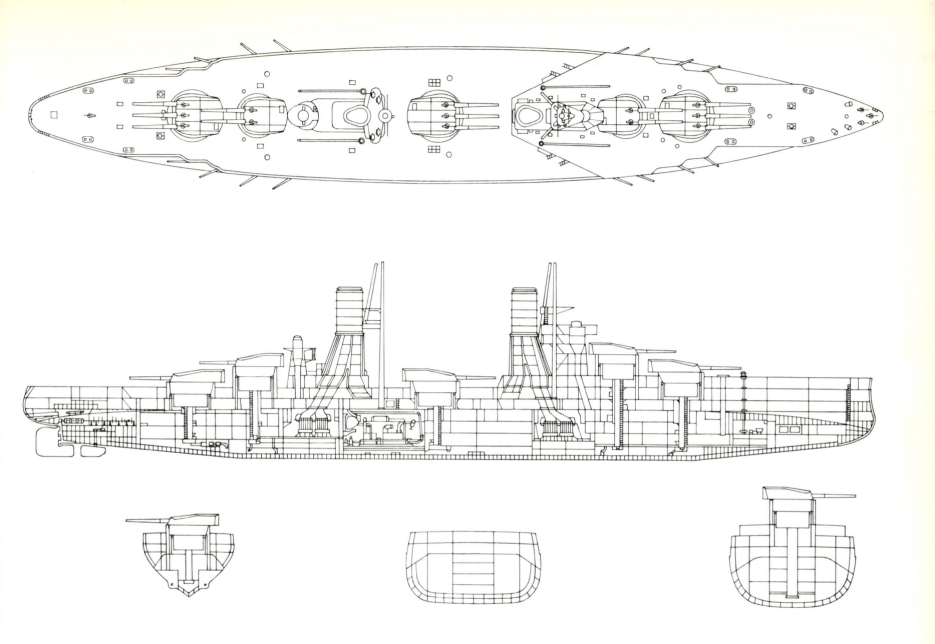

CAIO DUILIO

Italian super-dreadnought, one of four ships

of the *Giulio Cesare* class built during the First World War which were

to survive to be modernised and serve again

in the Second World War.

French super-dreadnought *Lorraine* (1913), mounting ten 13·4 inch guns. One of three ships of this class built by the French Navy before the onset of the First World War brought further construction to a halt.

Dante Alighieri (completed 1912) and the four ships of the *Giulio Cesare* class. A fifth ship, the *Leonardo da Vinci*, had been blown up in 1916, reputedly as a result of sabotage.

A similar standstill occurred in the United States with regard to capital ships in favour of other, more urgently needed types. The two *Pennsylvania*'s laid down in 1913–14 were completed in 1916; the next class, however, the three *Idaho*'s laid down in 1915 and the two *California*'s in 1916 and 1917, were not completed until after the end of the war. All mounted twelve 14-inch guns in triple turrets, and in their arrangement of armour protection they followed the pattern of 'all-or-nothing', set by the *Nevada*. With the *New Mexico* of the *Idaho* class, the U.S. Navy adopted the turbo-electric drive system which was to be followed in all subsequent capital ships for the next twenty years.

In spite of this virtual cessation of capital ship construction in the United States, decisions were taken in 1916 to begin a huge programme of naval expansion inspired by the announcement of a similar building programme adopted by the Japanese who announced that they intended to build and maintain a fleet of eight battleships and eight battle-cruisers none of which were to exceed eight years in age. The corresponding American programme of 1916 was for ten battleships and six battle-cruisers to be built in the next few years. Only one ship from this programme, the battleship *Maryland*, in April 1917, was laid down during the war. Between May 1919 and April 1921, nine battleships were laid down, but of these, seven were cancelled as a result of the Washington Treaty, discussed in the next chapter, and only the *Colorado* and the *West Virginia* were completed.

With a displacement of some 32,000 tons and a main armament of eight 16-inch guns, these ships were representatives of an age that was passing. Indeed, except for their increased main armament, they were very similar to the previous class, having a speed of only 21 knots. Their propulsion was by turbo-electric drive, superheated steam being supplied by eight small-tube boilers which were now taking the place, in all warships, of the numerous large-tube boilers previously fitted.

The German Navy had been the first to adopt this type of boiler, which conferred a great saving in weight and space. Thus whereas the British *Indefatigable* had required thirty-one boilers to provide a horse-power of 44,000, the *Queen Elizabeth* twenty-four boilers for 75,000 horse-power, the *Von der Tann* drew her 43,000 horse-power from only eighteen boilers and the *König* had twelve for the same power. The first British capital ship to have small-tube boilers was the *Hood*, their substitution in place of large-tube boilers giving her an extra 24,000 horse-power over the *Renown* class with the same weight of machinery. Super-heated steam, which had since been developed, permitted even fewer boilers.

The six battle-cruisers of the American 1916 programme were finally laid down after the end of the war, but again construction of them was suspended and finally abandoned as a result of the Washington Treaty, except for the *Lexington* and *Saratoga*, which were redesigned and completed as aircraft carriers.

The 1916 programme, in addition to these capital ships, had authorised the construction of ten 'scout cruisers' of the *Omaha* class, 7100-ton ships, oil-fired and turbine-driven to give a speed of 35 knots and mounting twelve 6-inch guns. A programme of more than eighty destroyers of the four-funnelled, flush-deck type, mounting four 4-inch guns and 12 torpedo-tubes, was authorised at the same time.

Meanwhile the Japanese were building the four 40,600-ton battleships *Nagato, Mutsu, Kaga* and *Tosa*, mounting eight 16-inch guns, to be added to the four modern battleships of the *Fuso* class. Provision was also made for four new battle-cruisers of 42,000 tons, *Amagi, Akagi, Atako* and *Takao*, the first two of which were laid down in 1920. At the same time a group of eight light cruisers of the *Kama* and *Natori* classes was authorised, ships of 5170 tons and a speed of 33 knots which mounted seven 5·5-inch guns. Three of these were launched during 1920 and the remainder had been begun.

In 1920 an additional programme was introduced, providing for four more battleships and four battle-cruisers to replace the *Fuso* and *Kongo* classes which were approaching the eight-year age limit, twelve further light cruisers and a great many destroyers and submarines.

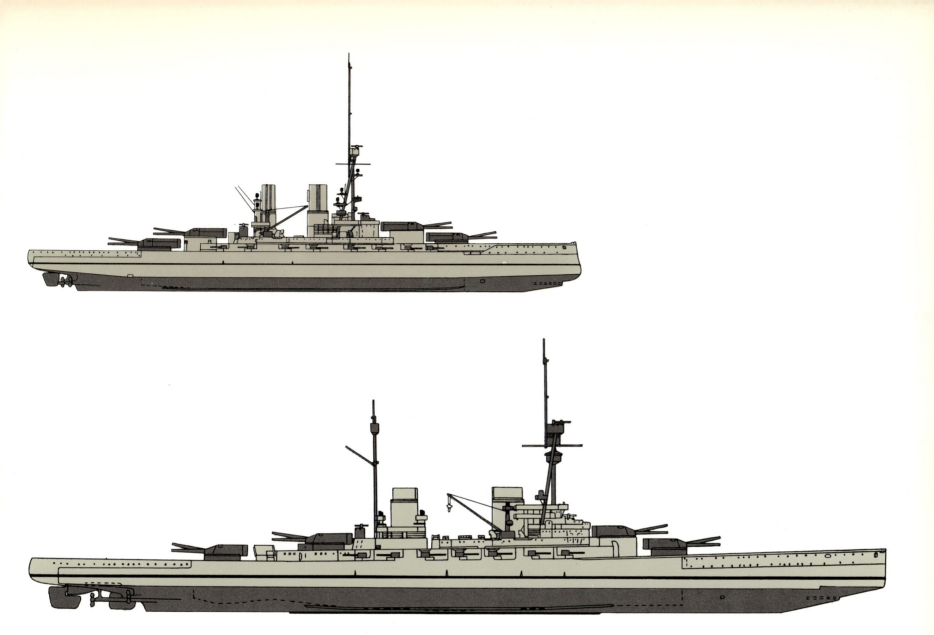

BAYERN/HINDENBURG

German super-dreadnought *Bayern*,
the first of her type mounting 15-inch guns to be built for
the Imperial German Navy.

German battle-cruiser *Hindenburg*,
the last to be added to the High Sea Fleet, sister to the
famous *Lützow* lost at Jutland.

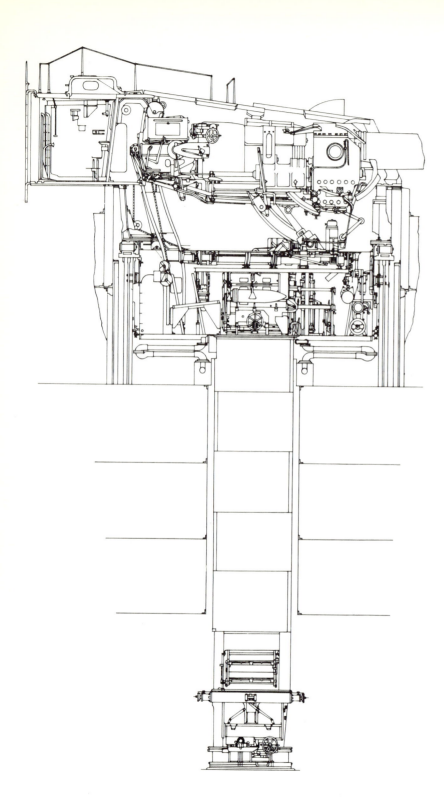

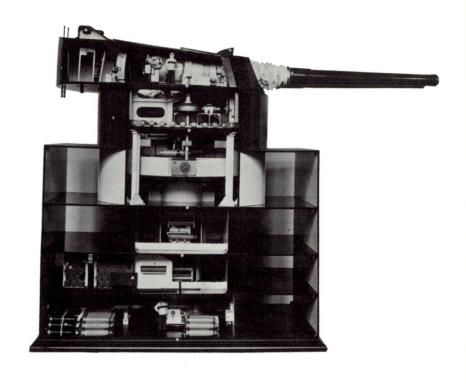

Left: Details of the mechanism of a 15-inch turret as mounted in the *Queen Elizabeth* (1913).

Right: Sectional view of a 15-inch turret of H.M.S. *Hood* (1918).

H.M.S. *Hood* (1918). Originally designed as a battle-cruiser with comparatively light armour protection, this beautiful ship finally emerged in 1920 as the prototype of the fast battleship which was to become the backbone of all modern navies in the Second World War. Lack of modernisation, however, left her outclassed in that war and she was sunk in battle by the German battleship *Bismarck* in 1941. (Photo from 1937.)

French light cruiser *La Galissonnière*. Mounting nine 6-inch guns in triple turrets, and with a speed of 36 knots, the six ships of this class were begun in 1931 in reply to the Italian *Condottieri* class.

THE WASHINGTON TREATY

The naval armaments race between Britain and Germany, which had come to an end with the defeat of the latter, had thus been taken up by the United States and Japan. By 1921, eleven huge battleships and six battle-cruisers were under construction in the U.S. shipyards. The Japanese had commissioned two battleships; two more as well as four battle-cruisers of their 'Eight-Eight' programme had been laid down. Two further battleships of 45,000 tons and mounting eight 18-inch guns were projected. Britain, not yet able to contemplate the end of her long-established sea supremacy, in spite of crippling economic difficulties, felt impelled to compete; her naval estimates for 1921 included provision for four battle-cruisers which were to mount nine 16-inch guns, to be followed by a group of 48,500-ton battleships with a main armament of nine 18-inch guns.

In 1921, however, the United States government called a conference to discuss a limitation of naval armaments. It opened in Washington on 12th November 1921, and continued until 6th February 1922 when a Treaty was signed by the five main naval powers who agreed to limit their capital ship tonnage in the proportion of 5 : 5 : 3 for the United States, Great Britain and Japan and 1·75 for France and Italy. In numbers of ships this permitted Great Britain to retain twenty-two until her two projected ships, *Nelson* and *Rodney*, were completed, when four earlier ships were to be scrapped. The United States was permitted to complete the *Colorado* and *West Virginia* to replace the old *North Dakota* and *Delaware* which would then be scrapped, leaving a total of eighteen under the American flag. The Japanese were to retain ten ships; France and Italy might build up to a similar number but, in the event, were content with fewer.

By the terms of the Treaty, all other capital ships built or building were to be scrapped except for any which might be appropriated for conversion to aircraft carriers; the Powers agreed not to build or acquire any further capital ships except in replacement of any which were lost or of those which reached the agreed age limit of twenty years. Such new ships were limited to a tonnage of 35,000 tons.

As an immediate consequence, besides scrapping the majority of her existing dreadnought fleet, Britain cancelled her projected battleship and battle-cruiser programme and set about designing the two 35,000-ton ships permitted by the Treaty, which were to emerge in 1927 as the *Nelson* and *Rodney*. They are of interest as the first example of battleships designed under the restrictions imposed by the Treaty. This led to the concentration of their three triple 16-inch turrets forward of the superstructure so as to be able to restrict the amount of armour required to establish a citadel on the 'all-or-nothing' principle. This arrangement did not prove very satisfactory, the bridge superstructure being almost uninhabitable when the after 16-inch guns were firing on the beam. A further saving of weight was achieved by the adoption of super-heated steam, which enabled the number of boilers to be reduced to eight, and of geared turbines of 45,000 horse-power. Another new feature was the mounting of their secondary armament of twelve 6-inch guns in power-worked twin turrets.

Forecastle of H.M.S. *Rodney*, British battleship. This ship and her sister H.M.S. *Nelson* were completed in 1927 under the restrictions imposed by the Washington Treaty. Though their armament of nine 16-inch guns was very powerful for their day, their moderate speed of 23 knots made them obsolescent before the Second World War broke out.

These ships can be said to have been the last battleships 'of-the-line', their moderate speed of 23 knots making them unable to take their place in the fast task forces which were to become the basic unit with the advent of the aircraft carrier.

The first navy to develop the concept of the fast battleship initiated by the *Queen Elizabeth* class was the French, when in 1932 it laid down the 26,500-ton *Dunkerque* and, two years later, her sister ship *Strasbourg*. To enable these ships to incorporate on this displacement the armour protection of a battleship and the 30 knots of a battle-cruiser, their main armament was restricted to eight 13-inch guns and, following the example of the British *Nelson* class, they were mounted forward of the bridge superstructure. By concentrating them in two quadruple turrets, however, greater space was made available between the turrets and between the after turret and the superstructure, thus obviating the damaging blast effect experienced in the *Nelson* and *Rodney*.

Profiting from the lessons of the First World War, armour protection on the side was sacrificed, the belt being a maximum of 11 inches thick, in favour of 5-inch upper and 2-inch lower armoured decks.

In the United States and Japan, advantage was taken of the clause in the Washington Treaty which permitted capital ships to be converted to aircraft carriers. It has been mentioned that the former selected the battle-cruisers *Lexington* and *Saratoga* for this purpose. Conversion of the Japanese battle-cruisers *Amagi* and *Akagi* was similarly begun. When the *Amagi* was heavily damaged in the devastating earthquake of 1923, she was scrapped and the hull of the unfinished battleship *Kaga* appropriated to replace her. The development of carriers, the number and size of which were also limited by the Washington Treaty, is examined on pages 205–17.

Cruisers were also limited in size by the definition of the capital ship established in the Treaty as any ship of more than 10,000 tons and/or with guns of more than 8·1-inch calibre. At the same time the largest gun which might be mounted in a cruiser was 8-inch. Inevitably the major navies set out to design cruisers mounting as many 8-inch guns as possible on this limited displacement. As high speeds and long endurance were also required, weight and space had to be saved in other directions. New techniques and the use of lighter metals where possible contributed to this; in the main either armour protection or hull strength had to be sacrificed. Even so, the officially declared 10,000 tons was often considerably more in reality.

The British Navy had produced ships of this size, laid down in 1916 but not completed until after the end of the war. These ships of the *Hawkins* class were quite extensively armoured over their whole length, but their speed was barely 29 knots and their main armament was limited to seven 7·5-inch guns on single, hand-worked mountings. Such guns were the biggest that could be hand-worked; indeed, their ammunition was too heavy for the average Japanese sailor to handle and it has been said that the 8-inch limit was particularly favoured by the Japanese so that the heaviest cruisers would necessarily have power-worked guns.

Power-worked 8-inch mountings absorbed a great deal of additional weight so that the first 'Washington Treaty' heavy cruisers of the British Navy, the five *Kent* class laid down in 1924, mounting eight 8-inch guns in twin turrets, were given virtually no armour. Designed primarily for service on foreign stations and for trade-protection duties, particular attention was paid to habitability and sea-keeping qualities, and they were given a very high freeboard. Coupled with their lack of armour protection, this caused them to be described as 'tin-clads'. They were followed by four more very similar ships of the *London* class, laid down in 1926.

Perhaps the most extreme examples of the 'tin-clad' style were the first heavy cruisers built by the French to Washington Treaty limitations, the two ships of the *Tourville* class, mounting eight 8-inch guns. Designed primarily for operation in the Mediterranean, however, by greatly reducing their endurance they were able to incorporate machinery of 120,000 horse-power, giving them a speed of more than 33 knots. Four similar ships of the *Suffren* class, laid down between 1926 and 1929, were given a small measure of protection, but with power reduced to 90,000 horse-power, a reduction of speed to 31 knots.

Japanese cruiser *Takao* (1930). Ostensibly limited to the 10,000 tons allowed by the Washington Treaty rules, she was actually more than 13,000 and so able to mount ten 8-inch guns and a fair degree of armour protection.

After this the French abandoned the 'tin-clad' design, with the *Algérie* which had side armour of $4\frac{1}{2}$ inches and a 3-inch armoured deck, and, with 84,000 horse-power, a designed speed of 31 knots.

Comparable ships of the Italian Navy were the two *Trento* class laid down in 1925 and followed between 1929 and 1931 by four *Zara* class. By sacrificing hull strength, however, the Italians were able to give these ships some armour protection, the former having 3-inch side armour as well as 3 inches on their turrets, while the latter with $5\frac{1}{2}$-inch side armour and 5 inches on their turrets were an improvement on the real 'tin-clads'. The most distinctive feature of Italian warships of this epoch was their extremely light construction, which sometimes led to damage as a result of heavy weather encountered during wartime operations.

More successful in producing well-balanced cruisers in the Washington Treaty period were the Japanese and the Americans, the former by secretly violating the terms and laying down four ships of the *Nachi* class in 1924 and 1925 which had a displacement of over 13,000 tons. At some sacrifice of speed as compared to French and Italian heavy cruisers they not only mounted ten 8-inch guns in twin turrets but had 3-inch armour on their sides and turrets and a 3-inch protective deck. This class was followed in 1927 and 1928 by four similar ships of the *Atago* class.

Similarly the Japanese light cruisers of the *Mogami* and *Tone* classes laid down in 1931 were given out to be 8500 tons displacement but were in reality 11,200 tons, which permitted them to mount twelve or fifteen 6·1-inch guns in triple turrets, later replaced by 8-inch guns in twin turrets and twelve 24-inch above-water torpedo tubes and to have a moderate degree of armour protection. The powerful battery of torpedo tubes to launch the high-performance 'Long Lance' torpedoes was a unique feature of Japanese cruisers and was to prove a very effective weapon during the Second World War.

That excellent ships within the Treaty limitations could be produced was shown by the two heavy cruisers *Furutaka* and *Kako*, designed by Vice-Admiral Hiraga and incorporating new techniques first tried out in the light cruiser *Yubari*, described below. Completed in 1925, these ships mounted six 8-inch guns in single turrets (later replaced by twin turrets) and twelve fixed 24-inch torpedo tubes (later replaced by two quadruple revolving mountings). Protection was supplied by a belt of 3-inch side armour, a 2-inch protective deck and 5 inches of armour on the turrets. In spite of these weighty characteristics, the standard displacement was only 9150 tons and a speed of 33 knots was achieved.

In America great pains were taken in the design of their heavy cruisers to save weight by the use of welding instead of riveting (first adopted by the Germans in the cruiser *Emden*) and by the use of aluminium alloy wherever possible. As a result their first two 'treaty' cruisers emerged with a displacement of only 9100 tons. Owing to the exceptionally narrow beam of these ships, their ten 8-inch guns were mounted in two twin turrets with triple turrets superimposed. The following six ships of the *Northampton* class saved further weight by grouping their nine 8-inch guns in three triple turrets and, in spite of increased length, were still little more than 9000 tons displacement.

The most interesting outcome of the treaty limitations on ships was the class built by the Germans, who were prohibited by the terms of the Treaty of Versailles from building any warships of more than 10,000 tons displacement. Unaffected by the Washington Treaty, they proceeded to build armoured ships ostensibly of this weight, mounting six 11-inch guns in two triple turrets, which came to be popularly known as 'pocket-battleships'. The first of the class was the *Deutschland*, later renamed *Lützow*, which was laid down in 1929 and was followed by two others, the *Admiral Scheer* and the *Admiral Graf Spee*. Electric welding was used in their construction to save weight and they were the first warships of such a size to have this feature.

Though they were in reality of some 12,000 tons displacement, it was nevertheless a most ingenious design which permitted them to mount such an armament together with 4-inch side armour and a secondary armament of eight 5·9-inch and six 4·1-inch guns as well as eight torpedo tubes. Great endurance and a speed of 26

knots, provided by eight sets of diesel engines of 6750 horse-power each, made them formidable ships in the role of commerce raiders.

Another essential component of a balanced fleet was the light cruiser with a main armament of guns of 6-inch calibre or less. The British, with their numerous ships of the *C*, *D* and *E* classes built or laid down during the war, contented themselves during the 1920s with completing the last four ships of the *D* class, mounting six 6-inch guns on a displacement of 4850 tons, and the *Emerald* and *Enterprise* (7500 tons, seven 6-inch) notable chiefly for the very high horse-power (for their day) of 80,000, which gave them a speed of 33 knots.

During the 1930s the British added a large number of light cruisers to their navy, beginning with five ships of the *Leander* class of 7000 tons with eight 6-inch guns in twin turrets. These were followed by larger ships of the *Southampton* and 'Colony' classes of from 8000 to 10,000 tons with twelve or nine 6-inch guns in triple turrets. All these ships had a moderate degree of protection including an armour belt of 4 to 2 inches and a speed of about 33 knots.

The Americans, who completed the ten ships of the *Omaha* class of their 1916 programme between 1923 and 1925, laid down no further light cruisers until 1935. The Japanese, after completing the eleven ships of the *Kuma* and *Natori* class of their 1917 and 1919 programme between 1920 and 1925, built three further ships of much the same size and armament—the *Jintsu* class—during the decade when the Washington Treaty was in force.

One further light cruiser was the interesting *Yubari*, designed by Vice-Admiral Y. Hiraga, which mounted a main armament of six 5·5-inch high-angle guns and four 24-inch torpedo tubes on a displacement of only 2890 tons with a speed of $35\frac{1}{2}$ knots.

The first light cruisers added to the French Navy during this period were the three 7249-ton ships of the *Duguay-Trouin* class, laid down in 1922–23, unarmoured, fast (33 knots) ships mounting eight 6·1-inch guns.

Having adopted a type of ship called *contre-torpilleur*, which was a super-destroyer or miniature cruiser, no further light cruisers were laid down for the French Navy until 1931 when, in reply to the Italian 'Condottieri' class of 6-inch cruisers, the *Émile Bertin* and the six *La Galissonnière* class were begun. Both types mounted nine 6-inch guns in triple turrets, but the former, of 5886 tons displacement, and unarmoured, achieved a speed of 39 knots on trials, whereas the latter, of 7700 tons, sacrificed 5 knots in favour of quite extensive protection including a belt of side armour $4\frac{3}{4}$ to 3 inches thick.

The Germans began the rebuilding of their navy with the light cruiser *Emden*, the first all-welded warship, completed in 1925, a ship of 5400 tons mounting eight 5·9-inch guns and protected by a belt of 2-inch to 4-inch armour. Geared turbines gave her a speed of 29 knots. Their next light cruisers, three ships of the *Köln* class laid down in 1926, were of similar size but faster (32 knots) and were the first cruisers to mount their nine 5·9-inch guns in triple turrets. The *Leipzig* and *Nürnberg* which followed were improved versions of this class.

Destroyers of the Washington Treaty period advanced little beyond those built during the last year of the First World War. The British had ended the war with a very large number of the *V* and *W* class ships of some 1500 tons mounting four 4·7-inch guns and six 21-inch torpedo tubes in two triple mountings with a top speed at deep load of some 31 knots. Sufficient of these were kept in service to make up the two main fleets—in home waters and the Mediterranean—and a flotilla on the China Station. It was not until 1924 that two prototypes of the post-war *A* class were begun, which were basically only improvements of the *W* class. They were followed at yearly intervals by flotillas of similar design up to the *I* class laid down in 1936. Destroyers of basically similar design were built by all the major navies.

The French Navy, for instance, laid down twenty-six *torpilleurs* of the *Simon* and *Alcyon* classes of much the same armament and size completed between 1926 and 1931. They also struck out on a new line by building between 1924 and 1925 a larger class of *contre-torpilleurs* of the *Tigre* class, of some 2126 tons and higher speed, 35 knots at normal displacement, and an armament of five 5·1-inch

The German light cruiser *Leipzig* (1929). Improved version of the *Köln* class laid down 1925, mounting nine 5·9-inch guns in triple turrets.

guns. These were followed between 1928 and 1934 by eighteen further ships of 2400 tons armed with five 5·5-inch guns all of which had a top speed of between 37 and 40 knots. Then came the six ships of the *Le Fantasque* class with a similar armament and the six 2900-ton *Mogador*'s which had a main armament of eight 5·5-inch and ten torpedo tubes, of which only two were completed. Both these classes achieved 43 to 45 knots on trials.

The United States Navy, with more than 240 of its war programme of flush-deck, four-funnelled destroyers completed between 1918 and 1921, contented itself until 1932 with these 1200-ton, 35-knot ships, mounting usually four 4-inch guns (a few had 5-inch) and two triple 21-inch torpedo-tube mountings on each side. It then began to modernise its destroyer fleet with eight ships of the *Farragut* class. With their raised forecastle and superimposed gun mountings, these were more conventional types of destroyers; but, incorporating five of the new 5-inch, 38-calibre, dual-purpose gun which was to become the standard U.S. destroyer main armament for more than ten years and twelve 21-inch torpedo tubes in quadruple mountings, they were more powerfully armed than contemporary ships abroad, while their 42,800 horse-power geared turbines and four high-pressure boilers gave them the satisfactory speed of 36½ knots at standard displacement.

Interesting destroyers of this period were the twelve Italian ships of the 'Navigatori' class laid down in 1927. They had a very high speed of around 40 knots. To secure this they were built with comparatively light scantlings even by Mediterranean standards. It was in reply to these ships that the French included in their 1930 programme six *contre-torpilleurs* of the *Fantasque* class described above.

The shipbuilding 'holiday' imposed by the Washington Treaty was the occasion for all the major naval powers to modernise those old battleships which, by the terms of the Treaty, they were allowed to maintain in service. The process included improvements in the range of main-armament guns by increasing their maximum elevation, and an increase in the number of anti-aircraft guns; modernisation of machinery, substituting oil fuel for coal where applicable, introducing high-pressure steam and high super-heat to achieve higher speeds or at least maintain original speed in spite of increased displacement resulting from increased horizontal armour protection and the incorporation of anti-torpedo bulges.

The ships were, indeed, transformed in the process. The Italians went furthest in the modernisation of their four pre-war super-dreadnoughts of the *Cavour* class in which they added 50 feet to the length of the hull and, with the substitution of new boilers and engines to raise the horse-power from 30,000 to 75,000, added five knots to their speed. At the same time the thirteen 12-inch, 46-calibre guns were replaced by ten 12·6-inch, 44-calibre guns of a new type on mountings which gave them greatly increased range.

The Japanese similarly transformed their capital ships, their battle-cruisers and battleships all emerging as fast battleships.

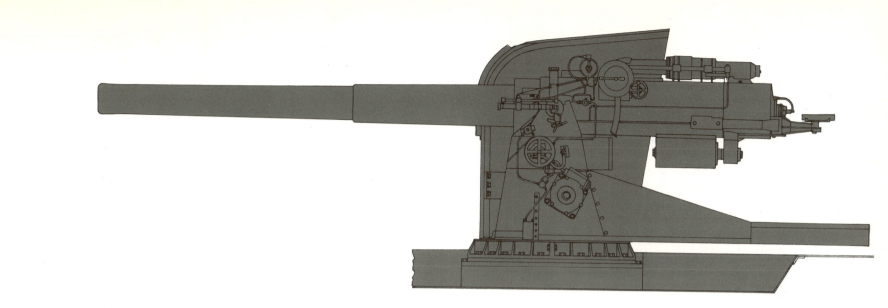

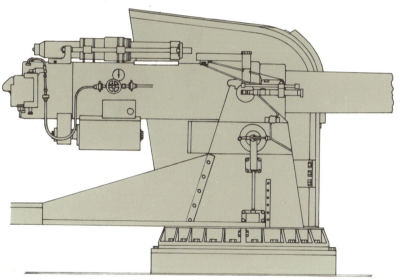

6-inch gun as fitted in cruisers and as secondary armament in battleships. It fired a 100-pound shell to a maximum range of 22,000 yards.

FARRAGUT

The American destroyer *Farragut* (1934),
one of the first of a huge programme of modernisation and
expansion of the U.S. Navy.

194

U.S.S. *West Virginia*, super-dreadnought of the 1916 programme. One of the last slow battleships to be built. Sunk at Pearl Harbor 1941—subsequently raised and repaired for service. (Photo from 1941.)

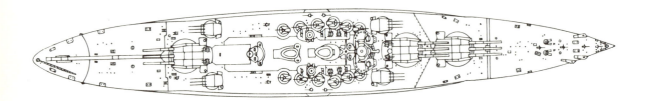

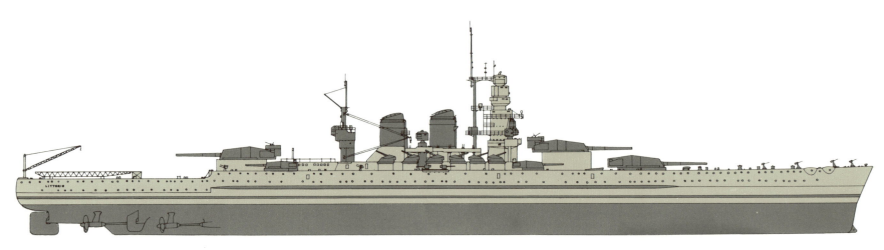

Admiral Angelo Iachino, C.-in-C. of the Italian Fleet for the greater part of the Second World War.

LITTORIO

The Italian battleship *Littorio*, *Vittorio Veneto* class (1937), one of the three fast (30 knots) battleships of 41,167 tons laid down after the lapsing of the Washington Treaty. Proved a very successful design.

BUILDING PROGRAMMES

FOR THE SECOND WORLD WAR

The Washington Treaty and its sequel, the London Naval Treaty of 1930, were due to terminate at the end of 1936. In the hope of continuing them, a conference on naval armaments was held in London in 1935. Long before this, however, the international situation indicated that success was unlikely. In 1934 the German Chancellor Hitler had publicly denounced the Versailles Treaty on the grounds that the ex-Allies had failed to fulfil the terms which called for a reduction in their armaments. In place of the naval restriction clauses he negotiated an agreement by which Germany might build up her navy to 35 per cent of the strength of the British Navy. As a first step there were laid down in that year the fast battleships *Scharnhorst* and *Gneisenau* of 31,850 tons standard displacement (officially declared as 26,000). Designed primarily for the *guerre-de-course* rather than for battle, their main armament was restricted to nine 11-inch guns in triple turrets in favour of very heavy armour and a top speed of over 31 knots, while diesel engines were incorporated for cruising, giving them a very large endurance.

Meanwhile both Italy and Japan had adopted aggressive attitudes which left little prospect of the naval conference achieving very much. The resultant Treaty of 1936, indeed, abolished all quantitative limitations on all categories of warships. Every major navy now felt impelled to join in an armaments race. The size of battleships was to have been restricted to 35,000 tons and their main armament to 14-inch calibre, by the 1936 Treaty. The United States, before deciding on the design of their new battleships, agreed to wait until the end of that year for Japan to ratify the Treaty. When she failed to do so the decision was taken to adopt the 16-inch gun as the main armament.

Britain, however, whence could be seen the war clouds gathering, felt unable to wait so long. In Germany the *Scharnhorst* and *Gneisenau* were nearing completion, while the Italians were well advanced with their two fast battleships, *Littorio* and *Vittorio Veneto*. The design for 14-inch guns in quadruple turrets for the projected British ships had been prepared. To change to 16-inch would delay them by at least a year. It was decided to go ahead and on 1st January 1937 the first two ships of the new *King George V* class were laid down.

The original design was for twelve 14-inch guns in three quadruple turrets to be mounted. When tests with improved shells disclosed the need for greater armour protection, however, the extra weight was accompanied by reducing the forward superfiring turret to a twin. Of 36,750 tons standard displacement when thus modified, the *King George V* and *Prince of Wales* had a massive armoured belt 15 inches thick over the magazines and 14 inches over the machinery spaces, 15-inch armoured bulkheads, turrets with 16-inch faces, 15-inch sides and 9-inch roofs and barbettes of 16 inches. Six inches of armoured deck covered the magazines, 5 inches the machinery spaces. The secondary armament of sixteen of a new type of 5·25-inch dual-purpose gun was mounted in twin turrets. Geared turbines developing 125,000 horse-power gave them a speed of $29\frac{1}{4}$ knots.

The Italian battleships *Littorio* and *Vittorio Veneto* mentioned previously had

Italian light cruiser *Armando Díaz* (1932), of 5,406 tons and 36·5 knots. An improved version of the *Condottieri* class.

been laid down in 1934 in reply to the French *Dunkerque* and *Strasbourg*. Ostensibly in conformation with Washington Treaty limitation of 35,000 tons, in practice their standard displacement was 41,167 tons, while their main armament was nine 15-inch guns. Designed by Umberto Pugliese, these ships combined a powerful armament, high speed (over 30 knots), good armour protection and a very elegant appearance. Their underwater protection in the form of ingeniously designed internal 'bulges' was particularly successful, and during the Second World War both the *Littorio* and *Vittorio Veneto* were to survive torpedoing with comparatively little damage. They were, nevertheless, of light hull construction, in the Italian style, and were to suffer for this when operating at high speed in heavy weather. A third ship, the *Roma*, completed during the war, was sunk by German radio-controlled glider bombs when she was *en route* to Malta to surrender to the Allies.

All the major naval powers began extensive building programmes with the lapsing of the Washington Treaty and the London Naval Treaties of 1930 and 1936 which stemmed from it.

The Japanese laid down in 1937 what were to emerge as the two most powerful battleships in the world during the Second World War. These were the *Yamato* and *Musashi* of 64,170 tons standard displacement, which had a main armament of nine $18 \cdot 1$-inch guns in triple turrets and a speed of $27\frac{1}{2}$ knots. In the event, the development of the aircraft carrier, resulting in the main fleet actions in the Pacific being fought at ranges far outside that of the biggest gun, prevented either of these monstrous ships from acting in the classic role for which they were designed—battleships-of-the-line. Both were sunk by naval air attack with bombs and torpedoes.

In Germany, also, following the Anglo-German Naval Agreement, two new battleships *Bismarck* and *Tirpitz* were laid down in 1936. Declared 35,000 tons standard displacement but actually some 42,000 tons, mounting eight 15-inch guns and with a speed of 30 knots, the most notable feature of these ships was their massive protection by a complete side belt of $12\frac{1}{2}$ inches (lower) and $5\frac{3}{4}$ inches (upper) armour, an armoured 4-inch deck and a degree of internal subdivision which was to make them virtually unsinkable by gunfire alone.

A programme of six further, larger battleships was also projected and two of these were laid down in 1939 but were never completed. They would have been of 56,200 tons standard displacement, mounting eight 16-inch guns. Three even larger ships, H.42, H.43 and H.44, never went further than the planning stage. The largest of these, H.44, was to have displaced no less than 122,000 tons and to mount eight 20-inch guns.

France and Italy had never built up to the limit allowed them until the latter laid down the *Littorio* and *Vittorio Veneto* in 1934 (described earlier). This impelled the French to follow suit and in 1935 the fast battleship *Richelieu*, of 35,000 tons standard displacement, was laid down, to be followed by the *Jean Bart*, *Clemenceau* and *Gascogne*. Only the first of these had been completed before the German occupation of France in 1940. The *Jean Bart* in an uncompleted state was hastily made seaworthy and steamed to Casablanca to prevent her falling into German hands. The *Clemenceau* lay, in an early stage of construction, throughout the war at Brest and was never completed. The *Gascogne* was never begun.

These ships, with a main armament of eight 15-inch guns, a speed of more than 30 knots, were in their general design enlarged *Dunkerque*'s, with the same massive superstructure and the same layout of their main armament, both quadruple turrets being sited forward—though this was to have been altered in the *Gascogne*. Though they enjoyed very heavy side armour, they were less well protected horizontally, their two armoured decks of 6 and 2 inches being less than was considered necessary a few years later in the face of the threat of aerial bombing and the plunging fire of long-range naval action, when we find the American *North Carolina* class with 6-inch and 4-inch decks.

The restriction of the first British fast battleships of the post-Washington Treaty era to guns of 14-inch calibre in accordance with the terms of the stillborn London

Top: U.S.S. *North Carolina*, one of six fast battleships of 35,000 tons laid down between 1937 and 1938 after the lapsing of the Washington Treaty. Each mounted nine 16-inch guns in triple turrets.

Bottom: British destroyer H.M.S. *Jupiter* (1938–40) of the similar *J* and *K* classes laid down as part of the re-armament programme prior to the Second World War.

Treaty of 1936 has been mentioned earlier. The United States was in less of a hurry to begin their battleship building programme, and when it became clear that the Japanese would not adhere to the new London Treaty, they laid down between 1937 and 1939 six fast battleships of 35,000 tons. Of these, the *North Carolina* and *Washington* were sister ships; the *Indiana, Massachusetts, Alabama* and *South Dakota* were quite different in appearance; but all mounted nine 16-inch guns and a secondary armament of twenty 5-inch, and had a speed of 28 knots. With these ships, the U.S. Navy finally abandoned electric drive in favour of geared turbines.

Between 1940 and 1941, four larger (45,000-ton) ships, *Iowa, Missouri, New Jersey* and *Wisconsin*—most graceful of all American battleships—were laid down. They had a speed of 32 knots and mounted, again, three triple 16-inch turrets, but of more powerful guns than in the earlier ships. Completed in 1943 and 1944, they were also given, as a result of war experience, no less than 120 close-range 40-mm. and 20-mm. automatic guns to support the twenty dual-purpose 5-inch guns in the anti-aircraft role.

Besides the battleships, mentioned earlier, and aircraft carriers, which have been given a section to themselves, there was a feverish building of other classes of men-of-war by the major navies in the years immediately before and during the Second World War. Following the completion of the eight cruisers of the *Southampton* class in 1936, the British built two similar ships of the *Belfast* class of 10,000 tons which mounted twelve 6-inch guns in triple turrets, had a speed of 32 knots and a high degree of protection from a 4 to 3-inch side belt. They then embarked on an extensive programme of 8000-ton light cruisers of the 'Colony' class with originally twelve, later nine, 6-inch guns in triple turrets, laid down between 1938 and 1939.

The growing influence of air power on war at sea had led to the conversion, in 1935, of the old British light cruisers of the *C* class into anti-aircraft cruisers by the substitution of high-angle 4-inch guns for their original 6-inch main battery. The British now went on to construct fifteen ships of the *Dido* class of 5700 tons and armed with ten or eight 5·25-inch dual-purpose (H.A./L.A.) guns in twin turrets.

The French and Italian navies built no further heavy cruisers mounting 8-inch guns following the completion of the *Algérie* by the former in 1934 and the *Zara* class by the Italians in 1932. Nor did either navy build any further light cruisers of the middle size after the six French *La Gallissonnière* class completed in 1935–1937 and the Italian 'Condottieri' class, ten of which were completed between 1931 and 1936. The Italians, however, embarked in 1939 on a programme of very small, fast light cruisers of the 'Capitani Romani' class of 3475 tons (standard) and a speed of 40 knots, which mounted eight 5·3-inch guns in twin turrets. Only three of the twelve laid down were completed before the end of the war.

The French equivalent of these ships were the six *Mogador*'s with a similar armament and speed, of which only two were completed in 1938; but with a displacement of only 2900 tons they were rated by the French as *contre-torpilleurs* and must be looked upon as super-destroyers.

The German Navy laid down five heavy cruisers between 1935 and 1937, though only three, *Blücher, Admiral Hipper* and *Prinz Eugen*, were completed. Ostensibly 10,000 tons displacement in accordance with treaty restrictions, they were actually 14,240 tons with a speed of 32 knots and a main armament of eight 8-inch guns.

By far the largest programme undertaken during the years immediately before and during the Second World War was that of the United States Navy where, besides the ten fast battleships, nine cruisers of the *Honolulu* class, mounting fifteen 6-inch guns on a standard displacement of 9700 tons, were completed during 1938 and 1939. At the same time a new type of light anti-aircraft cruiser, with a main armament of sixteen 5-inch dual-purpose guns (twelve in later ships of the class) and a speed of 35 knots, was introduced. Eleven of this *Atlanta* class were completed during the war. An even larger number (twenty-seven) of the

10,000-ton *Cleveland* class were built, mounting twelve 6-inch guns in triple turrets and twelve 5-inch in twin mounts.

Of heavy cruisers, there were twenty ships of the *Baltimore* class or similar of 13,600 tons which mounted nine of an improved type of 8-inch gun, firing a heavier shell, and twelve 5-inch.

Destroyers were, of course, built by all the combatant navies in considerable numbers. Typical of the period were the British *J, K, L* and *M* classes laid down before the war with a displacement of 1760 tons and an armament of six 4·7-inch guns and ten 21-inch torpedo tubes (reduced later to five in order to mount an increased anti-aircraft armament); the United States *Benson/Livermore* class of 1700 tons, mounting five 5-inch guns and ten 21-inch torpedo tubes (later reduced to four and five respectively), of which more than seventy were built, and the *Fletcher* class of 2050 tons, with five 5-inch and ten 21-inch torpedo tubes, of which 175 were completed; German destroyers of the *Z* type which on a displacement of 2600 tons mounted four or five 5·9-inch guns and eight 21-inch torpedo tubes; the Italian *Artigliere* class of 1620 tons, mounting five 4·7-inch guns (one being a light gun for firing star shells only), which, built in the Italian fashion of very light construction, had a speed of nearly 40 knots.

Apart from the major types of warship—battleships, cruisers, destroyers and aircraft carriers—a great many specialised craft were developed during the Second World War, such as motor torpedo boats and gunboats, minesweepers, etc., typical examples of which are illustrated. Probably the most important of these specialised types, owing to the role they played in the vital campaign fought by the German U-boats to cut the Allied life-line and on account of the large numbers in which they were built, were the escort vessels for protection of ocean convoys.

These were either specially designed for the purpose like the very numerous 'Flower', 'River', 'Loch' and 'Bay' classes of the British Navy which were primarily anti-submarine ships, the *Black Swan* class which were armed as anti-aircraft ships with six 4-inch high-angle guns, and the destroyer-escorts of the U.S. Navy, a number of which were also supplied to the British; or they were adapted from sloops designed for service on foreign stations such as the British *Grimsby* class, and from obsolescent destroyers given increased endurance by the conversion of one boiler room to oil bunkers and anti-submarine weapons at the expense of guns and torpedoes.

The U.S.S. *Missouri* firing a bombardment salvo from her 16-inch guns during the Korean War. All four of this ultimate class of U.S. battleships were subsequently de-commissioned. Now (1968), however, the *New Jersey* is being re-activated for a bombardment role in the Vietnam War.

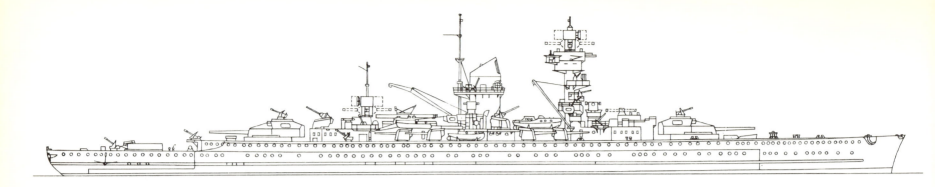

ADMIRAL SCHEER

The *Admiral Scheer*, one of the ingeniously designed German 'pocket battleships', which contrived to incorporate an armament of six 11-inch guns, a speed of 26 knots and a great endurance on a displacement of 12,000 tons.

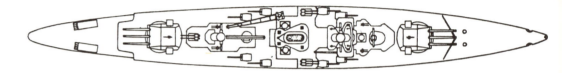

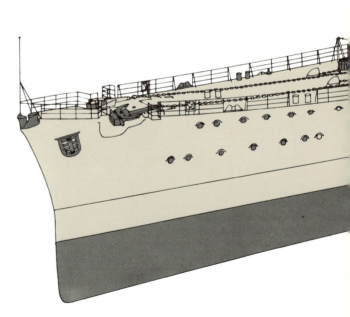

Left: Admiral Karl Dönitz, C.-in-C. of the U-boat arm of the German Navy in the Second World War until he superseded Admiral Raeder in January 1943.

Right: Admiral Erich Raeder, C.-in-C. of the German Navy under the Nazi régime and architect of its restoration following the repudiation of the Versailles Treaty.

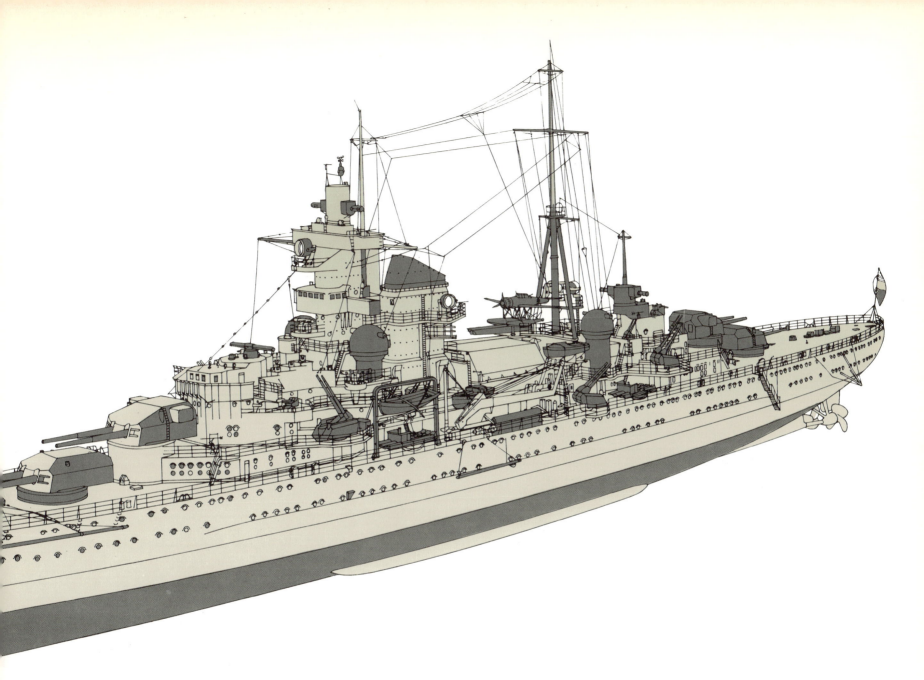

ADMIRAL HIPPER

German cruiser, ostensibly of 10,000 tons,
she and her sisters *Prinz Eugen* and *Blücher* were actually 14,240 tons
and, with a speed of 32 knots and a main armament of
eight 8-inch guns, were very formidable units.

Top: H.M.S. *Furious* (1918) as she appeared after her second conversion to an aircraft carrier with a flying-off deck forward and a landing deck aft.

Bottom: H.M.S. *Argus* (1917), converted from the uncompleted hull of a passenger liner to become the first flush-deck carrier and the first ship successfully to operate land planes.

THE AIRCRAFT CARRIER

The development during the First World War which was to have the most revolutionary consequences for sea warfare emerged so undramatically that it was given comparatively scant notice. In September 1918 a squat, ugly ship, immediately christened the 'flat-iron' from her shape, lacking masts and funnels, flush-deck from bow to stern, joined the British Grand Fleet. This was the *Argus*, the first aircraft carrier on which planes could both land and take off. Her design was the outcome of a long process of trial and error which had begun as long ago as 14th November 1910.

On that day an American civilian pilot, Eugene B. Ely, flew off from an 83-foot platform built over the bow of the U.S. light cruiser *Birmingham* in a Curtiss biplane powered by a 50 horse-power engine. The take-off run was only 57 feet and the primitive flying machine lost height after clearing the platform, actually touching the water just before it gained flying speed and climbed away to make a safe landing on shore.

Two months later Ely took the air again, on 18th January 1911, to make an even more epoch-making flight. On board the armoured cruiser *Pennsylvania* a wooden platform 119 feet long had been erected. Stretched across this platform, 12 inches above it, were twenty-two ropes with fifty-pound sandbags on the ends of each. Ely's plane had been fitted with three hooks intended to catch these ropes, which thus formed a simple form of arrester gear, and he now steered to make the first deck-landing in history. He skimmed over the first eleven ropes, but hooked the twelfth and successive ones which brought him to rest after a run of only 30 feet.

Ely received no pay for his exploit, only a letter of thanks from the Secretary of the Navy, and it is sad to relate he was killed a year later in an air crash. Furthermore, his achievement was not followed up by the U.S. Navy, which, like other navies, pinned its faith on seaplanes taking off from and alighting only on the water.

Meanwhile in England the first naval aviators had learnt to fly and, though they also only envisaged seaplanes for operation over water, one of them, Lieutenant Charles Samson, flew a Short S.27 biplane from a platform over the forecastle of the battleship *Africa* in January 1912, repeating the exploit from the *Hibernia* and the *London* while they were steaming at 10½ knots.

His aircraft had a wheeled undercarriage as well as air bags for alighting on the water; but when seaplanes with wooden floats were evolved, the ability to take off from a deck was preserved by means of detachable trolleys on which the plane ran for its take-off. During the First World War the British equipped a number of passenger boats to operate seaplanes in this way as well as small fighter aircraft on wheels. The largest of these was the ex-Cunard liner *Campania*. By an unfortunate signal mistake, she failed to sail with the British Grand Fleet for the Battle of Jutland. A smaller seaplane carrier, the *Engadine*, however, accompanied the Battle Cruiser Fleet from Rosyth and made history by operating one of her sea-

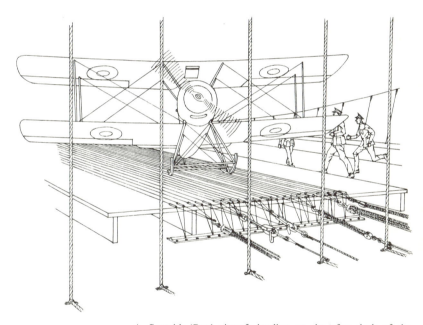

A Sopwith 'Pup' aircraft landing on the after deck of the *Furious*. Fore-and-aft wires on the deck and a rope barrier comprised an early (unsuccessful) arrester system.

planes on reconnaissance duties during the opening phase of the battle. The first important man-of-war to be so equipped was the so-called light cruiser *Furious* which had been designed to mount two 18-inch guns in single turrets, fore and aft. The forward turret was removed and the space devoted to a hangar over which was built a sloping flight-deck 228 feet long.

Operation of wheeled aircraft from these ships entailed the planes landing ashore or 'ditching', and though Squadron Commander E. H. Dunning succeeded in landing a little Sopwith 'Pup' fighter on the *Furious*'s deck, the manoeuvre could only be classed as a 'stunt' and on his second attempt at landing his plane went over the side and he lost his life. A clear deck on which to land was an obvious requirement and the *Furious* was now given one over her stern, the after turret being removed. Her funnel and bridge superstructure remained, rising up between the landing and flying-off decks.

This arrangement, however, proved a failure. A combination of turbulence in the airflow over the after end of the deck and of an absence of any airflow further forward, owing to the obstructing superstructure, led to a great many crashes and the scheme had to be abandoned.

In the meantime a liner which had been on the stocks in a British yard for Italy, the *Conte Rosso*, had been requisitioned and was being converted into the 14,450-ton *Argus* with a flight deck uninterrupted by any superstructure or funnel, the boiler smoke and gases being led through trunks and exhausted over the stern. Though the system of arrester gear fitted on her deck—an arrangement of fore-and-aft wires in which horns on the aircraft's undercarriages engaged—proved a failure, she was otherwise a great success and it proved feasible to land the lightly loaded aircraft of the day without it, relying upon the wind-speed down the deck to shorten their landing run.

This arrangement was to be retained for the next ten years or more in the British carriers which followed the *Argus*. The first of these to be completed was the *Eagle* in 1920 with a displacement of 22,600 tons, converted from a battleship which had been laid down for Chile. She was also the first to incorporate a bridge superstructure and funnels offset along one side, generally referred to as an 'island', so as to allow a clear flight deck over her whole length. So, too, did the 10,850-ton *Hermes*, the first ship to be laid down as an aircraft carrier and completed in 1923. The *Furious*, on the other hand, which had again been taken in hand for alteration at the end of the war, copied the flush-deck arrangement of the *Argus* in her next metamorphosis, in which shape she emerged in 1925.

With these four ships, *Argus, Eagle, Hermes* and *Furious*, the British Navy had established a clear lead over all others with regard to ship-borne aircraft. Progress came almost to a halt, however, as a result of the transfer of responsibility for naval aviation from the Admiralty in 1918 to the newly constituted Royal Air Force. Imbued with theories of the supersession of sea power by air power in the shape of the bomber aircraft, the new service refused to devote more than a small fraction of its available funds or talents to the development of carrier-borne types or the technique of operating them.

Meanwhile the United States and Japanese navies, profiting from the experience of the British, rapidly overhauled them and were soon in the lead. The Japanese entered the race when they laid down the 7470-ton *Hosho* in December 1919, which joined the fleet three years later. Carrying twenty-one aircraft, the *Hosho* had a small, conventional bridge structure (removed in 1923) and three funnels which swung to a horizontal position during flying operations.

The Americans' first carrier was the 11,050-ton *Langley* converted from the collier *Jupiter*, which had a small navigation platform to the side of her flight deck and, at first, a short funnel on each side, interconnected so that exhaust gases could discharge to port or starboard, depending on the direction of the wind. She was eventually given two port-side funnels which hinged outward during flying operations.

Besides the British *Argus* and *Eagle*, which were in service, and the *Hermes* and *Furious* under construction, these were the only two other carriers in existence when in 1922 the Washington Treaty for the limitation of naval armaments,

Top: The *Hosho*, first Japanese aircraft carrier, completed in 1922 and operated twenty-one planes.

Bottom: The *Langley*, first U.S. aircraft carrier (1922), converted from a collier for experimental purposes. Reclassed as a seaplane carrier in 1936. The above photo shows the *Langley* anchored off Christobal, Canal Zone, 1930.

discussed on pages 189–92, was signed. So far as carriers were concerned, this limited the tonnage of the five main naval powers to 135,000 tons for Britain and the United States, 81,000 tons for Japan and 60,000 tons for France and Italy. Individual carriers, newly constructed, were limited to a displacement of 27,000 tons. The United States, Britain and Japan, however, might each convert two warships which would otherwise be scrapped, into aircraft carriers of not more than 33,000 tons.

The immediate result of this was the selection by the Americans and Japanese of two of their projected capital ships for conversion. The former chose the battle-cruisers *Lexington* and *Saratoga*, which, with a main armament of eight 16-inch guns and a speed of 33 knots, were to have displaced 43,500 tons. Redesigned as 'island' carriers, their displacement was 36,000 tons, the extra 3000 tons over the Washington Treaty limit being legitimised by the U.S. Navy's claim that it represented the additional weight permissible in the terms of the Treaty on account of defence against air and submarine attack. With an overall length of 888 feet and a huge island superstructure on the starboard side, they were the largest warships afloat, while their speed of more than 33 knots set a record for large men-of-war. They were each designed to operate seventy-two aircraft and carried an armament of eight 8-inch guns in twin turrets, as well as twelve 5-inch anti-aircraft guns. They were notable for being the first carriers to incorporate their hangars and flight decks into the main hull structure instead of being added appendages above a hull which ended at the main deck level.

The Japanese, who had planned, prior to the Washington Treaty, to build two carriers of 12,500 tons each, now cancelled them, and substituted the uncompleted battle-cruisers *Akagi* and *Amagi* which had been designed to mount ten 16-inch guns on a displacement of 41,200 tons. When the latter was severely damaged in 1923 in the disastrous earthquake, her place was taken by the unfinished fast battleship *Kaga*.

The *Akagi* and *Kaga* emerged in 1927 and 1928 as carriers with three flight decks stepped up in tiers from forward aft, but in 1935 the main flight deck was extended to the full length of the ship. Each could operate sixty aircraft and had an armament of ten 8-inch and twelve 4·7-inch guns.

The British with no battle-cruisers on the stocks (though a few had been ordered) selected for conversion two existing ships which were something of 'white elephants'. These were the sister ships of the *Furious*, the *Courageous* and *Glorious*, lightly built, unarmoured cruisers which had been given two twin 15-inch turrets each and had been intended to operate in the shallow waters of the Baltic in pursuance of one of Admiral Fisher's still-born strategic concepts. They were now rebuilt as 'island' carriers, operating forty-eight aircraft from a main flight deck covering some two-thirds of their length and a lower flying-off deck forward of the hangar from which fighters could take off—a feature to be found also in the *Furious*. Their defensive armament consisted of sixteen 4·7-inch A.A. guns.

These two ships brought British carrier tonnage to within 20,000 tons of the permitted limit, and though the earlier ones were rapidly becoming outmoded, no further ships were laid down until the *Ark Royal* in 1935. This ship adopted the style inaugurated by the *Lexington* and *Saratoga* of incorporating her double hangars and flight deck in the main hull structure, a feature which was to be found in all future British carriers, whereas the U.S. Navy had reverted to the earlier system of superimposing the hangars and flight decks over the main hull structure. She could carry seventy-two aircraft, but it was found in practice that sixty was the maximum number that could be efficiently operated.

On the abrogation of the naval treaties of limitation at the end of 1936, four more carriers were ordered for the British Navy. These were the 23,000-ton ships of the *Illustrious* class which were of an entirely new design, being given extensive armour protection which made their single hangars into armoured boxes with sides 4½ inches thick and a 3-inch flight deck overhead. This arrangement entailed a reduction of operational capacity to thirty-six aircraft, though this was increased later to sixty when the system was adopted of having a deck 'park' forward of the landing area, separated from it by a crash barrier.

Two similar ships, *Implacable* and *Indefatigable*, laid down in 1939, had additional hangar space, which enabled them to operate seventy-two aircraft.

The French Navy did not decide to acquire aircraft carriers until 1922 when the battleship *Béarn*, one of the uncompleted super-dreadnoughts, was taken in hand for conversion. She was completed in May 1927 as an 'island' carrier of 22,146 tons standard displacement. Her machinery remained unaltered, consisting of two turbines for main propulsion and two reciprocating engines for cruising and manœuvring. These gave her the inadequate speed of only 21½ knots, which allowed her to operate simultaneously only a quarter of her forty aircraft.

It was not until November 1938 that the next French carrier, the *Joffre*, was laid down, and she had not been launched when the Franco-German armistice was signed in 1940, after which she was dismantled.

The U.S. and Japanese navies had meanwhile embarked on programmes to build carriers up to the allotted limits. The former planned to build five 13,800-ton ships at a rate of one a year from 1929 to 1933. The first of these, the *Ranger*, was not, however, laid down until 1931. She was comparatively slow (30 knots) and was distinguishable from other carriers by her small 'island' structure and six small funnels, three to each side and interconnected.

Before the *Ranger* was completed, the decision was reached that 20,000 tons was the minimum effective tonnage for aircraft carriers. The next two ships, therefore, the *Enterprise* and *Yorktown* laid down in 1934, were of roughly this size. The large 'island' design was re-adopted for these and all subsequent U.S. carriers. With three lifts or elevators working between flight deck and hangar, they could each operate eighty aircraft. Geared turbines gave them a speed of 34 knots. These two ships brought the U.S. Navy to within 14,500 tons of the total permitted carrier force. A final, smaller carrier, the *Wasp*, was therefore laid down, which actually emerged as an 'island' carrier of 14,700 tons and a maximum stowage of eighty-five aircraft.

The Japanese, following the two dreadnought conversions mentioned above, continued their carrier programme with the little *Ryujo* of only 10,600 tons, which was completed in 1933, to operate thirty-six aircraft. She had no 'island' structure as originally completed, and her boiler smoke and gases were discharged through two funnels of unequal size projecting from her starboard side.

Japan's next carrier was the *Soryu*, laid down in 1934, and two years later her near sister *Hiryu* was begun. The *Soryu* displaced 18,800 tons, her near sister was 1350 tons heavier and both measured 747 feet overall. Geared turbines drove them at a fraction over 34 knots and each had a main battery of twelve 5-inch anti-aircraft guns. Their standard aircraft capacity was fifty-three and fifty-seven respectively. The *Soryu* was completed in December 1937, and the *Hiryu* joined the fleet in the summer of 1939.

By this time the Japanese were ahead of all other navies in their appreciation of the importance and function of the carrier as the striking force of the fleet. It was envisaged that these two ships with the *Akagi* and *Kaga* would operate as a four-carrier formation. Therefore the *Akagi* and *Hiryu* had been given port-side 'island' superstructures while the other two had theirs to starboard, an arrangement which was expected to allow a compact formation with non-conflicting traffic patterns. The *Hiryu* and *Soryu* had their exhaust gases expelled from funnels built into their starboard sides.

The next two Japanese carriers were probably the most successful warships of this category the nation built. These were the *Shokaku* and *Zuikaku*. One or both participated in every major carrier action of the Pacific War except Midway. Indeed, even the decision for the date of the Pearl Harbor attack was based in part on the availability of these carriers. The Washington Naval Treaty expired at the end of 1936 and the absence of limitations led to their excellent designs.

The *Shokaku* was laid down in December 1937 and the *Zuikaku* the following May. Except for their bow configurations, the two ships were almost identical. They featured small 'island' structures on the starboard side of their flight decks and had two funnels trunked out and down aft of the 'island'. Each ship

Three United States battleships attest to the damage done by the Japanese attack on Pearl Harbor, 7th December 1941. At right the *Arizona*, which was a total loss; the *West Virginia* (*left*) was severely damaged and the *Tennessee* (*centre*) damaged.

displaced 25,675 tons, measured 846 feet overall and had geared turbines which could provide a speed of just over 34 knots. Sixteen 5-inch anti-aircraft guns, a large number of 25-mm. guns and a standard capacity of seventy-two aircraft formed their armament. The *Shokaku* and *Zuikaku* compared favourably with their U.S. contemporaries, the *Essex* class ships, the first of which was not laid down until more than three years after the *Shokaku* was started.

The next Japanese carriers to be completed were conversions, the first two, the *Zuiho* and *Shoho*, having been laid down as oilers. Converted to light carriers of 11,262 tons, a speed of 28 knots and a complement of some thirty aircraft, they joined the fleet in 1940 and 1942 respectively. Two much larger carriers, the *Hiyo* and *Junyo*, were converted from passenger liners and emerged with a displacement of 24,140 tons, a speed of $25\frac{1}{2}$ knots and up to fifty-three aircraft.

The German and Italian navies suffered from having to rely for air support upon an independent air force. In consequence they lagged behind other navies in the development of carriers. The former, however, laid down a 23,200-ton ship, the *Graf Zeppelin*, in 1937, which was launched at the end of 1938 and was 85 per cent completed when, early in 1940, further work on her ceased and she was never completed. A second ship of the same type was laid down in 1938, but work on her, too, was stopped in 1940.

The German Navy also projected the conversion of three passenger liners, *Europa*, *Gneisenau* and *Potsdam*, and the cruiser *Seydlitz*, which had been laid down in 1937 but was still uncompleted as a cruiser in 1942. Work only on the *Seydlitz* was ever begun and none of these projects was completed.

In Italy, plans to convert the trans-Atlantic liner *Roma* had been prepared in the middle of 1940. It was not, however, until the encounter between the Italian and British fleets off Cape Matapan on 28th March 1941, a disaster which the Italians ascribed with justification to a lack of fighter protection, that orders were given to proceed with the project. Renamed the *Aquila*, the ship would have had a displacement of some 27,000 tons and a speed of 30 knots and would have operated fifty-one 'Re 2001' fighter aircraft. Completion was delayed as a result of bomb damage in November 1942, but she was nearly completed when, at the Armistice on 9th September 1943, she was sabotaged by her crew and abandoned, to be captured by the Germans. Subsequently, in order to prevent her being sunk by the Germans as a blockship at the entrance to Genoa harbour, she was attacked by Italian frogmen and sunk at her berth.

The U.S. Navy did not take advantage of the removal of treaty limitations until September 1939 when the *Hornet* was laid down to a slightly modified *Yorktown* design. The veteran *Langley* was now relegated to the role of seaplane tender; so that when the United States entered the Second World War, though eleven further carriers of the *Essex* class had been laid down, the U.S. Navy had seven carriers in commission as compared to nine Japanese.

The U.S. Navy went rapidly ahead after this, however, with the 27,100-ton *Essex* class, 'island' carriers 876 feet long with a speed of 33 knots and a powerful array of up to 136 anti-aircraft guns of various calibres, including twelve 5-inch in twin turrets. No less than 110 aircraft could be operated with two centre-line and one ship-side lift opposite the 'island' to handle them. The first of these ships, the *Essex*, was commissioned on the last day of 1942.

To meet the urgent need for fast carriers, in early 1942 five light cruisers on the building ways (10,000-ton ships which were to mount twelve 6-inch guns) were taken in hand for conversion to light carriers. With four similar ships which were laid down shortly afterward, these light carriers were 11,000-ton, 610-foot warships capable of 32 knots and able to operate some thirty-five aircraft (only 40-mm. and 20-mm. guns were mounted). The first of these ships, the *Independence*, was completed in the first month of 1943.

By the end of the war, seventeen *Essex* and the ten *Independence* class carriers had been completed, one of the former taking just seventeen months from keel laying to commissioning. One of the light carriers was commissioned just twelve months after her keel was laid down.

In contrast, in mid-1942 the Japanese had only two fleet carriers under con-

H.M.S. *Ark Royal*, most famous British carrier of the Second World War. Played decisive part in sinking of *Bismarck* and operated with convoys to Malta until sunk by U-boat, November 1941.

struction, the 28,570-ton *Taiho* and the 17,150-ton *Unryu*. These were well-designed, fast and powerful ships, the former having an armoured flight deck, but they were not scheduled for completion until late June 1944 and late September 1944 respectively. In addition, a submarine tender was being converted to the 13,360-ton light carrier *Ryuho*. After the disaster at Midway, the Japanese Navy began a major carrier-building and conversion programme.

The unfinished battleship *Shinano* (to have been a 65,000-ton ship mounting nine 18·1-inch guns) was taken in hand for conversion and, at a later stage also, the unfinished heavy cruiser *Ibuki* (to have displaced 12,400 tons and mounted ten 8-inch guns).

Next, two *seaplane* carriers were taken in hand for conversion to light carriers, the *Chitose* and *Chiyoda* (as *aircraft* carriers each would displace 11,190 tons, be 610½ feet overall, have a speed of 29 knots, and operate thirty aircraft).

Plans were made for building five additional ships of the *Taiho* class (29,300 tons) and thirteen more similar to the 17,150-ton *Unryu*.

This was a most encouraging programme, but it was to fall apart as the war moved closer to the Japanese homeland, with shipyards cut off from raw materials, production facilities diverted to other projects, and tankers bringing oil to Japan sunk.

The *Shinano* emerged as the largest carrier of the Second World War with a displacement of 64,800 tons. From her 'island' superstructure on the starboard side a funnel slanted outwards at 26 degrees to keep the exhaust fumes away from the flight deck. With a 4-inch armoured deck and an armament of sixteen 5-inch and 156 25-mm. anti-aircraft guns, she was intended to operate as a floating air base rather than a fleet carrier, her primary function being to refuel, re-arm and repair aircraft from other carriers or from land bases. Her own aircraft complement was to have been only forty-two.

This huge ship, still uncompleted, was on passage from Yokosuka to Kure for final fitting out when, early on 29th November 1944, she was torpedoed and sunk by a U.S. submarine.

The *Taiho* joined the fleet just in time to take part in the great carrier Battle of the Philippine Sea on 19th and 20th June 1944, during which she was torpedoed by a U.S. submarine and sunk. Only the *Unryu* herself of the projected class of that name was completed and she was also sunk by a U.S. submarine in December 1944 before she had ever been in action.

Naval operations of the Second World War were to show that the aircraft carrier had emerged as the most important unit of the fleet, the 'capital ship', all other men-of-war becoming virtually their auxiliaries. Even in the *guerre-de-course*, fought out along the trade routes and round the convoys of merchantmen and transports, it was the addition to the escort forces of small auxiliary carriers converted from merchant-ship hulls and carrying either anti-submarine aircraft or fighters according to the opposition encountered, which finally ensured the defeat of the German attack.

The first of these auxiliary or 'escort' carriers was converted by the British in 1941 from a captured German merchant ship and renamed the *Audacity*. Though she did not survive long, being sunk by a U-boat during a convoy battle in December 1941, her success in convoy operations led to the initiation of a large programme of construction, no less than 110 being built in U.S. shipyards of which thirty-eight were supplied to supplement four British-built escort carriers. The first ones were converted merchantmen (or 18-knot oilers) but they were followed by improved, built-for-the-purpose ships. There were the fifty 'production-line' *Casablanca* class, the last commissioned on 8th July 1944, exactly a year after the first, and the 'ultimate' design—the *Commencement Bay* class ships. These last were 12,000-ton, 553-foot ships capable of 19 knots. Each had two elevators and could operate up to thirty-four aircraft.

In both ocean wars these escort carriers proved invaluable as convoy escorts, flagships of independent submarine killer groups, and aircraft transports. In the Atlantic they made a vital contribution to the battle against the German U-boats by providing convoy escort in the mid-ocean gap which shore-based aircraft could not adequately cover. They were also the core of submarine killer groups. As an example of their prowess, in the Atlantic the U.S. escort carriers *Bogue* and *Card* each destroyed eight U-boats with their planes (the *Bogue*'s planes helped kill two other submarines); in the Pacific the U.S.S. *Anzio*'s planes sank three Japanese submarines and teamed up with surface ships to finish off two others.

Another important role the escort carriers played was that of providing air cover and support to amphibious operations—in the Mediterranean off North Africa, Sicily, Salerno and Anzio, and in the Pacific at the assaults on Japanese-held island groups after 1943.

On the other side of the coin, six U.S. escort carriers were sunk in the Second World War—three by suicide planes, one by surface gunfire and two by submarine attack. German submarines sank two British escort carriers (including the pioneer *Audacity*) and a third was lost through an internal explosion.

The Japanese also had five escort carriers converted from merchantmen. They were used primarily for transport duties and all were lost—one to U.S. air attack, the others to U.S. submarine torpedoes.

It was in the main fleet operations, however, that the larger types of aircraft carrier were most notably successful. In the confined waters of the Mediterranean, where many naval authorities had considered them to be too vulnerable to shore-based air attack to survive, the few obsolete fighter aircraft put up in the early stages of the war by the veteran *Eagle* provided a degree of air defence without which the British Mediterranean fleet could hardly have operated. With the addition of the new carrier *Illustrious* to the fleet in November 1940, the British were able to mount a highly successful night attack by torpedo planes on the Italian fleet in the harbour of Taranto, as a result of which the battleship *Conte di Cavour* was sunk and the battleships *Littorio* and *Caio Duilio* were seriously damaged and put out of service for several months.

Nevertheless, when, two months later, the German Air Force from Sicily concentrated a large number of dive-bombers to attack the *Illustrious* they showed that single carriers, with their meagre complement of defensive fighters, could not afford to operate within easy range of shore air bases. The carrier was heavily damaged and put out of service for many months, only her armoured deck saving her from destruction.

In spite of this, British carriers, the famous *Ark Royal* in particular, constituted the principal defence in the hard-fought convoy operations from Gibraltar to Malta by which that island was enabled to survive, and though both the *Ark Royal* and the *Eagle* were sunk by submarine attack in the course of them, none were put out of action by air attack. At the other end of the Mediterranean, when the British and Italian fleets met off Cape Matapan on 28th March 1941, it was the presence of the *Formidable* with a small force of torpedo planes with the former and the absence of such a ship to provide fighter defence for the latter which led to the unwilling Italian fleet being brought partially to action, with the loss of the cruisers *Pola*, *Fiume* and *Zara* and two destroyers, and serious damage to the battleship *Vittorio Veneto*.

In the wider spaces of the Atlantic the carrier justified its position of pre-eminence even more when the German battleship *Bismarck* broke out in May 1941 and, after finding the *Hood*'s Achilles heel of inadequate armour protection and sinking her, defied the efforts of a large number of battleships and cruisers to locate her. It was only as a result of minor damage inflicted by the battleship *Prince of Wales* and an aircraft from the carrier *Victorious* which forced her to seek refuge in Brest, and further crippling damage by torpedo planes from the *Ark Royal*, that the giant battleship was at last brought to action, overwhelmed by superior numbers and finally sunk by gunfire and torpedoes.

Where the carrier sailed completely supreme, however, challenged only by its like in the enemy fleet, was the Pacific; and it was the carrier that opened the war in that theatre, by attacking Pearl Harbor early on the morning of Sunday 7th December 1941. A force of 361 torpedo planes, dive-bombers and fighters taking off from the decks of the *Akagi*, *Kaga*, *Soryu*, *Hiryu*, *Shokaku* and

Japanese aircraft of the Second World War: Aichi Type 99 (Val), dive-bomber of the kind which sank the British carrier *Hermes* and cruisers *Cornwall* and *Dorsetshire*.

Japanese aircraft carrier *Ryujo* (1931) incorporated improvements in design from experience gained with the *Akagi* and *Kaga*. She was, however, found to be top heavy on completion and was modified then, and again in 1935 when the forecastle was heightened. Sunk by U.S. carrier planes at Battle of Easter and Solomons.

The Japanese squadron entering Singapore Naval Base after its capture, 1942, led by the cruiser *Chokai*, flagship of Admiral Ozawa. Painting by Tokushiro Kobayakawa.

212

Zuikaku achieved complete surprise to eliminate the battleship force of the U.S. Pacific fleet and destroy Army, Navy and Marine aviation in Hawaii.

Decisive results eluded them, nevertheless. As luck would have it, the three U.S. carriers of the Pacific fleet, *Lexington, Enterprise* and *Saratoga*, were absent from Pearl Harbor at the time of the attack and so escaped damage. Furthermore the harbour facilities—the huge array of tanks brimming with oil fuel, the dry-docks and workshops—had not been damaged and remained available to provide the vital forward base for a reconstituted Pacific fleet. Meanwhile, however, the Japanese carrier force demonstrated the new shape of ocean warfare as it ranged far and freely over the Pacific and Indian Oceans, supporting the capture of Wake Island and the Japanese conquest of the south-west Pacific, devastating the Allied bases at Darwin in northern Australia, Colombo and Trincomalee in Ceylon. During these last attacks the striking power of carrier-borne dive-bombers was dramatically demonstrated by the speedy destruction of the British cruisers *Cornwall* and *Dorsetshire* and the veteran carrier *Hermes*.

During the four years of naval warfare in the Pacific which followed, except for a brief night encounter off Guadalcanal and another during the Battle of Leyte, the opposing battleship squadrons never came within shot or even sight of one another. The main actions were fought by the air groups of the opposing carrier forces at a range of several hundred miles and came about as a result of one navy acting in support of landing operations being attacked by its opponent. In the first of these, the Battle of the Coral Sea on 7th and 8th May 1942, the Japanese fleet was covering an expedition aimed at the occupation of the Allied base of Port Moresby in Papua. In opposition came the American carriers *Lexington* and *Yorktown*, the air groups from which sank the small carrier *Shoho* on the 7th while the Japanese striking force from the *Shokaku* and *Zuikaku*, failing to locate their primary target, sent a tanker and a destroyer to the bottom.

The next day the rival air striking forces found their enemies almost simultaneously. The *Lexington* was torpedoed several times and bombs set her ablaze to blow up and sink a few hours later. The *Yorktown* was damaged by a direct hit and many near misses by dive-bombers. In reply the *Shokaku* was heavily damaged by the American dive-bombers. Tactically it was a Japanese victory, but a Pyrrhic one in that it cost them so many planes and, more important, irreplaceable experienced aircrews, so that their two best carriers were out of action at a critical moment a month later. Strategically, the Coral Sea was an American success in that the Japanese expeditionary force turned back, foiled.

The Japanese plan to attack and occupy the mid-ocean island base of Midway and the Aleutian Islands led to the next carrier clash and one of the most decisive battles of history. The whole Japanese fleet took part in the operation, battleships and cruisers as well as all the available carriers. Even the veteran *Hosho* sailed with the battleships while the light carrier *Zuiho* accompanied the Midway Assault Force. The *Junyo* and the light carrier *Ryujo* were sent to strike Dutch Harbour in the Aleutians. But it was round the fast carrier force comprising the *Akagi, Kaga, Hiryu* and *Soryu* that the main events of the battle were to rage.

The Japanese plan was based on the assumption that it was completely unknown to the Americans. In fact the latter had long ago broken the Japanese codes and their every intention was known; and so, although the only force available to the Americans was the task force centred on the carriers *Enterprise, Hornet* and *Yorktown*, they were able to deploy them so as to achieve absolute surprise. The Japanese carriers were caught by the American carrier air strikes with their decks cluttered with aircraft being refuelled and rearmed. The defensive fighters which were in the air were able to annihilate the American squadrons of slow and unmanœuvrable torpedo planes; but while they were occupied low down, the swarm of dive-bombers arrived undetected high above.

In quick succession the *Akagi, Kaga* and *Soryu* were rent asunder and set on fire. In each case the flames proved impossible to control; after desperate hours of struggle the three ships were abandoned and scuttled. The fourth carrier, *Hiryu*, escaped damage long enough to despatch a small striking force in two waves; they

succeeded in crippling the *Yorktown*, which was subsequently torpedoed and sunk by a Japanese submarine when under tow.

Meanwhile the *Hiryu* had suffered the same fate as her squadron mates at the hands of the U.S. dive-bombers.

The Battle of Midway was an overwhelming American victory; it greatly reduced but did not eliminate the Japanese naval superiority, however, and, until the first of the new *Essex* and *Independence* classes began to join the Pacific fleet early in 1943, several hard-fought, drawn battles were fought at sea in the south-west Pacific in support of the campaign for possession of Guadalcanal, the key to control of that area. At the Battle of the Eastern Solomons on 24th and 25th August 1942 the light carrier *Ryujo* was sunk and the *Shokaku* slightly damaged at the cost of heavy damage to the *Enterprise*. A week later the *Saratoga* was torpedoed by a Japanese submarine and put out of action for some months. The *Wasp* was more unlucky. She sank when torpedoed by a Japanese submarine in her turn on 15th September.

The Americans in the South Pacific were thus reduced to only two carriers, the *Enterprise* and the *Hornet*, when the next clash occurred at the Battle of the Santa Cruz Islands on 26th October 1942. In the course of this action the light carrier *Zuiho* and the *Shokaku* were both heavily damaged and driven out of the action; but in reply the *Hornet* was sunk by a combination of bombs and torpedoes.

Neither of these battles was at first sight to the advantage of the Americans; but in fact Japanese losses of aircraft and aircrews were so heavy that their carriers were gravely reduced in efficiency. They were, in the short term, unable to carry out their task of supporting their ground forces on Guadalcanal, who soon were forced to give up the struggle for the island; in the longer term they had ceased to be a match for their opponents who, as reinforcements of *Essex* and *Independence* class carriers joined them early in 1943, were able to go over to the offensive.

When the greatest carrier battle of the war took place in June 1944 in the Philippine Sea, where the Japanese fleet advanced to attack the U.S. Pacific fleet supporting the landings on the Mariana Islands, the Americans could deploy seven fleet and eight light carriers to oppose three Japanese fleet carriers and six light. In the two-day battle the Japanese carrier planes were outclassed and slaughtered, inflicting no significant damage on any American ship. In reply, besides the *Shokaku* and *Taiho* sunk by submarine, the light carrier *Hiyo* was sunk and two other Japanese carriers heavily damaged by U.S. carrier planes. This marked the end of a viable Japanese carrier force. Though a number of carriers were still afloat, when the two fleets met in the wide-spread Battle of Leyte Gulf in October 1944, the Japanese carriers could only be used in a decoy role for lack of trained carrier pilots. In that battle American carrier pilots sent to the bottom the giant battleship *Musashi*, sister to the *Yamato*, as well as destroying the veteran carrier *Zuikaku* and the light carriers *Chitose, Chiyoda* and *Zuiho*.

By the end of the war the Japanese homeland was under daily attack from a huge Anglo-American carrier fleet to which the British contributed four fleet carriers and the Americans ten fleet and six light fleet carriers.

The British had made ambitious plans for additional carriers to be built during the war, including three 45,000-ton ships of the *Gibraltar* class and four *Audacious* class of 36,800 tons. As priority was given to other types of ship, particularly anti-submarine types and landing craft, however, this programme was deferred and by the end of the war all of the *Gibraltar* class were cancelled as well as all but two of the *Audacious* class which were eventually to be completed as the *Eagle* and *Ark Royal*, destined to be the last fleet carriers of the British Navy.

A further programme of ten *Colossus* class light carriers of some 13,300 tons, six *Majestic* class of 14,000 tons and eight *Hermes* class of 18,300 tons was similarly emasculated. Though five of the *Majestic*'s were completed, one was sold to the Indian Navy (*Vikrant*), two to the Royal Australian Navy (*Melbourne* and *Sydney*) and one to the Royal Canadian Navy (*Bonaventure*). All the *Colossus* class were eventually completed, though two were equipped as main-

Page 214: British Swordfish torpedo/reconnaissance plane of the type which crippled three Italian battleships at Taranto in November 1940.

Top: Hellcat F6F. The Grumman naval fighter which replaced the Wildcat F4F in U.S. carrier fighter squadrons in 1943, giving American Naval airmen superiority over the Japanese Zero for the first time. Also used as a fighter-bomber carrying two 500-pound bombs.

Centre: Douglas Devastator TBD-1. The type of torpedo plane with which U.S. carriers were equipped until 1942. Slow and relatively defenceless, they were massacred at Midway.

Bottom: A British Fairey Barracuda torpedo glide bomber of the type which inflicted heavy bomb damage on the German battleship *Tirpitz* in April 1944.

tenance carriers, and one each acquired by the Royal Netherlands Navy (*Karel Doorman*), the French Navy (*Arromanches*), the Argentine Navy (*Independencia*) and the Brazilian Navy (*Minas Gerais*). Four of the *Hermes* class were cancelled: the remainder were much delayed but were finally commissioned during the 1950s.

In contrast, by the end of the war the U.S. Navy had the veterans *Ranger*, *Saratoga* and *Enterprise* (the first two quickly being disposed of) plus seventeen of the *Essex* class and nine of the light *Independence* class carriers. Seven more of the *Essex* class were completed (the last in 1950). Two improved light carriers, the *Wright* and the *Saipan*, were commissioned in 1946–47. These were similar to the *Independence*, but larger (14,500 tons, 683½ feet, 33 knots, 50 aircraft). But the queens of the post-war carrier fleet were three *Midway* class 'battle' or large carriers completed in 1945–47.

The *Midway*'s were designed after the battle of that name. Because dive-bombers had sunk four Japanese carriers in that fight, the *Midway*'s were given armoured flight decks, the first U.S. carriers so built. They each displaced 45,000 tons, were 968 feet long, could steam at 33 knots and could operate up to 137 contemporary aircraft. They were the first U.S. warships designed too wide to pass through the Panama Canal (113 feet hull beam and 136 feet extreme width). Their aircraft-handling facilities were similar to those of the *Essex* class (two centre-line and one port-side, deck-edge elevators). However, their armament was considerably more potent than their predecessors, each of the *Midway*'s initially mounting fourteen or sixteen 5-inch anti-aircraft guns of a new, improved design, and eighty-four 40-mm. and twenty-eight 20-mm. anti-aircraft guns.

One of these large carriers deployed in the Mediterranean in 1946 carried 123 fighters and bombers—a striking force more powerful than the entire air force of the most powerful Mediterranean nation at the time!

Between the Second World War and the outbreak of the Korean War in 1950, progress in carrier development was confined to work in the United States on the design of a ship to be called the U.S.S. *United States*. As laid down on 18th April 1949 she was to have had an overall length of 1090 feet and a displacement of 65,000 tons, which would have made her the largest warship yet attempted. She was to have had an uninterrupted flight deck with funnels projecting from either side at the level of her flight deck, and a small bridge built on an elevator enabling it to be lowered flush with the deck. The flight deck was designed to permit simultaneous catapult launching of four aircraft—twice as many as previous carriers—and three elevators would be available for ranging up and striking down aircraft. Such a ship would be able to operate 50-ton bombers which could deliver nuclear bombs on targets 1500 to 2000 miles from the ship and return to land on board.

A government decision to allocate available defence funds to development of the B-36 intercontinental bomber for this strategic role led, however, to cancellation of the carrier five days after her keel was laid. The U.S. Navy thereupon turned to a programme of modernisation of the existing *Essex* class (and, later, *Midway* class) carriers for the operation of jet aircraft. Flight decks were strengthened, more powerful catapults were installed, increased deck space was provided by removal of some 5-inch gun mountings, elevator capacity was increased, jet blast deflectors provided and aviation fuel storage doubled.

The first jet deck landing had been made by the British on 4th December 1945 when a De Havilland Vampire was landed on the light fleet carrier *Ocean*. Supply of jet aircraft to the British Fleet Air Arm lagged, however, and it was not until September 1951 that they entered squadron service. In the interval, thought devoted to the requirements for handling the aircraft of the future with their greater weights and landing speeds had led to two important new British developments. In 1951 a new type of catapult relying upon steam for power had been fitted in the British carrier *Perseus* and, when demonstrated to the Americans, had been immediately taken up by them. At about the same time an improved system for handling aircraft on deck was conceived.

Up to now, the after two-thirds of the deck had been set aside as the landing area; the forward one-third, separated by a crash barrier from this landing area, had been reserved as an aircraft park. It was suggested that by angling the landing

Principal American naval commanders in the Pacific war with Japan.

From left to right:

Admiral Chester W. Nimitz, C.-in-C., Pacific.

Admiral Raymond A. Spruance, victor of the battles of Midway and the Philippine Sea.

Admiral William F. Halsey, C.-in-C., U.S. Third Fleet at the Battle of Leyte.

area the crash barrier could be dispensed with and any aircraft failing to pick up an arrester wire could fly on, circle and make a fresh approach. Trials carried out on such a space painted on the decks of the British *Triumph* and the U.S.S. *Midway* proved successful. In the second half of 1952 the flight deck of the 27,000-ton U.S.S. *Antietam* was modified to incorporate a canted deck jutting out over the port side. So successful was this 'angled' or 'canted' deck that it became a standard feature of all carriers from this time onward.

The U.S.S. *Forrestal*, first of a class of 59,500-ton carriers, which was under construction was redesigned. At a length of 1039 feet overall, with her angled deck she is able to have a large starboard 'island' structure which contains control spaces, antennae and funnel. There are two deck-edge elevators abaft her 'island', one forward of the 'island', and one on the port side, at the forward end of the angled deck. The four deck-edge lifts reduce the interruption of flight and hangar deck activities found in carriers with centre-line elevators. In addition, the *Forrestal* can land and launch aircraft with all three starboard lifts lowered (later ships have their port-side elevator on the port quarter to allow all to be used during operations). There are two steam catapults forward and two on the angled deck, allowing the ship to catapult four aircraft every thirty seconds.

Today the *Forrestal* class carriers operate some eighty aircraft: two fighter squadrons, three light attack squadrons, reconnaissance heavy attack squadron, a few airborne early-warning aircraft, and a helicopter detachment. The largest of these aircraft weighs just over thirty-five tons! (In terms of Second World War aircraft, a *Forrestal* class ship could handle almost two hundred planes!)

For close-in defence the *Forrestal* and her sisters were initially fitted with eight rapid-fire 5-inch guns, in single mounts on sponsons. However, the forward guns have now been removed from these ships to improve sea-keeping qualities. Later ships are fitted with a twin surface-to-air 'Terrier' missile launcher on each quarter.

The *Forrestal* was completed in September 1955. Six additional ships of this general design have followed her into service: the *Saratoga* (in 1956), *Ranger* (1957), *Independence* (1959), *Kitty Hawk* (1961), *Constellation* (1961), *America* (1965) and *John F. Kennedy* (1968).

But the queen of the super-carriers is the nuclear-powered *Enterprise* (74,700 tons, 1123 feet overall). She was begun in early 1958 and completed in late 1961 (built in less time than some of the smaller, oil-fuelled *Forrestal* type carriers). The *Enterprise* is similar in arrangement to the *Forrestal*'s, having an angled flight deck, four deck-edge elevators, four steam catapults, and a starboard 'island' structure. However, her 'island' is a box-like structure, easily distinguished by the fixed-array radar antennae on each side which look like advertising billboards. This 'square island' is topped by a dome studded with T-shaped electronic countermeasure antennae.

The *Enterprise* is powered by eight nuclear reactors which drive turbines turning four screws. With the reactor cores installed when she was built the *Enterprise* steamed for three years and more than 200,000 miles. She was 're-fuelled' in early 1965 and the cores now installed have about 25 per cent greater life. The cores now under development for the *Enterprise* will last more than thirteen years before they require replacement.

The United States plans to construct three additional nuclear-powered carriers, to commission at two-year intervals, all to be in service by the mid-1970s. These ships will be slightly smaller than the giant *Enterprise* and will be powered by only a two-reactor plant. However, this plant will have approximately the same capabilities as the *Enterprise* machinery and will initially have cores that will last thirteen years. Two further nuclear-powered carriers, *Nimitz* and *Dwight D. Eisenhower*, of a similar size were nearing completion in 1973. A third is projected. The machinery of each incorporates only two reactors, producing approximately the same power as the *Enterprise*'s eight.

By 1973 all the *Essex* class ships had been placed in reserve classified as Anti Submarine Warfare Aircraft Carriers (CVS). All light aircraft carriers of the *Independence* class had been retired. The *Saipan* had been converted to a com-

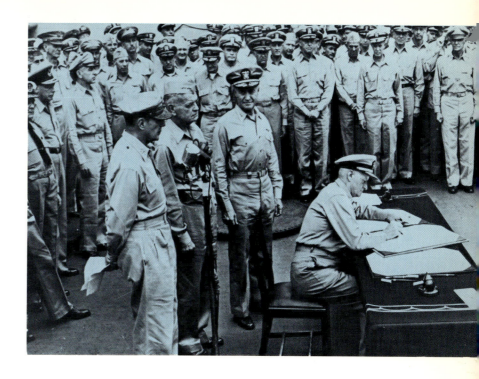

General Douglas MacArthur, Admiral William F. Halsey and Admiral Forrest Sherman look on as Admiral Chester W. Nimitz signs the Japanese surrender document aboard the U.S.S. *Missouri*, Tokyo Bay, 2nd September 1945.

H.M.S. *Ark Royal*, originally completed in 1955 as a sister to the *Eagle*. Modernised in 1959 and again in 1961.

Right: The British Navy's carrier-borne strike aircraft the Buccaneer, a rugged plane capable of carrying nuclear weapons, bombs, rockets and missiles at transonic speeds at low altitudes.

French aircraft carrier *Clemenceau*. Completed in 1961, she and her sister ship *Foch* were the first carriers to be designed and built in France and they incorporate the angled deck, mirror landing sights, steam catapults and deck-edge lift.

219

munications relay ship; the *Wright* to a command ship. The U.S. Navy had then in commission one nuclear carrier (CVN) and eleven attack carriers (CVA).

In the Royal Navy the requirement for jet-age carriers has been met by modernising the *Eagle* and *Ark Royal* (36,800 tons) and several smaller carriers which were unfinished at war's end in 1945. The *Eagle* was first completed in 1955 and subsequent modifications have been incorporated to the point that she is now a 44,100-ton, 812-foot, angled-deck carrier operating some forty-five modern aircraft and helicopters. She has two steam catapults (one forward and one on her angled deck), but only two elevators, both installed on her centre-line.

The *Ark Royal*, originally completed in early 1955, has similarly been modernised and now displaces 43,340 tons and has an overall length of $810\frac{1}{4}$ feet. She is similar in design to the *Eagle*. (As initially completed, the *Ark Royal* had two centre-line lifts and a starboard deck-edge elevator, the first British carrier with the latter feature. However, with her angled-deck conversion the side lift was removed.)

The other extensively modernised aircraft carriers of the Royal Navy were the *Hermes* (originally laid down as a light fleet carrier) and the Second World War veteran *Victorious*. The *Hermes*, completed in 1959, displaces 23,000 tons, is $744\frac{1}{4}$ feet overall, has two steam catapults forward, and two elevators (one centre-line and one at the forward end of her angled deck). She can only operate thirty contemporary aircraft and helicopters. Two other ships of this class, *Bulwark* and *Albion*, have been converted into helicopter carriers or 'commando ships' for amphibious operations.

As rebuilt in 1950–58, the *Victorious* (laid down in 1937 and completed in May 1941) resembles a modern ship, featuring an angled flight deck, two steam catapults forward, two centre-line lifts, and a capacity of some thirty-five aircraft and helicopters.

Replacements for the ageing carriers of the British Navy had been proposed, off and on, since 1950. Financial stringency and doubts as to their intended role and 'cost-effectiveness' caused repeated postponement, however, and in 1966 they were finally cancelled. All fleet carriers except the *Ark Royal* had been de-commissioned by 1973. Of the light fleet carriers, the *Hermes* has been converted to a Commando Carrier.

The French Navy, after a period during which she relied upon two *Independence* class light carriers lent by the United States and upon the ex-British *Colossus*, renamed *Arromanches* on being bought from the British and subsequently relegated to the role of helicopter carrier, laid down two new 22,000-ton carriers—the *Clemenceau* in 1955 and the *Foch* in 1957, which were completed in 1961 and 1963 respectively. Their geared turbines give them a speed of 32 knots. With angled decks and two steam catapults, one forward and one on the angled deck, they can operate some sixty modern aircraft.

The navies of Argentina, Brazil and the Netherlands each acquired from Britain a carrier of the *Colossus* class, renamed *Independencia*, *Minas Gerais* and *Karel Doorman* respectively. *Majestic* class ships form units of the navies of India (*Vikrant*), Canada (*Bonaventure*), Australia (*Melbourne* and *Sydney*, the latter functioning now as a troop transport).

So long as the fixed-wing aircraft remains a valid means of attack and defence at sea, the aircraft carrier must continue to be an essential component of any major fleet. Doubts have been raised, however, in the age of the nuclear-powered submarine, whether the carrier could survive in a naval war and, if she could, whether, in the age of the guided missile, the manned aircraft could be operated with reasonable safety.

Doubts have also been expressed, in view of the soaring costs of aircraft carriers and of the highly sophisticated aircraft required to operate from them, whether the carrier represents a wise expenditure of defence funds.

The British government, having decided that it was beyond its means and that when the *Ark Royal* reached the end of her useful life there would be no replacements, has had second thoughts. These have no doubt been inspired by the failure of the previously accepted concept that shore-based aircraft and ship-borne heli-

copters could provide all the required air defence of the fleet, and the successful development of a Vertical Take-Off and Landing (VTOL) fixed-wing aircraft, the Hawker 'Harrier'. Considerations are therefore being given (1973) to the adaptation of the projected helicopter carrier or 'through-deck cruiser' to operate aircraft of that type.

The French Navy has recently announced tentative plans also to acquire at least one V/STOL carrier before their present carriers come to an end of their useful life between 1985 and 1990.

The only navies that can examine the matter without the financial arguments outweighing the strategic are those of the Soviet Union and the United States. The former has, for the first time, an aircraft carrier nearing completion, the *Kiev*, a ship of some 45,000 tons. In the absence of any sign of fitment of catapults or arrester gear it is assumed that the approximately thirty-five fixed-wing aircraft which will use her angled flight deck will be of the Vertical or Short Take-Off (V/STOL) type. In addition she is expected to carry thirty-five helicopters. She will thus be a considerably cheaper proposition than the fixed-wing carriers still being built for the U.S. Navy; but her comparative effectiveness will depend upon the development of high-performance V/STOL fixed-wing aircraft.

Prior to laying down the *Kiev*, the Soviet Navy had limited her ship-borne air element to two helicopter-missile carriers and the one or two helicopters carried by various guided-missile cruisers and support ships. The helicopter-missile cruisers are the *Moskva* and *Leningrad* of 15,000 tons standard displacement, carrying between twenty and thirty helicopters and mounting two surface-to-air twin missile launchers and one twin launcher for either surface or anti-submarine missiles.

The United States has firmly decided in favour of prolonging the era of the aircraft carrier into the twenty-first century. The United States is also the only power of the Western bloc which is strong enough to accept the role of peace-keeper once played by Britain in the days of the *Pax Britannica*. Where gunboats and small landing parties of seamen and marines once sufficed to impose peace, amphibious operations on a considerable scale would be needed today: the essential air component of such operations would require a base somewhere in the area: on the score of mobility and availability, the aircraft carrier meets this requirement most adequately in the opinion of the U.S. government.

Whether this view will continue to be valid when nuclear-powered submarines become available to minor powers, or indeed whether manned aircraft will continue to be operable in the face of opposition by the ground-to-air missiles which minor powers are already acquiring, is a matter of varying opinion. Every new weapon tends eventually to evoke its antidote and thus it may be that the threat to the carrier and to the manned airplane will be overcome. Alternatively, improvement in the performance and capacity of VTOL fixed-wing aircraft may make it possible to provide ship-borne air elements of fleets in less expensive units such as Russia's *Kiev*.

It took the practical test of war to demonstrate that the pre-eminence of the battleship had passed. The same may apply to the carrier; but it must be remembered that the battleship was not immediately, entirely abolished: its function was changed from being the principal means of naval offence to the comparatively humble one of assisting in the defence of its supplanter. Similar ships, but with missile launchers replacing the guns, could still be necessary if a maritime war took place.

Therefore, though the fixed-wing aircraft carrier at present retains her pride of place in one of the world's two largest navies, it may be that the VTOL or V/STOL aircraft carrier will, sooner or later, supersede it. This would be able to dispense with many of the latter's expensive features, such as catapults, arrester gear, angled flight decks, etc.; it could be smaller and cheaper, so that several could be had for the price of one fixed-wing carrier and there would be fewer 'eggs in each basket'.

U.S.S. *Hancock*. One of five ships of the improved *Essex* class
launched in 1944. Modernised between 1954 and 1959 by addition of steam catapults, angled deck, enclosed bow and heavier
decks and larger lifts to operate bigger aircraft.

U.S.S. *Enterprise*, completed in 1961, the largest carrier in the world at 75,700 tons standard displacement. Nuclear-powered to provide 300,000 s.h.p., she has a radius of 400,000 miles at 20 knots and a maximum speed of 35 knots. Can operate up to 100 aircraft.

Details of the *Enterprise*'s square superstructure, into the sides of which are built eight fixed radar antennae, giving greatly increased ranges.

U.S.S. *America*, the first of the two latest conventionally powered U.S. attack carriers to be completed (1965). Embodies the most up-to-date radar, automatic landing and computerised tactical data systems. Operates up to ninety aircraft.

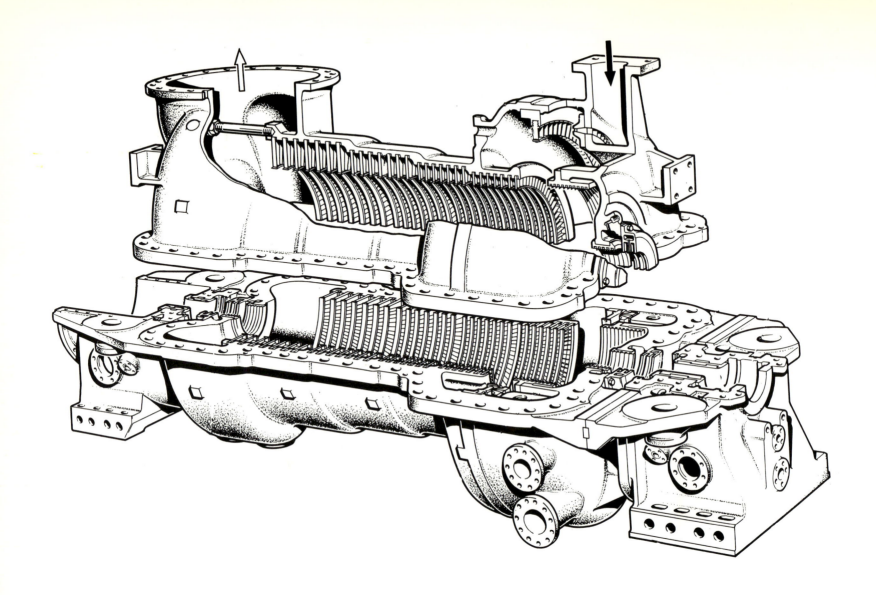

Casing and rotor of high-pressure combined impulse and
reaction steam turbine.

THE DEVELOPMENT OF

PROPULSION MACHINERY

By the end of the First World War, propulsion machinery for major warships had become virtually standardised with steam turbines driving propeller shafts through single-reduction gearing or through systems of electric drive.

Design was virtually static for a period after the First World War and then the naval powers started to improve steam machinery again. In Europe, the emphasis was on achieving the maximum power from a given weight and space, and therefore on maximum efficiency at full speed, whereas American warship machinery was designed to achieve maximum efficiency at medium power so that a greater cruising range was obtained for the same weight of machinery and fuel; this requirement was especially necessary for sea warfare over the vast distances of the Pacific Ocean.

The U.S. Navy was successful in utilising higher degrees of steam super-heating and steam pressures, which are important for good fuel economy.

A low degree of super-heated steam was originally introduced in early naval turbine installations with the object of obtaining really dry steam to avoid priming (the delivery to the engines of steam mixed with water). Investigations and experiments followed with ever-increasing temperatures of super-heat from which great savings in weight and space were to be expected as well as greater economy. It was in shore power stations, however, that increased super-heat, coupled with higher steam pressure, was first developed, followed by ships of the merchant navies. In the former, temperatures up to 1000°F and pressures as high as 2840 pounds were sometimes utilised. In the latter, a pressure of 1900 pounds was employed in the Italian liner *Conte Rosso* and temperatures as high as 750°F were not uncommon in merchant ships. Such ships, running continuously at near full speed, were able to achieve great improvements in economy and met few difficulties. In men-of-war, where great variations of speed are necessary, such high steam pressures involve the provision of more than two turbine units for each set of machinery and so give no saving in weight and space, or they necessitate either double reduction gearing or electric drive.

At the start of the Second World War, steam conditions of 400 pounds per square inch and 700°F temperature had become general, the three-drum boiler being almost the only design in use, with air pre-heaters in the larger ships.

A measure of the advances made in the previous twenty-four years is the change involved when the battleship *Queen Elizabeth* was re-engined and re-boilered in the course of modernisation in 1939. Her direct-drive turbines and twenty-four large-tube boilers were replaced by geared turbines and eight 3-drum, small-tube super-heated boilers with a saving of 50 per cent weight and $33\frac{1}{3}$ per cent space while her endurance at 10 knots was trebled. By the 1940s steam propulsion had advanced still further with steam pressures of 650 pounds per square

inch and temperatures of 850°F in ships of the U.S. Navy and in the German cruiser *Prinz Eugen* and German destroyers, driving small, high-speed turbines with double reduction gearing.

After the Second World War these developments were pursued by the British and other navies. With a further increase of steam temperatures to 950°F, however, the limit imposed by metallurgical considerations was reached. The gains to be made by increasing pressures were relatively small; nevertheless the U.S. Navy made use of pressures above 1400 pounds per square inch. However, costly research and development were required and acceptable levels of reliability were difficult to achieve.

On the other hand, with the virtual disappearance from most navies of large warships other than aircraft carriers, and a concentration on comparatively small ships which had, nevertheless, to house a multiplicity of new types of weapons and their complicated detection and control systems, the requirement to reduce the space occupied by propulsion machinery received fresh impetus.

Not only was a greater proportion of shipboard space required for the weapon and electronic communication equipment, but modern concepts also called for greatly increased crew accommodation to provide modern standards of habitability; at the same time, to achieve the necessary high manœuvrability, the displacement of the ship itself had to be strictly limited.

For smaller warships not requiring very high top speeds, propulsion by diesel engines, in which it was possible to achieve a weight/power ratio of 20 pounds per horse-power, provided an answer. For other ships of the frigate type which require as much as 30,000 horse-power, steam turbines were still necessary; these were reduced by 25 to 30 per cent in the weight and size of the machinery and fuel stowage as compared to earlier installations by reducing unnecessarily large safety margins and by applying the latest engineering techniques. As ships incorporated ever-greater weapons systems, much of whose weight was situated high up in the ship, further reductions were called for, particularly in the height of machinery space. The coming of the gas turbine offered the possibility of major improvements which could not be expected from the continued development of steam plant.

In the first application of gas turbines to major warships, no gas turbines with power and proven reliability sufficient to enable them altogether to supersede steam turbines were available and the British and German navies therefore adopted gas turbines in some types of frigates to enable the size of the steam plant to be reduced. The basic steam propulsion plant was designed to produce only half the power required for full speed and the balance was available from boost gas turbines, which could also be used for manœuvring if required. The addition of

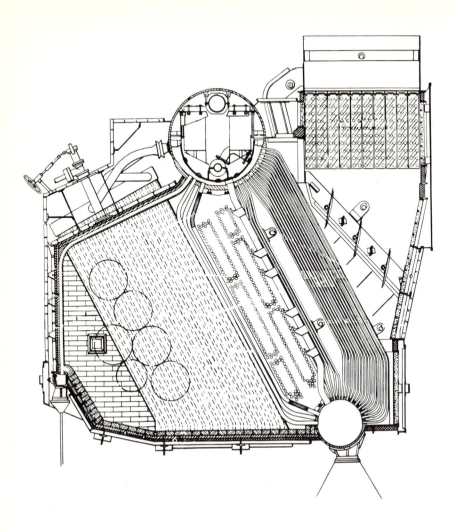

Diagram of a modern Babcock and Wilcox superheat water-tube boiler as fitted in warships.

gas turbines coupled to the propeller shafts also provided the desirable ability to get quickly under way from harbour in an emergency, which had previously been obtainable only by ships incorporating diesel drive.

Aircraft-type gas-turbine engines have now overcome their early shortcomings and many modern warships incorporate them as their only means of propulsion. The largest projected ship with this feature is the British 'through-deck cruiser' *Invincible*, a ship expected to displace between 19,000 and 20,000 tons.

Besides the great advantage over steam engines of being able to develop full power within a few minutes of being started up from cold, their operating costs are comparatively low; they occupy less space; defective engines can be rapidly replaced; and they require less manpower to operate and maintain. As gas turbines cannot use a reversible shaft, they are usually used in conjunction with variable-pitch propellers and can be controlled from the bridge.

For the smallest warships, those which come under the heading of 'coastal' craft, two types of engine were developed—the very light-weight (5 pounds per shaft horse-power) Deltic diesel engine and the gas turbine. The former was used in some British types of fast patrol boat for their main propulsion, as well as in the slower coastal minesweepers. Other British fast patrol boats had gas turbines to give them their high speed with Deltic engines for cruising.

The most revolutionary development of recent years has been the introduction of nuclear reactors in the place of normal boilers to provide steam power. Applied primarily to submarines, in which the advantage over other means of producing power when submerged are overwhelming, the system has since been applied in the U.S. Navy to guided-missile frigates, guided-missile cruisers and aircraft carriers. As in nuclear-powered submarines, their reactors generate steam to drive geared turbines.

The chief advantage of the system for surface ships is the ability it gives to the ship in which it is installed to operate at sustained high speeds for several years without refuelling.

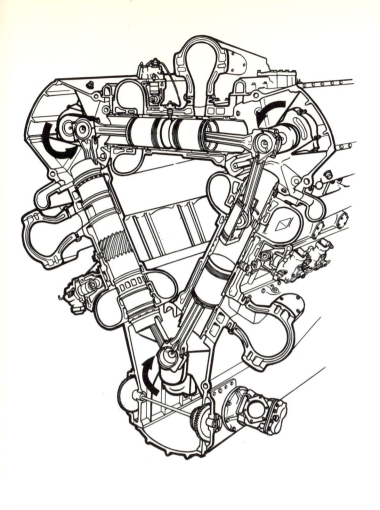

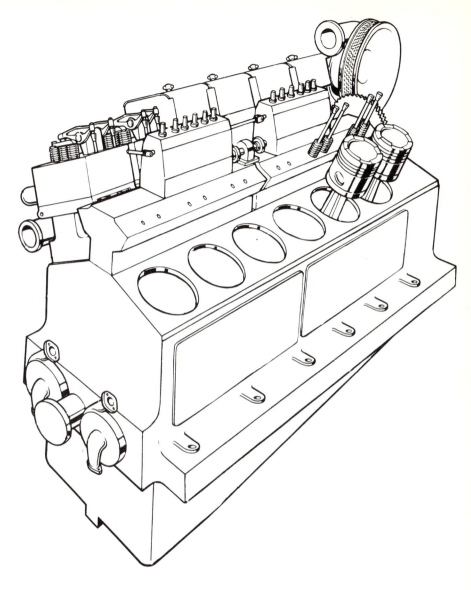

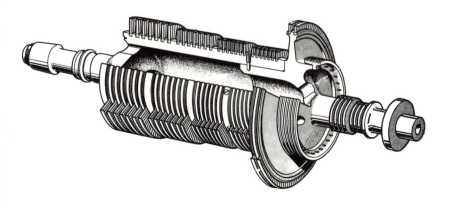

Top left: Deltic diesel engine, in which the nine cylinders, in each of which two pistons operate, are arranged in three units of three cylinders each, forming a triangle with a crankshaft at each end.

Top right: Large four-stroke supercharged diesel engine as used for marine propulsion.

Bottom left: Rotor of high-pressure combined impulse and reaction steam turbine.

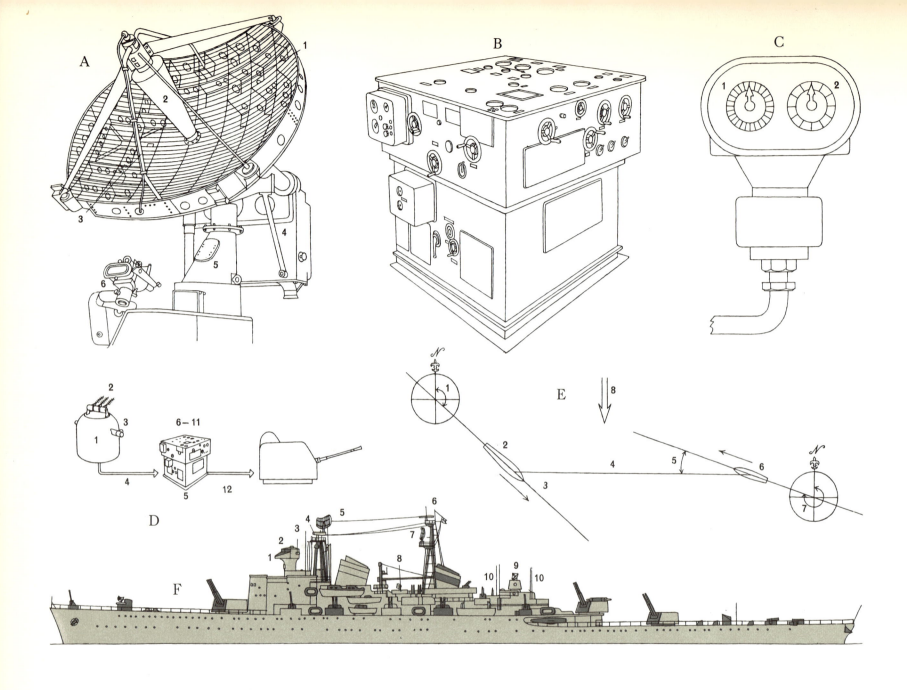

ACTION INFORMATION ORGANISATION

A *Fire-control radar*
1 Parabolic antenna
2 Radiator
3 Wave guide
4 Local stabiliser
5 Pedestal
6 Telescope

B *Predictor for ballistic data handling*

C *Range receiver*
1 Fine dial
2 Coarse dial

D *Principle of fire control*
1 Main director
2 Fire-control radar
3 Range finder
4 Range + deflection + elevation
5 Predictor
6–11 Data being handled in predictor

6 Wind direction and wind speed
7 Target's speed + inclination
8 Own course and speed
9 Powder temperature
10 Barometric pressure and air temperature
11 Spotting corrections
12 Firing data (gun elevation and angle of training) to guns

E *Basic fire-control principle*
1 Own course
2 Own ship
3 Deflection
4 Range
5 Inclination (angle on the target's bow)
6 Target
7 Target's course
8 Wind

F *Radar, range finders, etc.*
1 Fire-control radar for main armament (surface)
2 Forward director control tower (DCT)
3 Range finder
4 Navigation radar
5 Air-search (air-warning) radar

6 Surface-warning radar
7 Height-finding radar
8 Fine-control radar for close-range armament
9 After main director with range finder and fire-control radar
10 Aerials

While the Second World War was still being fought out at sea with conventional weapons (shells, bombs and torpedoes) with conventional means of delivery (guns and manned aircraft), developments had already taken place which were to change the whole concept of warfare and the function and armament of the various types of man-of-war.

Nuclear physics had produced an explosive of appalling power and destructiveness—so appalling, indeed, that it was hoped by many that it had made wars unthinkable. But when the victorious Allies split into two antagonistic camps, the free democracies led by the United States on one hand, the Communist world led by Soviet Russia on the other, the former found themselves faced by land forces so numerically superior that any aggression on their part could not be contained using conventional weapons.

The United States and Britain, however, held the advantage of a virtual monopoly of knowledge of the technique of production of atomic explosive. To redress the balance they pressed ahead with its development and that of the various means of its delivery, the United States soon outstripping her ally. Delivery of the nuclear bomb was entrusted at first to aircraft. Ever larger and faster bombers were built for the purpose for use by the U.S. Air Force, later by the British and, in more recent times, by the French.

Both the American and British navies, however, successfully demanded the right to play their part in wielding the main strike weapon by means of aircraft from their large carriers. Both navies, the American on a scale vastly greater than the British, built up the carrier group as the strike arm. The carriers themselves are described in the chapter devoted to the history of that type of ship. Here we examine the ships produced for the task of escorting them.

The process had begun during the war in the Pacific in which the carrier had established itself as the capital ship of the epoch. Cruisers and destroyers to screen them, built in great numbers, have been mentioned in the chapter devoted to that era. Many were placed in reserve at the end of the war; others continued to function in their original condition for the next six years, a period during which the world balance of power was maintained by the United States' unique possession of the nuclear bomb. It was always inevitable, however, that the Communists would, in time, also acquire the knowledge and technique to make it. This came about and coincided with the adoption of an aggressive policy by Soviet Russia. It was countered by the formation of the North Atlantic Treaty Organization amongst the Western democracies: massive naval rearmament programmes by both the opposing power groups followed.

The two principal features of these programmes were the adoption of guided missiles in place of guns and for launching anti-submarine devices, and the substitution of nuclear reactors in certain ships in place of conventional boilers to provide steam power for their turbines.

The technique of rocket and jet propulsion and radio guidance systems for

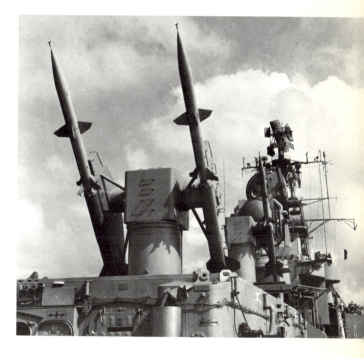

A twin Terrier missile launcher.

U.S.S. *Long Beach*, nuclear-powered guided-missile cruiser.
The first nuclear-powered surface warship in the world: radius
360,000 miles at 20 knots, 100,000 miles at full speed (30·5
knots).

Top: U.S.S. guided-missile frigate *Belknap* which mounts one twin Terrier/ASROC dual launcher forward (for missiles and A/S rockets).

Bottom: U.S.S. *Bainbridge.* Rated as a nuclear-powered guided-missile frigate, though her displacement (7600 tons) is more than that of an average light cruiser. Mounts two Advanced Terrier twin launchers forward and aft and an ASROC launcher forward. Radius 450,000 miles at 20 knots, 150,000 miles at full speed (30 knots).

231

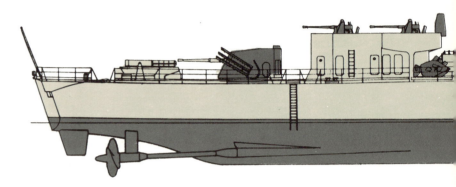

Top: Japanese guided-missile destroyer *Amatsukaze* (1963), 3050 tons. The first Japanese ship to be armed with guided missiles—one single Tartar launcher. Also carries dropping gear for A/S torpedoes. Powered by steam turbines, she has a speed of 33 knots.

Bottom: U.S.S. *Little Rock*, one of the six cruisers of the Second World War construction converted to 'single-ended' type of guided-missile cruiser between 1957 and 1960, mounting either one Talos twin launcher or one Terrier twin launcher aft.

flying bombs had been exploited by the Germans to produce their V.1 and V.2 weapons and air-launched glider bombs and by the Japanese for their rocket-propelled 'Baka' bomb. It was in response to the latter that American scientists began work, late in 1944, on an interceptor missile. To obtain supersonic speeds for it, propulsion by ram-jet was decided upon.

The ram-jet develops thrust just like the turbo-jet which powers a jet aircraft, but it does it without the complex, expensive turbine and compressor in the latter for injecting the air needed to burn the fuel. Instead, the ram-jet uses compressed air pushed into its front end by the forward motion of the missile itself. In the combustion section kerosene is mixed with the incoming air and burned, thus keeping up the required pressure. The hot gases from the combustion chamber are thrust out of a nozzle to the rear to provide the power for supersonic speed.

Physicists had known of the ram-jet principle for decades, but had never been able to fly one owing to the difficulty of giving it the initial high speed required to start it functioning. The answer to the problem was found in a booster rocket and, on 15th June 1945, a 6-inch wide exhaust-pipe from an F.47 Thunderbolt fighter spurted off the sand dunes at Island Beach, New Jersey, and reached a speed of 1200 miles per hour. This exhaust-pipe turned into a ram-jet should not have flown, just as a bumble-bee is in theory aerodynamically unable to fly. It does so nevertheless. So the ram-jet programme became known as 'Project Bumblebee'. When a radar guidance system was added to the resultant ram-jet missile, the first fully guided supersonic flight of the Terrier anti-aircraft missile was achieved in 1948.

As it first became operational the Terrier had a range of just over ten miles and was capable of intercepting aircraft flying more than 600 m.p.h.. at more than

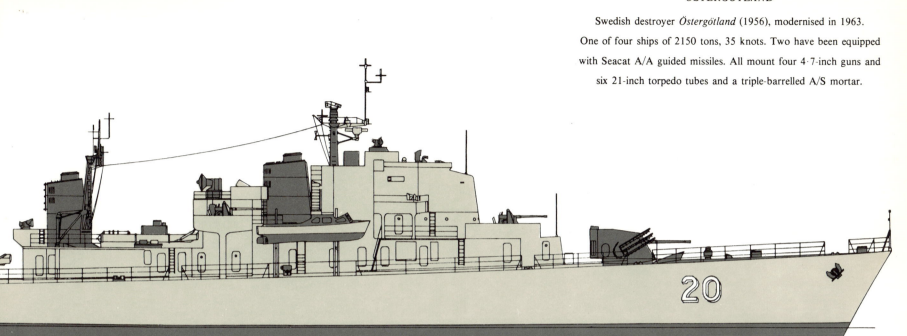

Swedish destroyer *Östergötland* (1956), modernised in 1963. One of four ships of 2150 tons, 35 knots. Two have been equipped with Seacat A/A guided missiles. All mount four 4·7-inch guns and six 21-inch torpedo tubes and a triple-barrelled A/S mortar.

50,000 feet. The missile's maximum speed is approximately two and a half times the speed of sound. The 15-foot Terrier is launched with an 11-foot booster which drops off after a few seconds of flight when the missile has sufficient speed for ram-jet ignition. Weight of the missile, complete with high-explosive warhead and booster, is 1100 pounds.

This missile armed the world's first guided-missile warships, the U.S. cruisers *Boston* and *Canberra*. Originally completed in 1943 as 13,600-ton cruisers armed with nine 8-inch guns, a dozen 5-inch dual-purpose guns, and seventy-one 40-mm. and 20-mm. weapons, these ships were converted to 'guided-missile heavy cruisers' between 1952 and 1956.

As missile ships they retain their two triple 8-inch turrets forward and have a conventional secondary battery of ten 5-inch guns and twelve 3-inch anti-aircraft weapons. However, they were provided with two large lattice masts to support the multitude of antennae required in their new role and their after guns have been re-placed in each ship with two twin Terrier missile launchers. To be loaded, the twin launcher comes to a vertical position facing aft. The missiles rise through deck hatches and engage lugs on the guide rails of the launcher. The missiles themselves, believed to be some 144 per ship, are stored in two rotating magazines below decks. Each launcher can fire two missiles every thirty seconds.

The *Boston* and *Canberra* were thus the first ships of a fleet of missile-armed screening ships for the U.S. Navy's carriers. They were followed by six additional cruiser-conversions of *Cleveland* class light cruisers completed during the war. These were originally 10,500-ton ships, mounting twelve 6-inch guns, an equal number of 5-inch dual-purpose guns, and forty-seven 40-mm. and 20-mm. weapons. Like the *Boston* and *Canberra*, these ships were 'single-end' conversions, retaining guns forward and being fitted with missiles aft.

The *Springfield, Providence* and *Topeka* of this series were armed with one twin Terrier launcher aft. The first two, also modified to serve as fleet flagships, retained only one triple 6-inch mount forward while the *Topeka* kept two 6-inch mounts forward.

Soon after the development of the Terrier got under way, the scientists began work on an improved anti-aircraft missile, one capable of exploding a nuclear war-head some sixty-five miles from the launching ship. This resulted in the Talos, a 3000-pound, ram-jet missile also fired with a booster rocket. One twin Talos launcher was installed in the former light cruisers *Little Rock, Oklahoma City* and *Galveston*. Again, the first two are fitted as fleet flagships and retain three 6-inch guns while the *Galveston* has six of these guns forward. These six 'single-end' conversions joined the fleet during 1958–60.

They were followed closely by four 'double-enders', essentially all-missile-armed cruisers. Three of these ships have also been converted from war-built heavy cruisers, the *Albany, Chicago* and *Columbus*. However, they differ from the earlier conversions in that during their reconstruction they were stripped entirely to their main deck and rebuilt with aluminium superstructures topped with twin 'macks'—combination masts and stacks (funnels).

H.M.C.S. *Skeena*, destroyer escort of the *St. Laurent* class of the Canadian Navy, equipped with variable-depth sonar submarine-detection equipment, A/S helicopter and Limbo A/S mortars. Steam-turbine propelled.

Netherlands cruiser *De Zeven Provincien*, launched 1950 and converted in 1964 to mount a twin Terrier missile launcher. Also mounts four fully automatic 6-inch radar-controlled guns. Steam-turbine propelled with a speed of 32 knots.

Built as 13,600 to 13,700-ton heavy cruisers mounting nine 8-inch guns, they rejoined the fleet in 1962–64, a few hundred tons lighter, carrying a twin Talos launcher forward and a twin Talos launcher aft. Amidships each ship was fitted with two short-range Tartar missile launchers (which will be discussed in detail later). After American entry into the Vietnamese War in the mid-1960s, when the so-called 'gun-gap' in the fleet became apparent, each of these ships was refitted with two open-mount 5-inch dual-purpose guns.

But the most advanced missile cruiser in the United States fleet is the *Long Beach*, the world's first nuclear-powered surface warship, the only cruiser built by the United States after the Second World War and—at 330 million dollars—the second most expensive warship in history. (The dubious distinction of being the most expensive goes to the 456 million dollar nuclear-powered carrier *Enterprise*.)

The *Long Beach* was originally planned as a large nuclear-powered 'destroyer' of about 7800 tons displacement. In early 1956, as she was being proposed to Congress in a shipbuilding programme, the decision was made to capitalise on the capabilities of nuclear propulsion and her displacement was increased to 11,000 tons. Increases in her armament caused further 'growth' and by the time she was ordered in October 1956 her displacement had grown to 14,000 tons. She was completed in late 1961 as a guided-missile cruiser with a displacement of 14,200 tons, and an overall length of $721\frac{1}{4}$ feet. Her design incorporates several advanced features, among them a 'square' superstructure the sides of which are formed by fixed radar antennae which give improved performance over the normal rotating antennae.

Armament for this ship consists of two twin Terrier launchers forward and a twin Talos launcher aft. As an afterthought, two single 5-inch guns were installed amidships. These, although enclosed mounts, are of limited value because of their limited arcs of fire.

The design of the *Long Beach* provided space for eight Polaris missile tubes, but the decision was made not to install these weapons (the 5-inch guns utilise some of this space). The most revolutionary feature of the *Long Beach* is her nuclear power plant. She has steam-turbine machinery with two pressurised water reactors in place of conventional boilers. On her initial reactor cores the *Long Beach* could steam 360,000 miles at 20 knots or 100,000 miles at continuous full power. Improved cores have now been installed which will increase considerably her endurance on a single 'fuelling'. The *Long Beach*'s speed is in excess of 30 knots, similar to the 32- or 33-knot speeds of the converted missile cruisers.

During the 1950s the navy briefly installed the Regulus I jet-propelled missile in a few all-gun heavy cruisers. This 500 m.p.h., 500-mile missile was fired from a launcher fitted to the ships' sterns. However, the operational life of the missile was relatively brief and it was soon removed from cruisers and employed only aboard submarines, for which it was primarily designed. An improved, supersonic Regulus II was planned for the nuclear-powered *Long Beach*, but this project was cancelled before the missile became operational. (Both versions are described in more detail in the submarine section of this volume.)

After the Second World War the United States Navy began constructing large destroyers with improved sea-keeping capabilities to operate with the newer carriers of the *Midway* and *Forrestal* classes. The first of these large destroyers were the four *Mitscher* class ships, 3500 tons and 493 feet overall, and armed with two rapid-fire 5-inch guns and four rapid-fire 3-inch guns. These were sleek ships of relatively conventional design powered by steam turbines capable of 35 knots.

While these ships were still on the building ways they were reclassified as 'destroyer leaders', a designation long on the navy's books but never formally assigned to ships. Then the designation system was thoroughly confused when, in 1955, shortly after the four *Mitscher*'s were completed, the classification 'frigate' was applied to these large destroyer-type warships. Heretofore in the steam age, the term 'frigate' referred to ships of smaller size and power than destroyers, such as those designated destroyer-escort in the U.S. Navy. Indeed, except for some

ASW ships built in the Second World War, the Americans had not used the expression 'frigate' since the era of sails and wooden hulls. Conversion of two of the *Mitscher* class to guided-missile destroyers brought their displacement up to 5200 tons, full load.

Inevitably the frigates which followed the *Mitscher*'s were larger and missile-armed. Between 1959 and 1961 the ten *Farragut* class frigates were completed, having a displacement of 4700 tons standard on a hull 512½ feet long, and carrying an armament of one 5-inch gun forward and a twin Terrier launcher aft.

Next came nine *Leahy* class ships of 5670 tons standard, 533 feet overall, and fitted with 'macks' in lieu of separate funnels and masts. These ships were 'double-enders' with a twin Terrier launcher forward and another aft. Amidships they each had two twin 3-inch gun mounts for close-in defence.

Following these ships the United States Navy built a single nuclear-powered frigate, the *Bainbridge*. She is considerably larger than her contemporaries, having a displacement of 7600 tons standard and an overall length of 564 feet. She follows a relatively conventional design, albeit without funnels, and is armed with twin Terrier launchers forward and aft and four 3-inch guns amidships. Again, she has the advantages of virtually unlimited endurance, being capable of more than 30 knots for 150,000 miles or 20 knots for 400,000 miles.

The realisation that warships must still have conventional guns in the missile age to cope with low-performance aircraft and for shore bombardment requirements led to the next series of frigates, the *Belknap* class, being 'single-end' ships. Again, the size of the ships increased with the nine *Belknap*'s, having a displacement of 5340 tons and a length of 547 feet. Forward is a twin Terrier launcher and aft a single rapid-fire 5-inch gun. Two single 3-inch guns are also mounted amidships.

When this series was proposed by the navy, Congress, with Administrative support, insisted that one of the series should be nuclear-powered, which led to the construction of the United States Navy's fourth nuclear-powered surface warship, the frigate *Truxtun*. Completed in 1967, she is an 8250-ton, 565-foot warship, larger than many cruisers of the Second World War era. Her armament is similar to that of the conventionally powered *Belknap*.

An effort was now made to adapt the Terrier-Talos missiles to smaller, conventional destroyer designs. The *Gearing* class destroyer *Gyatt* (2390 tons, 390½ feet) was armed with a twin Terrier launcher aft in 1956, retaining two twin 5-inch mounts forward and two twin 3-inch mounts amidships. Her missile system had a relatively small magazine capacity (twelve missiles) and limited fire control equipment. Although the *Gyatt* operated as a missile ship for some five years, the decision was made to develop a smaller anti-aircraft missile for destroyer use.

Thus the Tartar was developed. To avoid the use of a booster, a small-stage rocket motor was developed which provides high-thrust, short-duration initial burning and then lower-thrust, long-duration burning. The missile weighs just over 1200 pounds at launch, is 15 feet long, has a range of just over ten miles, and a 'burn-out' speed of Mach 2·5.

The Tartar was installed initially in the twenty-three *Adams* class guided-missile destroyers (3200 tons, 432 feet). The early ships of this class have a twin launcher but a single-arm launcher is installed in later ships, an arrangement that saves some sixteen tons of weight at the cost of only two fewer missiles. These destroyers also have two 5-inch guns. Twin Tartar launchers are also installed as a secondary missile battery in the three double-ended missile cruiser conversions (*Albany, Chicago, Columbus*), and a single-arm Tartar launcher has been installed in six (destroyer) escorts. Two of the early *Mitscher* class frigates are fitted with Tartar missile launchers.

The U.S. Navy's next series of frigates after the *Truxtun* also mount Tartar systems. The first two, *California* and *South Carolina*, to be commissioned at the end of 1973 and 1974 respectively, some 10,000 tons at full load, 596 feet overall, have two single Tartar D surface-to-air launchers firing Standard MR missiles. Their main A/S weapon is an ASROC (see later) eight-tube missile launcher. The *Virginia* and *Texas*, slightly smaller ships still under construction (1973), have two combination twin Tartar/ASROC launchers, firing a later mark

of MR missiles. All these ships, unlike the *Truxtun*, pay tribute to a returning belief in the need for a gun armament by mounting two 5-inch, single, dual-purpose guns.

All the missile-armed cruisers, frigates and destroyers are intended primarily for all-weather, anti-aircraft defence of carrier task groups. Most have been equipped with an effective anti-submarine armament; but, in the U.S. Navy, the task of submarine defence is primarily undertaken by land- and carrier-based fixed-wing aircraft and helicopters and non-missile destroyers and escorts.

There are two main anti-submarine weapons aboard U.S. warships: torpedoes and ASROC missiles. There are several torpedoes in service which are long-range weapons that, upon entering the water, 'home' acoustically on to a submarine. Torpedo launchers for these weapons have been mounted in the four double-ended missile cruisers, all frigates, destroyers and escort ships. The single-end missile frigates *Little Rock* and *Providence* have also been fitted with sonar and torpedo launchers.

ASROC—for 'anti-submarine rocket'—is actually a missile booster for an anti-submarine homing torpedo or a nuclear depth charge. The ASROC rocket booster with torpedo measures about 15 feet and weighs 1000 pounds.

The firing ship's sonar data are fed into a computer which charts the target's course, range and speed, and presents a firing solution for the missile. When fired the ASROC follows a ballistic trajectory. As it nears the water, the booster separates from the torpedo at a predetermined point and a parachute opens to slow the torpedo's descent. The ASROC torpedo's battery is activated on contact with salt water and the weapon automatically begins an acoustical homing search for the submarine. If an atomic depth charge is fitted to the ASROC booster the depth charge sinks to a predetermined depth and then detonates. Range of the ASROC is 'several' miles.

Eight-tube ASROC launchers—referred to as 'pepper boxes'—are mounted in the navy's four double-ended cruisers, guided-missile cruisers of the *Leahy/Bainbridge* series, the *Adams* class guided-missile destroyers, seventy-nine modernised Second World War era destroyers, and all of the new escort ships. The latest frigates can fire five ASROC from their Terrier or Tartar combined launchers.

Another anti-submarine weapon system that was developed by the U.S. Navy was DASH—Drone Anti-Submarine Helicopter. Like ASROC, this system was designed to enable ships to take advantage of the increased detection ranges which were becoming available with improved sonar gear. The DASH concept consisted of a radio-controlled, unmanned helicopter carrying a homing torpedo to the area in which the submarine had been detected and, on command, releasing the weapon. DASH was developed from a one-man helicopter design: the first operational DASH unit—two helicopters—went to sea in 1963. It suffered major problems with its 'black box' electronics equipment, however, and it is probably owing to this that, though facilities for it were fitted in 125 destroyers of Second World War vintage under the FRAM modernisation scheme, it is no longer in operation.

A final significant post-Second World War man-of-war in the U.S. surface-fleet has been the escort ship (formerly known as destroyer escort). The first ship in this programme was the *Dealey*, completed in 1954. She is a 1280-ton, 314½-foot ship capable of 25 knots. As built, her armament consisted of two twin 3-inch gun mounts plus a 12·75-mm. depth-charge mortar (Weapon Able, later Weapon Alpha); this has also been installed in some destroyers and early frigates, but subsequently replaced by more advanced weapons.

The *Dealey* was followed during the next decade by eighteen additional escort ships of varying design, all single-screw ships with a speed of 23 or 25 knots, and armed with 3-inch guns and anti-submarine weapons.

In 1962 the keel was laid down for the *Garcia*, the first ship in a major building programme to add sixty-two escort ships to the U.S. Navy. This, the largest American shipbuilding programme of essentially one design since 1945, was completed when the *Julius A. Furer* was commissioned on 11th November 1967.

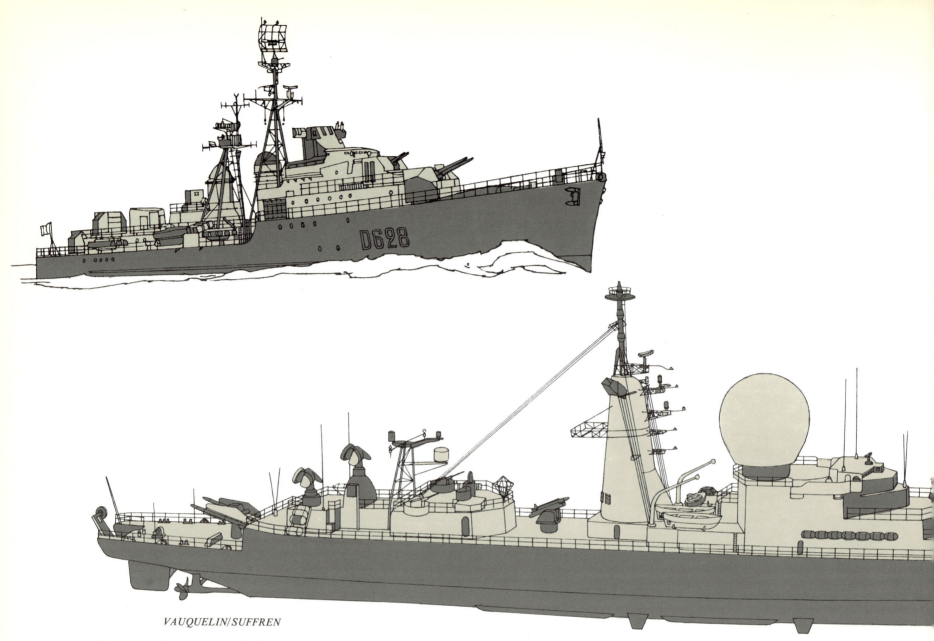

VAUQUELIN/SUFFREN

Top: French destroyer *Vauquelin* of the *Surcouf* class,
some of which mount single Tartar missiles aft; others, including
the *Vauquelin*, are being equipped as A/S vessels with
Malafon missile launchers, tubes for A/S torpedoes and two sonars.

Bottom: French guided-missile frigate *Suffren*,
equipped with a twin launcher for the Masurca A/A missiles, Malafon
rocket/homing torpedo launcher, tubes for A/S homing torpedoes,
two sonars including variable depth and the SENIT tactical information
system as well as the latest type of radar.

236

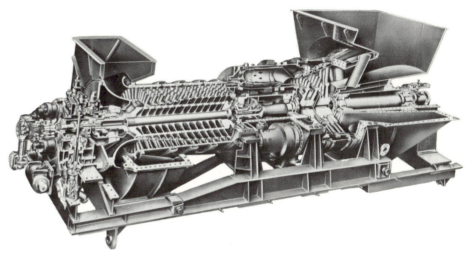

CAIO DUILIO

Italian guided-missile cruiser *Caio Duilio*,
completed 1964, equipped for defence against submarines (four A/S helicopters,
six A/S torpedo tubes) and aircraft (one Terrier twin launcher
and eight 3-inch fully automatic guns).

Sectional illustration of a marine gas-turbine propulsion unit.

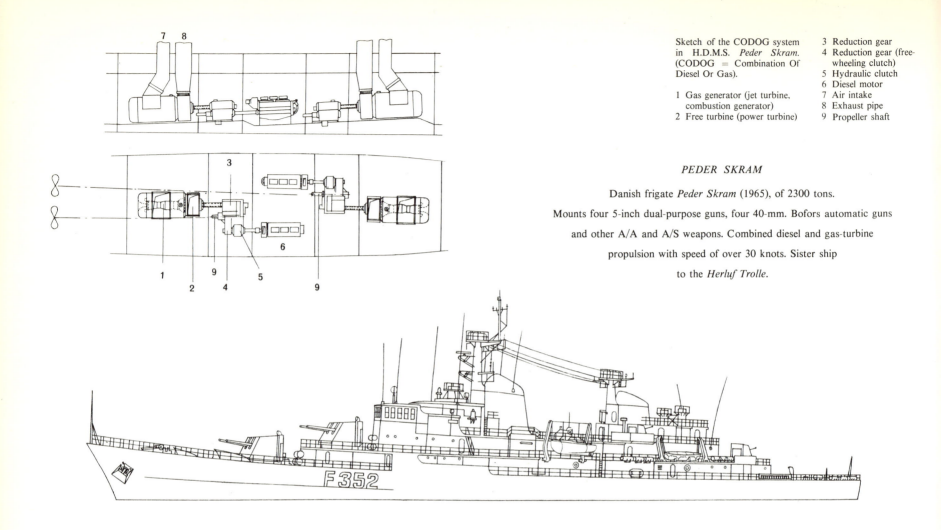

Sketch of the CODOG system in H.D.M.S. *Peder Skram*. (CODOG = Combination Of Diesel Or Gas).

1 Gas generator (jet turbine, combustion generator)
2 Free turbine (power turbine)
3 Reduction gear
4 Reduction gear (free-wheeling clutch)
5 Hydraulic clutch
6 Diesel motor
7 Air intake
8 Exhaust pipe
9 Propeller shaft

PEDER SKRAM

Danish frigate *Peder Skram* (1965), of 2300 tons.
Mounts four 5-inch dual-purpose guns, four 40-mm. Bofors automatic guns
and other A/A and A/S weapons. Combined diesel and gas-turbine
propulsion with speed of over 30 knots. Sister ship
to the *Herluf Trolle*.

The *Garcia* and fifteen of her sister ships have a displacement of 2620 tons, an overall length of 414½ feet, and a single-screw propulsion system featuring an advanced pressure-fired boiler which provides a speed of 27 knots. Ten of these ships are armed with two 5-inch guns, an eight-tube ASROC launcher and anti-submarine torpedo launchers. The six other ships have a single-arm Tartar missile launcher in lieu of the after 5-inch gun. (High costs have prevented this feature from being included in additional ships.)

The later escort ships, led by the U.S.S. *Knox*, are 3011-tonners, 438 feet over-all, but otherwise similar in basic design to the *Garcia* class. Other differences are non-pressure-fired boilers in the newer ships and only one 5-inch gun. All except the original ten *Garcia*s are fitted with a multiple launcher for Sea Sparrow, a modification of the navy-developed air-to-air Sparrow missile.

These escort ships are specially designed for anti-submarine operations and have several interesting features, among them large bow sonar domes for the SQS-26 equipment and two torpedo tubes built into their stern counters to facilitate the firing of wire-guided torpedoes without the danger of fouling the screw. They also have special devices to reduce the noise of their hulls passing through water, thus reducing vulnerability to submarine-fired homing torpedoes.

It is interesting to note how, in the fifteen-year period between the *Dealey* and the *Knox*, the displacement of the escort-ship designs has almost tripled and their length has increased by more than a quarter, until the *Knox* class ships are larger than many destroyers. These ships are nevertheless classified as escorts on account of their single propeller shaft and relatively slow speeds. The fact that these ships will be the replacement for the 4- and 6-gun, 2-shaft, 34-knot FRAM destroyers has aroused dismay in some quarters of the navy.

We cannot move on from discussing ships of one of the world's two largest navies without a look at some of the multifarious ships with specialised functions either of supporting the main fighting units or of operating in coastal or riverine waters.

The ever-increasing complexity of control of naval task forces has called for larger staffs for their commanders, served by a huge system of communications and electronic surveillance and counter measures. It has become more difficult to accommodate these staffs and facilities in the fighting units. Special Command and Communication Ships have therefore been provided.

The first ship of this category was the heavy cruiser *Northampton*, which was converted to a Task Force Command Ship while still under construction in

1948–53. Fitted with an elaborate combat information centre (CIC) with the latest electronic equipment, and with accommodation for a fleet commander and his staff, she was employed as flagship of the Second Fleet in the Atlantic until October 1961. Her place was taken by the *Wright*, converted to a Command Ship (CC) in May 1963. The *Wright*'s sister, the *Saipan*, was to have been similarly converted, but eventually emerged as a Major Communications Relay Ship fitted with communications relay equipment capable of giving support to major commands afloat or ashore. All these ships are at present (1973) in reserve. Still in active service is the *La Salle*, converted in 1972 from an Amphibious Transport Dock (LPD) to serve as flagship for the Commander of the U.S. Middle East Force. She has elaborate command and communications facilities and is specially equipped for operations in the extreme heat of the Persian Gulf, where she is based at Bahrain.

The next and much more numerous group of supporting ships are collectively known as Amphibious Warfare Ships. This group originated during the Second World War, a vast array of vessels ranging from landing craft and ships of many types, capable of being beached to off-load troops, tanks and artillery, and many of them mounting batteries of supporting artillery or rocket launchers, to amphibious transports, converted from large, fast freighters.

There are still many types of minor landing craft—too many to be listed here. There are also Landing Ships of various types, the older of which are kept in reserve. Those in service mostly date from 1966 when the first of the *Newport* class of 20-Tank Landing Ships (LST) was laid down; and in the following year, the first of the *Anchorage* class of Dock Landing Ships (LSD). These ships of some 10,000 tons (light) and a speed of 20 knots can accommodate three landing craft in a dock well, and several more on deck or on davits. Over the dock is a removable flight deck for the operation of helicopters. Of much the same size are Amphibious Transport Docks (LPD). All these ships are designed to carry and launch a balanced landing force.

More massive support for landing forces is provided by Amphibious Cargo Ships (LKA). Large numbers of these, built during the Second World War, are held in reserve. A new generation of them was initiated by the laying-down between 1966 and 1968 of five 20,000-ton ships of the *Charleston* class which can accommodate eighteen landing craft and 226 troops, while two heavy-lift cranes and a number of booms are available to hoist out the items of heavy equipment for a landing force carried in the holds.

The main body of any 'intervention force' would today be brought to the scene of action in Amphibious Assault Ships (LPH) and landed by the squadron of some thirty helicopters carried. They are in design similar to light aircraft carriers of early days with a flight deck over a hangar but with no angled flight deck, arrester gear or catapults. Indeed, those operated by the British Navy, H.M.S. *Hermes* and *Bulwark*, are converted from light aircraft carriers. The six ships of the *Iwo Jima* class of the U.S. Navy, of 17,000 tons light displacement and a speed of 22 knots, were designed specifically for the purpose. A further five ships of the much larger (39,300 tons full load) *Tarawa* class, which may operate Vertical or Short Take-Off and Landing (V/STOL) fixed-wing aircraft as well as helicopters, are under construction.

Following the war, the British Navy, at a slower pace and on a much smaller scale, followed in the footsteps of the U.S. Navy. A number of carriers under construction were brought to completion, as described in the chapter on those ships. Cruisers, destroyers and frigates of the Second World War period continued to serve with the fleet while three cruisers of the *Tiger* class laid down in 1944–45 were brought slowly to completion between 1959 and 1961 and some destroyers of the *Battle* and *Weapon* classes, laid down during the war, were completed between 1946 and 1948. The first post-war additions to the fleet were the eight destroyers of the *Daring* class, large for their day at 2800 tons and conventionally armed with six 4·5-inch guns in three twin turrets, fully automatic and radar-controlled. Their most interesting feature was, perhaps, their propelling machinery

consisting of steam turbines of the most advanced design, and the adoption by the Royal Navy for the first time of steam pressures of 650 pounds per square inch and temperatures of 850°F. All these ships were suitable as escorts for the carriers and for the battleships which were retained in commission for some years. The experiences of two world wars, however, caused the British Navy to lay emphasis on the naval task of convoy protection against submarine attack. A number of wartime-built destroyers of the *R*, *T*, *U*, *V*, *W* and *Z* classes were therefore converted between 1951 and 1954 to anti-submarine frigates by the removal of all but two 4-inch guns, the fitting of two Limbo 3-barrelled anti-submarine mortars aft and modifications of the superstructure and masts.

The first frigates of post-war design were the twelve ships of the Type 14, A/S Utility Type completed in 1956 and 1957, whose main weapons were, again, two Limbo mortars. These were followed by the Type 12, *Whitby* and *Rothesay* classes, the hull design of which was so successful that it was used as the basis of a number of general-purpose frigates of the *Leander* class, completed between 1963 and 1967. All these, like the 'Tribal' class of general-purpose frigates, have a main gun armament of two 4·5-inch guns and one Limbo anti-submarine mortar. Some were initially equipped with, and all will eventually mount, a quadruple launcher for the Seacat, a short-range radio-guided surface-to-air missile.

The 'Tribal' class broke new ground in the field of propulsion machinery by the addition of a gas turbine of 20,000 horse-power to boost their single-geared steam turbine for high-speed steaming and to allow the ships to get under way instantly in an emergency. Both types are also equipped to operate a Wasp light helicopter. Other frigates added to the fleet between 1958 and 1960 were four Type 61 aircraft direction frigates and four Type 41 anti-aircraft types. The gun armament in each of these types consists of two 4·5-inch guns and two 40 mm. Bofors automatic weapons, the latter to be replaced eventually by the Seacat missile.

The guided-missile era for the British Navy was ushered in by the development of the Seaslug long-range surface-to-air missile which, driven by a solid-fuel rocket propellant, rides a radio-beam to its target at a speed of Mach 2 and has a range of some seventeen miles. To mount this new weapon the guided-missile destroyer *Devonshire* of 5200 tons was laid down in March 1959 and has been followed by seven others of the same class. Like the 'Tribals', these ships incorporate a combination of steam and gas turbines to give a top speed of 32½ knots. A twin launcher for the Seaslug is mounted aft.

The short-range Seacat, for which two quadruple launchers are also mounted, is guided visually to its target by radio command, the most recent models at supersonic speed. The decision to discard fixed-wing aircraft carriers (discussed elsewhere) left the Royal Navy critically lacking in ship-strike capability, as no surface-to-surface missile had been developed. It has been necessary, therefore, to acquire French Exocet missiles and launchers, and these are being fitted in the *Devonshire* and three others of the class.

The latest British surface-to-surface air missile, the Seadart, which is propelled by ram-jet after initial boosting by solid-fuel rockets, has a certain anti-ship capability. It was round this weapon that the type 82 light cruiser was designed. Owing to shortage of funds, however, only one of this class has been built, the *Bristol*, a 6750-ton (full load) ship with combined steam and gas turbine propulsion.

Another weapon fitted in the *Bristol* is the Australian-developed Ikara anti-submarine missile which carries a torpedo to the vicinity of a detected submarine.

The French Navy, development of which came to a standstill during the war, started its resuscitation by completing construction of the 9380-ton cruiser *De Grasse* which had lain uncompleted at Lorient throughout the German occupation. After a further delay she was completed in 1955 as an anti-aircraft cruiser mounting sixteen 5-inch guns and equipped as a fleet command and air direction ship. Recently she has been modified to operate as flagship of the Pacific Experimental Nuclear Centre.

Fast patrol boats of the *Jaguar* class of the West German Navy. They are variously equipped as fast gunboats, torpedo boats or minelayers.

The French Navy's only cruiser of post-war design, the 8500-ton (standard) *Colbert*, is primarily an anti-aircraft ship with a gun armament of two 100-mm. single automatic weapons and twelve 57-mm. guns in six twin mountings. She also mounts two Exocet surface-to-surface and one twin Masurca surface-to-air missile launchers.

France's most recent frigate is the *Suffren* of 5200 tons. Launched in 1965, this ship of ultra-modern appearance became operational in 1967. Her double-reduction geared turbines driving two shafts at a total horse-power of 70,000 and taking steam at a pressure of 640 pounds per square inch and a super-heat temperature of 842°F, give her a speed of 34 knots. Two types of missile are mounted. A twin launcher for a Masurca surface-to-air, two-stage rocket with solid-fuel propellant, giving it a range of 22 miles at a speed of Mach 2·2, is mounted aft. For anti-submarine purposes there are Malafon acoustic-homing torpedoes, launched initially by two solid-fuel radio-controlled booster rockets and thereafter gliding down to start their submerged homing run. They have a range of seven miles. In addition other homing torpedoes can be launched from fixed tubes. Her sister ship *Duquesne* became operational in 1970.

The classification 'destroyer' has disappeared from the French Navy List. Ships which might previously have been so designated are now classified as 'frigates' like the *Suffren*, 'corvettes' such as the five 3000-ton ships of the *Aconit* class, or *escorteurs d'escadre* such as the 2750-ton *Surcouf* and her numerous improved successors. The most recent of these, *La Galissonnière*, completed in 1962, mounts two 4-inch automatic guns, a quadruple anti-submarine mortar, six 21-inch anti-submarine torpedo tubes, a launcher for Malafon anti-submarine missiles and a helicopter. Her geared turbines developed 72,000 horse-power on trials, giving her a speed of 38 knots.

Smaller types are the *escorteurs rapides* of the 1290-ton *Le Corse* and *Le Breton* classes which, completed between 1955 and 1960, were too early to receive the Malafon anti-submarine system, their anti-submarine weapon consisting either of sextuple launchers for Bofors rocket projectiles or quadruple anti-submarine mortars. Another, more recent class of escort are the *avisos-escorteurs* of the *Commandant Rivière* class, slower (26·5 knots maximum), diesel-driven and of good endurance with an armament of three of the 4-inch automatic anti-aircraft guns, a quadruple anti-submarine mortar and six anti-submarine torpedo tubes. These ships are designed also to take part in local 'peace-keeping' or 'police' operations, being fitted out for extreme climatic conditions, to operate a helicopter and to transport a commando force of seventy men with their equipment.

Finally, the French Navy has also a class of fourteen *escorteurs-cotières* of moderate speed (22 knots maximum), diesel-driven, built to the design of American P.C. boats, armed with light automatic weapons and an anti-submarine mortar.

The Italian Navy has completed two missile-armed 'escort cruisers', the *Andrea Doria* and *Caio Duilio*, of 6000 tons standard displacement. In addition to a twin launcher for Terrier missiles mounted forward, they have eight single turrets for 3-inch, fully automatic guns of a new pattern. Geared turbines of 60,000 horse-power drive them at 31 knots.

One further guided-missile cruiser of 8850 tons, the *Vittorio Veneto*, was completed in April 1969. She has a similar gun armament to the *Doria* class but with ASTER (a combination of ASROC and the Terrier Missile) replacing the Terrier system, and a speed of 32 knots. In addition she has four tubes for launching ballistic missiles of the Polaris type. The pre-war built cruiser *Giuseppe Garibaldi* of 9800 tons, which was converted in 1962 to operate a twin Terrier launcher, is also fitted with four tubes to launch ballistic missiles.

The most recently completed destroyers of the Italian Navy are the four 3200-ton guided-missile ships of the *Impavido* class, which have a Tartar missile system for their main armament. For anti-submarine operations they carry a light helicopter and are equipped with two triple tubes for anti-submarine torpedoes. Geared turbines of 70,000 horse-power give them a top speed of 34 knots. Two smaller ships are the *Indomito* and *Impetuoso* of 2755 tons, completed in 1958. Originally equipped with four 5-inch guns and anti-aircraft rocket launchers, their conversion to guided-missile destroyers with Tartar missiles is projected.

Fast frigates for the Italian Navy built since the war include the four 1680-ton, steam turbine driven ships of the *Centauro* class, completed in 1957 and 1958. These have recently been modernised and are now similarly armed to the improved *Centauro* or *Soldato* class ships *Alpino* and *Carabiniere* which were launched in 1967 and equipped to operate two anti-submarine helicopters as well as six launching tubes for anti-submarine torpedoes. Following the *Centauro* class came four ships of the *Bergamini* class, completed in 1961 and 1962, which had the distinction of being the first of any navy to operate anti-submarine helicopters.

The Italians have also built an interesting type of coastal escort, the diesel-driven *De Cristofaro* class of 840 tons and a speed of 23½ knots which mount two 3-inch fully automatic guns and two triple tubes for anti-submarine torpedoes.

The only other navy, besides that of Russia (which is examined later), to have in commission a cruiser completed since the end of the Second World War, is that of the Netherlands, which in 1953 completed two 9529-ton ships, *De Ruyter* and *De Zeven Provincien*, whose construction had been held up during the war. The *De Ruyter* was later sold to Peru. Her sister ship was converted in 1962–64, and again modernised in 1971–72. She now mounts a twin Terrier missile launcher on her quarter-deck and four six-inch guns in two twin turrets forward.

Sweden has also built, since the war, two types of fast destroyer or frigate. Completed in 1955 and 1956 were the two 2700-ton *Halland* and *Småland* which steam turbines of 55,000 horse-power drive at 35 knots. Their armament includes four automatic 4·7-inch dual-purpose guns, eight torpedo tubes and a twin Bofors anti-submarine rocket-projectile launcher. Two years later came the four 2150-ton *Östergötland* class of similar performance and armament, but with the addition of a twin Seacat surface-to-air launcher on two of the class. The Chilean Navy acquired the ex-Swedish cruiser *Göta Lejon* in 1971.

The West German Navy began its post-war reconstruction with the acquisition of six American destroyers of the *Fletcher* class between 1958 and 1960. Following this, six frigates of German design of the 1750-ton *Köln* class were laid down in the Stülcken yard at Hamburg, being completed between 1961 and 1964. Mounting two French 4-inch automatic guns, Dutch radar systems, a Swedish Bofors anti-submarine rocket launcher and four anti-submarine torpedo tubes, they have four 16-cylinder MAN diesel engines developing 3000 horse-power each and two Brown-Boveri gas turbines each developing 12,000 horse-power. Their maximum speed is 32 knots with 20 knots on diesels alone.

Most recent addition to West Germany's surface fleet are the four *Hamburg* class of 3400-ton destroyers. These have steam turbines and a speed of 35 knots. Like the *Köln* class they have gone abroad to obtain their armament of French 4-inch guns, Dutch radar and Swedish anti-submarine rocket projectiles.

The Royal Australian and Royal Canadian navies until recently acquired their major warships from British yards and to British design. Since the end of the Second World War, however, the former has built in Australian yards six 2000-ton *Yarra* class frigates to the design of the British *Leander* class and has had three American *Charles F. Adams* guided-missile destroyers built in the United States. The Canadian Navy has advanced still further by launching between 1951 and 1963 twenty frigates of Canadian design from Canadian shipyards. These are the 2360-ton *Saint Laurent* class, the design of which altered during the long programme to keep abreast of modern developments. These include the substitution of the new British 3-inch, 70-calibre guns in enclosed turrets. In the two most recent ships, however, the addition of helicopter platforms and hangars and the towed, variable-depth sonar has entailed reduction of the anti-submarine armament to a single Limbo mortar and of the gun armament to a twin 3-inch 50-calibre mount. During 1972–73 the Royal Canadian Navy also took delivery of four destroyers of the 4200-ton *Iroquois* class. These mount two twin launchers for the American Sea Sparrow missile, and operate two Sea King anti-submarine helicopters. They are powered by Pratt and Whitney gas turbines.

An interesting design of frigate is that of the 2200-ton Danish *Peder Skram* and *Herluf Trolle*. Driven by two diesel engines of 4800 horse-power and two gas turbines of 44,000, they have a top speed of over 30 knots and mount four 5-inch dual-purpose guns in twin turrets.

The Japanese began to rebuild their navy in 1954. They now (1973) have one guided-missile destroyer, *Amatsukaze*, and twenty-six 'conventionally' armed destroyers in commission, all of which were designed and built in Japan. The *Amatsukaze*, completed in 1965, mounts a single Tartar launcher, four 3-inch guns in twin mountings, two twin ASROC and mountings for A/S torpedoes. Another guided-missile destroyer was laid down in February 1973.

The largest class of recent destroyers are the eight 2150-ton ships of the *Minegumo* and *Yamagumo* class. These mount four 3-inch guns, ASROC and two triple mountings for A/S torpedoes. Diesel engines of 26,500 horse-power drive them at 27 knots maximum. Four more recent destroyers of the *Takatsuki* class are of 3050 tons displacement. Their primary A/S function is served by a helicopter, an octuple ASROC and two triple mountings for A/S homing torpedoes. Finally an even larger (4700 tons) destroyer, *Haruna*, completed in February 1973, can operate three A/S helicopters, and mounts an ASROC multiple launcher and two triple torpedo mountings.

Turning to examine the Russian Navy, today (1974) the most powerful in the world, we find ourselves studying a meteoric rise in size and quality since 1951, when the first of the *Sverdlov* class of 16,000-ton conventionally armed cruisers, of the large class of 3000-ton *Skoryi* class destroyers and of the *W* class conventionally powered submarines were all launched or laid down.

In the past, with brief periodical exceptions, the Russians, with their vast terri-

torial empire, contented themselves with a navy of a suitable size and composition only to defend the seaward flanks of their land forces and the coasts of Russia herself. Today, in support of her ideologically motivated pursuit of dominance, she has acquired, besides the greatest army, the most powerful navy ever assembled, which she is deploying world-wide in the fashion of maritime imperial powers.

Ships of all the types necessary for balanced task forces have been built. The first Soviet aircraft carrier, now fitting out, is discussed in the chapter on that class of vessel. Prior to the development of the Polaris ballistic missile launched from submarines, the chief sea-borne threat to Russia was the NATO carrier strike force. It was no doubt in response to this that the fourteen large cruisers of the *Sverdlov* class were built. These ships mounted twelve 6-inch guns in triple turrets and ten 21-inch torpedo tubes in two quintuple mountings. Their geared steam turbines developed 130,000 horse-power and gave them a speed of 34 knots. A smaller, 11,500-ton type of cruiser, the *Tchapaev* class, three of which were completed between 1950 and 1951, also mounted twelve 6-inch guns.

The most recent additions to the Soviet cruiser force are three 10,000-ton guided-missile cruisers, the first to be completed being the *Nikolayev* which carries eight launchers for surface-to-surface missiles of the latest supersonic, radar-controlled type in two mountings, and four surface-to-air launchers. She operates one helicopter for which a hangar is provided aft. Her main gun armament is four 3-inch in twin mountings. She is believed to have gas turbine machinery and a speed of some 34 knots. Under NATO nomenclature, these ships are named the *Kara* class.

Previous classes are the *Kresta II* missile cruisers, of 6000 tons standard, of which the first three have been completed. They have the same helicopter and surface-to-surface missile armament as the *Kara* class, but only four surface-to-air launchers. Steam turbine machinery of 100,000 s.h.p. drives them at 33 knots. Slightly smaller and with only four surface-to-surface missiles of an obsolescent type, but otherwise of similar capability, four of the class were launched between 1966 and 1968. Smaller again are the light cruisers completed between 1962 and 1965 of the *Kynda* class, mounting eight surface-to-surface missiles and one twin mount for surface-to-air.

The Soviet Navy's destroyer force of more than 110 ships was begun in 1954, when the first of the conventionally armed *Skoryi* class were completed. A little under 3000 tons standard displacement, they and the mass-produced *Kotlin* class which followed between 1954 and 1957 had a main gun armament of four 5·1-inch in twin mounts and a torpedo armament of ten 21-inch tubes. Later *Kotlin* class vessels were re-designed to mount missile launchers, surface-to-surface in the *Kildin*, surface-to-air in the *Sam Kotlin* class.

During the following years improved designs were completed of which the standard displacement was increased to 3700 tons, and the main armament was either surface-to-surface or surface-to-air missiles. These are given the NATO names of *Krupnyi* and *Kanin* classes. All the above ships were driven by geared steam turbines of some 80,000 s.h.p. In 1962, however, the Soviet Navy completed the first of nineteen ships of the *Kashin* class, the first warships in the world depending solely on gas-turbine propulsion which gives them a speed of 34 knots. With a standard displacement of 4300 tons they mount two twin surface-to-air missile launchers as well as four 3-inch guns and five 21-inch tubes for A/S torpedoes. The most recent Soviet destroyers are the *Krivak* class of 4800 tons, which mount four surface-to-surface missile launchers as well as two surface-to-air. Their gas turbines give them a speed of 38 knots.

The Soviet Navy has also acquired a large force of anti-submarine frigates, the majority of which belong to the 1200-ton *Riga* class built between 1952 and 1959, and the *Mirka* class of 950 tons standard displacement. Besides a gun armament of three 3·9-inch guns in the former, and four 3-inch (AA) in the latter, they mount A/S rocket launchers and A/S torpedoes. The *Riga* class are driven by geared steam turbines giving them a speed of 28 knots. The *Mirka* class have a combination of diesel and gas-turbine propulsion, the latter giving them a speed of 33 knots.

241

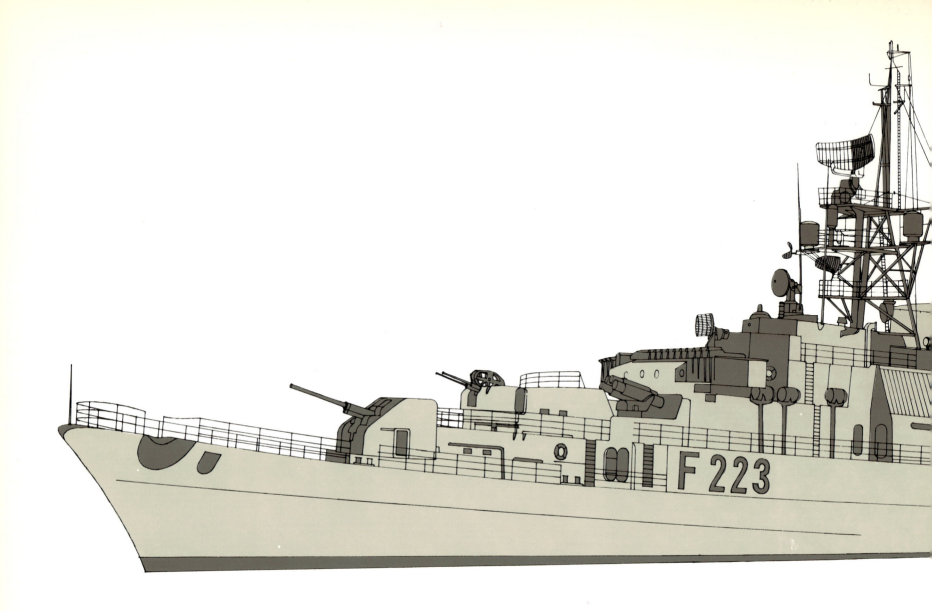

KARLSRUHE

German fast frigate *Karlsruhe* of the *Köln* class (1959),
one of a class of six ships of 2100 tons, mounting two 3·9-inch dual-purpose
guns and automatic weapons, two Bofors 4-barrelled A/S mortars and
two tubes for A/S torpedoes. Combined diesel and gas-turbine
propulsion gives a maximum speed of 30 knots.

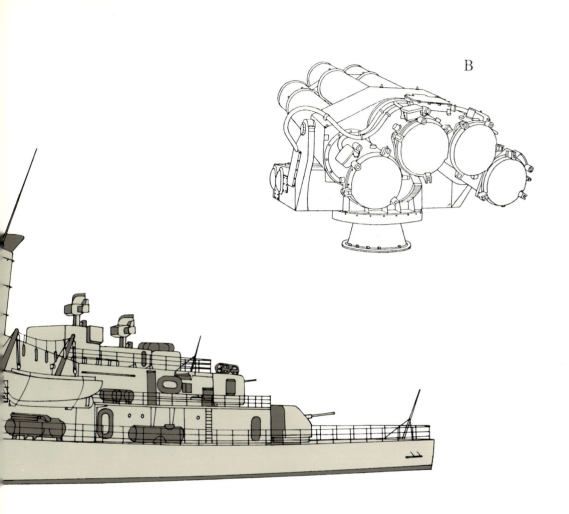

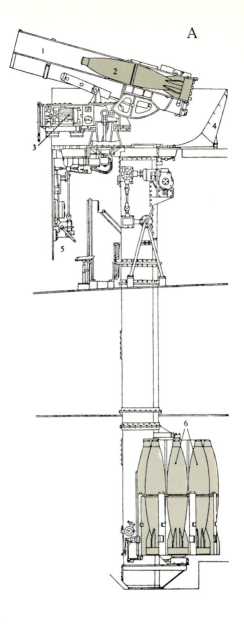

A *Anti-submarine rocket launcher*

1 Barrel
2 A/S rocket
3 Training motor
4 Flash shield
5 Training gear
6 Magazine

B Same as four-tube launcher

Navies of today depend upon a support force of ships as numerous as the actual fighting men-of-war. This includes Underway Replenishment Ships, large freighters and tankers to bring supplies of ammunition, victuals, engineering stores and fuel, and transfer them at sea, thus obviating the fleet's return to harbour during operations. There is no space here for a description of these many types of ships, and it is a moot point whether they are, in any case, 'men-of-war'.

Types that must be given a brief mention, however, are Mine Warfare Ships and Patrol Craft. The former, comprising mainly a large number of minesweeping and mine-hunting craft of less than 800 tons, form an essential element of all navies. To enable them to sweep for magnetically actuated mines without damage to themselves, they are built of non-magnetic materials. Influence mines have become so difficult to sweep, however, that minesweepers are often converted to mine-hunters in which sonar equipment accurately locates the mines, which can then be destroyed at a safe distance.

Patrol Craft originated in the First World War as high-speed Motor Torpedo Boats, and achieved numerous successes in that role in both World Wars. They were often opposed by Motor Gunboats. In recent years their ability to mount ship-to-ship, radio-guided supersonic missiles has made them of greater significance than ever. They are of particular value to small navies, providing a considerable striking power at low cost. They are also very difficult to counter, owing to the small target they offer to detection or to counter weapons. They are one of the major reasons why a fleet needs to have its own force of readily available fighter aircraft for its own defence.

The U.S. Navy has only a small number of such craft in commission, but it is experimenting with several types of hydrofoil missile boats and has projected a 2000-ton hovercraft or Surface Effect Ship (SES).

The Russians, on the other hand, have led the world in construction of missile-firing types, of which the most numerous, 170-ton boats known as the *Osa II* class, have been supplied to satellite powers and other minor navies. One of them, under the Egyptian flag, made history by sinking the Israeli destroyer *Eilat* on 21st October 1967 with a Styx missile, a subsonic solid-fuel rocket with a maximum range of 23 miles and an active radar homing device. Similar units also proved effective in the hands of the Indian Navy during the war with Pakistan at the end of 1971. Another numerous class of missile boats is the 70-ton *Komar*, which also mounts the Styx missile. More recent is the *Nanuchka* class of 800-ton craft which carry two triple launchers for supersonic surface-to-surface missiles, and a launcher for surface-to-air missiles. All the above craft are powered by diesel engines; the *Osa* and *Nanuchka* classes have a speed of 32 knots, the *Komar*'s, 40.

The Russians have used the same hulls as the *Osa* and *Komar* classes as MTB's, mounting torpedo tubes instead of missile launchers. They have also hydrofoil patrol boats of some 70 tons, which are reported to attain 50 knots driven by diesel engines of 6000 b.h.p.

Top: Norwegian corvette *Aeger* of the Sleipner class of 600 tons (1963–67). One of two submarine chasers of this class, armed with the Terne ASW system. Diesel-driven, with a speed of over 20 knots.

Bottom: Russian *Kotlin* class destroyer (1955), one of a class of thirty mass-produced ships mounting four 3·9-inch and ten 21-inch torpedo tubes. Steam-turbine driven with a maximum speed of 36 knots.

Russian cruiser *Sverdlov* (1951) of a class of fourteen similar ships of 15,450 tons, mounting twelve 5·9-inch and twelve 3·9-inch dual-purpose guns and ten 21-inch torpedo tubes.

245

British guided-missile destroyer *Devonshire* (1960), first of eight
County class, 5200 tons, equipped with Seaslug and Seacat A/A
missiles and four 4·5-inch guns. Carries an A/S helicopter.
Combined steam- and gas-turbine propulsion with a speed of
32 knots. Picture shows *Devonshire* firing a Seaslug missile.

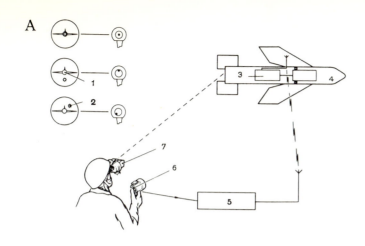

A

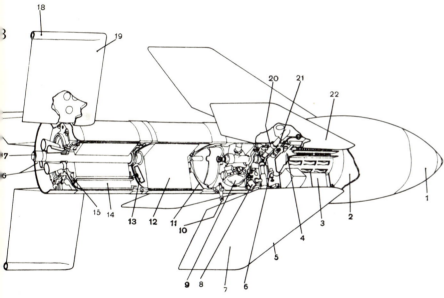

A *Aimer's view   Flight controller*
1 Target
2 Missile
3 Guidance system
4 Control system
5 Command link transmitter
6 Flight controller
7 Binocular sight

B *Seacat missile*
1 Fuse
2 Warhead
3 Electronic pack
4 Thermal battery
5 Contact fuse (in all control surfaces)
6 Control surface position potentiometer

7 Guidance receiver aerial
8 Hydraulic actuator
9 Roll gyroscope
10 Missile support pin
11 Hydraulic accumulator
12 Sustainer charge
13 Sustainer charge igniter
14 Boost charge
15 Boost charge igniter
16 Boost charge nozzles
17 Sustainer charge nozzles
18 Flare tube
19 Fin
20 Control surfaces actuator assembly
21 Control surface stub
22 Cable duct

Seacat ship-to-air missile and mounting being prepared for firing.

Diagrams showing mechanism of the Seacat close-range A/A missile which is in use in several European navies. The missile is visually guided to its target by a controller operating a 'joystick' and is kept in view by means of flares along the tips of the fins.

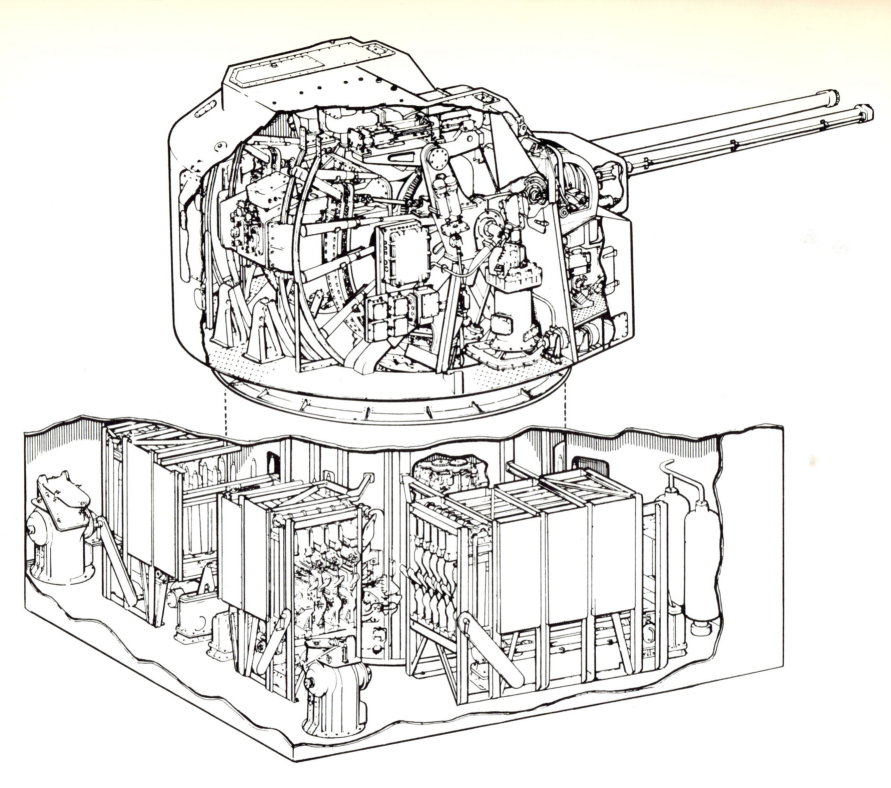

Warships' guns today are often fully automatic, requiring no crew in the gunhouse to load or fire them. Here is a sectional drawing of a Vickers 3-inch high-angle twin mounting showing the gun mechanism in its protective gunhouse and the gunbay situated below it.

The invention and early development of the Whitehead torpedo, its acquisition by all the major navies and their resultant adoption of the various types of 'torpedo-craft' have been considered earlier. By 1914, though the propelling machinery as developed varied from country to country, the torpedo had become a steam- or vapour-driven weapon, usually of 18 or 21 inches diameter and some $17\frac{1}{2}$ or 22 feet in length, capable of speeds up to 44 knots for 3750 yards or 28 knots for a range of 10,000 yards.

In the British torpedo a form of radial reciprocating engine—'the Brotherhood'—was driven by a mixture of gas and air produced by burning oil fuel in compressed air. The U.S. Navy on the other hand developed the Bliss-Leavitt torpedo, named after its inventors, in which steam, generated by forcing a spray of water through an alcohol torch, drove a turbine.

During the twenty years following the end of the First World War, the torpedoes generally in use made little advance on these types, though experiments to improve their performance were made. The British, American and German navies developed a type of actuating mechanism or 'pistol' for the warheads which was operated by the change of magnetic field as the torpedo passed under a ship. In each case, under war conditions, the device proved unreliable and a reversion was made to the earlier form of pistol, operated by impact.

The first major change in the design of the torpedo between the wars was made by the Germans, who developed one electrically propelled for use in their submarines. This had the great advantage of leaving no track to betray its approach. The British meanwhile experimented during the 1930s with a torpedo in which the propellant fuel was liquid oxygen: the system was expected to give greatly increased speed and range, but the danger inherent in the handling of the fuel was eventually considered too great and the experiments were abandoned. They were followed up, however, by the Japanese, who finally produced what was to be the most effective torpedo used during the Second World War—the 24-inch liquid-oxygen-propelled 'Long-Lance', which carried a warhead containing 1000 pounds of high explosive at 36 knots for 22 miles or at 49 knots for 11 miles.

By the beginning of the Second World War nearly all torpedoes in use could be pre-set to change course after firing, making the track independent of the course of the firing surface ship or submarine. The Germans took this principle further by adapting their torpedoes to run on a zig-zag course, to trace a figure of eight or to track to and fro across the target's course. They also devised a torpedo with an acoustic sensor which caused it to steer for the noise of a target ship's propellers.

This was the first of the new generation of torpedoes depending upon electronics for their direction to the target by means of passive or active 'homing' devices or, in co-operation with electronic sensors, by wire guidance, which have largely replaced the earlier types with their pre-set, hit-or-miss, course patterns.

The U.S. Navy's standard anti-shipping torpedo for use by submarines is a

An anti-submarine helicopter equipped with a Mark 46 A/S torpedo (U.S. Navy).

development of the 21-inch weapon in use at the end of the war. Propelled at extremely high speeds by machinery using hydrogen peroxide for its fuel, it carries a 732-pound warhead.

The acoustic-homing torpedo first adopted by the U.S. Navy was a 19-inch weapon electrically propelled for submarine launching and a similar one designed for launching from fixed-wing aircraft against submarine targets.

In the search for a weapon to counter the modern, deep-diving submarine, the Americans next produced a surface-launched 21-inch torpedo, $13\frac{1}{2}$ feet in length, weighing 1800 pounds, which sought its target by an active acoustic device or 'sonar'. The advance of 'miniaturisation' enabled the next torpedo, electrically driven, suitable for surface or submarine launching and possessing passive or active guidance systems, to revert to the 19-inch diameter, only 13 feet in length and weighing only 1430 pounds. Modified as a wire-guided anti-submarine torpedo, it is 16 inches longer and 260 pounds heavier.

A more recent type of anti-submarine torpedo (Astor) for use only by submarines is also an electrically driven 19-inch weapon but has a higher speed, greater range and improved deep-diving capabilities; it can be set to run straight against surface targets or it can be wire-guided to seek out a fast, deep-diving submarine and can be armed with a nuclear warhead.

At the same time as these larger torpedoes were being produced, a light-weight type was also being developed, primarily for launching from helicopters and later to be carried by anti-submarine missiles. Starting with a little, electrically driven 10-inch type, 92 inches in length and weighing only 265 pounds, American engineers went on to produce a somewhat larger, $12\frac{3}{4}$-inch torpedo, also electrically propelled and incorporating an active acoustic guidance system which can be launched from surface ships, from fixed- or rotary-wing aircraft, including the unmanned, radio-controlled helicopter (DASH), or it can be carried to the estimated position of a submerged submarine by an anti-submarine rocket (ASROC) whence it will begin its submarine-seeking run.

A more recent type of light-weight torpedo, of much the same size, though somewhat heavier, employs a solid-propellant, hot-gas generator both for propulsion and to provide electric power for the active guidance system and hydraulic power for steering control mechanism. A variation of this torpedo uses, instead of the solid propellant, a liquid monopropellant called Otto fuel, a monopropellant being a chemical fuel which contains its own oxidiser. This type of fuel and machinery is also likely to be used in future types of large torpedoes.

A SUBROC (anti-submarine rocket delivered homing torpedo) being loaded into the nuclear-powered submarine U.S.S. *Permit*.

By the time the outbreak of the First World War was impending, the submarine had become an ocean-going man-of-war, the largest being the French *submersibles d'escadre* of some 800 tons surface displacement and a surface speed of 19 knots. Except for a few French boats which still relied on steam for surface propulsion, the diesel engine had become the standard.

Nevertheless, few foresaw the revolution in naval warfare that they were to bring about. The French, to be sure, envisaged their large *submersibles d'escadre* accompanying their surface fleet on operations; but it was in the role of solitary, secret assailant that the submarine was first to make its mark, the invisible threat forcing surface ships to follow irregular zig-zag courses, and major units to surround themselves with screens of destroyers. They made harbours unsafe also, forcing the adoption of defensive booms and nets. They then assumed the classic corsair's role in the *guerre-de-course* in which they were nearly decisively successful until their opponents relearnt the lessons of the past and herded their merchant ships in escorted convoys. As a consequence, navies found it necessary to develop a new type of surface warship, the convoy escort, considered on pages 239–71.

Apart from the ordinary attack submarine which altered only in detail during the war, a number of unconventional types were built. The Germans built some large cargo-carrying submarines to run the Allied blockade with strategic raw materials such as rubber, the best known being the *Deutschland* which made two successful voyages to the United States before that country entered the war. The British built the *R* class of small submarine-hunting submarines which, equipped with unusually large electric batteries and a powerful electric motor driving a single screw, had the high underwater speed of 15 knots. The single diesel engine for which space remained, however, gave them only $9\frac{1}{2}$ knots on the surface. At the other end of the scale, the British constructed the *K* class which, driven on the surface by oil-fired boilers and steam turbines, had a speed of 24 knots, the intention being that they should accompany the Grand Fleet. These boats, with their comparatively great length of 337 feet, were liable to get out of control when diving and suffered a number of disastrous accidents. Equally unlucky were the submarine monitors of the *M* class which were armed with a single 12-inch gun in a fixed turret which could be fired with only the gun muzzle protruding above the surface. One of the three of this class was accidentally rammed and sunk in the English Channel; another, which had been converted to carry a seaplane in place of her gun, was lost through some mishap with the watertight doors of the hangar; only the third survived to die a natural death in the breaker's yard. Soon after the war the British also built an experimental submarine cruiser, the *X.1*, which was armed with four 5·25-inch guns in two turrets. With a surface displacement of 3050 tons and a length of 363 feet, she was the biggest submarine to have been built up to that time. Nearly as large was the French *Surcouf* of 2880 tons displacement, armed with two 8-inch guns in a turret and provided with a hangar

The German Molch one-man U-boat, at a factory where this type of U-boat was assembled.

Italian midget submarine CB 12, Second World War.

housing a small seaplane. The American mine-laying submarine *Argonaut*, completed in 1928, was longer than the *X.1* by 17 feet but 170 tons less in surface displacement.

Dwarfing all of them, with a length of 400 feet and a surface displacement of 3530 tons, were the Japanese submarines *1400–402*, which carried three assembled aircraft, components for a fourth and a launching catapult. These were the largest submarines built prior to the advent of the nuclear-powered submarines of today.

Such craft were the exception, however, the majority being much smaller with surface displacements varying between 2000 tons and 500 for ocean-going types and 250 tons for coastal types of limited range. In the first decade following the end of the First World War, navies tended to build large submarines, the size dictated mainly by that of the machinery necessary to give them the desired speed: but with improvements in the design of diesel engines, small submarines suitable for operation in the restricted waters of the Mediterranean and North Seas were preferred by the British, French, Italian and German navies. The U.S. and Japanese navies, requiring submarines of large endurance for operation in the Pacific, continued to build craft of 1500 tons or more

The principal Second World War developments in submarine construction were the introduction of the *schnorkel* breathing tube which permitted a submarine to run its diesel engines for propulsion and battery-charging while remaining submerged; the achievement of high submerged speeds and great submerged endurance; and the construction of miniature submarines for attacks inside enemy harbours.

The *schnorkel* was originally an invention of Commander I. I. Wichers of the Royal Netherlands Navy and was incorporated in Dutch submarines prior to 1939. The Germans adopted it in 1943 during the war and by the end of it had fitted the majority of their submarines. The Germans were also the pioneers in achieving high submerged speed and endurance. By means of streamlining and incorporation of powerful electric motors of 2500 horse-power driven by batteries of exceptionally light construction and large capacity, their Type XXI submarines were given a submerged speed of 16 knots, which could be maintained for one hour, and an endurance of more than three days at 4 knots. These submarines would undoubtedly have presented a formidable problem to the anti-submarine forces of the Allies if they had been perfected earlier, but only a few were in commission by the time the war came to an end.

Even more remarkable was the development by the German Professor Hellmuth Walter of engines utilising hydrogen peroxide for fuel with which it was possible to achieve submerged speeds of the order of 25 knots or more. Five Type XVIIB U-boats, incorporating such an engine, had been launched but not perfected when the war came to an end. Taken over by the British, trials were carried out in which very high submerged speeds were obtained. There were considerable hazards, however, in using so unstable a substance as hydrogen peroxide, and these drawbacks had not been satisfactorily overcome when nuclear power arrived on the scene to supersede it.

The other principal development in the submarine field during the Second World War was that of miniature types, mainly for delivering attacks on ships in harbour. The British, Germans, Italians and Japanese all utilised such craft. The Japanese were the first to do so when several two-man craft transported to the vicinity in mother submarines were launched to penetrate Pearl Harbor simultaneously with the air attack which began the Pacific War. These 'midgets' carried torpedoes with which unsuccessful attacks were made. Towards the end of the war, the Japanese built large numbers of similar craft to make a 'last ditch' defence against the Allied invasion fleet; unlike the earlier midgets, these were intended only for suicide attack missions; surrender came, however, before they could be used.

The British *X* craft of 35 tons carried explosive charges to be laid under their targets; their most notable exploit was when two of them succeeded in September 1943 in seriously damaging the German battleship *Tirpitz* lying in a Norwegian

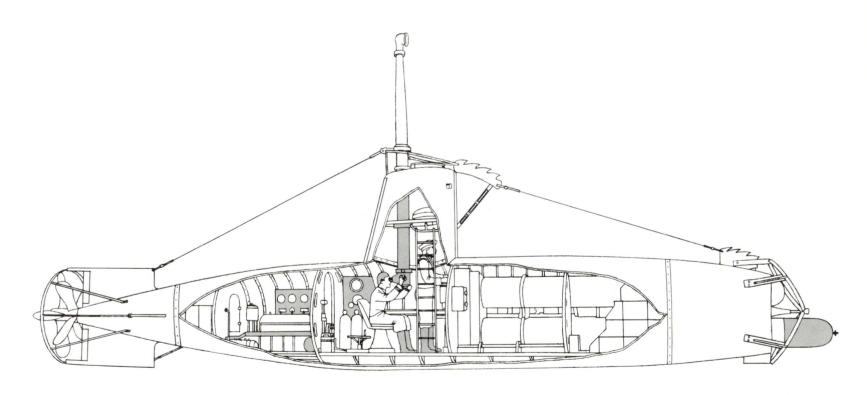

Top: Japanese two-man midget submarine Type A of Second World War. This type of boat was carried by a 'mother' submarine and was used in attacks on Pearl Harbor, Sydney (New South Wales) and Diego Suarez.

Bottom: Japanese midget submarine, Second World War. Sectional view of the submarine, showing interior. The officer in charge sits at the periscope, while the engineer stands by the torpedo release.

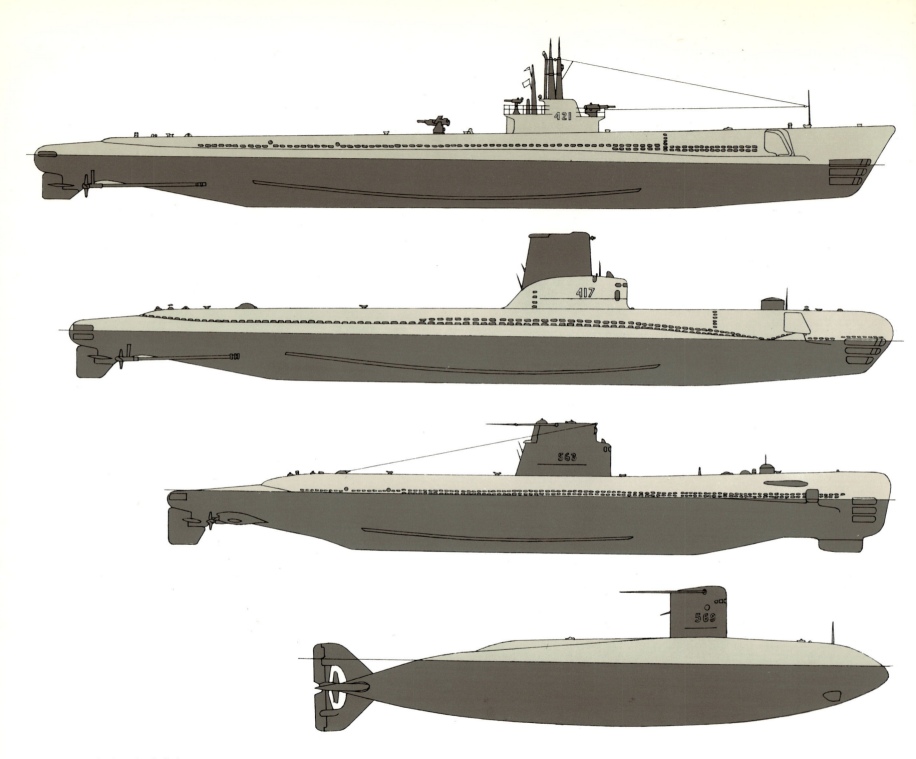

Development of submarine hull shapes:

Second World War U.S. fleet type.
'Guppy', fleet type modified for high underwater speed.
Post-war high-speed type.
'Teardrop' hull for the experimental *Albacore*.

fiord. The Germans did not develop such craft until late in the war when four different types were produced, the one-man *Biber* of 6·3 tons and *Molch* of 10¾ tons, the two-man *Seehund*, a craft of 16 tons displacement, 39 feet in length and carrying two 21-inch torpedoes, and the two-man *Hecht* of 12·2 tons, carrying one torpedo or one mine. These latter craft were sufficiently seaworthy to make offensive cruises in the Channel where they had some minor successes. Other types were in course of production when the war came to an end.

The Italian midget submarine played an insignificant part in the war; but it was the Italian Navy which had the most notable success with the smallest type of underwater craft, the 'human-torpedo' or 'chariot' in English parlance, called 'slow-speed torpedoes' or familiarly 'sows' (*maiale*) by the Italians. Launched from a parent submarine off Alexandria, three of them penetrated the harbour to attach their explosive charges to the hulls of the battleships *Queen Elizabeth* and *Valiant*, both of which were heavily damaged and put out of action. Others were launched off Gibraltar, where they achieved a number of successes against merchant ships. British 'chariots' were also successfully operated against ships in Palermo harbour and Japanese cruisers at Singapore. German human torpedoes, *Neger* and *Marder*, also had some minor successes against the Allied ships engaged in the Normandy landings in 1944.

Submarine development since the end of the Second World War has been largely the monopoly of the United States and Soviet navies. The latter contented themselves at first by copying and developing the German Type XXI. The U.S. Navy broke fresh ground in 1951 when they constructed the experimental submarine *Albacore* which successfully demonstrated the high-speed capabilities of a so-called 'pear-drop'-shaped hull having a length/beam ratio of 7·6 to 1 as compared to 11·5 to 1 of contemporary craft. Driven by a single screw, the *Albacore* achieved very high underwater speeds and great manœuvrability.

Between 1951 and 1954 submarines for specialised duties such as radar-picket and missile-launching submarines were built having conventional diesel-electric drive. At the same time, however, the first two nuclear-powered vessels, *Nautilus* and *Seawolf*, were under construction and when they were commissioned, in 1954 and 1957 respectively, they became the first true submarines, able to operate submerged without any contact with the atmosphere almost indefinitely and with speed and endurance as high or higher submerged than on the surface. After four more nuclear submarines had been completed during 1957–59, ships of conventional design of 2300 tons displacement and 268 feet in length, nuclear propulsion and the *Albacore* hull were finally combined to produce the six *Skipjack* class submarines of 1959–61.

All these ships are classified as 'attack' submarines (as opposed to the ballistic-missile type). Their main weapon is still the torpedo; but today the majority of these are either acoustically 'homed' to their target or they are guided by electronic commands passed to them over a threadlike wire which is paid out by the torpedo as it moves forward.

One type of acoustic homing weapon for use by these submarines against other underwater craft is SUBROC. Fired from a conventional torpedo tube in the general direction of an enemy submarine, it leaves the water and travels through the air propelled by a rocket on a ballistic trajectory. Re-entering the water slowed down by a small parachute, its acoustic homing device then guides it to track down its target. Alternatively, a nuclear device can be fitted to explode just after the missile enters the water. The range of SUBROC is unofficially stated to be from ten to twenty-five miles.

Various specialised types of nuclear-powered submarines were added at about this time, including the huge radar-picket *Triton* of 5850 tons displacement and 447½ feet in length, a guided-missile submarine, *Halibut*, and an anti-submarine hunter-killer, *Tullibee*, as well as several less-specialised 'attack' submarines.

In the meantime the nuclear bomb had been developed and means of delivering it by ballistic missile were sought. Although in the early stages both the missile, powered by a highly volatile liquid fuel, and the nuclear warhead were very large and unwieldy, plans were made to arm surface ships and submarines with them.

Top: U.S. submarine *Grayback* as fitted to operate the Regulus surface-to-surface missile.

Bottom: U.S.S. *Skipjack*, nuclear-powered attack submarine steaming at high speed. Launched in 1958, she was the first of a class of six incorporating the streamlined hull configuration developed from the experimental *Albacore* (see page 254).

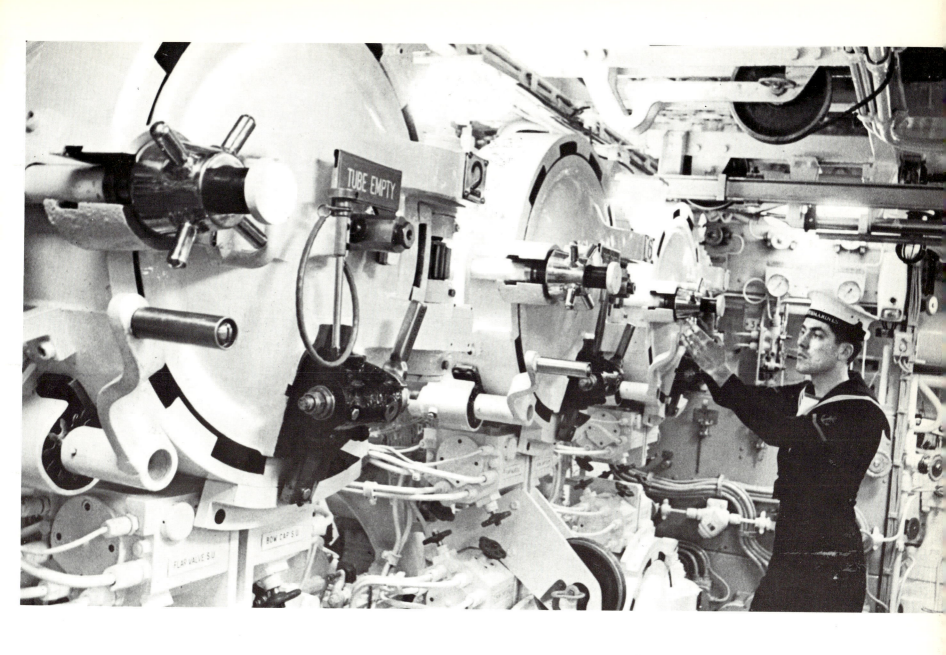

H.M.S. *Dreadnought* (1960), the first British nuclear-propelled submarine, designed specially to hunt and destroy other submarines. Has a speed of about 30 knots and is equipped with six 21-inch torpedo tubes in the bow.

Top: Italian submarine *Enrico Toti* (1967), first post-war Italian submarine. Diesel-electric drive with a speed of 14 knots on surface, 15 knots submerged.

Bottom: *Le Redoutable*, first French nuclear-powered submarine, which became operational in December 1971. Two others have been launched (1973), and two more are projected. The first two are equipped with sixteen M-1 ballistic missiles. The remainder will have the larger M-2 missiles.

The latter would have to displace some 8000 tons to carry and launch the 60-foot Jupiter missile.

Before plans had been perfected, however, on the expectation of much smaller nuclear warheads being devised, the U.S. Navy set out to develop the smaller solid-fuel missile which would be adequate to lift them, and to adapt an existing submarine design to house and launch them. The 'gamble' came off: the Polaris missile, only 28 feet long and weighing 28,000 pounds, was the result.

On the slipway the *Skipjack* class submarine *Scorpion* was cut asunder and additional compartments inserted to house additional control and navigation equipment, extra auxiliary machinery and a battery of sixteen missile tubes arranged in two rows.

The final result was the first ballistic-missile submarine *George Washington*, which successfully fired a Polaris missile for the first time from a submerged position on 20th July 1960. Four further submarines of similar type, five of the larger *Ethan Allen* class and thirty-one of the even larger *Lafayette* class of 7520 tons have been commissioned. In the meantime the original A-1 model Polaris with a range of 1200 nautical miles (1380 statute miles) was first replaced by the A-2 with a 1500-mile range and then by the A-3 with a range of 2500 nautical miles. Many of these submarines are having their Polaris missiles replaced by the Poseidon with a range of some 3000 nautical miles and carrying a 'multiple warhead' enabling it to strike several targets with the one missile.

An entirely new submarine-launched ballistic-missile system, named the 'Trident', is under development. The first nuclear-powered submarine for it is to be commenced during 1974 and is expected to be operational in 1979.

Progress with Soviet submarines started a few years behind that of the U.S. Navy, but, following a similar path in most respects, it has now (1974) surpassed it. There are forty-five nuclear-powered ballistic-missile submarines in service as compared to forty-one in the U.S. Navy. The Soviet Navy has only twenty-six nuclear-powered 'attack' submarines as compared with eighty-four American; but it has a huge preponderance in diesel-electric patrol submarines—233 as compared to thirty-two. It also has forty-two nuclear-powered submarines carrying anti-ship (or 'cruise') missiles. The majority of these mount medium-range (300 nautical miles maximum) missiles which require the co-operation of aircraft for guidance to the target. The latest class, which has been completed at a rate of three every year since 1968, carries short-range (30 nautical miles) missiles, which can be launched from under water. These submarines must be able to guide their missiles to their target without outside aid or information. No other navy has any submarines of this type, which must bid fair to revolutionise naval warfare. The U.S. Navy has realised the critical shortcoming in its lack of them, and has begun design of a prototype.

Both the British and French navies similarly advanced from the streamlined, fast, diesel-electric drive attack or patrol submarines to nuclear-powered hunter-killer anti-submarine submarines or nuclear-powered ballistic-missile submarines. By accepting American nuclear reactors and propulsion machinery, the British were able to commission their first nuclear attack submarine, H.M.S. *Dreadnought*, in April 1963 and laid down their first Polaris type the following year. They now (1974) have seven 'attack' and four ballistic-missile submarines in commission. Three further 'attack' submarines are under construction. The French, relying upon their own resources, first built an experimental diesel-electric ballistic-missile submarine, the *Gymnote*, completed in 1966, and in March 1964 laid down their first nuclear-powered type, *Le Redoutable*, to be followed by four sisters and, later, a prototype nuclear-powered 'attack' submarine to be named *Rubis*.

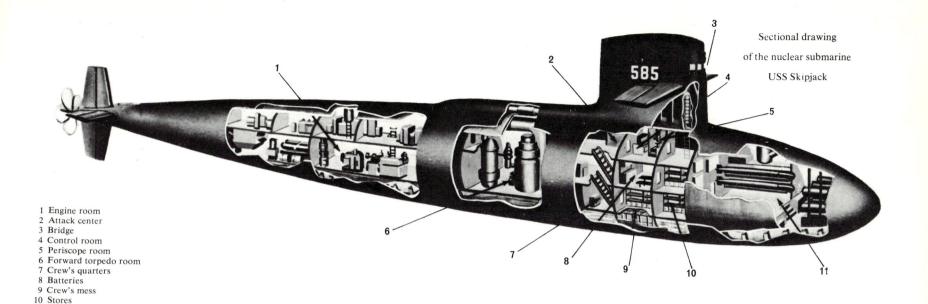

Sectional drawing
of the nuclear submarine
USS Skipjack

1 Engine room
2 Attack center
3 Bridge
4 Control room
5 Periscope room
6 Forward torpedo room
7 Crew's quarters
8 Batteries
9 Crew's mess
10 Stores
11 Reactor room

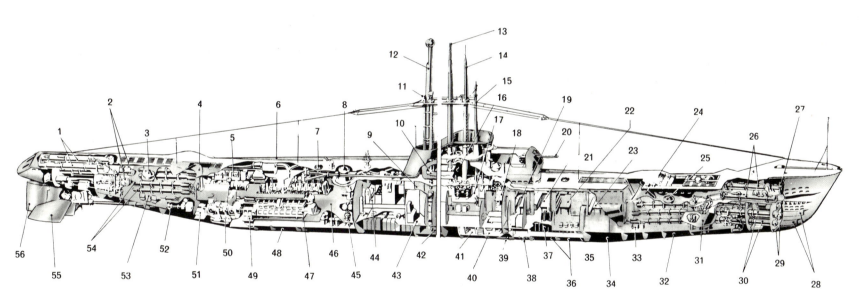

1 External torpedo tubes	29 Bow caps	15 Radar mast	43 Radar office
2 Internal torpedo tubes	30 Internal torpedo tubes	16 Conning tower	44 Galley
3 Escape hatch	31 Hydroplane	17 Control room	45 Ballast pump
4 Torpedo loading hatch	32 For' diving trim tanks	18 Wardroom	46 Engine-room
5 Switchboard	33 Escape sets	19 E.R.A.s' mess	47 Main engine
6 Ballast tanks	34 Fuel oil	20 4-inch gun	48 Lubricating oil
7 Indicator buoy	35 Escape sets	21 C. and P.O.s' mess	49 Engine clutch
8 Escape hatch	36 Fuel oil	22 Engineering mechanics' mess	50 Main motor
9 Wireless office	37 No. 1 battery	23 Seamen's mess	51 Tail clutch
10 Captain's cabin	38 H.P. air bottles	24 Torpedo loading hatch	52 Stern gland
11 Snort exhaust	39 Log	25 Escape hatch	53 Escape sets
12 Snort mast	40 Auxiliary machinery space	26 External torpedo tubes	54 Reload torpedoes
13 Search periscope	41 Magazine	27 Bow buoyancy tanks	55 Hydroplane
14 Attack periscope	42 Sperry compass	28 Bow shutters	56 Rudder

Sectional drawing
of the interior arrangement of a typical
conventionally powered
submarine.

U.S.S. *Lafayette*, name ship of a class of thirty-one nuclear-powered ballistic-missile submarines launched between 1962 and 1965 with sixteen tubes for Poseidon missiles.

Right: A Polaris ballistic missile being fired from a U.S. submarine.

U.S.S. *California*, one of two nuclear-powered guided-missile frigates commissioned in the United States Navy during 1974. They mount two Tartar surface-to-air launchers for which some eighty missiles are carried. Anti-submarine weapons comprise Mk. 45 torpedoes and an ASROC eight-tube launcher. Subsequent ships of this category, the *Virginia* class, will mount combination Tartar/ASROC launchers.

THE PRESENT AND THE FUTURE

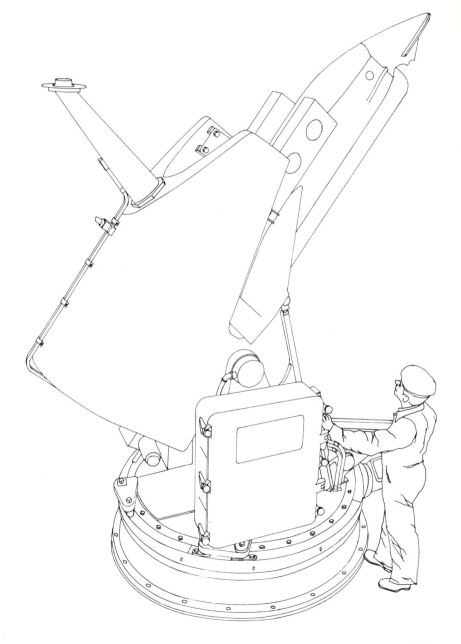

IKARA, an Australian-developed long-range anti-submarine system comprising a dual-thrust, solid propellant rocket missile carrying an American type 44 acoustic homing torpedo which is directed to the vicinity of a submerged target by information from a sonar fed through an Action Data Automation (ADA) system.

The distribution of maritime strength between the major powers of the world today (1974) clearly emphasises the assumption of a position of rivalry for dominance between the two super-powers, the U.S.S.R. and the U.S.A.

The latter rose during the Second World War to be a naval power of seemingly unchallengeable supremacy, displacing, at last, the British Royal Navy. At the conclusion of the war, maritime superiority remained essential for the United States to enable her to support her individually weak allies and to pose a sea-borne deterrent threat to the vastly superior and unmatchable land power of the Soviet Union. When the hitherto negligible Soviet Navy began a programme of naval construction in 1951, it seemed at first to represent a resurgence of the traditional Russian strategy of provision of a navy primarily defensive against the NATO threat, comprising as it did a surface fleet centred on heavy cruisers and a rapidly expanding submarine force.

As time passed, however, it became clear not only that the Russian submarine strength was being increased to a size far beyond any purely defensive requirements, but also that a powerful balanced fleet was being accumulated. Year by year the Soviet Navy increased in size and quality until, by 1973, it was numerically superior in cruisers, escort vessels (destroyers/frigates/corvettes), guided-missile-firing submarines, diesel-electric patrol submarines, missile-firing fast patrol boats, minesweepers and depot/repair/maintenance vessels. Only in aircraft carriers, 'fleet' or 'attack' submarines, landing ships and craft, supply ships and large replenishment tankers is the U.S. Navy now superior.

The disparity in carrier strength is symptomatic of the different attitude to sea power of the inherently maritime nations of the west, and, in the past, that of the primarily land nation, Russia. While the major land powers of Europe—firstly Spain, then France and finally Germany—strove in turn to impose their rule on the Continent, their defeat at sea by smaller powers such as the Netherlands and Britain played a crucial part in frustrating their ambitions. Russia's contribution was mainly terrestrial.

Thus when a ship-borne air element was added to the equipment of sea power during the First World War, it was the British Royal Navy that developed the aircraft carrier and acquired a number of such ships before any other navy. The other primarily maritime great power, Japan, quickly followed suit and soon outstripped Britain between the wars, as did the United States. During the war that followed, while Russian energies had to be concentrated on land-based opposition to the invasion of her territory by German armies, the struggle between Japan

Soviet guided-missile destroyer of the *Krivak* class (NATO code-name). Ships of this class first appeared in 1971. They displace 4800 tons standard and mount four surface-to-surface and two surface-to-air missile launchers and eight 21-inch torpedo tubes in two quadruple mounts. Anti-submarine rockets are launched from two 12-barrelled mountings forward. Eight sets of gas turbines driving two propeller shafts give these ships a top speed of 38 knots.

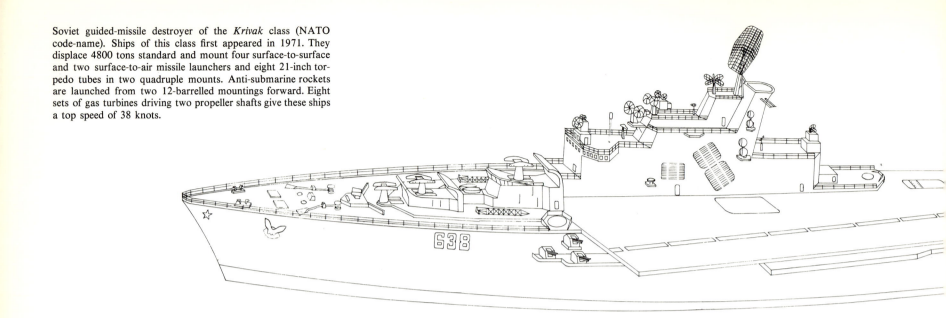

and the western allies in the Pacific, led by the United States, was largely dominated by the ship-borne air power of both sides. The outcome left the allies possessors of unchallengeable sea power and huge fleets of all types of warships.

The most expensive of these and requiring the greatest expertise and experience to build and operate was the carrier: so that, when the western world split into two opposing, ideologically influenced power blocs, the Soviet bloc evidently shrank from the attempt to achieve parity in ship-borne air strength. Having seen the maritime alliance suffer nearly fatal wounds from the attack by German U-boats during the war, they concentrated on building the greatest submarine fleet the world had ever seen. And when the guided missile became a practical proposition, it was upon them, rather than tactical, ship-borne aircraft, that the Russians relied for long-range defence of their fleet against air or surface attack.

Today, therefore, we see the navies of the western alliance composed of warships whose armament depends for real effectiveness upon the backing of ship-borne tactical aircraft which, except in the case of the U.S. Navy, no longer exist. This gap in armament is in the process of being filled up by the addition of surface-to-surface missiles and an ever-increasing number of surface-to-air missiles; but for the time being there is a marked imbalance, with the Russian fleet far better equipped than any other. Meanwhile a new development has made

its appearance—the V/STOL fixed-wing aircraft—which may once again transform the whole scene.

Dominating the present situation is the vast accretion to the two major navies of their huge numbers of submarines, the majority nuclear-powered and equipped with either ballistic or cruise missiles. Upon the former rests the main hope of a deterrent balance of power to prevent the destruction of the civilised world in an atomic war; the latter, difficult as they are to detect or to counter, bid fair to revolutionise the nature of naval warfare.

Another notable feature of the present day is the great increase in defensive naval power conferred upon even the most minor powers by the possession of surface-to-surface missiles so compact that they can be mounted in small, cheap vessels such as fast patrol boats, yet possessing the hitting power of and far greater accuracy than the 16-inch batteries of battleships of a previous generation. With the at least temporary eclipse in most navies of ship-borne tactical aircraft (the most effective antidote to such a threat), this has given these minor powers a defensive naval capability greater than any ever before possible.

Thus future developments in the design of the man-of-war must seemingly centre on two features—surface-to-surface guided missiles and the V/STOL fixed-wing tactical aircraft.

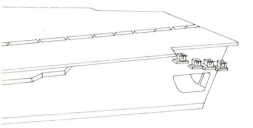

The V/STOL Hawker 'Harrier' aircraft hovering over the helicopter deck of the British cruiser *Blake*. This is the first effective fixed-wing aircraft of its type with a payload and speed sufficient to provide ship-borne tactical air support to a fleet. It can alight on any ship's helicopter pad, but would require the facilities of some simple form of aircraft carrier, such as the projected *Invincible*, for its maintenance and operation.

U.S.S. *Garcia*, an escort vessel of a building programme which added sixty-two ships of basically similar design to the U.S. Navy between 1962 and 1967. Ships of this class mount one or two 5-inch dual-purpose guns, ASROC launchers and either a Sea Sparrow or Tartar missile-launching anti-aircraft system. Though they vary between 2620 and 3011 tons standard displacement, they are classified as escort vessels on account of their single propeller shaft and limited (27 knots) speed.

ASROC, the standard American ship-borne, anti-submarine weapon. It is a ballistic, solid-propellant rocket directed by a control computer in accordance with information received from sonar and carrying either an acoustic homing torpedo or a nuclear depth-charge. It is mounted in the majority of United States cruisers, destroyers and escort vessels, the launcher being sometimes a combined Tartar/ASROC launcher.

Soviet guided-missile cruiser of the *Kresta II* class (NATO code-name). One of a number of ships of this class, five of which were commissioned between 1970 and 1973. Displacing some 6000 tons, they are powered by a conventional steam-turbine system and have a maximum speed of 34 knots. They are armed with two quadruple surface-to-surface missile launchers and two twin surface-to-air; their anti-submarine weapons are rockets fired from two twelve-barrelled launchers forward and two six-barrelled aft. A helicopter is operated from a pad in the stern, and there is a hangar forward of it.

Soviet cruise-missile, nuclear-powered submarine. This type of submarine, of which the Russians have forty-five nuclear-powered and twenty-two diesel-electric driven, are perhaps the most significant item in the development of warships since 1958, posing, as they do, an almost unanswerable threat to a surface fleet. This is particularly true of the most recent types whose missiles can be launched from beneath the surface of the sea and require no external guidance.

Soviet guided-missile cruiser *Nikolayev*, which was laid down in 1969 and entered service during 1973. Displacing some 10,000 tons and powered by gas turbines, she has a speed of more than 30 knots. She mounts eight surface-to-surface and four surface-to-air missile launchers, as well as launchers for anti-submarine rockets and two quadruple 21-inch torpedo mountings. A helicopter is operated from a pad right aft with a hangar just forward of it.

267

Marine gas turbines widely used for ship propulsion by the British Royal and other Navies. The Olympus provides between 22,000 and 27,000 shaft horse-power to give high-speed propulsion; the Tyne some 4000 to 5000 s.h.p. for economical cruising. Over a steam-turbine system the gas turbine has the advantages of instant readiness at all times, of requiring less space and manpower, and of being lighter.

Soviet Helicopter Carrier *Moskva*, one of two of this type of ship which joined the Russian fleet in 1967. They operate eighteen helicopters and are themselves well equipped for anti-submarine operations. When a Russian fixed-wing V/STOL aircraft of sufficient capability becomes available, it may also be embarked.

Artist's impression of H.M.S. *Invincible*, the projected British 'through-deck' or 'general purpose' cruiser now under construction (1974). It will combine the functions of a Fleet Command and Control Ship, a carrier of large anti-submarine helicopters such as the Sea King and probably of fixed-wing V/STOL tactical aircraft such as the Hawker 'Harrier'. Her Sea Dart missile system will give her an area air-defence capability.

H.M.S. *Hermes*, laid down in 1944 as a light carrier, but not completed until 1959 when she emerged as a small strike carrier equipped to operate the most advanced aircraft types. She is seen here in her later role as a helicopter carrier to which she was converted between 1971 and 1974.

BIBLIOGRAPHY

ABELL, SIR WESTCOTT
    The Shipwright's Trade. Cambridge 1948
ALBION, R. G.
    Forests and Sea Power. The Timber Problem of the Royal Navy, 1652–1862. Hamden 1965
ALBOLDT, E.
    Die Tragödie der alten deutschen Marine. Berlin 1928
ANDERSON, R. C.
    Rigging of Ships 1600–1720. London 1927
    Catalogue of Ship-Models. Scale Models. London 1952
    Oared Fighting Ships. London 1962

BAKER, W. A.
    The Development of Wooden Ship Construction. Quincy, Massachusetts 1955
BANGH, D. A.
    British Naval Administration in the Age of Walpole. Princeton 1965
BARFOD, HALFDAN
    Vor Flaade i Fortid og Nutid. København 1941
BARFOD, JØRGEN H.
    Orlogsflåden på Niels Juels Tid. 1648–1699. København 1963
BATTINE, R.
    Method of Building and Rigging Ships of War. London 1684
BAXTER, JAMES PHINNEY
    The Introduction of the Ironclad Warship. University of Harvard
BLANCKLEY, T. R.
    The Naval Expositer. London 1750
BRAGADIN, M.
    Che ha fatto la Marina? Milano 1955
BRIN, B.
    La nostra Marina Militare. Roma 1881
BRØGGER, A. W. & SHETELIG, H.
    The Viking Ships. Oslo 1951
BROWNE, DOUGLAS G.
    The Floating Bulwark. The Story of the Fighting Ship 1514–1942. London 1963
BUGLER, ARTHUR
    H.M.S. Victory. London 1966

CASSON, L.
    The Ancient Mariners. London 1959
    Scheepvaart in de oudheid. Utrecht 1964
CHAPELLE, HOWARD I.
    The Baltimore Clipper, Its Origin and Development. Salem, Massachusetts 1930
    The History of the American Sailing Ships. New York 1935
    The History of the American Sailing Navy. New York 1949
    The Search for Speed under Sail, 1700–1855. New York 1967
CHAPMAN, F. H. af
    Architectura Navalis Mercatoria. Stockholm 1768
CHARNOCK, J.
    History of Marine Architecture. London 1800–02
CHASSELOUP-LAUBAT, M. de
    Les Marines de guerre modernes. Paris 1903
CIPOLLA, C. M.
    Guns and Sails in the Early Phase of European Expansion, 1400–1700. London 1965

CLERC RAMPAL, GEORGE
    La Marine française pendant la grande guerre 1914–1918. Paris 1919
CLOWES, G. S. L.
    Sailing Ships. London 1932
CLOWES & LAIRD, W.
    The Royal Navy, A History. London 1897–1903
COOPER, JAMES FENIMORE
    The History of the Navy. Philadelphia 1847
COWBURN, PHILIP
    The Warship in History. London 1966

Danmarks Søfart og Søhandel
(Red. Bering Liisberg)
DEANE, A.
    Doctrine of Naval Architecture. London 1670
DEGENKOLV, H.
    Oplysninger vedrørende Den Danske Flaade i sidste Aarhundrede. København 1906
DERRICK, C.
    Memoirs of the Royal Navy. London 1806
DI GIAMBERARDINO, OSCAR
    L'arte della guerra sul mare. Roma 1938
DOLBY, JAMES
    The Steel Navy—A History in Silhouette—1860–1963. London 1965

EIDEM, O. & LÜTKEN, O.
    Vor Sømagts Historie. København 1905
ELIAS, J. E.
    Schetsen uit de geschiedenis van ons Zeewezen. 's-Gravenhage 1916–30
ESPAGNAC du RAVAY
    Vingt ans de Politique navale 1919–1939. Paris-Grenoble 1942
EVERS, F. J. H.
    Oorlogsschepen. Amsterdam 1902
EVERS, HEINRICH
    Kriegsschiffbau. Berlin 1943

FAHEY, JAMES C.
    The Ships and Aircraft of the U.S. Fleet. New York, etc., 1939–65
FALCONER, W.
    Universal Dictionary of the Marine. London 1769 & 1815
FERNÁNDEZ-DURO, CESÁREO
    Armada Española. Madrid 1903
FINCHAM, J.
    History of Naval Architecture. London 1851
FIORAVANZO, GIUSEPPE
    La Marina Militare nel suo primo secolo di vita. Roma 1961
Flåden gennem 450 År (Red. R. Steen Steensen, G. Honnens de Lichtenberg & M. Friis Møller). *København 1961*
Flåden, administration, teknik og civile opgaver (Red. K. G. Konradsen, G. Honnens de Lichtenberg & M. Friis Møller). *København 1962*
FURTTENBACH, J.
    Architectura Navalis. Ulm 1629

GARDE, H. G.
    Efterretninger om den danske og norske Søemagt. I–IV. København 1832–35
GAROFALO, F.
    Nozioni di Storia Navale. Bologna 1934
GELDER, M. J. de
    Elementair overzicht van bouw der hedendaagsche oorlogsschepen. Amsterdam 1897
GIORGERINI, G. & NANI, A.
    Le Marine Militari nel Mondo. Milano 1960
    Le Navi di Linea Italiane. Roma 1961
    Gli Incrociatori Italiani. Roma 1964
GÓMEZ NÚÑES, SEVERO
    La Guerra Hispano-Americana. Madrid 1899
GRÖNER, ERICH
    Die deutschen Kriegschiffe 1815–1945. München 1966–67

HEDDERWICK, P.
    Treatise on Marine Architecture. Edinburgh 1830
HOLMES, G. C. V.
    Ancient and Modern Ships. London 1910
HUTCHINSON, W.
    Treatise of Naval Architecture. Liverpool 1794

IRIONDO, EDUARDO
    Impresiones del viaje de circunnavegación de la fragata blindada 'Numancia'. Madrid 1927

JAMES, W.
    Naval History of Great Britain. London 1860
JONGE, J. C. de
    Geschiedenis van het Nederlandsche Zeewezen. Harlem 1858–62
JOUAN, RENÉ
    Histoire de la Marine Française (2 volumes). Paris 1932

KJØLSEN, F. H.
    Da Danmarks Flaade blev saenket. København 1945
    Fregatten fortaeller. København 1962
KLEM, KNUD
    De Danskes Vej. København 1941
KNOX, DUDLEY W.
    A History of the United States Navy (revised). New York 1948
KREBS, H.
    Verdenskrigens Søkrigshistorie, I–III. København 1927–42
KVARNING, LARS-AKE
    Wasa. Stockholm 1968

LACOUR GAYET, G.
    La Marine militaire de la France pendant le règne de Louis XV. Paris 1905

La Marine militaire de la France pendant le règne de Louis XVI. Paris 1909

LANDSTRÖM, B.
The Ship. Stockholm & London 1961

LANE, F. C.
Venetian Ships and Shipbuilding of the Renaissance. Baltimore 1934

LA ROÉRIE, G. & VIVIELLE, J.
Navires et Marins (de la rame à l'hélice). Paris 1930

LARSEN, KAY
Vore Orlogsskibe fra Halvfemserne til nu. København 1932

LAUBEUF, MAXIME & STROH, HENRI
Sous-marins. Paris 1923

LAUGHTON, L. G. C.
Old Ship Figureheads and Sterns. London & New York 1925

LE FLEMING, H. M.
Warships of World War I. London 1961

LE MASSON, HENRI
Histoire du torpilleur en France 1872–1940. Paris 1967
La Marine de guerre moderne (porte-avions, sous-marins, escorteurs). Paris 1950

LENTON, H. T. & COLLEDGE, J. J.
Warships of World War II. London 1964

LEVER, D.
Young Sea Officer's Sheet Anchor. London 1808

LEWIS, MICHAEL
The Navy of Britain. London 1948
The Spanish Armada. London 1960
Armada Guns. London 1961

LOIR, MAURICE
La Marine française. Paris 1893

LUBBOCK, B.
Barbow's Journal 1659–1703. London 1934

LUND, KAJ
Damp kl 5 (Søvaernets Maskinvaesen 1834–1959). København 1959

LÜTKEN, O.
Søkrigsbegivenhederne i 1864. København 1896

MACBRIDE, ROBERT
Civil War Ironclads. Philadelphia 1962

MAHAN, A. T.
The Influence of Sea Power upon History, 1660–1783. New York 1962

MANNING, T. D. & WALKER, C. F.
British Warship Names. London 1959

MARLIANI, MANUEL
El combate de Trafalgar. Madrid 1850

MARSTRAND, V.
Arsenalet i Piraeus. København 1922

MOLLI, G.
La Marina Antica e Moderna. Genève 1906

MOORE, A. H.
Sailing Ships of War, 1800–1860. London & New York 1926

MORDAL, JACQUES
25 Siècles de guerre sur mer. Paris 1959

MUNCHING, L. L. von
Oorlogsschepen van vandaag. Amsterdam 1949
Moderne Oorlogsschepen. Alkmaar 1962
Vliegkampschepen. Alkmaar 1964

NICOLAS, L., REUSSNER, A. & de BELOT, R.
La puissance navale dans l'histoire (3 volumes). Paris 1958, 1960, 1963

NØRREGAARD, G.
Fregatten Falster ved Marokko 1753. København 1956

OPPENHEIM, M.
Administration of the Royal Navy, 1509–1660. London 1896

PÁRIS, EDMOND
Souvenirs de Marine (6 volumes). Paris 1882–1908

PATRONE, G.
Antichi Modelli Navali Italiani. Roma 1961

PERAL, ANTONIO ISAAC
El profundo Isaac. Madrid 1934

PESCE, G.-L.
La Navigation sous-marine. Paris 1912

PÒ, G.
La Guerra sui Mari. Bologna 1940

POLMAR, NORMAN
Atomic Submarines. Princeton 1963

POTTER, EDWARD B. (Ed.)
The United States and World Sea Power. Eaglewood Cliffs, New York 1955

RÁLAMB, Á. C.
Skeps Sbyggerij eller Adelig Öfning X. Stockholm 1691

RANDACCIO, CARLO
Storia Navale Antica e Moderna. Roma 1891

REINHARD, KAY
Kortfattet Haandbog i Søkrigshistorie. København 1906

RITTMEYER, R.
Seekriege und Seekriegswesen in ihrer weltgeschichtlichen Entwicklung. Berlin 1907–11

ROBINSON, S. S. & ROBINSON, MARY L.
A History of Naval Tactics from 1530 to 1930. The Evolution of Tactical Maxims. Annapolis, Maryland 1942

RONCIÈRE, CHARLES de la
Histoire de la Marine française. Paris 1898–1932

RONCIÈRE, CHARLES de la & CLERC RAMPAL, GEORGE
Histoire de la Marine française. Paris 1935

ROSELL, CAYETANO
Combate Naval de Lepanto. Madrid 1853

ROSSELL, H. E.
Types of Naval Ships. London 1945

SALAUN, H.
La Marine française 1871–1932. Paris 1934

SCHAFFALITZKY de MUCKADELL, C.
Haandbog i Nordens Søkrigshistorie. København 1911

SCHOERNER, G.
Regalskeppet. Stockholm 1964

SCHULTZ, J. H.
Den danske Marine 1814–1848. I–IV. København 1930–50
Skibbygning og Maskinvaesen ved Orlogsvaerftet gennem 250 Aar. København 1942

SLOAN, EDWARD W.
Benjamin Franklin Isherwood, Naval Engineer. Annapolis, Maryland 1965

STALKARTT, M.
Naval Architecture. London 1781

STEEL, D.
Elements and Practice of Rigging and Seamanship. London 1794
Naval Architecture. London 1804

STEEN STEENSEN, R.
Alverdens Krigsskibe. København 1942 and 1953
Hangarskibe. København 1944
Søkrigsvåben. København 1946
Flaadens Skibe 1950. København 1950
Vore Torpedobaade gennem 75 år. København 1953

Vore Undervandsbåde gennem 50 år. København 1960
Orlogsmuseet. København 1961
Fregatten Jylland. København 1965
Vore Panserskibe. 1863–1943. København 1968

STENZEL, A.
Seekriegsgeschichte in ihren wichtigsten Abschnitten mit Berücksichtigung der Seetaktik. Hannover/Leipzig 1907–11

STEVENS, J. R.
Old Time Ships. Toronto 1949

SUTHERLAND, W.
Shipbuilding Unveiled. London 1717
Svenska Flottans Historia (publ. by A.-B. Allhems Förlag). Malmö 1942–45

SWANN, LEONARD A.
John Roach, Maritime Entrepreneur. Annapolis, Maryland 1965

THOMAZI, A.
Napoléon et ses Marins. Paris 1950

VECCHI, A. V.
Storia Generale della Marina Militare. Livorno 1895

VREUGDENHIL, A.
Koningen, Scheepsbouwers en Zeevaarders. Amsterdam 1951

WANDEL, C. F.
Søkrigen i de dansk-norske Farvande 1807–1814. København 1915

WATTS, ANTHONY J.
Japanese Warships of World War II. London 1966

ZACHARIAE, G. H.
Orlogsvaerftets Historie (før og Nu 1924). København 1924

ÅKERLUND, H.
Nydamskeppen. Göteborg 1963

DICTIONARIES, PERIODICALS, REFERENCE WORKS

Almanacco Navale (Ed. Giorgerini, G. & Nani, A.). Roma 1962–67
The American Neptune. Salem, Massachusetts 1941 onwards
Dictionary of American Naval Fighting Ships. I–II. Washington 1959 & 1963
Les Flottes de Combat. Paris 1897 onwards
Jane's Fighting Ships. London 1897 onwards
Journal de la Marine, le Yacht. Paris 1878 onwards
La Marina Italiana nella Seconda Guerra Mondiale. Roma 1947–67
Marine-Archiv: Der Krieg zur See. Berlin/Frankfurt 1922–66
Marine Rundschau. Zeitschrift für Seewesen. Frankfurt/Main 1955–1967
The Mariners Mirror. Cambridge 1911 onwards
Nauticus—Jahrbuch für Deutschland Seeinteressen. Berlin 1899–1914
Neptunia. Paris 1947 onwards
Publications, Navy Records Society. London 1894 onwards
La Revue Maritime (Revue Maritime et Coloniale 1861–1896). Paris 1861–1914, 1920 onwards
Svensk Marinkalender. Stockholm 1931 onwards
Taschenbuch der Kriegsflotten (B. Weyer)—Weyers Flottentaschenbuch. München 1899–1967
Tidsskrift for Søvaesen. København

GENERAL INDEX

Figures in italics refer to illustrations

PICTURE ACKNOWLEDGEMENTS

We wish to thank the following persons, museums and institutions for their kindness in placing picture material (on pages indicated) at our disposal.

Aquilera, Alfredo, Valencia 126
Associazione Marinara 'Aldebaran', Trieste 173, 258
Bayeux, City of, France 22
Bokgillet, Uppsala, Sweden. Reprinted from Olaus Magnus, *Carta Marina*, 1539, facsimile and translation 1964 26–27
British Museum, The Trustees of, London 10, 15, 16, 17
Bundesministerium der Verteidigung, Bonn 240
Canadian Armed Forces 234
Delius, Klasing & Co., Bielefeld and Berlin. Reprinted from *Der Brandtaucher. Ein Tauchboot—von der Idee zur Wirklichkeit* by Hans-George Bethge 164
Deutsches Archäologisches Institut, Rome 18–19
Die deutsche Marine vom dritten Jahrhundert bis zum Dritten Reich by Alexander Kircher. Reprint 152–53
Elias, Vicente, Bilbao 94
Établissement Cinématographiques des Armées, Ivry-sur-Seine 258
Foto-Drüppel, Wilhelmshaven, West Germany 139, 176, 192, 203
Fraccaroli, Aldo, Pura, Switzerland 100, 197
Frans Halsmuseum, Haarlem 52
Fukui, Shizuo, Yokohama 127, 190, 206, 253
Giorgerini, Giorgio, Genoa 196, 252
  Redrawn from G. Giorgerini and A. Nani
      Le Navi di Linea Italiane 101, 118, 138, 163, 183, 196
      Gli Incrociatori Italiani 148–49
Goodyear Aerospace Corporation, U.S.A. 250
Green, William, Chislehurst, Kent, England 211
Hawker Siddeley Aviation Ltd. 265
Heeresgeschichtliches Museum, Vienna 2, 106–07, 134–35
Her Britannic Majesty's Stationery Office, by permission of the Controller. British Crown Copyright 218, 246, 247, 269
  Reprinted from *Naval Engineering Practice*, Volumes I and II 224–27, 237, 259

Hodder and Stoughton Ltd., London. Reprinted from *The Life and Letters of David, Earl Beatty* by W. S. Chalmers 176
Imperial Japanese Navy, official paintings reproduced by courtesy of Shizuo Fukui 124, 130–31, 212
Imperial War Museum, London 116, 137, 163, 179, 180, 186, 187, 189, 198, 199, 204, 209, 211, 214, 215, 251, 253
Jane's Fighting Ships, Sampson Low, Marston & Company, London 232
Koninkluke Marine, The Hague 234
J. F. Lehmanns Verlag, Munich. Redrawn from *Die deutschen Kriegsschiffe 1815–1945*, Volume I, by Erich Gröner 114, 139, 176, 181, 185, 202
Le Masson, Henri, Neuilly-sur-Seine, France 77, 90, 105, 108, 109, 112, 128, 132, 146, 155, 175
Magdalene College, The Master and Fellows of, Cambridge 31
Marine Française 219
      Constructions Navales Cherbourg 175
          ,,   ,, Lorient 188
The Maritime Museum, Gothenburg, Sweden 74
The Maritime Museum, Karlskrona, Sweden 63
Musée de la Marine, Paris 54, 70–71, 84, 97, 151, 184
Museo Naval, Madrid 113
National Maritime Museum, Greenwich 9, 36, 49, 60, 64, 66–67, 81, 82, 102, 103
      Greenwich Hospital Collection 64
      Richard Perkins Collection 125, 136, 140
National Maritime Museum—The Wasa Dockyard, Stockholm 34, 56–57, 58, 59, 171
The National Museum (Svenska Porträttarkivet), Stockholm 34
Naval Material Administration, Stockholm 233
Nederlandsch Historisch Scheepvaart Museum, Amsterdam 60
Nordisk Pressefoto, Copenhagen 256–57

Norton & Company, Inc., W. W., New York. Reprinted from *The History of American Sailing Ships* by Howard I. Chapelle. Copyright 1935 by W. W. Norton & Company, Inc., copyright 1963 by Howard I. Chapelle 68
Prentice–Hall, Inc., Englewood Cliffs, New Jersey, U.S.A. Redrawn from *Sea Power. A Naval History*. Eds. E. B. Potter and Chester W. Nimitz. Copyright 1960 128
Rolls-Royce (1971) Ltd., Bristol Engine Division, U.K. 268
The Royal Danish Navy 238
The Royal Library, Copenhagen. Ny Kgl. Saml. 101, fol., Rud. van Deventer, *Bericht von Pulver und Feuerwerken* 40, 41
The Royal Norwegian Navy 244
Sakai & Co., Tokyo 121
Science Museum, London. British Crown Copyright 12, 16, 24, 48, 69, 89, 92, 118, 144, 161
      Redrawn by permission of the Maritime Museum, Haifa 14
      Lent to Science Museum by C. Cochrane & Co., Birkenhead 168
      ,,   ,,   ,, Yarrow & Company (1922) Limited, Glasgow 92
Short Brothers & Harland Limited, Belfast 247
The Smithsonian Institution, United States National Museum, Washington, D.C. 215
Swedish Naval Staff, Stockholm 244–45
United States Naval Institute, Annapolis, Maryland 148
United States Navy, official photographs 138, 156, 195, 199, 201, 206, 208, 215, 216, 217, 221, 222, 223, 229, 230, 231, 232, 249, 254, 255, 258, 260–62, 266–68
Vickers Limited, London 96, 99, 111, 117, 119, 122, 138, 193, 248, 268

LIST OF SHIPS MENTIONED IN TEXT AND ILLUSTRATIONS
Figures in italics refer to illustrations

Name/Class	Launching Date/Era	Nationality/Type
A CLASS	1902–03	*British Submarines* 173
ABOUKIR	1848	*British 90-gun Ship* 69
ACONIT CLASS	1955	*French Aircraft Direction Corvettes* 239
ACTIF	1862	*French Sloop* 91
ADLER	1566	*Hanseatic Galleon* 51
ADMIRAL CLASS	1884–86	*British Battleships* 115, 120
ADMIRAL GRAF SPEE	1934	*German Pocket Battleship* 191
ADMIRAL HIPPER	1937	*German Heavy Cruiser* 200, *202–03*
ADMIRAL SCHEER	1933	*German Pocket Battleship* 191, 194, *202*
ADZUMO	1899	*Japanese Armoured Cruiser* 126
AEGER	1967	*Norwegian Corvette* 244
AETNA	1856	*British Ironclad* 80
AFFONDATORE	1865	*Italian Coast-defence Vessel* 105, *107–08*
AFRICA	1911	*British Battleship* 205
AGAMEMNON	1852	*British Steam-sail Ship of the line* 76, 82
AGINCOURT	1913	*British Battleship* 177–78
AGORDAT	1899	*Italian Torpedo Cruiser* 154
AIGRETTE	1904	*French Submarine* 170
AKAGI	1925	*Japanese Battle-cruiser, later Fleet Carrier* 184, 190, 207, 210, 213
ALABAMA	1940	*U.S. Battleship* 200
ALARM	1758	*British Frigate* 62
ALBACORE	1953	*U.S. Submarine* 254, 255
ALBANY	1944	*U.S. Guided-missile Cruiser, formerly Heavy Cruiser* 233, 235
ALBION	1842	*British 90-gun Ship* 69, 72
ALBION	1947	*British Light Fleet Carrier, later Commando Ship* 220
ALCYON CLASS	1926–29	*French Destroyers* 191
ALECTO	1839	*British Paddle-sloop* 76, 80
ALEXANDRA	1875	*British Battleship* 110
ALGÉRIE	1932	*French Heavy Cruiser* 191, 200
ALGÉRIEN	1901	*French Submarine* 170
ALMIRANTE LATORRE	1911	*Chilean Battleship* 178
ALMA CLASS	1867–68	*French Cruisers* 147
ALPINO CLASS	1967–68	*Italian Frigates* 240
AMAGI	1920	*Japanese Battle-cruiser* 184, 190, 207
AMALFI	1908	*Italian Cruiser* 151
AMATSUKAZE	1963	*Japanese Guided-missile Destroyer* 232, 241
AMERICA	1964	*U.S. Attack Carrier* 217, *223*
AMETHYST	1903	*British Cruiser* 132, 143
AMIRAL BAUDIN	1884	*French Battleship* 116
AMIRAL CHARNER CLASS	1892–95	*French Cruisers* 151
AMIRAL DUPERRE	1879	*French Battleship* 97, 116
ANDREA DORIA	1963	*Italian Guided-missile Cruiser* 240
ANDREA DORIA CLASS	1884–85	*Italian Battleships* 120
ANDROMAQUE	1841	*French Frigate* 72
ANGUILLE	1904	*French Submarine* 170
ANSON	1886	*British Battleship* 110
ANTIETAM	1952	*U.S. Fleet Carrier* 217
ANZIO	1943	*U.S. Escort Carrier* 210
AQUILA	1943	*Italian Fleet Carrier* 208
ARCHER CLASS	1885–86	*British Light Cruisers* 147
ARETHUSA	1849	*British Frigate* 72
ARETHUSA CLASS	1913–14	*British Light Cruisers* 154
ARGONAUT	1927	*U.S. Mine-laying Submarine* 251
ARGUS	1900	*French River Gunboat* 155
ARGUS	1917	*British Aircraft Carrier* 204–06
ARKANSAS	1911	*U.S. Battleship* 133
ARK ROYAL	1937	*British Fleet Carrier* 207, 209, 210
ARK ROYAL	1955	*British Fleet Carrier* 213, 218, 220
ARLINGTON	1945	*U.S. Light Fleet Carrier, later Command Ship*
ARMANDO DÍAZ	1932	*Italian Light Cruiser* 197
ARMINIUS	1864	*Prussian Coast-defence Vessel* 105, 118
ARROGANT	1848	*British Screw Frigate* 76, 80
ARROMANCHES	1943	*French Light Fleet Carrier* 220
ARTIGLIERE CLASS	1937–38	*Italian Destroyers* 200
ASAHI	1900	*Japanese Battleship* 125
ASTRAEA CLASS	1893	*British Light Cruisers* 150
ATAGO CLASS	1930–31	*Japanese Heavy Cruisers* 191
ATLANTA CLASS	1941–44	*U.S. Light Cruisers* 200
AUDACITY	1938	*British Escort Carrier* 209
AZUMA	1900	*Japanese Cruiser*
B CLASS	1904–06	*British Submarines* 173
BADGER	1911	*British Destroyer* 144
BAINBRIDGE	1961	*U.S. Guided Missile Frigate* 231, 235
BALTIMORE	1888	*U.S. Cruiser* 150
BALTIMORE CLASS	1942–45	*U.S. Heavy Cruisers* 200
BARHAM	1914	*British Battleship* 178
BARROSA CLASS	1889	*British Cruisers* 150
BATTLE CLASS	1946–48	*British Destroyers* 239
BATOUM	1880	*Russian Torpedo Boat* 158
BAY CLASS	1944–45	*British Anti-submarine Ships* 200
BAYAN	1900	*Russian Cruiser* 126
BAYARD	1879	*French Cruiser* 150
BAYERN CLASS	1915	*German Battleships* 182, *185*
BÉARN	1927	*French Battleship, later Fleet Carrier* 207
BEAVER	1911	*British Destroyer* 144
BELFAST CLASS	1938	*British Heavy Cruisers* 200
BELKNAP CLASS	1964–65	*U.S. Guided Missile Frigates* 231, 235, 239
BELLE POULE	1834	*French Frigate* 72
BELLEROPHON	1865	*British Ship-of-the-line* 107
BELLEROPHON CLASS	1907	*British Battleships* 133
BELLONA CLASS	1908	*British Light Cruisers* 154
BENBOW	1885	*British Battleship* 110
BENEDETTO BRIN	1901	*Italian Battleship* 120
BENSON/LIVERMORE CLASS	1939–41	*U.S. Destroyers* 200
BERGAMINI CLASS	1960	*Italian Frigates* 240
BERTHE DE VILLERS	1884	*French River Gunboat* 155
BIBER CLASS	1944–45	*German Midget Submarines* 255
BIRMINGHAM CLASS	1911–13	*U.S. Light Cruisers* 205
BISMARCK	1939	*German Battleship* 182, 198, 210
BLACK PRINCE	1860	*British Ship-of-the-line* 80
BLACK SWAN CLASS	1939–42	*British Anti-aircraft Ships* 200
BLAKE	1889	*British Cruiser* 147, 150
BLANCHE CLASS	1909–11	*British Light Cruisers* 154
BLÜCHER	1908	*German Armoured Cruiser* 154, 177
BLÜCHER	1937	*German Heavy Cruiser* 200
BOBILLOT	1884	*French River Gunboat* 154
BOGUE CLASS	1941–42	*U.S. Escort Carriers* 210
BOMBE CLASS	1885	*French Torpedo-boat Destroyers* 158
BONAVENTURE	1945	*Canadian Light Fleet Carrier* 213, 220
BORODINO CLASS	1915–16	*Russian Battle-cruisers* 182
BOSTON	1942	*U.S. Guided-missile Cruiser, formerly Heavy Cruiser* 232
BOUCLIER	1909	*French Destroyer* 159
BRANDENBURG CLASS	1891–92	*German Battleships* 120
BRANDTAUCHER	1850	*German (Prussian) Submarine* 165
BRENNUS	1891	*French Battleship* 118
BRESLAU CLASS	1911	*German Light Cruisers* 154
BRETAGNE CLASS	1913	*French Battleships* 137, 182
BRISTOL CLASS	1909–10	*British Light Cruisers*
BRITANNIA	1682	*English 100-gun Three-decker* 53
BRITANNIA	1762	*British 100-gun Ship* 62
BROOKLYN	1895	*U.S. Cruiser* 154
BUFFEL	1868	*Dutch Armoured Ship* 115
BULL	1546	*English Galleass* 35
BULLDOG	1845	*British Steam-sail Warship* 79
BULWARK	1807	*British 74-gun Ship* 66, 79
BULWARK	1948	*British Light Fleet Carrier, later Commando Ship* 220, 239
BUSSARD CLASS	1890–95	*German Cruisers* 150
C CLASS	1908–10	*British Submarines* 173
CAESAR	1793	*British 80-gun Ship* 66
CAIO DUILIO	1913	*Italian Battleship* 183, 210
CAIO DUILIO	1962	*Italian Guided-missile Cruiser* 237, 240
CALEDONIA	1808	*British 120-gun Ship* 66
CALIFORNIA CLASS	1901	*U.S. Cruisers* 123
CALIFORNIA CLASS	1919	*U.S. Battleships* 137, 184
CALLIOPE CLASS	1914–15	*British Light Cruisers* 154
CAMBRIAN	1797	*British Frigate* 63
CAMPANIA	1908	*British Liner, later Seaplane Carrier* 205
CAMPERDOWN	1885	*British Battleship* 110
CANADA	1913	*British Battleship* 178

Name/Class	Launching Date/Era	Nationality/Type
CANBERRA	1943	U.S. Guided-missile Cruiser, formerly Heavy Cruiser 232
CANOPUS	1796	French, later British 84 gun Ship 72
CAPITANI ROMANI CLASS	1940–42	Italian Light Cruisers 200
CAPTAIN	1869	British Sail-rigged Turret Ship 103, 109–10, 118
CARABINIERE	1967	Italian Frigate 240
CARD	1944	U.S. Escort Carrier 210
CASABLANCA CLASS	1943–44	U.S. Escort Carriers 210
CASQUE CLASS	1910–14	French Destroyers 159
CASSARD CLASS	1893–96	French Cruisers 150
CATHERINE II	1887	Russian Battleship 118
CAVOUR CLASS	1911	Italian Battleships 192
CENTAURO CLASS	1954–56	Italian Frigates 240
CERBÈRE	1868	French Coast-defence Vessel 105
CHARLEMAGNE CLASS	1895–96	French Battleships 118
CHARLES F. ADAMS CLASS	1959–63	U.S. Guided-missile Destroyers 239, 241
CHARLES GALLEY	1676	English Galley 37
CHARLESTON	1888	U.S. Cruiser 150
CHARLOTTE DUNDAS	1801	British Paddle-tug 75
CHASSEUR CLASS	1908–11	French Destroyers 159
CHATEAU RENAULT	1897	French Cruiser 150
CHICAGO	1882	U.S. Cruiser 147
CHICAGO	1944	U.S. Guided-missile Cruiser, formerly Heavy Cruiser 233, 235
CHITOSE	1898	Japanese Cruiser 150
CHITOSE	1928	Japanese Seaplane Tender, later Light Fleet Carrier 210, 213
CHIYODA	1928	Japanese Seaplane Tender, later Light Fleet Carrier 210, 213
CHOKAI	1931	Japanese Cruiser 212
CHRISTOPHER OF THE TOWER	c. 1412	English Warship 30
CICOGNE	1904	French Submarine 170
CIVETTA	1826	Austrian Steamship 76
CLEMENCEAU	1957	French Light Fleet Carrier 219, 220
CLERMONT	1807	U.S. Steamboat 75
CLEVELAND CLASS	1901–03	U.S. Cruisers 150
CLEVELAND CLASS	1941–44	U.S. Light Cruisers, later Guided-missile Cruisers 200, 232
COATIT	1899	Italian Torpedo Cruiser 154
COBRA	1899	British Torpedo-boat Destroyer 159
COLBERT	1875	French Battleship 116
COLBERT	1956	French Anti-aircraft Cruiser 239
COLLINGWOOD	1882	British Battleship 110
CÓLN CLASS	1908–09	German Light Cruisers 154
COLOMBE	c. 1480	French Carrack 30, 53
COLONY CLASS	1939–40	British Light Cruisers 191, 200
COLORADO	1921	U.S. Battleship 184, 189
COLORADO CLASS	1903–04	U.S. Cruisers 154
COLOSSUS	1910	British Battleship 133, 136
COLOSSUS CLASS	1943	British Light Fleet Carriers 213, 220
COLUMBUS	1944	U.S. Guided-missile Cruiser 233, 235
COMET	1822	British Paddle-steamer 76
COMMANDANT RIVIÈRE CLASS	1958–62	French Dual-purpose Frigates 240
COMMENCEMENT BAY CLASS	1944–45	U.S. Escort Carriers 210
COMMERCE DE MARSEILLE	1788	French 118-gun Ship 62, 66
COMUS CLASS	1878	British Light Cruisers 150
CONDOR	1884	French Torpedo Cruiser 154
CONDOTTIERI CLASS	1936–40	Italian Light Cruisers 191, 200
CONGRESS	1841	U.S. Frigate 85
CONSTANCE	1846	British Frigate 72, 91
CONSTANTINE	1878	Russian Armoured Steamer 157
CONSTANT WARWICK	1645	English Warship 58
CONSTELLATION	1960	U.S. Attack Carrier 217
CONSTITUTION	1797	U.S. Frigate 70, 72
CONTE DI CAVOUR	1911	Italian Battleship 210
CORAL SEA	1945	U.S. Attack Carrier
CORNWALL	1926	British Cruiser 213
CORNWALLIS	1903	British Battleship 119
CORSE	1842	French Despatch-vessel 76, 89, 90
COUNTY CLASS	1960–65	British Guided-missile Destroyers 246
COURAGEOUS	1916	British Cruiser, later Fleet Carrier 182, 207
COURBET, ex-FOUDROYANT	1882	French Battleship 116
COURBET	1913	French Battleship 140
COURONNE	1860	French Ironclad 80
CRESCENT CLASS	1891–92	British Cruisers 150
CRESSY CLASS	1899–1900	British Cruisers 151
CRUIZER	1828	British Brig 72
CUMBERLAND	1842	U.S. Frigate 85
CYGNET	1585	English Warship 48
D CLASS	1908–11	British Submarines 174
DANDOLO	1878	Italian Battleship 97, 110, 120
DANTE ALIGHIERI	1910	Italian Battleship 137, 138
DANTON CLASS	1909	French Battleships 137
DARING	1844	British Brig 72
DARING	1893	British Destroyer 158
DARING CLASS	1949–52	British Destroyers 239
DAUNTLESS	1847	British Screw Frigate 76
DEALEY CLASS	1954–59	U.S. Destroyer Escorts 235, 238
DECOY	1893	British Destroyer 158
DE CRISTOFARO CLASS	1964–65	Italian Corvettes 240
DEFENCE	1907	British Cruiser 177, 180
DE GRASSE	1946	French Command and Air Directions Cruiser 239
DELAWARE	1909	U.S. Battleship 133, 189
DELFIN	1903	Russian Submarine 174
DELFINO	1896	Italian Submarine 174
DEMOLOGOS	1815	U.S. Steam Frigate 75, 78
D'ENTRECASTEAUX	1896	French Cruiser 150
DERFFLINGER	1913	German Battle-cruiser 141, 177–78, 180–81
DE RUYTER	1946	Dutch Cruiser 240
DESCARTES CLASS	1894–97	French Cruisers 150
DESTRUCTOR	1886	Spanish Torpedo Gunboat 91, 94, 158
DEUTSCHLAND	1874	German Armoured Frigate 118
DEUTSCHLAND	1916	German Cargo Submarine 251
DEUTSCHLAND	1931	German Pocket Battleship 191
DEVASTATION	1871	British Battleship 97, 110, 116
DEVASTATION	1855	French Floating Battery 80, 97
DEVASTATION	1879	French Battleship 116
DEVONSHIRE	1960	British Guided-missile Destroyer 239, 246
DE ZEVEN PROVINCIEN	1665	Dutch Warship 60
DE ZEVEN PROVINCIEN	1950	Dutch Guided-missile Cruiser 234, 240
DIDO CLASS	1895–96	British Cruisers 150
DIDO CLASS	1939–40	British Light Cruisers 200
DIMITRI DONSKOI	1883	Russian Cruiser 150
DOGALI	1886	Italian Cruiser 91, 95, 150
DORSETSHIRE	1927	British Heavy Cruiser 213
DREADNOUGHT	1875	British Battleship 97, 110
DREADNOUGHT	1906	British Battleship 125, 132, 137, 143 et al.
DREADNOUGHT	1960	British Nuclear-powered Attack Submarine 256–57
DUBUQUE	1904	U.S. Gunboat 154
DUGUAY TROUIN	1877	French Cruiser 147, 151
DUGUAY TROUIN CLASS	1923–24	French Light Cruisers 191
DUGUESCLIN CLASS	1879–82	French Cruisers 150
DUILIO	1876	Italian Battleship 97, 101, 110, 120, 157, 163 et al.
DUNKERQUE	1935	French Battleship 190
DUPUY DE LÔME	1890	French Cruiser 91, 123, 125, 150–51
DUQUESNE	1876	French Cruiser 147
DURANDAL CLASS	1898–1900	French Destroyers 159, 162
E CLASS	1928	British Destroyers
EAGLE	1776	British 64-gun Ship 165
EAGLE	1918	British Fleet Carrier 205–06, 210
EAGLE	1951	British Fleet Carrier 213, 220
EBER CLASS	1903	German Sloops 154
ECLAIREUR	1877	French Cruiser 147
EDEN	1903	British Destroyer 159
EDGAR CLASS	1890–92	British Cruisers 150
EDGAR QUINET	1907	French Cruiser 154
EMDEN	1925	German Light Cruiser 191
EMERALD	1920	British Light Cruiser 191
ÉMILE BERTIN	1933	French Light Cruiser 191
ENDYMION	1797	British Frigate 65, 70
ENGADINE	1914	British Seaplane Carrier 205
ENRICO TOTI	1967	Italian Submarine 258
ENTERPRISE	1919	British Light Cruiser 191
ENTERPRISE	1936	U.S. Fleet Carrier 207, 213, 216, 217
ENTERPRISE	1960	U.S. Nuclear-powered Attack Carrier 217, 222, 234
EREBUS	1856	British Ironclad 80
ERIN	1913	British Battleship 178
ERZHERZOG FERDINAND MAX	1865	Austrian Warship 106–08
ESMERALDA	1883	Chilean Cruiser 150
ESPIEGLE	1844	British Brig 72
ESPIEGLE CLASS	1900–03	British Sloops 154
ESSEX CLASS	1942–45	U.S. Fleet Carriers 208, 213, 216
ETHAN ALLAN CLASS	1960–62	U.S. Ballistic-missile Submarines 258
ETNA CLASS	1885–86	Italian Cruisers 150
EURYALUS	1853	British Warship 83
FADERNESLANDET	1783	Swedish Warship 63
FAIDHERBE	1897	French River Gunboat 154
FARFADET CLASS	1899–1901	French Submarines 170
FARRAGUT CLASS	1934–35	U.S. Destroyers 192, 194
FARRAGUT CLASS	1958–60	U.S. Guided-missile Frigates 234
FIREBRAND	1842	British Steam Frigate 76
FIUME	1930	Italian Heavy Cruiser 210
FLETCHER CLASS	1940–41	U.S. Destroyers 200, 240
FLORIDA	1910	U.S. Battleship 133
FLOWER CLASS	1939–42	British Anti-submarine Ships 200
FLY CLASS	1915–16	British River Gunboats 155
FLYING FISH	1844	British Brig 72
FOCH	1960	French Light Fleet Carrier 220

Name/Class	Launching Date/Era	Nationality/Type
FORBAN CLASS	1895–98	French Torpedo Boats 158
FORELLE	1903	Russian Submarine 174
FORMIDABLE	1884	French Battleship 116
FORMIDABLE	1939	British Fleet Carrier 210
FORRESTAL	1954	U.S. Attack Carrier 217, 234
FÖRSIKTIGHETEN	1784	Swedish Warship 63
FORTE	1841	French Frigate 72
FORTH	1813	British Frigate 72
FOUDRE	1895	French Torpedo Boat Carrier 157
FOUDROYANT	1882	French Battleship 116
FRANÇAIS	1900	French Submarine 170
FRANCESCO FERRUCCIO	1902	Italian Cruiser 151
FRANKLIN D. ROOSEVELT	1945	U.S. Attack Carrier
FREDERICUS QUARTUS	1699	Danish 110-gun Three-decker 53
FRIEDRICH DER GROSSE	1874	German Armoured Frigate 118
FRIEDLAND	1840	French 120-gun Ship 69
FRIEDLAND	1873	French Battleship 116
FUJI	1896	Japanese Battleship 125
FURIOUS	1916	British Cruiser, later Fleet Carrier 204–206
FÜRST BISMARCK	1897	German Cruiser 152–3, 154
FURUTAKA	1925	Japanese Heavy Cruiser 191
FUSHIMI	1903	Japanese River Gunboat 155
FUSO CLASS	1914–15	Japanese Battleships 137, 184
G.137	1905	German Destroyer
GALLEON OF VENICE	16th C.	Venetian Galley 37
GALLEY SUBTYLLE	1544	English Galley 35
GALVESTON	1942	U.S. Guided-missile Cruiser 233
GANGES	1821	British 84-gun Ship 69
GANGUT CLASS	1911	Russian Battleships 137
GARCIA CLASS	1963–66	U.S. Escort Ships 235, 238
GAZELLE	1900	German Cruiser 150
GEARING CLASS	1944–45	U.S. Radar Picket Destroyers 235
GEORGE WASHINGTON CLASS	1959–60	U.S. Ballistic-missile Submarines 258
GIOVANNI BAUSAN	1883	Italian Cruiser 150
GIULIO CESARE CLASS	1911	Italian Battleships 137, 184
GIUSEPPE GARIBALDI	1899	Italian Cruiser 148–49, 151
GLASGOW	1814	British Frigate 72
GLATTON	1871	British Coast-defence Vessel 102, 105
GLAUCO	1905	Italian Submarine 173, 174
GLOIRE	1859	French Steam Frigate 80, 83, 97 et al.
GLORIOUS	1916	British Cruiser, later Fleet Carrier 207
GNEISENAU	1906	German Cruiser 154, 177
GNEISENAU	1935	German Battleship 197
GOITO CLASS	1887–89	Italian Torpedo Cruisers 154
GOKSTAD SHIP	9th C.	Norwegian Longship 20, 21
GOLIATH	1842	British Frigate 70
GOOD HOPE	1901	British Cruiser 154, 177
GORGON	1837	British Steam Sloop 76, 88, 89
GOUBET I—GOUBET II	1886–87	French Submarines 167
GRÂCE DIEU	1418	English Warship 29, 30
GRAF ZEPPELIN	1939	German Fleet Carrier 208
GRASSHOPPER CLASS	1887	British Torpedo Gunboats 158
GRAYBACK	1957	U.S. Guided-missile Submarine 255
GREAT GALLEY	1515	English Galley 35
GREAT HARRY (HENRY GRÂCE À DIEU)	1514	English Carrack 31, 32
GREAT MICHAEL	1511	Scottish Carrack 32
GRIMSBY CLASS	1933	British Sloops 200
GROMOBOI	1899	Russian Cruiser 151
GROSSER KURFÜRST	1875	German Armoured Frigate 118
GROSSER KURFÜRST	1913	German Battleship 180
GUERRIERE	1813	U.S. Frigate 70, 72
GUICHEN	1897	French Cruiser 150
GUSTAVE ZÉDÉ	1893	French Submarine 169
GYATT	1945	U.S. Guided-missile Destroyer 235
GYMNOTE	1888	French Submarine 167, 169, 175
GYMNOTE	1964	French Ballistic-missile Submarine 258
HABSBURG	1865	Austrian Warship 107–08
HAJEN	1904	Swedish Submarine 174
HALIBUT	1959	U.S. Nuclear-powered Guided-missile Submarine 255
HALLAND	1952	Swedish Destroyer 240
HALSNØY BOAT	1st and 2nd C.	Scandinavian Longship 21
HAMBURG CLASS	1960–63	German Destroyers 241
HANCOCK	1944	U.S. Aircraft Carrier 221
HARUNA	1913	Japanese Battle-cruiser 141
HATSUSE	1899	Japanese Battleship 125
HAVOCK	1893	British Torpedo Boat Destroyer 158, 163
HAVFRUEN	1789	Danish Frigate 61
HAWKINS CLASS	1917–20	British Cruisers 190
HECHT CLASS	1944–45	German Midget Submarines 255
HELENA	1895	U.S. Gunboat 154
HENRI IV	1899	French Battleship 136
HENRY GRÂCE À DIEU (GREAT HARRY)	1514	English Warship 31, 32
HERCULE	1836	French Three-decker 69
HERCULES	1868	British Ship-of-the-line 108
HERCULES	1910	British Battleship 133
HERLUF TROLLE	1966	Danish Fast Frigate 241
HERMES	1919	British Light Fleet Carrier 205, 213, 220, 239
HERMES CLASS	1947–53	British Light Fleet Carriers 213, 216, 220
HERON	1897	British River Gunboat 155
HIBERNIA	1804	British 110-, later 120-gun Ship 66
HIBERNIA	1908	British Battleship 205
HINDENBURG	1915	German Battle-cruiser 182, 185
HIRYU	1937	Japanese Fleet Carrier 207, 210
HIYEI	1912	Japanese Battle-cruiser 141
HIYO	1941	Japanese Fleet Carrier 208, 210, 213
HOCHE	1886	French Battleship 116
HOLIGOST OF THE TOWER	c. 1412	English Warship 29
HOLLAND NO. 1, 7, 8, 9	1875–1902	U.S. Submarines 172, 173
HONOLULU CLASS	1936–38	U.S. Cruisers 200
HOOD	1891	British Battleship 115, 182
HOOD	1918	British Battle-cruiser 182, 186–87, 210
HORNET	1893	British Torpedo Boat 158
HORNET	1940	U.S. Fleet Carrier 208, 213
HOSHO	1922	Japanese Light Fleet Carrier 206, 213
HOTSPUR	1870	British Coast-defence Vessel 102, 105
HOUSATONIC	1864	U.S. (Federal) Warship 166
HOWE	1815	British 120-gun Ship 66
HOWE	1885	British Battleship 110
HUASCAR	1864	Peruvian Monitor 123, 147, 158
HUNLEY	1864	U.S. (Confederate) Submarine 166
HVALEN	1909	Swedish Submarine 174
HYUGA	1913	Japanese Battleship 137
I 400–402	1943–44	Japanese Submarines 252
IBUKI	1943	Japanese Heavy Cruiser 210
IDAHO CLASS	1917	U.S. Battleships 184
IDZUMO CLASS	1899	Japanese Armoured Cruisers 123, 126
IKAZUCHI CLASS	1897–1900	Japanese Destroyers 132
IKOMA	1906	Japanese Battleship 141
ILLUSTRIOUS CLASS	1939	British Fleet Carrier 207, 210
IMPAVIDO CLASS	1962–68	Italian Guided-missile Destroyers 240
IMPERATRITSA MARIA	1913	Russian Battleship 137
IMPETUOSO	1956	Italian Destroyer 240
IMPLACABLE	1939	British Fleet Carrier 207
INCONSTANT	1868	British Frigate, later Cruiser 147
INDEFATIGABLE	1909	British Battle-cruiser 141, 178, 181–82 et al.
INDEFATIGABLE	1939	British Fleet Carrier 207
INDEPENDENCE	1954	U.S. Attack Carrier 217
INDEPENDENCE CLASS	1943	U.S. Light Fleet Carriers 208, 213, 216, 217
INDEPENDENCIA	1944	Argentine Light Fleet Carrier 220
INDIANA	1940	U.S. Battleship 200
INDOMITABLE	1907	British Battle-cruiser 141
INDOMITABLE	1939	British Fleet Carrier
INDOMITO	1955	Italian Destroyer 240
INFLEXIBLE	1876	British Battleship 97–98, 110, 118, 120, 123
INFLEXIBLE	1907	British Battle-cruiser 136, 141, 154, 177, 182
INSECT CLASS	1915–16	British River Gunboats 155
INVINCIBLE	1907	British Battle-cruiser 141, 154, 177, 180–82
INVINCIBLE	c. 1740	French 74-gun Ship 62
IOWA	1942	U.S. Battleship 200
IRENE	1887	German Cruiser 150
IRIS	1878	British Despatch-ship 91
IRON DUKE CLASS	1912	British Battleships 136, 178, 179
ISE	1916	Japanese Battleship 137
ISMAIL	1915	Russian Battle-cruiser
ITALIA	1880	Italian Battleship 110, 120, 150
IVAR HVITFELD	1886	Danish Coast-defence Vessel 157
IWATE	1900	Japanese Armoured Cruiser 126
J CLASS	1938–29	British Destroyers 200
JAGUAR	1898	German Sloop 154
JAGUAR CLASS	1957–64	German Fast Patrol Boats 240
JAMES GALLEY	1676	English Galley 37
JASON CLASS	1892–93	British Gunboats 158
JAURÉGUIBERRY CLASS	1893–96	French Battleships 116
JAVA	1813	U.S. Frigate 70, 72
JAVA	1815	British Frigate 70
JEAN BART	1939	French Battleship 198
JEAN BART CLASS	1889–91	French Cruisers 150
JEAN BART CLASS	1911–12	French Battleships 137, 182
JEANNE D'ARC	1899	French Cruiser 149, 151
JEMMAPES	1840	French Warship 69
JESUS OF THE TOWER	c. 1412	English Warship 29
JINTSU CLASS	1923–25	Japanese Light Cruisers 191
JOFFRE	1961	French Fleet Carrier 207
JOHN F. KENNEDY	1968	U.S. Attack Carrier 217

Name/Class	Launching Date/Era	Nationality/Type
JUNYO	1941	Japanese Fleet Carrier 208, 213
JUPITER	1913	U.S. Collier, later Aircraft Carrier 144, 206
JUPITER	1938	British Destroyer 199
JURIEN DE LA GRAVIÈRE	1899	French Cruiser 154
K CLASS	1916–18	British Fleet Submarines 251
K CLASS	1938–39	British Destroyers 200
KAGA	1925	Japanese Battleship, later Fleet Carrier 184, 190, 207, 210, 213
KAISER	1858	Austrian Screw-driven Two-decker 108
KAISER	1873	German Armoured Frigate 118
KAISER CLASS	1911	German Battleships 136, 139
KAISER FRANZ JOSEPH I	1889	Austrian Cruiser 150
KAISER FRIEDRICH III	1896	German Armoured Frigate 120
KAISERIN ELISABETH	1890	Austrian Cruiser 150
KAKO	1925	Japanese Heavy Cruiser 191
KAMA CLASS	1920	Japanese Light Cruisers 184
KAMBALA	1907	Russian Submarine 174
KARASS	1905	Russian Submarine 174
KAREL DOORMAN	1943	Dutch Light Fleet Carrier 213, 220
KARLSRUHE	1960	German Frigate 242
KARP	1906	Russian Submarine 174
KASAGI	1897	Japanese Cruiser 150
KASHIN CLASS	1962–64	Russian Guided-missile Frigates 241
KASUGA	1902	Japanese Cruiser 151
KAWACHI	1910	Japanese Battleship 137
KENT CLASS	1926	British Heavy Cruisers 190
KERSAINT	1897	French Sloop 154
KING GEORGE V CLASS	1911	British Battleships 136
KING GEORGE V CLASS	1939–40	British Battleships 197
KIRISHIMA	1913	Japanese Battle-cruiser 141
KITTY HAWK	1960	U.S. Attack Carrier 217
KNIAZ MININ	1869	Russian Sail-rigged Turret Ship 118
KNIAZ SOUVAROFF	1903	Russian Battleship 128
KNOX CLASS	1966	U.S. Destroyers 235, 238
KÖLN CLASS	1927–28	German Light Cruisers 191
KÖLN CLASS	1958–62	German Frigates 240, 241, 242
KONGO CLASS	1912–13	Japanese Battle-cruisers 141, 184
KÖNIG CLASS	1913–14	German Battleships 136, 184
KÖNIGSBERG	1905	German Light Cruiser 154
KÖNIG WILHELM	1868	German (Prussian) Broadside Ship 118
KOTLIN CLASS	1955–58	Russian Destroyers 241
KRAB	1912	Russian Submarine Minelayer 174
KRUPNYI CLASS	1960–64	Russian Guided-missile Frigates 241
KUMA CLASS	1919–20	Japanese Light Cruisers 191
KVALSUND SHIP	8th C.	Scandinavian Longship 21
KYNDA CLASS	1961–62	Russian Guided-missile Frigates 241
L CLASS	1938–39	British Destroyers 200
LA COURONNE	1638	French 72-gun Two-decker 43, 53
LAFAYETTE CLASS	1962–66	U.S. Ballistic-missile Submarines 258, 260
LA GALISSONNIÈRE	1960	French Squadron Escort Destroyer 239
LA GALISSONNIÈRE CLASS	1933–35	French Light Cruisers 188, 191, 200
LA GRANDE FRANÇOISE	1527	French Carrack 32
LANGLEY	1920	U.S. Aircraft Carrier 206, 208
LA POMONE	c. 1790	French Frigate 65, 73
LAVE	1855	French Floating Battery 80, 97
LA VICTORIEUSE	1875	French Armoured Cruiser 146
LEAHY CLASS	1961–63	U.S. Guided-missile Frigates 235
LEANDER	1813	British Frigate 70
LEANDER CLASS	1882	British Cruisers 150
LEANDER CLASS	1931–33	British Light Cruisers 191
LEANDER CLASS	1961–65	British General-purpose Frigates 239
LE BON		French 50-gun Ship 37
LE BRETON CLASS	1954–57	French Fast Escort Frigates 239
LE CORSE CLASS	1952–53	French Fast Escort Frigates 239
LE DIABLE MARIN	1855	Russian Submarine 164, 166
LE FANTASQUE CLASS	1933–34	French Destroyers 192
LE FOUGUEUX CLASS	1954–59	French Patrol Vessels
LEIPZIG	1929	German Light Cruiser 191, 192
LEONARDO DA VINCI	1911	Italian Battleship 184
LEONIDAS	1914	British Destroyer 184
LEPANTO	1883	Italian Battleship 110, 118, 120, 150
LE PLONGEUR	1863	French Submarine 166, 169
LE SOLEIL ROYAL	1669	French Warship 54
LE VALMY	1847	French 120-gun Ship 70–71
LEVRIER	1891	French Torpedo Boat Destroyer 158
LEXINGTON	1925	U.S. Carrier 184, 190, 206, 213
LIFFEY	1814	British Frigate 72
LIFFEY	1856	British Screw Frigate
LIGHTNING	1876	British Torpedo Boat 157, 161
LION CLASS	1910	British Battle-cruisers 141, 177, 181
LITTLE ROCK	1942	U.S. Guided-missile Cruiser, formerly Light Cruiser 232, 233, 235
LITTORIO	1937	Italian Battleship 196, 197, 198 210
LIVERPOOL	1813	British Frigate 72
LOCH CLASS	1943–44	British Anti-submarine Ships 200
LOIRET	1863	French Naval Transport 91
LOMBARDIA CLASS	1890–98	Italian Cruisers 150
LONDON CLASS	1927–28	British Heavy Cruisers 190
LONG BEACH	1959	U.S. Guided-missile Cruiser, Nuclear-powered 230, 234
LONG SERPENT	c. 1000	Norwegian Longship 21
LORRAINE	1913	French Battleship 184
LÜBECK	1903	German Light Cruiser 132, 143
LUCIFER	1914	British Destroyer 144
LÜTZOW	1913	German Battle-cruiser 177–78, 180, 181
LÜTZOW	1931	German Pocket Battleship 191
M CLASS	1918–19	British Submarine Monitors 251
M CLASS	1938–39	British Destroyers 200
MACKENSEN	1917	German Battle-cruiser 182
MAGENTA	1861	French Battleship 80, 105, 108
MAGENTA	1890	French Battleship 116
MAJESTIC	1843	British Frigate 70
MAJESTIC CLASS	1895	British Battleships 115, 116, 123, 151
MAJESTIC CLASS	1944–45	British Light Fleet Carriers 213, 220
MALAYA	1914	British Battleship 178, 180
MARCEAU	1887	French Battleship 116
MARENGO	1869	French Battleship 109
MARKGRAF	1913	German Battleship 180
MARS	1563	Swedish Galleon 51
MARSALA	1911	Italian Light Cruiser 154
MARYLAND	1920	U.S. Battleship 184
MARY ROSE	1509	English Carrack 29, 32
MASSACHUSETTS	1940	U.S. Battleship 200
MEDEA CLASS	188'	British Cruisers 150
MEDUSA CLASS	1911	Italian Submarines 174
MELBOURNE	1945	Australian Light Fleet Carrier 213, 220
MERCURY	1878	British Despatch-ship 91
MERRIMAC	1855	U.S. (Confederate) Steam Frigate 74, 84, 85
MERSEY CLASS	1885–86	British Cruisers 150
MICHIGAN	1909	U.S. Battleship 133
MIDWAY	1945	U.S. Attack Carrier 216–17, 234
MIKASA	1900	Japanese Battleship 125–26, 127, 131
MINAS GERAIS	1944	Brazilian Light Fleet Carrier 220
MINOTAUR CLASS	1906	British Cruisers 154
MISSOURI	1942	U.S. Battleship 200, 201, 217
MITSCHER CLASS	1952	U.S. Destroyers 234–35
MOGADOR CLASS	1936–37	French Destroyers 192, 200
MOGAMI CLASS	1934–36	Japanese Light Cruisers 191
MOLCH CLASS	1944–45	German Midget Submarines 251, 255
MOLTKE	1910	German Battle-cruiser 141, 177
MONARCH	1868	British Sail-rigged Turret Ship 109
MONITOR	1862	U.S. (Federal) Turret Ship 74, 83–85, 105
MONMOUTH	1901	British Cruiser 154, 177
MONOCACY	1914	U.S. River Gunboat 155, 156
MONTEBELLO	1812	French 120-gun Ship 69
MORSE	1899	French Submarine 170
MOSQUITO	1890	British River Gunboat 155
MUSASHI	1940	Japanese Battleship 197, 213
MUTINE	1844	British Brig 72
MUTSU	1920	Japanese Battleship 184
NACHI CLASS	1927–28	Japanese Heavy Cruisers 191
NAGATO	1919	Japanese Battleship 184
NAIADE CLASS	1903–04	French Submarines 170
NAIWA	1885	Japanese Cruiser 118, 150
NAPOLÉON, later CORSE	1842	French Despatch-vessel 76, 89, 90
NAPOLÉON	1850	French Steam Ship-of-the-line 76
NARVAL	1899	French Submarine 169, 170, 174, 175
NASSAU CLASS	1908	German Battleships 132, 136, 139
NATORI CLASS	1921–23	Japanese Light Cruisers 184, 191
NAUTILUS	1800	French Submarine (Fulton) 165, 167
NAUTILUS	1954	U.S. Nuclear-powered Submarine 255
NAVIGATORI CLASS	1928–30	Italian Destroyers 192
NELSON	1814	British 120-gun Ship 66
NELSON	1876	British Cruiser 147
NELSON	1925	British Battleship 189–90
NEMBO	1901	Italian Destroyer 162
NEPTUNE	1887	French Battleship 116
NEPTUNE	1909	British Battleship 133

Name/Class	Launching Date/Era	Nationality/Type
SOVEREIGN OF THE SEAS (ROYAL SOVEREIGN)	1637	*English 104-gun Three-decker* 51, 53
SPANKER CLASS	1889–91	*British Torpedo Gunboats* 158
SPHINX	1830	*French aviso* 76, 79
SPRINGFIELD	1942	*U.S. Guided-missile Cruiser, formerly Light Cruiser* 232
SQUALO	1906	*Italian Submarine* 174
ST. LAURENT CLASS	1950–52	*Canadian Anti-submarine Frigates* 234, 241
ST. VINCENT	1815	*British 120-gun Ship* 66, 72
ST. VINCENT	1908	*British Battleship* 133
STORA KRONAN	1672	*Swedish 128-gun Three-decker* 53
STORE KRAFWELN	1532	*Swedish Carrack* 32
STRASBOURG	1936	*French Battleship* 190, 197
SUFFREN CLASS	1927–30	*French Heavy Cruisers* 190
SUFFREN CLASS	1965–66	*French Guided-missile Frigates* 236, 239
SUMIDA	1903	*Japanese River Gunboat* 155
SUPERB	1842	*British 80-gun Ship* 72
SUPERBE	c. 1670	*French 74-gun Ship* 53
SURCOUF	1929	*French Submarine* 251
SURCOUF CLASS	1953–54	*French Squadron Escort Destroyers* 236, 239
SUTLEJ	1855	*British Frigate* 72
SVERDLOV CLASS	1951–58	*Russian Cruisers* 241, *245*
SYDNEY	1944	*Australian Light Fleet Carrier* 213, 220
T CLASS	1943	*British Destroyers, later Anti-submarine Frigates* 239
TAGE	1847	*French Three-decker* 69
TAIHO	1942	*Japanese Fleet Carrier* 210, 213
TAKAO	1930	*Japanese Heavy Cruiser* 184, *190*
TCHAPAEV CLASS	1941–47	*Russian Cruisers* 241
TCHESMÉ	1887	*Russian Battleship* 118
TÉMÉRAIRE	1876	*British Battleship* 110
TENNESSEE	1919	*U.S. Battleship* 137, *208*
TENNESSEE CLASS	1903–05	*U.S. Cruisers* 151
TERRIBLE	1881	*French Battleship* 98
TERRIBLE	1895	*British Armoured Cruiser* 150
TERROR	1856	*British Ironclad* 80
TEXAS	1912	*U.S. Battleship* 136
THÉSÉE	1758	*French 74-gun Ship* 32
THUNDERBOLT	1856	*British Ironclad* 80
THUNDERER	1872	*British Battleship* 110, 112, *117*
TIGER	1913	*British Battle-cruiser* 141, 178
TIGER CLASS	1944–45	*British Cruisers, later Helicopter Carriers* 239
TIGRE CLASS	1924–25	*French Destroyers* 191
TIRPITZ	1939	*German Battleship* 198, *252*
TOKIWA	1898	*Japanese Armoured Cruiser* 126
TONE CLASS	1937–38	*Japanese Light Cruisers* 191
TONNANTE	1855	*French Floating Battery* 80, 97
TONNERRE CLASS	1875	*French Turret Ships* 105
TOPEKA	1942	*U.S. Guided-missile Cruiser, formerly Light Cruiser* 232
TORBORG	1772	*Swedish Galley* 34
TORDENSKJOLD	1880	*Danish Coast-defence Vessel* 157
TORTOISE BOAT	16th C.	*Korean Warship* 78
TOSA	19?	*Japanese Battleship* 184
TOURVILLE	1876	*French Cruiser* 147
TOURVILLE CLASS	1925–26	*French Heavy Cruisers* 190
TOWN CLASS	1909–14	*British Light Cruisers* 154
TRAFALGAR	1841	*British 120-gun Ship* 72
TRAFALGAR	1887	*British Battleship* 115
TRENTO CLASS	1926–27	*Italian Heavy Cruisers* 191
TRIBAL CLASS	1908–10	*British Destroyers* 161
TRIBAL CLASS	1959–62	*British General-purpose Destroyers* 239
TRIDENT	1876	*French Battleship* 116
TRINITY ROYAL OF THE TOWER	1416	*English Warship* 29
TRIPOLI	1886	*Italian Torpedo Cruiser* 154
TRITON	1958	*U.S. Nuclear-powered Radar Picket Submarine* 255
TRIUMPH	1561	*English Galleon* 48
TRIUMPH	1944	*British Light Fleet Carrier* 217
TRUXTUN	1964	*U.S. Guided-missile Frigate, Nuclear-powered* 235
TSAREVITCH	1901	*Russian Battleship* 118
TSINGTAU	1903	*German River Gunboat* 155
TSUKUBA	1905	*Japanese Battle-cruiser* 141
TULLIBEE	1960	*U.S. Nuclear-powered Anti-submarine Hunter-killer Submarine* 255
TURBINIA	1897	*British Turbine-driven Craft* 143, 159
TURTLE	1776	*U.S. Submersible* 165, *166*
TYPE A	1938–42	*Japanese Midget Submarines* 253
TYPE 14	1953–57	*British Anti-submarine Frigates* 239
TYPE 41	1954–57	*British Anti-aircraft Frigates* 240
TYPE 61	1953–59	*British Aircraft Direction Frigates* 240
TYPE 82	1968–69	*British Guided-missile Destroyers* 239
TYULEN CLASS	1913–14	*Russian Submarines* 174
U CLASS	1943	*British Destroyers, later Anti-submarine Frigates* 239
U.1	1905	*German Submarine* 174
UNITED STATES	1797	*U.S. Frigate* 70
UNITED STATES	1964	*U.S. Attack Carrier*
UNRYU	1943	*Japanese Fleet Carrier* 210
UTAH	1909	*U.S. Battleship* 133
V CLASS	1943	*British Destroyers, later Anti-submarine Frigates* 191, 239
VALIANT	1914	*British Battleship* 178, 255
VALKYRIEN	1888	*Danish Cruiser* 157
VANGUARD	1835	*British 80-gun Ship* 69, 72
VARESE	1899	*Italian Cruiser* 151
VATERLAND	1903	*German River Gunboat* 155
VAUQUELIN	1956	*French Squadron Escort Destroyer* 236
VERNON	1832	*British Frigate* 72
VICE-ADMIRAL POPOV	1875	*Russian Coast-defence Ship* 105
VICTORIA	1887	*British Battleship* 91, *94–5*, 110
VICTORIOUS	1939	*British Fleet Carrier* 210, 220
VICTORY	1765	*British 100-gun Ship* 62
VIGILANTE	1900	*French River Gunboat* 155
VIKRANT	1945	*Indian Light Fleet Carrier* 213, 220
VILLARS CLASS	1879	*French Cruisers*
VILLE DE PARIS	1795	*British 110-gun Ship* 66
VIPER	1899	*British Torpedo Boat Destroyer* 143, *145*, 159
VIRGINIA	1855	*U.S. (Confederate) Steam Frigate* 84
VIRIBUS UNITIS	1911	*Austrian Battleship* 134–35, 137
VITTORIO VENETO	1969	*Italian Guided-missile Cruiser* 240
VITTORIO VENETO CLASS	1937	*Italian Battleships* 196, 197, 198, 210
VLADIMIR MONOMACH	1882	*Russian Cruiser* 150
VON DER TANN	1908	*German Battle-cruiser* 141, 154, *181*, 184
VULCAN	1895	*British Torpedo Boat Carrier* 157
W CLASS	1944	*British Destroyers* 191, 239
WAMPANOAG	1867	*U.S. Cruiser* 147, *148*
WARRIOR	1860	*British Steam Frigate* 80, 83, 86–87, 97 et al.
WARSPITE	1913	*British Battleship* 180
WASA	1628	*Swedish Galleon* 32, 47, 51, 56–59
WASHINGTON	1940	*U.S. Battleship* 198, 200
WASP	1937	*U.S. Fleet Carrier* 207, 213
WATERWITCH	1832	*British Brig* 72
WATTIGNIES	1891	*French Torpedo Cruiser* 154
WEAPON CLASS	1946–48	*British Destroyers* 239
WEST VIRGINIA	1921	*U.S. Battleship* 184, 189, *195*, 208
WHITBY CLASS	1954–57	*British Anti-submarine Frigates* 239
WISCONSIN	1942	*U.S. Battleship* 200
WOODCOCK	1897	*British River Gunboat* 155
WOODLARK	1897	*British River Gunboat* 155
WRIGHT	1945	*U.S. Light Fleet Carrier, later Relay Ship* 216, 217, 238
WYOMING	1911	*U.S. Battleship* 133
X.1	1922	*British Experimental Submarine* 251–52
XXI CLASS	1944–45	*German Submarines* 252, 255
XVII B CLASS	1944	*German Submarines* 252
X CRAFT	1943	*British Midget Submarines* 252
YAKUMO	1899	*Japanese Armoured Cruiser* 126
YAMASHIRO	1915	*Japanese Battleship* 137
YAMATO	1939	*Japanese Battleship* 198
YARRA CLASS	1961–65	*Australian Anti-submarine Frigates* 241
YASHIMA	1896	*Japanese Battleship* 125
YORKTOWN	1936	*U.S. Fleet Carrier* 207, *208*, 213
YUBARI	1923	*Japanese Light Cruiser* 191
Z CLASS	1945	*British Destroyers, later Anti-submarine Frigates*
Z TYPE	1930–39	*German Destroyers* 200
ZARA CLASS	1930	*Italian Cruisers* 191, 200, 210
ZELÉE CLASS	1900	*French Sloops* 154
ZUIHO	1940	*Japanese Submarine Tender, later Light Fleet Carrier* 208, 213
ZUIKAKU	1939	*Japanese Fleet Carrier* 208, 213

Talleres Offset Nerecan, S.A. – Printed in Spain